RESEARCH IN ORGANIZATIONAL CHANGE AND DEVELOPMENT

Volume 1 • 1987

RESEARCH IN ORGANIZATIONAL CHANGE AND DEVELOPMENT

An Annual Series featuring Advances in Theory, Methodology and Research

Editors: RICHARD W. WOODMAN
Department of Management
Texas A & M University

WILLIAM A. PASMORE
Department of Organizational Behavior
Case Western Reserve University

VOLUME 1 • 1987

 JAI PRESS INC.

Greenwich, Connecticut   *London, England*

CONTENTS

LIST OF CONTRIBUTORS

Chris Argyris

Graduate School of Education
Harvard University

L. David Brown

Department of Organizational
Behavior
School of Management
Boston University

R. J. Bullock

Department of Psychology
University of Houston

David L. Cooperrider

Department of Organizational
Behavior
Weatherhead School of Management
Case Western Reserve University

Jane Gibson Covey

Institute for Development Research
Boston University

Thomas G. Cummings

Graduate School of Business
Administration
University of Southern California

Wilfred H. Drath

Center for Creative Leadership
Greensboro, North Carolina

Robert E. Kaplan

Center for Creative Leadership
Greensboro, North Carolina

Joan R. Kofodimos

Center for Creative Leadership
Greensboro, North Carolina

Susan A. Mohrman   Center for Effective Organizations
                                                Graduate School of Business
                                                    Administration
                                                University of Southern California

Jerry I. Porras   Graduate School of Business
                                                Stanford University

Peter Robertson   Graduate School of Business
                                                Stanford University

Suresh Srivastva   Department of Organizational
                                                    Behavior
                                                Weatherhead School of Management
                                                Case Western Reserve University

Mark E. Tubbs   Department of Psychology
                                                University of Missouri at St. Louis

EDITORIAL STATEMENT

This annual series is intended to provide an outlet for scholarly articles dealing with processes of organization development, transformation, innovation, or change through the application of behavioral sciences to human issues in organizing. Articles will be primarily of a conceptual nature, making ground breaking contributions to the development of new research or action paradigms. Empirical work that leads directly to theory development will also be published.

The specific topics chosen for inclusion in each annual volume will reflect current trends and emergent issues in the field of organizational change and development. Articles addressing change methods and processes, inquiry/research methods, and cutting-edge issues or topics will be published. Broad license will be given to authors who can help produce a shift in our thinking about the field, leading to new targets of inquiry or action. Chapters published in the series will be longer than articles published in most journals, allowing authors the opportunity to develop their ideas more fully.

To differentiate this annual series from other JAI publications dealing with organizational behavior and personnel/human resources, it should be stressed that we are soliciting contributions which have as their basic thrust issues of change in organizations. We are not interested in descriptions of organizations as they currently exist, except in order to point toward issues that might affect change processes, nor are we interested in ways of recruiting, selecting or managing personnel unless such methods are part of a systemic approach to transforming organizational processes. In Weick's terminology, we are interested in pieces that emphasize think"ing"—that is, that place emphasis on actions that can be taken by researchers or practitioners to expand the scope of our current approaches to organization development.

PREFACE

This first volume of *Research in Organizational Change and Development* contains seven chapters. While these cover a wide range of topics, they all have at least one thing in common—each challenges our accepted paradigms and comfortable understandings and invites us to view the change and development area from new perspectives.

In the opening chapter, Jerry Porras and Peter Robertson suggest that OD theories can be categorized as either implementation theories or theories of change processes. Each category of theory is carefully delineated and analyzed. Specific suggestions for needed theory development should be instructive for the field. Next, Dave Brown and Jane Covey describe a type of organization that does not fit neatly into the conventional OD paradigm. They suggest that the change and development area has much to learn from the experiences of "development organizations."

The third chapter, by Chris Argyris, focuses on the use of defensive reasoning processes by OD professionals. Argyris argues that such defensive reasoning will prevent the OD professional from providing the necessary help to client organizations. David Cooperrider and Suresh Srivastva argue for expansion and revision of the OD paradigm. They see action research has having failed, in large part, to fulfill its earlier promise, and propose "appreciative inquiry" as an alternative to action research grounded in a positivistic science. Action researchers should find their essay provocative.

R. J. Bullock and Mark Tubbs challenge some aspects of the traditional research paradigm in OD. They propose the application of meta-analysis to evaluate cumulative findings from case studies of organizational change. A detailed description of the case meta-analysis method should allow researchers to apply this innovative methodology. The next chapter, by Bob Kaplan, Joan Kofodimos, and Bill Drath, examines the role and implications of executive development in organizational change. They propose a new method of inquiry— "Biographical Action Research"—which can be used to assess the developmental needs of executives and to deal with the forces affecting executive development. Finally, Tom Cummings and Susan Mohrman develop a strategy for implementing quality-of-work-life innovations in organizations. The traditional innovation adoption process, utilized by most organizations, is viewed as a particularly inappropriate approach to QWL innovation. Cummings and Mohrman advocate a "self design" approach to innovation suitable for QWL and other fundamental changes in organizations.

These chapters, then, are Volume 1. It is our hope that this scholarly forum will help to move the change and development field into productive areas for research and action.

Richard W. Woodman
William A. Pasmore
Series Editors

ORGANIZATION DEVELOPMENT THEORY:

A TYPOLOGY AND EVALUATION

Jerry I. Porras and Peter J. Robertson

ABSTRACT

Two types of Organization Development theory are identified and discussed in this chapter. The first, implementation theory, focuses on the intervention activity required to carry out effective planned change efforts in organizations. The second, change process theory, attempts to explain the dynamics through which the organization changes as a response to any intervention activity. Evaluations of both types of theory suggest that implementation theory is more fully developed than change process theory. However, improved theoretical development is needed in both areas. For implementation theory, further work is needed in the development of more comprehensive diagnostic models, in the specification of conditions for effective change, and in the establishment of useful criteria for change agents. Since change process theory is in such a fragmented state, all facets of it require further

Research in Organizational Change and Development, Vol. 1, pages 1–57.
Copyright © 1987 by JAI Press Inc.
All rights of reproduction in any form reserved.
ISBN: 0-89232-749-9

theoretical advancement. Substantial improvement in the quality of both types of OD theory are needed to enhance the efficacy of planned change processes in organizations.

INTRODUCTION

Throughout the past decade, numerous writers have commented unfavorably on the state and quality of theory in the field of Organization Development (e.g., Friedlander & Brown, 1974; Burke, 1976, 1982; Margulies & Raia, 1978; Lundberg, 1978; Golembiewski, 1979). The general consensus seems to be that, at present, OD theory is inadequate and does not provide the rich concepts needed to understand and guide complex organizational change processes. As Lundberg (1978, p. 9) notes, "OD's 'theory' is largely uneven and insufficient". Or as Porras and Patterson (1979, p. 44) state, "at present no generally accepted theory of organizational change exists."

The lack of a comprehensive, well-formulated theory impedes practice, evaluation, and research in OD, the major activities of the field. Effective OD practice is inhibited because, instead of being guided by relevant theory, the activities of change agents are influenced by their personal goals and values (Tichy, 1975), their cognitive styles (Slocum, 1978), or their familiarity and facility with specific techniques (Porras & Patterson, 1979). In other words, the methods used by change agents may be more a function of who they are than of what is most appropriate given the situation. What change agents should do can only be ascertained through the application of well-developed theory.

Inadequate theory also hinders the evaluation of OD programs. Bass (1983) suggests two potential problems. He points out that unless theory specifies what outcomes constitute success, evaluation is problematic. Also, without theory-based predictions regarding the timing of the outcomes, measurement of them at the wrong time can lead to inaccurate conclusions concerning the success of any change program.

An additional problem in evaluation stems from the possibility that different types of interventions have their most pronounced effects on different kinds of variables (Woodman & Muse, 1982). For example, process interventions may be more likely to produce measurable changes in process variables (Woodman & Wayne, 1985), since there is little evidence for changes in outcome variables resulting from process interventions (Kaplan, 1979; Woodman & Sherwood, 1980). Evaluations of OD programs need to be guided by established theory regarding such relationships. Otherwise, in circumstances where a relationship between the particular interventions and variables of interest would not be expected, evaluations may conclude pessimistically that OD has no effect.

Research on OD is also affected by the lack of an adequate theoretical base. Porras and Roberts (1980) indicate that an outgrowth of the theoretical poverty in

OD is a lack of an organized thrust in the investigation of the change process. More specifically, Porras and Patterson (1978) claim that the selection of variables for investigation is typically an arbitrary process. For example, Porras and Berg (1978) found that while the vast majority of interventions used in OD programs focused on groups, a relatively small number of group variables were targets of assessment research.

Well-developed theory is critical, then, to effective practice, evaluation, and research of Organization Development. However, OD theory in its current state does not meet these needs. There are some important reasons why this situation exists. First, and probably most important, no broadly accepted theory of organizations has yet been developed, so that a theory of organizational change at this stage is a bit problematic. Second, the processes of change are so complex that, given our current understanding of social system dynamics, it has been extremely difficult to postulate a theory of Organization Development. And finally, there is some confusion over exactly what is meant by the concept of theory in OD. There appear to be different types of theory in this field and, as of yet, those types have not been clearly delineated. It is upon this last point that we base our efforts to assess OD theory.

Bennis (1965) recognized the existence of different types of theory when he distinguished between a theory of change and a theory of changing. If in fact two different types of theory exist, an evaluation of "the state of overall theory in OD" is not very meaningful. Instead, a clear specification and evaluation of the two separate types and their level of development would be more useful.

Such an evaluation is a critical first step in generating the necessary improvements in the theory base upon which OD activities rest. By specifying different types of theory, and noting the strengths and weaknesses of each, future theoretical development can be directed toward filling any gaps identified. By strengthening theory, OD practice, evaluation, and research will subsequently be improved.

The purpose of this chapter, then, is to provide an evaluation of current theory in OD in order to facilitate future theoretical development in the field. More specifically, our objectives here are: to suggest a typology of OD theory; to use this typology to understand the current state of theory development; and to indicate where improved theoretical development is most needed. It is our hope that the present framework and analysis will serve not only to facilitate, but to motivate as well, the theoretical advancements critical to improved understanding and practice of the process of planned organizational change.

Before beginning, we should note that the scope of this effort is limited to theory concerning *planned* change in a *formal* organizational context. Because of this focus, theory of adaptation processes (Leavitt, Dill & Eyring, 1973), evolutionary or natural selection change (Hannan & Freeman, 1977), and diffusion of innovations (Rogers, 1983) is not considered. Furthermore, given our organizational level intent, we will not examine community and social change. Theory of individual change is considered only if it takes place within an organizational context (e.g., management development) and excluded if it takes on any other character (e.g., change as a result of a psychotherapeutic relationship).

While not attempting an exhaustive review of the field, an effort was made to conduct a thorough investigation of the major theoretical contributions to the OD literature. It was our intent to evaluate the present condition of theoretical development in OD and to do so based on the major available works.

Towards a Typology

It is our contention that, consistent with Bennis (1965), two broad types of change theory exist. The first of these we label *implementation theory*, (Bennis' theory of changing). This type can be defined as theory that focuses on activities change agents must undertake in effecting planned change. It is theory that describes what must be done to induce change and how to best insure the success of a change attempt.

Implementation theory can be contrasted with the second major type, *change process theory*, (Bennis' theory of change). This theory explains the dynamics of the change process by specifying (a) the variables that are manipulable in the change effort, (b) the intended outcomes of the change attempt, (c) the causal relationships between manipulable, mediator, and outcome variables, and (d) the effects of relevant moderator variables. Whereas implementation theory is centered around what must be done to induce change, change process theory describes the underlying dynamics by which change occurs.

Ideally, change process theory should guide implementation theory in the identification of variables to target for change. Since it describes the fundamental nature of the social system to be altered, it should inform the approaches used to change that social system. Although the two types of theory are thus related, for our purposes each type will be discussed separately below.

IMPLEMENTATION THEORY

Three subcategories of implementation theory can be found in the planned organizational change literature: (1) strategy theories; (2) procedure theories; and (3) technique theories. These subcategories correspond to three different levels of specificity regarding the activities of planned change attempts.

Table 1 shows a listing of prominent theories in each of these subcategories. Theories are represented by bibliographic references and listed alphabetically. The various technique theories are further subdivided according to broad focus of the technique described. Note that the theories listed under the intervention technique section of the third column represent only a small subset of the broad range of available perspectives. Each of the three subcategories will be discussed in turn using the referenced theories as examples.

Table 1.   Prominent Implementation Theories

Strategy Theories	Procedures Theories	Technique Theories
Bennis (1966)	Argyris (1970)	Diagnostic Techniques
Chin & Benne (1969)	Beckhard (1969)	Emery & Trist (1978)
Greiner (1967)	Beckhard & Harris (1977)	Nadler & Tushman (1977)
Hornstein et al. (1971)	Beer (1980)	Weisbord (1976)
Margulies & Raia (1978)	Blake & Mouton (1968)	
Walton (1965)	Bowers & Franklin (1972)	Planning Techniques
	Bowers et al. (1975)	Jayaram (1976)
	Burke (1982)	Krone (1975)
	Cummings & Srivastva (1977)	Porras & Harkness (1985)
	French & Bell (1978)	
	Lawrence & Lorsch (1969)	Intervention Techniques
	Likert (1967)	Beckhard (1967)
	Lippitt et al. (1958)	Dyer (1977)
	Margulies & Raia (1978)	Galbraith (1973)
	Nadler (1981)	Schein (1969)
	Tichy (1983)	Steele (1973)
		Walton (1969)
		Evaluation Techniques
		Armenakis & Zmud (1979)
		Bedian et al. (1980)
		Golembiewski et al. (1976)
		Randolph (1982)
		Schmitt (1982)
		Terborg et al. (1980)

Strategy Theories

At the most general level of implementation theories are what we refer to as strategies of change. Various typologies of change strategies have been proposed. Many include or are based on the way power is used in implementing change (Walton, 1965; Bennis, 1966; Greiner, 1967; Chin & Benne, 1969). Others focus on the broad organizational factors targeted for change (Hornstein et al., 1971; Margulies & Raia, 1978) or on the cognitive mechanisms used to bring about alterations in individual behavior change (Chin & Benne, 1969; Walton, 1965). In all of these cases, broad perspectives on how to approach the change task are prescribed by the theories.

Although these strategies are included under our category of implementation theory, they do not provide guidelines for specific change agent activity. As Margulies and Raia (1978, pp. 44–45) point out, these typologies tend to be "descriptive methods for categorizing either approaches to change or in some global sense methods for bringing about change . . . (They) do not appear to adequately provide a functional model for implementing and directing change in organizations." However, under proper conditions, change can be accomplished through use of any of these different strategies. And, at a general level, different strategies suggest different activities in which change agents should engage in order to induce the change. In any case, the need for more specific guides to change agent action has spawned a second set of theories to which we now turn.

Procedure Theories

The second subcategory of implementation theories is at the middle level of specificity and includes theories which are more functional for directing change. These theories, which we call procedure theories of change implementation, are concerned with the entire scope of a change attempt. It is this group to which the term implementation theory most aptly applies.

These theories are more specific than change strategies in that particular steps and procedures are outlined, often with recommendations as to how these steps can best be carried out. The action research model, for example, consists of scouting, entry, data collection, data feedback, diagnosis, action planning, action implementation, and evaluation (Frohman, Sashkin, & Kavanagh, 1976). It provides the foundation on which most procedure theories are based. This category and some representative theories will be discussed in greater detail shortly.

Technique Theories

The final and most specific subcategory of implementation theories is that group which emphasizes *only one* of the steps of the entire process included in the procedure theories of change. Although the greatest number of these theories concentrate on either the diagnosis or the intervention step, theories of planning and evaluation exist as well.

Diagnostic Theories

Various diagnostic models have been proposed. Perhaps the most popular is Weisbord's (1976), which focuses on analyzing the gap between the formal and informal properties of six key organizational characteristics. Nadler and Tushman (1977) take a similar approach by proposing that important organizational problems can be identified by determining the degree of congruence existing between pairs of key organizational components. Emery and Trist (1978) also focus on fit between organizational components, but use the notion of joint optimization of social and technical systems design. In all of these cases, a diagnosis is achieved through an analysis of the relationship between critical organizational variables.

Planning Theories

Relatively few theories of planning exist. Two prominent ones are derived from the open systems work of the Tavistock Institute: open system planning (Jayaram, 1976) and open system redesign (Krone, 1975).

A third, more recent approach (Porras & Harkness, 1985), has been proposed as a method for concretely establishing action plans and using them to guide action. It also draws on systems theory, but translates this perspective into graphical representations of plans and their interrelationships.

All three of these planning theories are predicated on the fact that change is organic in nature and that severe limitations exist on planning in the traditional manner. Nevertheless, plans can keep change directions more in focus and thus facilitate organization development.

Intervention Theories

Numerous "mini-theories" of intervention exist and have been well documented by French and Bell (1978), Huse (1980), and Burke (1982). Several have been particularly popular for over a decade and all describe a rather circumscribed approach to actually intervening into an organizational system (Schein, 1969; Beckhard, 1967; Walton, 1969; Dyer, 1977). Others, although broader in scope, nevertheless are relatively clearly bounded in their perspective and focus (Galbraith, 1973; Steele, 1973).

Clearly the theories mentioned above are only a small subset of a rather large group of concrete intervention techniques for organizational change. Nevertheless, they are representative of the types of theories which guide techniques and, as such, reflect the more bounded nature of this set of implementation theories.

Evaluation Theories

Most recently, emphasis has grown on the evaluation of planned change efforts. With it, theories of evaluation have developed. Evaluation of change was the focus of theoretical work by Golembiewski, Billingsley, and Yeager (1976), who distinguished between three types of change that can result from OD efforts. Numerous methodologies for measuring these different types of changes have been proposed (Armenakis & Zmud, 1979; Bedian, Armenakis, & Gibson, 1980; Terborg, Howard, & Maxwell, 1980; Schmitt, 1982; Randolph, 1982). These efforts, based on theoretical perspectives of change and of research methodology, have been developed and applied to the very complex phenomena of organizational change.

PROCEDURE THEORIES

Having described briefly the three subcategories of implementation theory, we want to look in more depth at the group of theories at the middle level of specificity, the procedure theories. These are our primary focus because, as indicated above, they conform most closely to what we mean by implementation theory.

On the one hand, unlike the more general change strategy theories, procedure theories suggest specific activities which must be undertaken in planned change attempts. On the other hand, unlike the more specific technique theories which consider only one stage of the change process, procedure theories focus on the *entire* process of planned change implementation.

Table 2 presents important theoretical information drawn from selected procedure theories. The set of theories included is not intended to represent a complete list of the theories available in the planned organizational change literature. However, we believe that the list is fairly comprehensive, that it does include the most prominent theories to be found, and that, as a group, these theories are representative of this type of theoretical work. The discussion below presents some generalizations about this set of theories, but for more specific information regarding any particular theory, the reader should consult Table 2.

Intervention Phases

We will begin our discussion of procedure theories by first considering the various steps generally proposed as important in a successful change effort. Table 3 provides a comprehensive list of the stages of intervention contained in the theories as a set. The particular steps included by each theory are also indicated. We should note that in this table, the diagnosis stage incorporates the activities of data collection, analysis, and feedback, even though some theories consider them distinct steps.

From the table, one can see that the diagnosis and action/intervention stages are the two most frequently incorporated into procedure theories. This is not surprising, as these two sets of activities form the foundation of any rationally planned change attempt (i.e., determining what the problem is and then trying to correct it). Our earlier conclusion that diagnosis and intervention receive the greatest attention in technique theories is consistent with this observation.

After diagnosis and intervention, the activities included most often in the various procedure theories are action planning and evaluation of the change effort. Over half the theories contain one or the other, and just under half include both. Considering all 4 of these steps together, we see that 6 of the 16 theories include all of them, while 5 theories include 3 of the 4. Thus there seems to be substantial agreement among theorists that the procedure for implementing planned change has at its core the activities of diagnosis, action planning, intervention, and evaluation of the change effort.

Beyond these four activities, however, there is much less agreement. Only five theories mention one of the early stages of change implementation (i.e., selection of client, entry, or contracting). It could be that the remaining theories consider the establishment of the relationship between client and change agent as a given or as a prerequisite to the implementation of a planned change attempt.

The formation of an ideal model as a prelude to conscious action is mentioned only twice. The infrequent use of this tactic in planned intervention is consistent

(*text continues on page 21*)

Table 2. Procedure Oriented Implementation Theories in Organization Development

Theory	Steps Included	Diagnostic Variables	Intervention Choice Criteria	Conditions for Effective Change	Criteria for Change Agents
Argyris (1970)	Help client generate valid data Enable client to have free, informed choice Help client generate internal commitment to choices made	Criteria of System Competence: Awareness of relevant information Understanding by the relevant parties Manipulability of information Cost of information is within the system's capacity Problems are solved such that they don't recur The above are met without decreasing effectiveness of problem-solving, decision-making, and implementing processes	Time Resources Organizational health Interventionist competence (implied) Decrease restraining forces of change Decrease dysfunctionality and organizational pressures Increase probability of performing primary tasks	Deviance from existing norms High degree of unfreezing New system required to be self-corrective High degree of involvement of relevant clients High degree of personal and system discomfort	Confidence in own intervention philosophy Accurate perception of stressful reality Acceptance of the client's attacks and mistrust Trust in own experience of reality Investing stressful environment with growth experiences
Beckhard (1969)	Diagnosis Strategy planning Education Consulting and training	Processes: Decision-making Communication patterns	Not specified	Pressure for change from environment Some strategic people are "hurting" &	Not specified

(continued)

9

Table 2. (Cont.)

Theory	Steps Included	Diagnostic Variables	Intervention Choice Criteria	Conditions for Effective Change	Criteria for Change Agents
	Evaluation	Relationships between groups Conflict management Goal setting Planning methods		willing to diagnose problem Leadership exists Collaborative problem identification between line and staff Willingness to take risks Realistic, long-term time perspective Willingness to face data and work with it System rewards for effort in addition to results Tangible intermediate results	
Beckhard & Harris (1977)	Diagnosing present condition Setting goals and defining new state after change Defining transition state between present and future	Processes: attitudes, practices policies, structures & rewards	Not specified	Organizational leadership must be aware of need for change & its consequences for their actions It must have a relatively clear idea of the changed condition desired	Not specified

	Developing strategies and action plans for managing transition Evaluating change effort Stabilizing the new condition			
Beer (1980)	Selection of client Entry and contracting Data collection and diagnosis Feedback of data Developing and testing possible solutions Action planning Managing organizational transitions Evaluation Institutionalization	Environment Organizational outcomes Human outputs Organizational behavior and process Organizational structures People Culture Dominant coalition Consequence between the elements in the diagnostic model In regards to sequencing of interventions: Maximize diagnostic data, effectiveness, efficiency, speed and relevance, and minimize psychological & organizational strain of change	Dissatisfaction with the status quo A new model for managing or organizing A planned process for managing change Early success which is intrinsically rewarding Early reinforcement through extrinsic rewards Strong leadership which sets new expectations, induces new behaviors and reinforces desired behaviors Slack resources must exist Political resources must exist Change resources must match size and kind of change	Outside perspective Model discrepent behavior such that creative tension arises which induces change in the client Be aware of assumptions and models underlying practice Systems orientation Role and person characteristics: Generalist/specialist Integrator Neutrality Credibility Marginality

(continued)

11

Table 2. (Cont.)

Theory	Steps Included	Diagnostic Variables	Intervention Choice Criteria	Conditions for Effective Change	Criteria for Change Agents
Blake & Mouton (1968)	Grid seminar Team development Intergroup development Development of an ideal strategic model Planning and implementation (of the ideal model) Systematic critique	Supervisory styles/communication Stragegic plan/planning	Not specified	Led from the top, yet include active and concentrated effort of all organizational members, based on a belief in its importance	Key people should be line managers, with long-range potential and ability to work in a 9, 9, way
Bowers & Franklin (1972)	Formation of a model of (ideal) organizational functioning Selection of a goal Assessment of the situation Formation of diagnosis Feedback Adjustment Reevaluation	Not specified	Based on diagnosis	Not specified	Interpersonal skills Ability to provide link between scientific knowledge regarding solving problems & the problems exhibited in the immediate situation Source of information Ability to facilitate groups processes

12

Bowers, Franklin & Pecorella (1975)	Diagnosis Intervention	Problem behaviors: support, goal emphasis, work facilitation, interaction facilitation Precursors: information, skills, values, situation	Congruence, matching of interventions with problems and precursors		Not specified
Burke (1982)	Entry Contracting Diagnosis Feedback Planning change Intervention Evaluation	Norms Roles Values Rewards Power	Determining the client's readiness for change Making certain the change is tied to power points in the organization Arranging for internal resources to help manage, monitor and maintain the change process	Not specified	Ability to: Tolerate ambiguity Influence Confront difficult issues Support and nurture others Listen well and empathize Recognize one's own feelings and intuitions quickly Conceptualize Discover and mobilize human energy Teach or create learning opportunities Maintain a sense of humor Be self-confident Be interpersonally competent

(*continued*)

Table 2. (Cont.)

Theory	Steps Included	Diagnostic Variables	Intervention Choice Criteria	Conditions for Effective Change	Criteria for Change Agents
Cummings & Srivastva (1977)	Defining an experimental system Sanctioning an experiment Forming an action group Analyzing the system Generating hypotheses for redesign Implementing and evaluating the hypotheses Making the transition to normal operating conditions Dissemenating results	*Production system:* Work unit Production processes Key variances Social system Worker's perceptions of their roles Environment *Service systems:* Work unit Objectives Work roles Grouping of roles Workers' perceptions of their roles Environment	Not specified	Climate must support and enhance behavior that is interpersonally open, experimental, and high in trust and risk-taking Organizational members at lower levels are actively engaged in change process	Not specified
French & Bell (1978)	Diagnosis Action Process maintenance	Communication patterns, styles and flows Goal setting Decision-making, problem-solving and action-planning Conflict resolution and management Managing interface relations	Overall change goals Readiness and receptivity of the target Key leverage points Most pressing problems Resources	Perception of organizational problems by key people Introduction of an external behavioral scientist-consultant Initial top level support or involvement Active involvement of work team leaders Operationalizing of the	Be an expert in the sense of being competent to present a range of options Be able to practice and develop effective behavior

		Superior-subordinate relations Organization's culture Interpersonal, group, and intergroup processes Skills for task accomplishment		action-research model and early successes An open educational philosophy about OD Acknowledgement of the congruency with previous good practice Involvement of personnel people and congruency with personnel policy and practice Development of internal resources Effective management of the OD process Monitoring the process and measuring results	Interpersonal skills that allow them to relate effectively both to top management and to organizational members
Lawrence & Lorsch (1969)	Diagnosis Action planning Implementation Evaluation	Environmental and task demands facing organization Needs of individual contributors Level of differentiation Problems in achieving integration	Better fit between the organization & environmental demands, or between the organization and needs of individuals	Commitment to change by key participants Top managers are involved and committed Participants must understand need for change and how	Must be educator, diagnostician and

15

(continued)

Table 2. (Cont.)

Theory	Steps Included	Diagnostic Variables	Intervention Choice Criteria	Conditions for Effective Change	Criteria for Change Agents
		Methods of conflict resolution Sources of individual satisfaction and dissatisfaction Adequacy of individual contribution contracts		change will be rewarding for them	consultant
Likert (1967)	Diagnosis Action	Use of supportive relationships Use of high standards Group structure Methods of decision-making and supervision Type or rewards Principles of organization Competency of superiors Adequacy of selection process, training resources and capital and equipment Members' expectations regarding work	Focus first on changing causal rather than intervening variables	Sufficient time allowed Modify all components of the managerial system to remain internally consistent Change operating procedures which bind an organization to present management system	Not specified

Lippitt, Watson & Westley (1958)	Development of need for change Establishment of change relationship Working toward change: a. diagnosis b. establishing goals and intentions of action c. transformation of intentions into change efforts Generalization and stabilization of change Achieving terminal relationship	Internal distribution of power Internal mobilization of energy Internal communication Correspondence between internal and external reality (perceived and actual environment) Goals and values for action Skills and strategies for action	Members' attitudes and motivation Interaction-influence system Performance variables Financial variables Goals Control system Communication	Choice of initial leverage point based on accessibility and linkages between the leverage point and the change objective	Not specified	Sensitivity to change and resistance forces in the client system Clear understanding of his/her own motivations Self-insight to guide ethical decisions Conceptual-diagnostic skill Orientation to theories and methods of change Operational and relational skills
Margulies and Raia (1978)	Prework Data collection Diagnosis Intervention	Structure Processes (task, management, and human)		Not specified	Existing management philosophy and practices The organization's culture	Personal characteristics: empathy, awareness, social sensitivity and the ability to listen

(continued)

Table 2. (Cont.)

Theory	Steps Included	Diagnostic Variables	Intervention Choice Criteria	Conditions for Effective Change	Criteria for Change Agents
			The objectives of the OD effort Size of the organization and the number of the people involved Experience the organization has had with the process of self-assessment Availability of time and resources Orientation and skills of the available consultative help		Problem-solving capabilities Client-related expertise
Nadler (1981)	Diagnosis Design future state Implement the transition	Inputs: environment, resources, history Outputs: organizational performance, group performance, individual behavior and affect Consistency among organizational components: task, individual, formal	Maintain congruency between organizational components	Must effectively deal with issues of resistance, control and power	Not specified

18

		organization, infor-mal organization			Not specified
Tichy (1983)	Diagnosis Developing change strategies and selecting techniques for carrying out the strategies Implementation Monitoring and evaluating	Output Input: history, environment, resources Mission/strategy Tasks Prescribed networks People Organizational processes Emergent networks	Strategic change lever targeted Degree to which intervention is understood by change manager Depth of the intervention Degree to which conditions necessary for success of the intervention are present	System approach: keep all systems aligned, within and between them	Not specified

19

Table 3. Stage Content of Procedure Oriented Theories

Stages in Implementation Procedure	Lippitt, Watson & Westley (1958)	Likert (1967)	Blake & Mouton (1968)	Beckhard (1969)	Lawrence & Lorsch (1969)	Argyris (1970)	Bowers & Franklin (1972)	Bowers, Franklin & Pecorella (1975)	Beckhard & Harris (1977)	Cummings & Srivasva (1977)	French & Bell (1978)	Margulies & Raia (1978)	Beer (1980)	Nadler (1981)	Burke (1982)	Tichy (1983)
Client Selection										×			×			
Entry	×												×		×	
Contracting		×								×		×	×		×	
Formation of An Ideal Model			×				×									
Diagnosis	×			×	×	×	×	×	×	×	×	×	×	×	×	×
Designing Alternatives									×				×			×
Goal Selection	×			×	×	×	×		×	×						
Planning			×	×					×				×	×	×	×
Action/Intervention	×	×	×	×	×	×	×	×	×	×	×	×	×	×	×	×
Monitoring and Evaluation			×		×		×		×	×	×		×	×	×	×
Institutionalization/Stabilization	×								×	×			×			

20

with the observation by Tichy and Hornstein (1976) that change agents too rarely use an explicit model of organizational functioning. Certainly this fact can have a profound effect on the efficacy of any change interventions.

Selecting a goal and designing alternatives to achieve it can easily be considered part of the planning process, and this may account for the relative infrequency with which these are mentioned. Yet, it has been our experience that, all too often, clear goals for change are not established and the variety of ways for achieving them not specified. Frequently, in the former case, this is caused by a rush to action, while in the latter, it is due to limitations in the change agent's repertoire of intervention techniques.

Finally, the institutionalization and stabilization of change has only recently begun to be recognized as a critical activity in the implementation of change (Goodman, Bazerman & Conlon, 1980). This may explain why it was included in only a few, relatively recent theories.

Diagnostic Variables

A second area of interest in the various theories is the variables suggested as being key to effective problem diagnosis. A quick scan of the *Diagnostic Variables* column in Table 2 shows a diverse set of variables suggested by the various theorists. In order to reduce this diversity, we have used the seven elements of an organizational model proposed by Porras (in press) in an attempt to more parsimoniously categorize the many variables listed.[1] These elements are the organization's: (1) environment; (2) purpose; (3) organizing arrangements; (4) social factors; (5) technology; (6) physical setting; and (7) outcomes (both individual and organizational). Specific definitions of each variable category are given in Table 4.

Table 5 indicates which theories include which of these diagnostic variables.[2] Every theory includes both organizing arrangements and social factors as important potential problem areas. This is not surprising, since these categories are fairly broad, incorporating a wide range of variables, and since historically OD has focused primarily on these aspects of organizational functioning.

There is much less agreement on the remaining variables, however. Technology is included nine times, while the environment is considered in only six theories. These two variables have become more prominent as the conceptualization of organizations as open sociotechnical systems has become more prevalent. Yet the fact that they are not incorporated into more diagnostic models may reflect the early dominant focus of OD on human-processual factors.

Furthermore, the fact that outcomes also are not included very frequently may well indicate the degree to which OD has been primarily process-oriented, assuming that by focusing on organizational processes, the outcomes will take care of themselves. However, recent findings have tended to discount this assumption (Porras, 1979; Porras & Wilkins, 1980). Outcome improvements are found to

Table 4.

ENVIRONMENT	The external conditions with which the organization must deal including its market, customers, technology, stockholders, government regulations, and the social culture and values in which it operates.
PURPOSE	The focusing element gathering together the contributions of diverse members of a system into a unified effort.
ORGANIZING ARRANGEMENTS	The more formalized guidelines for cooperative action which include the formal structure, policies and procedures, administrative systems, reward system, evaluation system, goals, and strategies.
SOCIAL FACTORS	The human related characteristics and processes in the organization including the organization's culture (which consists of values, norms, symbols, stories, myths, and rituals), interpersonal, group, and intergroup processes, individuals' attitudes, behavioral skills, informal communication networks, and status and influence patterns.
TECHNOLOGY	The process involved in the transformation of inputs into outputs including tools, equipment, machinery, technical expertise, job design, work flow design, technical procedures, and technical systems.
PHYSICAL SETTING	The actual physical environment in which work gets done, including the building, division of space, light, heat, and noise, etc., decorations, furniture, colors of walls, and architecture.
OUTCOME	The system's outputs which are the products of the efforts of the organizational members operating in conjunction with the above characteristics of the organization. They include organizational related outcomes such as productivity, performance, turnover, absenteeism, and grievance rates, and individual related outcomes such as satisfaction and self-realization/actualization.

occur without the concomitant improvement in human processes. Thus the link between processes and outcomes is not clear, and outcome improvements may not necessarily result from process improvements.

The organization's purpose and its physical setting are each included as a diagnostic variable only once. Historically, these variables have lacked importance in OD theory. Today, however, this points to areas where future theorizing and research efforts might be channeled.

All in all, Table 5 indicates that there is, in general, a lack of agreement on a

Table 5. Diagnostic Variables in Procedure Oriented Theories

Diagnostic Variable	Lippitt, Watson & Westley (1958)	Likert (1967)	Blake & Mouton (1968)	Beckhard (1969)	Lawrence & Lorsch (1969)	Argyris (1970)	Bowers & Franklin (1972)	Bowers, Franklin & Pecorella (1975)	Beckhard & Harris (1977)	Cummings & Srivastva (1977)	French & Bell (1978)	Margulies & Raia (1978)	Beer (1980)	Nadler (1981)	Burke (1982)	Tichy (1983)
Environment	X				X					X			X	X		X
Purpose																X
Organizing Arrangements	X	X	X	X	X	X		X	X	X	X	X	X	X	X	X
Social Factors	X	X	X	X	X	X		X	X	X	X	X	X	X	X	X
Technology	X	X			X			X		X	X	X		X	X	X
Physical Setting								X								
Outcomes		X											X	X		X

23

model of organization that can be used for diagnostic purposes. And while this lack of agreement pertains to the relatively broad variables that make up the model used here, the problem is much more acute when considering the more specific variables listed in Table 2. Furthermore, there seems to be little evidence that, across time, a coalescence on common variables is occurring. Neither is there any evidence that an expansion across all the variable sets is evolving. The variables considered important in the late 1970s and early 1980s are not much more varied than those emphasized in the 1950s and 1960s. This is certainly an area needing considerable future theoretical development.

In sum, then, there has been neither a narrowing of focus on a few key sets of variables, nor a proliferation of new variables to consider. Instead, there appears to be a stagnation in our understanding of the fundamental factors most relevant as targets of change efforts.

Choice of Intervention

The third column in Table 2 lists the criteria suggested by each theory for choosing which particular intervention(s) to use in the change effort. Although a considerable amount of overlap exists across theoretical perspectives, there nevertheless appears to be substantial diversity of viewpoints on how one goes about selecting a particular approach. What is needed, therefore, is a means by which the various selection methods might be integrated and assessed. Figure 1 presents just such a framework. It is derived from the theories presented in Table 2 and suggests that the decision regarding which intervention(s) to use is actually a two-stage process.

In the first stage, a broad set of potentially appropriate interventions can be delineated by a consideration of the general problem areas or organizational variables targeted for change. Criteria pertaining to this step can be classified into two general approaches: (1) the gap between actual and desired organizational states; and (2) the congruency among relevant organizational characteristics. In the second stage, selection of the particular intervention(s) to be used

Decision Stage	
Selection of a feasible intervention set, based on:	Selection of particular interventions, based on:
1. Gap between actual and desired organizational states 2. Congruency among relevant organizational characteristics.	1. Readiness of the target system 2. Leverage points 3. Skill of the change agent

Figure 1.   Framework for Choosing Intervention Approaches

occurs. Here, the criteria fall into three categories: (1) readiness of the target system; (2) leverage points; and (3) skills of the change agent. When taken together, these five conditions form a set of guidelines for choosing specific interventions. Each of these conditions is discussed more fully below.

Organizational Gaps

The first, and most common, means of identifying those areas which are to be the target of change is to note where gaps exist between actual and desired organizational states. By locating such gaps, the change agent together with the client system will have a clearer idea concerning which interventions will be most helpful. Thus, awareness of the desired states is important, and interventions should be chosen on the basis of these goals and objectives (French & Bell, 1978; Margulies & Raia, 1978).[3]

Determining the gaps between actual and desired states is likely to pinpoint particular organizational variables that need to be changed. Tichy (1983) refers to these variables as strategic change levers, and he recommends that interventions be chosen which are clearly tied to the identified levers. Bowers, Franklin, and Pecorella (1975) expand a bit on this notion by introducing the concept of precursors, and maintain that interventions should be selected to deal with precursors as well as with problems.

This gap analysis approach can be quite useful for identifying a broad set of potentially appropriate intervention techniques, but in and of itself does not specify one particular action to use.

Organizational Congruence

As an alternative to choosing intervention sets on the basis of the gaps or problems that are identified, actions can be selected with the intention of achieving congruence between relevant current aspects of the organization. From this perspective, improved organizational functioning is a result of such congruence. Thus, interventions can be chosen to bring about congruence between the organization and environmental demands, or between organizational and individual needs (Lawrence & Lorsch, 1969). Or, interventions can be selected to achieve congruency among various organizational components (Nadler, 1981) or diagnostic variables (Beer, 1980). In these theories, the guide for intervention selection is the congruency one wishes to achieve. Intervention techniques are chosen to focus on the desired congruencies.

As indicated above, focusing on gaps or on incongruous variables may suggest a set of appropriate interventions, but it may also leave open the question of which particular intervention to use. In other words, two or more different interventions might be available to address the same problem area or to achieve congruence between the same variables. The second stage of the decision process, then, is to choose between the available interventions. Three categories of criteria by which to choose can be identified.

Target System Readiness

The first and broadest of these criteria might be referred to as the readiness of the target system for the particular intervention under consideration (Burke, 1982; French & Bell, 1978). Conditions necessary for the success of the intervention should be present (Tichy, 1983). Probably key among these conditions is the availability of sufficient resources to support the change process (Burke 1982; French & Bell, 1978). In addition to tangible resources, sufficient time on the part of key organizational members must also be available to contribute to the intervention activities (Argyris, 1970; Margulies & Raia, 1978). Other factors suggested as affecting an organization's readiness for an intervention are the organization's health (Argyris, 1970); the consistency of the intervention with current culture and management philosophy (Margulies & Raia, 1978); the experience the organization has had with self-assessment (Margulies & Raia, 1978); and the degree of intervention depth the organization can tolerate (Tichy, 1983).

Leverage Points

The second criterion influencing the selection of specific intervention techniques has to do with the notion of leverage. Leverage points are aspects of the organization which are amenable to change and which have some concrete linkage to the change objective (Lippitt, Watson, & Westley, 1958).

A determination of the key leverage points in the organization is crucial in deciding *where* to intervene in the system and *how* to sequence interventions (French & Bell, 1978). Leverage will be gained by linking the change process to the power points in the organization (Burke, 1982). These include the individuals who are central to the main problems identified in the diagnosis, for example, human resource specialists when the reward system is a main area of concern. Also, greater leverage will be achieved by focusing on causal rather than intervening variables (Likert, 1967).

Change Agent Skill

Finally, interventions should be chosen on the basis of the skill of the change agent. His or her competence (Argyris, 1970), orientation (Margulies & Raia, 1978), and degree of understanding of the intervention possibilities (Tichy, 1983) are all important factors in determining whether the change agent should attempt to use a particular intervention. Often failures in intervention occur because the change agent attempts some action he or she is not competent to carry out. Knowing the limits of one's capabilities is a final criterion for selection of specific change techniques.

Conditions for Effective Change

The next column in Table 2, *Conditions for Effective Change,* poses greater difficulties in forming generalizations. This is because many of the characteristics mentioned in one theory are included in, if any, only one or two others.[4] We believe that this does not reflect disagreement over these issues as much as it indicates that many factors apparently are operating in change efforts and that there is no consensus on which factors are crucial for successful change. However, to give some indication of what might be the important characteristics, we will point out those which were considered in at least three theories.

The most commonly acknowledged factor necessary for effective change has to do with the quality of the client system involvement in the change program. Some theorists emphasize top level support (French & Bell, 1978; Lawrence & Lorsch, 1969), and focus on the need for strong leadership in the change effort (Beckhard, 1969; Beer, 1980). Others focus on lower level members (Cummings & Srivastva, 1977), and some note the need for commitment and involvement of the entire client system (Argyris, 1970; Blake & Mouton, 1968). In all these cases, however, the emphasis is on the client system providing the energy for the change process, *not the change agent*. In order for effective change to occur, the system members must want to make it happen.

Also receiving emphasis as an important factor is the recognition of a need for change. There needs to be a dissatisfaction with the status quo (Beer, 1980), which can come about through an awareness by key people of organizational problems (French & Bell, 1978), through a high degree of personal and/or system discomfort (Argyris, 1970), or through pressure from the environment (Beckhard, 1969). It should be emphasized that, in addition to recognizing a need for change (a deficiency oriented perspective), there should be some attraction toward the positive characteristics of a changed situation (Lawrence & Lorsch, 1969).

A third condition for effective change suggested in some of the theories is a willingness to break away from old patterns of operating and to take risks with new patterns. People must be open to deviating from existing norms (Argyris, 1970) and to taking risks (Beckhard, 1969). Operating procedures which bind the organization to its present managerial system must be altered (Likert, 1967). And finally, a climate must be created which supports behavior that is open, experimental, and high in trust and risk-taking (Cummings & Srivastva, 1977).

A final condition for effective change is simply the existence of early success and reinforcement (Beer, 1980; French & Bell, 1978) or, as Beckhard (1969) puts it, tangible intermediate results. This requires, of course, that the OD process be monitored and results measured (French & Bell, 1978).

Characteristics of Effective Change Agents

The final column in Table 2 also poses some difficulties in generalization for the same reasons as noted above regarding Conditions for Effective Change. However, a few patterns of interest emerged when analyzing this dimension.

Four characteristics of change agents surfaced as important. The first of these is simply interpersonal competence (Bowers & Franklin, 1972; Burke, 1982; Lawrence & Lorsch, 1969), or what Lippitt, Watson, and Westley (1958) call relational skills. These skills include the abilities to support and nurture others and to confront difficult issues (Burke, 1982); to influence others and to listen well and empathize (Burke, 1982; Margulies & Raia, 1978); to be highly aware and socially sensitive (Margulies & Raia, 1978); and to be able to facilitate group processes (Bowers & Franklin, 1972).

A second criterion for change agents is the ability to provide a link between scientific knowledge regarding solving problems and the problems present in the organization in which the planned change will take place (Bowers & Franklin, 1972). Thus, both problem-solving capabilities and client-related expertise are important criteria (Margulies & Raia, 1978). The former requires an ability to conceptualize (Burke, 1982) and diagnose (Lawrence & Lorsch, 1969), and an orientation toward theories and methods of change (Lippitt, Watson, & Westley, 1958), while the latter relies on an ability to present a range of options to the client system (French & Bell, 1978).

Third, the change agent must be an educator (Lawrence & Lorsch, 1969). He or she needs to be able to teach or create learning experiences (Burke, 1982) and invest the environment with growth experiences (Argyris, 1970). One means by which this might be accomplished is by modeling discrepant behavior which creates tension and thus induces change (Beer, 1980). Therefore, it is important that the change agent be able to practice and develop effective behavior (French & Bell, 1978).

Finally, a change agent needs to be in touch with himself or herself. Being aware of the assumptions and models underlying one's practice is central (Beer, 1980), as is the ability to recognize one's own feelings and intuitions quickly (Burke, 1982), and to have a clear understanding of one's motivations (Lippitt, Watson, & Westley, 1958). Self-insight serves as a necessary guide to ethical decisions in the course of any change program.

Summary of Implementation Theory

In summary, then, we have seen that implementation theory can be broken down into three subcategories. At the most general level are change strategies which, although concerned with the activities involved in change, do not provide much guidance for change agents regarding specific actions to take. At the most specific level are technique theories. These theories focus on only one phase of the entire change process, a process which is the subject of the third, more intermediate level of theories, the subcategory labeled procedure theories.

 An in-depth look at procedure theories as a group produced four major generalizations. The first is that there is considerable consensus on what steps are important in a planned change attempt. These steps are diagnosis, planning, intervention, and evaluation, four phases which form the core of the action research model.

The second is that there is much less agreement on which variables should be analyzed for an effective diagnosis of the organization. The multitude of diverse variables described in the set of theories we assessed was classified into the seven elements of a model by Porras (in press). Yet even then, agreement across this more general set of variables was only partial. Organizing arrangements and social factors were considered important by all the theories; technology and environment were included about half the time; and outcomes, purpose, and physical setting received very little support. We view inattention to these latter variables as a weakness of the diagnostic aspect of implementation theory.

A third finding was that even less agreement exists regarding both the conditions necessary for effective change and useful characteristics of change agents. Four conditions and four characteristics that garnered marginal support were discussed. All in all, however, the myriad of suggestions indicates that adequate systematic knowledge regarding these two categories has not been obtained. Of critical importance for the field is a theoretical understanding of the interactive effects of the particular problems being corrected, the conditions present within the situation and the change process, and the characteristics of the change agent.

In contrast to this discouraging assessment, the final generalization we can make reflects an area on which relative agreement exists among the theorists. This has to do with the criteria for choosing interventions. Although the original composite list appeared somewhat diverse, we were able to organize the many criteria into five categories which correspond to two stages in the intervention selection process. We believe that this two stage process, along with the five criteria, can serve as a useful guide to change agents for selecting the interventions they will use in an attempt to improve system functioning.

The purpose of implementation theory, as indicated earlier, is to provide guidance to change agents regarding the activities they should engage in to successfully bring about change in organizational systems. Our examination of this type of theory suggests that it partially fulfills its purpose insofar as it provides an outline of the steps that need to be performed and a framework for choosing interventions. However, it falls short of its goal by failing to specify an adequate diagnostic model and by not achieving a systematic understanding of the conditions necessary for change or of the characteristics imperative for change agents to be effective.

CHANGE PROCESS THEORY

We turn now to the second broad type of theory in our proposed typology, change process theory. To restate the definition, change process theory is theory that explains the dynamics of the change process by specifying (a) the variables that are manipulable in the change effort, (b) the intended outcomes of the change attempt, (c) the causal relationships between manipulable, mediator, and outcome or target variables, and (d) the effects of relevant moderator variables.

The theories on which our analysis is based are presented in Table 6. The format of the table has been designed to facilitate the subsequent discussion. Therefore, it is necessary at this point to digress for a moment to explain the rationale behind the table and the meaning of the format used. The columns in the table correspond to one of four types of variables that constitute a change process theory: (1) target variables; (2) manipulable variables; (3) mediator variables; and (4) moderator variables. These variables are defined as follows.

> *Target variables* are those which a change program is geared to ultimately affect in its attempt to improve organizational functioning. These are typically variables that are viewed as outcomes of system functioning.
>
> *Manipulable variables* are change levers, elements which can be directly influenced and which are thought to lead, through the causal mechanisms, to change in the target variables.
>
> *Mediator variables* are those variables that comprise the middle of the causal chain. Change in a manipulable variable must lead to change in the relevant mediator variable(s) if there is to be subsequent change in the target variables.
>
> *Moderator variables* are variables which impact the causal relationship between two other variables. Whether or not change in one variable leads to change in the variable that follows in the causal sequence depends on the state of the relevant moderator variables. They are not part of the causal chain themselves, in that they do not have to change, but they have an important bearing on the extent to Which the causal mechanism operates successfully.[5]

The relationships among these four types of variables are schematically represented in Figure 2A, which attempts to show the key connections that exist between the four sets of variables. We should note that theories can vary in the number of mediator variables included at each stage, how many different causal stages or links exist, the number of moderator variables thought to be relevant to a particular causal link, or which causal links have any moderator variables relevant to them at all.

Figure 2B builds on the relationships shown in Figure 2A, and represents how a theory modeled in that format could be presented in tabular rather than schematic form. The dotted lines in Figure 2B separate the various stages of the causal chain. For example, the first link in Figure 2A consists of manipulable variable(s) A impacting mediator variable(s) B, and this link is moderated by moderator variable(s) C. In Figure 2B, this is shown in the table cell above the top horizontal line.

The second link in Figure 2A then consists of mediator variable(s) B impacting mediator variable(s) D, moderated by moderator variable(s) E. This is represented in Figure 2B with the information between the two dotted lines. B is driving D so D is placed directly below B to signify this relationship. E is on the

(A)   Schematic Representation

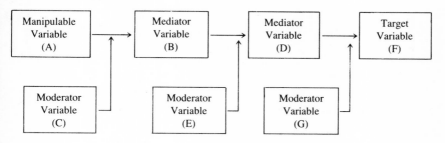

(B)   Tabular Representation

Theory	Target Level	Target Variables	Manipulable Variables	Mediator Variables	Moderator Variables
Doe(198X)	Organization	F	A	B	C
				D	E
					G

Figure 2.   Process Variables in OD Theory

same horizontal level as D because it provides the moderating context for the B→D relationship.[6]

The final link in this model is the connection of mediator variable(s) D to target variable F. This relationship is moderated by moderator variable(s) G. This is represented in the figure by placing G below the bottom horizontal dotted line.[7] This reflects the fact that the last mentioned mediator variable D is related to the target variable F with the relationship moderated by the variable at the bottom of the moderator variable column.[8]

Table 6 presents the theories on which our analysis will be based. In contrast to the list of implementation theories, we have included in this table *all* of the substantive change process theories which were found in an extensive search of literature relevant to OD.[9]

To examine this group of theories, we will follow a similar course as was taken in the evaluation of implementation theory. That is, we will take each column of Table 6 and try to summarize and evaluate the information obtained from the theories. For information on particular theories, however, the reader should refer to the table.

Table 6. Change Process Theories In Organization Development

Theory	Target Level	Target Variables	Manipulable Variables	Mediator Variables	Moderator Variables
Cartwwright (1951)	Individual	Behavior, attitudes, beliefs and values	Group norms and standards Leadership style Emotional atmosphere Stratification into cliques and hierarchies	Shared perception of need for change	
				Pressure to conform Threat of punishment for nonconformity	
					Strong sense of belonging to the group Attractiveness of the group Relevance of change target to basis of group's attractiveness Prestige of influencer
Dalton (1970)	Individual	Behavior and attitudes, re-inforced and internalized	Information	Testing out proposed changes	Internal tension, felt need for change Authority and prestige of influencer
					Objectives become more specific Relationships form which support intended changes

Goodman & Dean (1982)	Organizational	Information	Knowledge	Self-esteem improves Motivation for change becomes internalized
	Institutionalization of behavior			Credibility of the communicator Content of the communication Relationship between content and prior experiences or current attitudes and beliefs
			Adoption/performance of behavior	Perceived ability to perform new behavior Perceived relationships between behavior and rewards Attractiveness of the rewards
			Preference for and continuation of the behavior	Congruency between actual and expected rewards Level of commitment to new behavior
			Normative and value consensus	Social comparison processes Social threshold Attributions about appropriateness

(continued)

33

Table 6. (Cont.)

Theory	Target Level	Target Variables	Manipulable Variables	Mediator Variables	Moderator Variables
House (1967)	Organizational	Performance	Information	Knowledge	Lateral and vertical generalization Communication and persuasion
				Attitudes	Motivation to learn Ability to learn Method of instruction
					Ego involvement/flexible attitudes Discussion of application and benefits Superior's attitude Top managment philosophy Cultural conditions
				Skills	Adaptability Practice of desired abilities Corrective training Superior's attitude
				Individual's performance	On-the-job practice and feedback of results Coaching and counseling by superior Top management philosophy and practices

34

Lawler (1982)	Organizational	Operating effectiveness	Organizational design features: Organizational structure Job design Information system Career system Selection and training policies Reward system Personnel policies Physical layout	Understanding of reward system Knowledge of and responsibility for organizational performance that is meaningful Extrinsic and intrinsic rewards tied to organizational performance Motivation for skill building Learning opportunities Preemployment skills Motivation and mechanisms for communication, coordination, and self-control
				Primary group norms Coordination of individuals' performances toward organizational goals Performance appraisal based on new practices New practices rewarded Top management support Informal group attitudes
				Motivation for organizational performance

(continued)

35

Table 6. (*Cont.*)

Theory	Target Level	Target Variables	Manipulable Variables	Mediator Variables	Moderator Variables
		Quality of work life	The above organizational design features	Individual performance capability Communication, coordination, and self-control Meeting of people's existence, social, and growth and control needs	
Miles et al. (1969)	Organizational	Organizational health	Information fedback through meetings, with a focus on process analysis	Corroboration or disconfirmation of feelings Inquiries why responses on which data are based were as they were Meetings run by relevant work groups Success experiences Increased interaction between peers, and between superiors and subordinates Process legitimized as content Cognitive awareness of process issues	

36

(continued)

				Collaborative data collection
			Attention, concern and acceptance of data Liking of task and others Conformity pressures Pressure for clarification of own and other's position Development of problem-solving norms and practice of problem-solving behavior through process feedback	
			Development of change goals Development of change-supporting norms and skills	
			Action decisions Development of new change-supporting structures	
Nadler (1977)	Individual	Behavior	Information, through the processes of data collection and feedback	Expectations that data collection will affect desired outcomes Disconfirmation of perceptions Changes in external and internal reward expectancies	Importance of data to relevant power groups Perceived accuracy of data

37

Table 6. (Cont.)

Theory	Target Level	Target Variables	Manipulable Variables	Mediator Variables	Moderator Variables
				Motivation to perform measured behavior	Goal setting is facilitated Comparison data is included Task is challenging Perceived accuracy of data Clear link between performance and rewards Rewards are valued Psychological safety Level of performance is attainable

Targets of Change

The first two columns in the table indicate what is to be the target of change, described by level of analysis (i.e., individual or organizational, and as specific variables). Each theory presented attempts to explain how change takes place in the designated target variable. Three of the theories focus on the individual as the change target and specify characteristics of the individual as variables of interest. Cartwright (1951) focuses on individual change, both behavioral and cognitive. Likewise, the Dalton (1970, p. 155) model explains change in behavior and attitudes of individuals, although he makes it clear that the final goal is organizational change, which requires "the significant alteration of the behavior patterns of a large part of the individuals who constitute the organization." Nadler (1977) suggests that his model explains how data collection and feedback can lead to the change of behavior of individuals, groups, and the organization. However, he does not address the issue of how group or organizational behavior can be defined in terms other than the behavior of individual members, and thus the theory appears to be explaining only individual change.

The remaining four theories target the organization as the focus of change. Although Goodman and Dean (1982) consider behavior change as the target variable, the level they focus on can best be described as organizational. They describe the process by which individuals make the decision to adopt new behaviors, but, in contrast to Nadler (1977), they also attempt to explain how the behavioral changes made by individuals in the organization are translated into the institutionalization of the behavior. An institutionalized act is one which persists over time, is performed by two or more individuals in response to a common stimulus, and exists as a social fact (Goodman, Bazerman, & Conlon, 1980). Also explaining change at the organizational level are Miles, Hornstein, Callahan, Calder, and Schiavo (1969), who emphasize organizational health; House (1967), whose target variable is organizational performance[10]; and Lawler (1982), who looks at both performance and quality of work life.

The targets of change in these theories, then, are predominantly of two types, either individual behavior or some form of organizational effectiveness. Furthermore, as indicated above, change in individual behavior is often seen as a key means of improving organizational effectiveness, although this linkage has not been conceptualized by these theorists.

We should note that the primary individual level change target in these theories is behavior and not psychological health or self-actualization. Historically, for implementation theorists, OD has had the dual goals of improving *both* organizational performance and the psychological health of the organizational members, the latter primarily through greater opportunities for self-actualization. Yet the goal of psychological health has not received much theoretical attention as a target of change. Lawler (1982) does include as a change target the quality of work life, which he points out is a function of meeting peoples' existence, social, and growth and control needs. Other than this, though, the theories remain silent on the matter. Two useful avenues of theoretical development would be to explain the dynamics by which improved individual psychological health is attained, and to explore the relationship between more effective individual behavior in the organization and increases in psychological health.[11]

Manipulable Variables

A composite list of the manipulable variables proposed by all the theories combined turns out to be somewhat sparse. Information seems to be the primary variable and is the only one included by House (1967) and by Goodman and Dean (1982). Dalton (1970) does not explicitly specify information as being the manipulable variable, but it can be inferred from his emphasis on influence attempts as the initial cause of change. Information is the important variable in Nadler's (1977) approach, as he analyzes the mechanisms by which data collection and feedback lead to behavior change. Similarly, Miles et al. (1969), in considering the impact of survey feedback on the organization, propose that the manipulable variable is information—either information about the organization fedback to its members or information generated through the process analyses conducted at these feedback meetings.

Only two theories propose manipulable variables other than information. Lawler (1982) proposes an extensive list of organizational design variables that he groups into the eight categories noted in Table 6. And Cartwright (1951) considers four characteristics of groups that are instrumental in bringing about change in group members.

A few observations can be made about the above set of manipulable variables. First, to reiterate, the list is rather limited. It leads to the impression that there should be many more variables recognized as being important change levers. In fact, a comparison to the diagnostic variables discussed in the implementation theory section seems useful. There, the model by Porras (in press) was used to classify the many variables that had been suggested as important for effective organizational diagnosis. Of these, five of them—purpose, organizing arrangements, social factors, technology, and physical setting—are obviously manipulable in a planned change program.

Similarly, other writers have addressed the issue of what characteristics of an organization can be the focus of planned change. Leavitt (1965, pp. 1145–46), for example, divides change strategies into structural, technological, and people approaches. As Leavitt points out, all three approaches share "an expressed interest in improving organizational behavior, through improved performance of tasks." Yet the three approaches can be differentiated by, among other things, their different points of entry into the organization.

The important point here is that, regardless of the organizational model or the particular variables selected, a comprehensive theory of change process should designate a broad set of variables that could be manipulated by those trying to induce change. A review of current planned change theory (i.e., the seven theories presented here) shows that this requirement is not adequately met. The range of manipulable variables specified in these theories is much too restricted.

Part of the problem in these perspectives is the emphasis on information. It is not clear whether information can accurately be referred to as a variable, in the sense that a change in information will create, through whatever causal mechanisms might be operating, a change in a target variable such as behavior. In two of the theories, namely Nadler (1977) and Miles et al. (1969), information does seem to fit this description. In both cases, it is a change of information available to organizational members, gained through the process of feedback, which directly induces them to at least consider changing their behavior. This happens through the creation of a state of tension which results from a conflict between old perceptions and feelings, and new ones that arise from the new information.

For the other three theories in which information also seems to be the main manipulable variable, the change trigger takes the form of information to the organizational member about possible new behaviors he or she could adopt. Sometimes, this information is viewed as coming in an attempt to influence the recipient to adopt the new behavior (Dalton, 1970; House, 1967). However, information is not always *explicitly* suggested as a variable to manipulate (Dalton, 1970; Goodman & Dean, 1982). Instead, it has to be inferred, given the first stage of the causal sequence. For example, Dalton (1970) points out that individuals first test out the proposed changes advocated by the person trying to influence their behavior. In advocating change, the influencer must transmit information. In House (1967) and in Goodman and Dean (1982), the first stage is labeled "knowledge of the behavior," which suggests that this also is preceded by some form of transmission of information regarding the behavior.

In this sense, information seems less like a specific variable that is changed by the change agent in order to induce other types of changes. Instead, information regarding new behaviors most likely is a consequence of changes in variables such as those included in the diagnostic model. For example, changes in policies and procedures (i.e., changes in organizing arrangements) certainly provide new information to employees concerning what behaviors are appropriate. Similarly, the replacement of equipment (i.e., technological change) will invariably be accompanied by information on how to correctly operate the new equipment.

In light of this, specification of these manipulable variables by change process theorists would be necessary for achieving a greater understanding of change dynamics. Different types of changes (i.e., the manipulation of different variables) would provide different information to individuals and would trigger different sets of conditions that would have an important impact on how the remainder of the causal mechanism operated.

While the task of specifying all these differences a priori is likely to be too difficult, a useful starting point would be for change process theory to specify these variables so that the differences could then be tested empirically. It is a major weakness of these theories, individually, that so few variables are specified. Collectively, there can be no movement towards consensus on what the important manipulable variables are unless individual theories propose more variables.

Mediator Variables

The third column in Table 6 shows the mediator variables hypothesized to link manipulable variables to target variables. As explained earlier, a causal chain may have several stages or links, and each link itself may have one or several mediator variables. For our present purposes, however, we will not distinguish the variables by the stage of the causal chain in which they are found. Instead, they will be considered as one set, and the following discussion will pertain to the entire set, although they will be grouped into three broad categories: (1) motivational factors; (2) social influence factors; and (3) individual attributes.[12]

Motivational Factors

Motivation is an important variable included in the causal chain. Motivating factors driving individual behavior change take two forms in the theories presented. First are those variables that are related in one way or another to rewards. For example, Lawler (1982) suggests that individuals must understand the reward system, and also that intrinsic and extrinsic rewards should be tied to organizational performance. Nadler (1977) points out that there must be expectations that the data collection process will affect outcomes desired by individuals, and that changes in both internal and external reward expectancies must result from the feedback of the data. Miles et al. (1969) include success experiences (implied is the notion that success will be rewarding) as important to a continuation of the change process that has already begun. In all of these cases, the notion of rewards motivating behavior change plays a key role.

A second motivational factor has to do with the recognition of a need for change. If data fed back to individuals disconfirms their feelings (Miles et al., 1969) or perceptions (Nadler, 1977), a desire to change typically results. Certainly this outcome requires individual acceptance of the data, and may also involve inquiries as to why responses were as they were (Miles et al., 1969) before behavior change occurs.

On the more proactive side, the development of change goals (Miles et al., 1969) can lead people to see where change is needed by clarifying the gap between a desired state and the present situation. Another method of generating a need for change can come about through the use of the small group in the organization. Using the group to generate a shared need for change results in stronger motivational force for change in the individual (Cartwright, 1951).

Social Influence Factors

These mediator variables reflect the role of other organizational members in influencing an individual to alter his or her behavior. These variables are found in three of the theories, and each describes a somewhat different mechanism for change. Cartwright (1951) sees pressure to conform and threat of punishment for nonconformity as helping to bring about change in individuals. Goodman and Dean (1982) take a more positive view of the process and suggest that normative and value consensus regarding the appropriateness of new behaviors are the key mechanisms for achieving institutionalization of those behaviors.

Miles et al. (1969) hypothesize a dynamic that incorporates a portion of both of these first two perspectives. They suggest that the survey feedback process will lead to increased interaction between peers, and between superiors and subordinates. With increased interaction, there will be enhanced liking of the task and other group members, resulting in increased pressures to conform and for clarification of the positions held by the various members. These in turn will lead to the development of problem solving norms and change-supporting norms and structures.

Individual Attributes

This final category of mediator variables can be broken down into three subcategories: (a) cognitive characteristics; (b) skills; and (c) behaviors.

Cognitive characteristics include knowledge and attitudes. Knowledge, or awareness and understanding of new behaviors, appears to be a key initial mediator variable (House, 1967; Goodman & Dean, 1982). In addition, knowledge of and responsibility for meaningful organizational performance is important in generating motivation to perform well (Lawler, 1982). However, positive attitudes regarding new practices and concepts must follow awareness of them if behavior is to change (House, 1967). Once the initial change has accrued, preference for, and thus continuation of, a new behavior is an important part of the longer term institutionalization process (Goodman & Dean, 1982).

Skills must change along with attitudes in order for individuals to improve their performance (House, 1967). Individual performance capabilities are a function of pre-employment skills, learning opportunities, and motivation for skill building. As such, they are a key determinant of operating effectiveness, and must improve if the effectiveness of the organization is to improve (Lawler, 1982).

Operating skills are not the only ones critical for organizational improvement. Skills in facilitating change are also critical if change is to endure. Miles et al. (1969) point out that development of problem-solving skills will in turn lead to the development of change-supporting skills as well.

The third individual attribute is behavior, an area which contains some very contradictory points of view. In Goodman and Dean's (1982) model, the adoption of the behavior is the second mediator variable, following knowledge of the behavior. Only after a behavior is adopted can an individual determine whether the results of the new behavior are sufficiently rewarding to continue performing it. In other words, the attitude about the behavior follows its performance.

House (1967), on the other hand, suggests that the process works the opposite way. He maintains that an individual, after becoming aware of a new behavior, will need to develop a positive attitude regarding it before performing it. Thus, change in individual performance is the last mediator variable in his model rather than the first.

The only mediator variable indicated by Dalton (1970) is the testing of proposed changes in behavior or attitude. This follows advocation of the change, and precedes reinforcement and internalization of the new behavior or attitude.

Miles et al. (1969), while not explicitly describing a behavior, identify action decisions as a mediator variable. We include it here because it implies that actions (behaviors) will follow. There are no other mediator variables specified between action decisions and the target variable of greater organizational health in the Miles et al. formulation.

Moderator Variables

Listed in the last column in Table 6, moderator variables are conceived of as having an impact on the relationship between any two variables in the causal chain. As with the mediator variables, we break the list of moderator variables into three categories: (1) characteristics of the information generation and transmission process; (2) propensity to change factors; and (3) social influence factors.[13]

Information Generation and Transmission

Our discussion of manipulable variables highlighted the fact that the predominant variable included in these theories was information. Because of this, many characteristics of the information itself and of the process through which it is generated and transmitted have been hypothesized as affecting how individuals react and change.

Three broad categories of the information generation and transmission process seem to have been emphasized: (a) characteristics of the data; (b) characteristics of the individual who is using the data to influence others; and (c) characteristics of the process through which the data are collected and given to the organization being influenced.

For the data to be influential, they must be perceived as accurate (Nadler, 1977), relevant (Goodman & Dean, 1982), meaningfully comparable to other data (Nadler, 1977), credible in terms of how they relate to the receiver's prior experiences or current attitudes and beliefs (Goodman & Dean, 1982), and viewed as important by the power groups in the organization (Nadler, 1977). These characteristics of the data themselves strongly affect the impact they have.

The traits of the individual using the data to influence others also play an important moderator role in the change process. The authority and prestige of the influencer have an important bearing on whether or not proposed changes are adopted (Cartwright, 1951; Dalton, 1970). The credibility of the communicator also plays an important role in the receipt, modification, or rejection of the information transmitted (Goodman & Dean, 1982). One should not expect that the power of the data themselves are sufficient to influence change, but rather that the person using the data plays an important role as well.

Finally, the process itself through which data are collected and shared with the target system has an effect on the degree of influence which occurs. Collaboration of the client group in the collection of data will increase its acceptance. Data collected without direct involvement of the organizational members in the process tends to not be as central as if the same data were collected in collaboration with the client group (Miles et al., 1969).

The method of instruction (i.e., the means by which information is communicated,) can affect what is learned. For example, the development of positive attitudes about new behaviors will be enhanced if individuals can discuss with others how these behaviors can be applied and what benefits will accrue if they are adopted (House, 1967).

All of these contextual characteristics will affect the degree to which information will influence individuals to change their behavior on the job.

Propensity to Change Factors

This next category of moderator variables focuses on internal aspects of the individual rather than on the external dynamics described above. It consists of three subcategories of variables: (a) those influencing an individual's ability to change; (b) those affecting his or her motivation to change; and (c) variables involving rewards.

Regarding the ability of people to change, Goodman and Dean (1982) maintain that the perceived ability to perform a new behavior will moderate whether or not the behavior is adopted. Similarly, Nadler (1977) views motivation to perform a behavior as being dependent in part on whether or not the level of performance is attainable.

Ability to learn plays an important role in the extent to which knowledge regarding new behaviors and practices will be acquired (House, 1967). Furthermore, whether knowledge can be converted into skills will depend on the individual's adaptability, the opportunities he or she has to practice new skills, and training to correct any undesirable behavior patterns. On-the-job practice and feedback of results is important in converting skills into improved performance.

While ability focuses on whether or not people can change, a motivational issue is whether they are willing to change. Thus, motivation to change is the second subcategory of propensity to change. A felt need for change and the internalization of motivation to change are important moderators (Dalton, 1970). Motivation to learn is another important factor influencing the acquisition of new knowledge (House, 1967).

Conditions that facilitate goal setting also can be significant moderating variables (Nadler, 1977), since goals can provide motivation. Along the same vein, as objectives become more specific, it is more likely that new behaviors and attitudes will be established and maintained (Dalton, 1970).

Three final variables that can be related to motivation to change are the level of ego involvement, which moderates attitudinal change (House, 1967); the level of commitment, which affects whether or not individuals will continue to perform adopted behavior (Goodman & Dean, 1982); and the degree to which a task is challenging, which can influence the extent to which its attainment is desirable (Nadler, 1977).

The third subcategory of propensity to change factors is closely tied to the second. The variables included here are those that involve rewards, which have an important influence on motivation. These variables deal with the question of what will happen if people do change. The perceived relationship between performance or behavior and rewards will play a crucial role in determining whether or not behaviors will change (Goodman & Dean, 1982; Nadler, 1977). Thus, organizational performance will improve if performance appraisal is based on the new practices and if the new behaviors are directly rewarded (House, 1967). Congruency between expected and actual rewards will impact the decision regarding continuation of an adopted behavior (Goodman & Dean, 1982). And last but certainly not least, the value of the rewards will have a major bearing on decisions regarding change (Goodman & Dean, 1982; Nadler, 1977).

Social Influence Factors

This final category of moderator variables takes into account characteristics and processes of the social system in which the change is taking place. Psychological safety must exist for people to be willing to change (Nadler, 1977). In addition, change will be more likely if relationships form which support the intended changes (Dalton, 1970). Cultural conditions, primary group norms, and informal group attitudes are also important moderators of change (House, 1967).

Management plays a key part in the success of any change effort. For example, the immediate superior's attitude towards the change plays an important direct role in the process. Whether he or she coaches and counsels individuals trying to change strongly influences the success of any effort. Furthermore, top management philosophy and practices have a much broader yet strongly influential effect on the development effort (House, 1967).

The individual's co-workers are also a component of the context in which change takes place. If the group is attractive to the individual, if the change target is relevant to the basis of attraction, and if the individual has a strong sense of belonging to the group, he or she will be much more likely to change in response to pressures for conformity (Cartwright, 1951).

Goodman and Dean (1982), in an attempt to explain how behaviors adopted by individuals in an organization become institutionalized acts, list six mechanisms that moderate the development of a normative and value consensus regarding the behaviors:

1. social comparison processes help people validate their beliefs about the value of a new behavior;
2. a social threshold exists such that the percentage of people adopting a new behavior becomes large enough that the costs of not adopting it become too great;
3. attributions about appropriateness work to verify that the behavior should be performed;
4. lateral generalization helps to allow attributions of appropriateness to generalize to new behaviors that are similar to behaviors which are already considered appropriate;
5. vertical generalization ensures that these behaviors then become valued (i.e., seen as being "good");
6. communication and persuasion serve to augment the other five mechanisms as system members communicate with each other about beliefs, behaviors, preferences, norms, and values.

These mechanisms indicate that the impact of other members of the social system is a critical element in this process.

Summary of Change Process Theory

The preceeding examination of the four types of variables that comprise change process theory produced the following generalizations. First, the variables that are the targets of change in these theories are generally of two types, either individual behavior or organizational performance or effectiveness. Individual psychological growth or self-actualization is not considered at all, despite its importance historically as one of the basic goals of Organization Development.

The weakest aspect of these theories as a group is the paucity of manipulable variables suggested. The majority of the models contain information as the sole manipulable variable. We agree that the information available to organizational members is an important ingredient in any changes that occur within the system. Furthermore, it can be argued that a change in information will accompany a change in any other variable that could potentially be considered a manipulable variable, e.g., structure or technology. However, since information change will always be present, a primary focus on information reduces the usefulness of the theory. What is important instead is the ways in which changes in manipulable organizational characteristics have differential impacts on information and other variables in the causal mechanism. Therefore, change process theory could be improved by specifying these key variables, so that these differences in the operation of the causal mechanisms could be hypothesized and tested empirically.

In contrast to the manipulable variables, a substantial range of both mediator and moderator variables has been hypothesized as playing an important role in the dynamics of organizational change. Also, within each type, nearly all the variables could be placed into one of three categories, reflecting agreement on the nature of the variables that are likely to be consequential in change processes.

It is interesting to note, however, that there is substantial overlap between variables specified as mediators and those specified as moderators. Both types have a category of social influence variables, and while the specific variables are not necessarily the same, the foci are similar. For instance, the norms of the system in which change is occuring, the extent to which an individual likes being involved in the system, and the degree to which aspects of the system support the change are all factors that are included as both mediators and moderators.

Similarly, the relationships between performance and rewards, and the expectations that people develop regarding how changes will affect the rewards they receive, are included in both lists of variables. Finally, motivation to change, the perception of a need for change, and the role of goal setting in helping to achieve change have all been suggested both as being a part of the causal mechanism and as moderating a causal link.

An implication of this overlap is that, while there is some agreement on the nature of variables important to change processes, there is still confusion regarding how the causal mechanisms operate. In other words, the interchangeability of some classes of variables between mediators and moderators demonstrates that change process theory, at its present state of development, is unable to adequately specify the dynamics underlying planned change in organizational settings.

A focus of future theoretical work should be to determine more accurately which variables are part of the causal sequence and which variables moderate the process. Awareness of the former would enable change agents to more finely tune their interventions and to monitor the change to make sure it is ''taking,'' while an understanding of the latter would allow them to better predict whether a change attempt is likely to succeed in a given situation. Both of these benefits would serve to improve the chances for planned change attempts to be successfully administered.

We conclude our summary of change process theories with a few general observations. First, it is important to note that the number of theories attempting to explain the dynamics of change is relatively small. In our search of the literature, a few additional theories focusing on change dynamics were found (e.g., Schein, 1964; Kimberly & Nielsen, 1975), but their levels of specification of the causal mechanisms were insufficient to be considered as a change process theory.

Even among the theories we have included here, there is quite a bit of variance in the degree of specification of variables and their relationships. The theories range from Dalton (1970), who specifies 1 mediator and 6 moderator variables, to Miles et al. (1969), who describe 15 mediator variables in 5 stages, and House (1967), who includes 21 moderator variables moderating 5 causal links. This variance in the complexity of the theories is further evidence of the evaluation made above that the dynamics of change are not yet adequately understood.

In addition to complexity, the generality of the theories is another dimension by which they can be differentiated. Most of these theories have limited generality because they have a particular intervention strategy as an underlying guiding framework. Miles et al. (1969) and Nadler (1977) are based on survey feedback; Cartwright (1951) is grounded in group dynamics; House (1967) focuses on management development; and Lawler (1982) is concerned with increasing worker involvement as a means to improved organizational effectiveness. Only two theories, Dalton (1970) and Goodman and Dean (1982), attempt to explain changes in behavior without linking these changes to particular methods. It would be beneficial if future theoretical development focused on building more generalized models, models which could explain change dynamics regardless of the strategy used to induce the change.

A fourth characteristic of these theories is that they do not seem to build on each other. By considering them in chronological order, one can not see any signs of evolution toward a parsimonious theory of change processes. This is no doubt due in part to the fact that most of them are associated with particular intervention strategies. But it may also indicate that there is no shared view of what the more relevant fundamental theories might be. For instance, a theory of change dynamics will of necessity have to incorporate elements of motivation theory. Yet various theories of motivation are represented in these theories. Expectancy theory is the most prominent, but traces of need theory and theory of goal-setting can be found as well. Agreement on what the most useful underlying theories are could help theorists build on each other's work to develop a more parsimonious change process theory.

FUTURE DIRECTIONS

Drawing on the above analysis, we next turn to a discussion of those areas of OD theory in which improved theoretical development is most needed. We will first address the specific needs that have emerged from our assessment. Then we will discuss in more general terms the need for an integrated, parsimonious theory of organizational change processes.

Regarding implementation theory, one area ripe for improvement is the development of a comprehensive diagnostic model, consensually supported as the most appropriate framework for viewing an organization. Currently, there are a number of models from which to choose, reflecting a lack either of understanding or of agreement about which organizational characteristics are critical determinants of an organization's effectiveness or the psychological well-being of its members. Furthermore, some potentially important factors, such as an organization's purpose or its physical setting, have, up to this point, been given very little attention. When agreement develops regarding the set of key variables most fruitfully explored in the diagnostic process, the choice of which model to use will no longer have to be such an arbitrary process. Furthermore, if the model is sufficiently comprehensive, it will insure that no critical variables are overlooked.

A second need is for greater clarification of the conditions necessary for change and the characteristics required of change agents. As indicated in the analysis above, a broad range of factors has been suggested in both of these categories. Since all the factors may at one time or another be critical to the success of a planned change program, it would be useful to clarify the interactive effects of the nature of the problem, the conditions necessary to successfully address the problem, and the change agent characteristics required to effectively facilitate the desired changes. This would allow a more accurate a priori assessment regarding the likelihood of change and a better match between change agents and situations.

Although implementation theory can use some important fine tuning, in general it is in relatively decent shape. In contrast, our analysis of change process theory suggests that substantial further theoretical development is needed in all areas. The goal of change process theory is to explicate the causal mechanisms through which changes in various organizational characteristics lead to desired changes in the targeted outcomes. A well-developed theory would specify the set of variables which can be manipulated by change agents, the set of outcomes which these interventions are intended to impact, and the dynamics through which these changes occur, including the relevant mediator and moderator variables.

One need, then, is improved specification of a set of manipulable variables. In practice, change agents' initial interventions impact a wide variety of organizational characteristics (e.g., structure, job design, decision-making processes, management style, etc.). Yet the theories discussed above do not reflect this diversity. As there may be overlap between the variables examined in a diagnosis and those manipulated by the change agent, theoretical development in each of these areas could draw upon work done in the other.

In addition to manipulable variables, a complete set of target variables must also be specified. As indicated earlier, individual behavior and various aspects of organizational effectiveness were the targets identified in the theories considered here. In light of this, a number of issues need to be addressed. First, as pointed out above, psychological health was not included. Since this has traditionally been a stated goal of OD, inclusion in change process theories seems paramount.

A second issue has to do with whether or not individual behavior change should in fact be considered a target variable. If individuals changed their behavior, yet there were no resulting changes in organizational performance or psychological well-being, would the change program be considered a success? If not, then individual behavior change remains a mediator variable, and the mechanisms through which changed behavior leads to changes in the target variables must be identified as well.[14]

Finally, it may be that organizational effectiveness should not be considered as a single target variable. Effectiveness can be measured along a number of dimensions (e.g., profitability, growth, quality of work life, etc.), and the factors leading to change along one of these dimensions may not bring about change along others. A similar caveat applies to the relationship between organizational effectiveness and psychological health. While it is often assumed that these two outcomes go hand in hand, this may not be the case and the change dynamics underlying each may be very different.

Perhaps the most important yet most difficult theoretical development needed is greater clarification of the nature of the underlying dynamics of change. The importance of this task rests in the potential utility of such a theory for assessing the progress of change programs as they occur. By indicating the causal linkages between manipulable and target variables, the theory could be used to help monitor the change effort. It could indicate where breakdowns in the process have occurred, and provide guidance regarding steps to take to get the program back on track.

Specification of the causal mechanisms is a difficult task, however, because of the complexity of organizational change processes. As indicated above, quite a few variables have been proposed as mediators and as moderators of the relationships between manipulable and target variables. Furthermore, there was a fair amount of overlap between these two sets of variables. Not surprisingly, there are also some similarities between these variables and the factors that were mentioned in the implementation theories as conditions for effective change. This may be because of the conceptual similarity between "moderators" and "conditions necessary for change."

Identification of the causal mechanisms will require sorting through the broad range of variables that have been suggested, in order to ascertain which of them form the causal links between manipulable and target variables and which ones serve to moderate these relationships. To achieve parsimony, the many specific variables may need to be aggregated to higher levels of abstraction. Towards this end, the categories identified above in the respective sections may serve as a useful starting point.

Taken together, all of these recommendations add up to a prescription for the development of a comprehensive, integrated, and parsimonious theory of planned organizational change. Therefore, we wish to conclude this chapter with a few words concerning why we believe attempts should be made to develop the theory base of organizational change toward this end, rather than maintaining the current state of diversified and unconnected pieces of theory. One could argue that fragmented theory is the best that can be done in the organizational change field and that it gives maximum flexibility to the change agent in deciding the best actions to take. We do not support this position and thus need to elaborate on our perspective.

First of all, we believe that integration and parsimony can and should be achieved in change process theory.[15] We maintain that an organizational world is bounded by a manageable set of variables which can be manipulated in attempts to produce desired outcomes. Furthermore, we believe that the dynamics by which these outcomes are achieved follow relatively stable and consistent patterns which can be known. These patterns can be formulated into theory by identifying the critical mediator and moderator variables and determining the interactions between them.

In addition to being possible, we believe that development of an integrated, parsimonious theory would prove beneficial to the research, evaluation, and practice of Organizational Development. As noted earlier in the introduction, an inadequate theory base has impeded each of these activities to one degree or another. Improved theory, then, could improve the ability of scholars and practitioners to effectively perform them. More specifically, research that was theory driven could become more focused, as the theory would highlight which variables to measure when studying particular relationships. Evaluation of change programs could be improved, since the theory would allow specific predictions regarding the relationships between particular types of interventions and outcomes of interest.

Improvements in identification of the variables for study and in the specification of relationships among these variables would establish the basis for advances in research methodology. Standardized instruments for measuring variables are more likely to be developed if the variables of interest remain the same over time. Innovative research designs are more possible if the relationships under study are more clearly specified. The whole area of research methods could receive a substantial boost if the theory of OD processes were clearer and broadly accepted.

As an additional consequence of the existence of improved theory, the way Organizational Development is practiced also would improve. As better research in the field was done and as more effective evaluations of change programs were performed, new knowledge would be generated out of which improved implementation theory would evolve. A better theoretical base could directly lead to a more effective use of theory by change agents to guide their choices of interventions, instead of these choices being based on personal values, preferences, or cognitive styles. They would be able to track change programs more accurately, learn from them, and make the necessary adjustment to insure the success of their efforts. Planned organizational change would no longer have to be a shotgun, hit or miss, highly intuitive approach. Instead, the ability to consistently intervene in organizational systems to enhance system functioning and/or individuals' well-being could become more systematic and effective.

After all, this is the ultimate goal of those involved in the field of OD, to develop organizational systems such that individuals can work together in ways that allow for the achievement of both personal and organizational goals. It is our strong belief that an improved theoretical understanding of the dynamics under-lying planned organizational change will considerably enhance our ability to create and maintain such systems. It is this belief which has inspired the recom-mendations proposed here.

NOTES

1.　Not all of the diagnostic variables in Table 1 were neatly classified into one of the seven categories in Porras' model. Some, for example workers' perceptions of their roles (Cummings & Srivastva, 1977), were hard to place in any category, and others, for example the situation (Bowers, Franklin, & Pecorella, 1975), were broad enough to include aspects of more than one category. However, these difficulties would have little, if any, impact on Table 5, from which the following generalizations are derived.

2.　Bowers and Franklin (1972) do not include any diagnostic variables.

3.　It should be noted, however, that only Blake and Mouton (1968) and Bowers and Franklin (1972) actually prescribe a stage in the intervention process which focuses on the formation of an "ideal model" or desired end state. In order to effectively use gap analysis as a guide to intervention, members of the client system will need to make explicit the ideal state they wish to achieve.

4.　Not all theories specified conditions for effective change or the final category of information, criteria for change agents.

5.　The definitions of mediators and moderators reflect the distinctions between these two types of variables as specified by James and Brett (1984).

6.　If, however, there were no moderator variables influencing this link, the space where E is included would be left blank. For example, in Cartwright (1951), shared perception of a need for change leads to conformity pressures and threat of punishment for non-conformity, but no moderator variables are suggested.

7.　If the variable(s) G did not exist, the final dotted line would be omitted, denoting that the final mediator variable was linked to the target variable without being moderated by moderator variables [see, for example, Nadler (1977) or Miles et al. (1969)].

8.　Of the seven theories, only two need further explanation. In House (1967), knowledge changes can lead to changes in both attitudes and skills, which then combine to influence individual performance. Thus, attitudes and skills are at the same stage of the causal chain, but two different sets of moderator variables regulate the impact of knowledge on them. In Lawler (1982), a second target variable, quality of work life, is influenced by the same set of manipulable variables through the one mediator variable (meeting people's needs).

9.　Included in this search were approximately 40 books focusing on Organization Development or on organizational change in general. Any reader desiring a copy of a list of these books should contact the authors. The search also included the last twelve years of six prominent journals in the field of organizations and organizational change (*Journal of Applied Behavioral Science, Academy of*

Management Review, Administrative Science Quarterly, Group and Organization Studies, Human Relations, and *Organizational Dynamics*). However, because of the possibility that a theory or theories were overlooked, we again cannot claim with certainty that the list is exhaustive.

10.   Actually, House (1967) proposes that four variables may be the target of change: knowledge, attitudes, skills, or individual performance. However, he also indicates that improved organizational performance is a result of changes in these variables, and he specifies the causal sequence through which these changes are thought to occur. Because of this, we have taken organizational performance to be the target variable, and knowledge, attitudes, skills, and individual performance are considered to be mediator variables.

11.   This relationship has recently begun to be explored in literature on stress.

12.   Three variables did not fit well into any of the above categories. These were: awareness of process issues, which are legitimized as acceptable content for discussion (Miles, et al., 1969); mechanisms and motivation for communication, coordination, and self-control (Lawler, 1982); and the meeting of individuals' existence, social, growth, and control needs (Lawler, 1982). While the latter could be considered to be related to rewards, it is not directly related to motivation, since it is included as a mediator variable that leads to the improvement of quality of work life.

13.   Two variables which could not be classified in any of the above categories were the coordination of individuals' performance toward organizational goals (House, 1967) and the improvement of self-esteem (Dalton, 1970).

14.   Recent work by Porras and Hoffer (1986) has identified a set of behaviors, proposed to be generalizable across change settings, which tend to improve in successful change efforts. In addition, Hoffer (1986) has demonstrated the positive relationship between these behaviors and an elaborate set of organizational performance measures. Both of these efforts are intended to explore the existence and role of behavior change in effective planned organizational change processes.

15.   The emphasis in our comments below will explicitly be on change process theory, although most of what we say is relevant to implementation theory as well. We choose to highlight change process theory since it is both the most underdeveloped of the two types of theory and, in our opinion, the most important to improve.

REFERENCES

Argyris, C. (1970). *Intervention theory and method*. Reading, MA: Addison-Wesley.

Armenakis, A. A., & Zmud, R. W. (1979). Interpreting the measurement of change in organizational research. *Personnel Psychology, 32*, 709–723.

Bass, B. M. (1983). Issues involved in relations between methodological rigor and reported outcomes in evaluations of organizational development. *Journal of Applied Psychology, 68*, 197–199.

Beckhard, R. (1967). The confrontation meeting. *Harvard Business Review, 45*, 149–153.

Beckhard, R. (1969). *Organization development: Strategies and models*. Reading, MA: Addison-Wesley.

Bedian, A. G., Armenakis, A. A., & Gibson, R. W. (1980). On the measurement and control of beta change. *Academy of Management Review, 5*, 561–566.

Beer, M. (1980). *Organization change and development*. Santa Monica, CA: Goodyear.

Bennis, W. G. (1966). *Changing organizations*. New York: McGraw-Hill.

Blake, R. R., & Mouton, J. S. (1968). *Corporate excellence through grid organization development*. Houston: Gulf.

Bowers, D. G., & Franklin, J. L. (1972). Survey-guided development: Using human resources measurement in organizational change. *Journal of Contemporary Business, 1*, 43–55.

Bowers, D. G., Franklin, J. L., & Pecorella, P. A. (1975). Matching problems, precursors, and interventions in OD: A systemic approach. *Journal of Applied Behavioral Science, 11,* 391–409.

Burke, W. W. (1976). Organization development in transition. *Journal of Applied Behavioral Science, 12,* 22–43.

Burke, W. W. (1982). *Organization development.* Boston: Little, Brown.

Cartwright, D. (1951). Achieving change in people: Some applications of group dynamics theory. *Human Relations, 4,* 381–392.

Chin, R., & Benne, K. D. (1969). General strategies for effecting changes in human systems. In W. G. Bennis, K. D. Benne, & R. Chin (eds.), *The planning of change,* (2nd ed.) New York: Holt, Rinehart and Winston.

Cummings, T. G. and Srivastva, S. (1977). *Management of work: A socio-technical systems approach.* San Diego: University Associates.

Dalton, G. W. (1970). Influence and organizational change. In *Organizational Behavior Models Comparative Administration Research Institute Series No. 2,* Bureau of Economic and Business Research, Kent State University.

Dyer, W. E. (1977). *Team-building: Issues and alternatives.* Reading, MA: Adison-Wesley.

Emery, F. E., & Trist, E. L. (1978). Analytical model for sociotechnical systems. In W. A. Pasmore & J. J. Sherwood (Eds.), *Sociotechnical systems.* San Diego: University Associates.

French, W. L., & Bell, C. H., Jr. (1978). *Organization development* (2nd ed.) Englewood Cliffs, NJ: Prentice-Hall.

Friedlander, F., & Brown, L. D. (1974). Organization development. *Annual Review of Psychology, 25,* 313–341.

Frohman, M. A., Sashkin, M., & Kavanagh, M. J. (1976). Action-research as applied to organization development. *Organization and Administrative Sciences, 7,* 129–142.

Galbraith, J. (1973). *Designing complex organizations.* Reading, MA: Addison-Wesley.

Golembiewski, R. T. (1979). *Approaches to planned change.* New York: Marcel Dekker.

Golembiewski, R. T., Billingsley, K., & Yeager, S. (1976). Measuring change and persistence in human affairs: Types of change generated by OD designs. *Journal of Applied Behavioral Science, 12,* 133–157.

Goodman, P. S., Bazerman, M., & Conlon, E. (1980). Institutionalization of planned organizational change.'' In B. M. Staw & L. L. Cummings (eds.), *Research in Organizational Behavior,* Vol. 2. Greenwich, CT: JAI Press.

Goodman, P. S., & Dean J. W., Jr. (1982). Creating long-term organizational change. In P. S. Goodman and Associates (Eds.), *Change in organizations.* San Francisco: Jossey-Bass.

Greiner, L. E. (1967). Patterns of organization change. *Harvard Business Review, 45,* 119–130.

Hannan, M. T., & Freeman, J. H. (1977). The population ecology of organizations. *American Journal of Sociology, 82,* 929–964.

Hoffer, S. (1986). Behavior and organizational performance: An empirical study. Ph.D. dissertation, School of Education, Stanford University.

Hornstein, H. A., Bunker, B. B., Burke, W. W., Gindes, M., & Lewicki, R. J. (1971). *Social intervention: A behavioral science approach.* New York: The Free Press.

House, R. J. (1967). *Management development.* Ann Arbor, MI: The University of Michigan.

Huse, E. F. (1980). *Organization development and change,* (2nd ed.) St. Paul: West.

James, L. R., & Brett, J. M. (1984). Mediators, moderators, and tests for mediation. *Journal of Applied Psychology, 69,* 307–321.

Jayaram, G. K. (1976). Open systems planning. In W. G. Bennis, K. D. Benne, R. Chin, & K. Corey (Eds.), *The planning of change,* 3rd ed. New York: Holt, Rinehart and Winston.

Kimberley, J. R., & Nielsen, W. R. (1975). Organization development and change in organizational performance. *Administrative Science Quarterly, 20,* 191–206.

Kaplan, R. E. (1979). The conspicuous absence of evidence that process consultation enhances task performance. *Journal of Applied Behavioral Science, 15,* 346–360.

Krone, L. G. (1975). Open systems redesign. In J. D. Adams (Ed.), *New Technologies in organization development: 2.* La Jolla, CA: University Associates.

Lawler, E. E. (1982). Increasing worker involvement to enhance organizational effectiveness. In P. S. Goodman and Associates, *Change in organizations.* San Francisco: Jossey-Bass.

Lawrence, P. R., & Lorsch, J. W. (1969). *Developing organizations: Diagnosis and action.* Reading, MA: Addison-Wesley.

Leavitt, H. J. (1965). Applied organizational change in industry: Structural, technological and humanistic approaches. In J. G. March (Ed.), *Handbook of organizations.* Chicago: Rand McNally.

Leavitt, H. J., Dill, W. R., & Eyring, H. B. (1973). *The organizational world.* New York: Harcourt, Brace, Jovanovich.

Likert, R. (1967). *The human organization.* New York: McGraw-Hill.

Lippitt, R., Watson, J., & Westley, B. (1958). *Dynamics of planned change.* New York: Harcourt, Brace.

Lundberg, C. C. (1978). Organization development theory: A strategic and conceptual appraisal. Unpublished ms. Oregon State University.

Margulies, N., & Raia, A. P. (1978). *Conceptual foundations of organizational development.* New York: McGraw-Hill.

Miles, M. B., Hornstein, H. A., Callahan, D. M., Calder, P. H., & Schiavo, R. S. (1969). The consequence of survey feedback: Theory and evaluation. In W. G. Bennis, K. D. Benne, & R. Chin (Eds.), *The planning of change,* (2nd ed.) New York: Holt, Rinehart, and Winston.

Nadler, D. A. (1977). *Feedback and organization development: Using data-based methods.* Reading, MA: Addison-Wesley.

Nadler, D. A. (1981). Managing organizational change: An integrative perspective. *Journal of Applied Behavioral Science, 17,* 191–211.

Nadler, D. A., & Tushman, M. L. (1977). A diagnostic model for organization behavior. In J. R. Hackman, E. E. Lawler, & L. W. Porter (Eds.), *Perspectives on behavior in organizations.* New York: McGraw-Hill.

Porras, J. I. (1979). The comparative impact of different OD techniques and intervention intensities. *Journal of Applied Behavioral Science, 15,* 156–178.

Porras, J. I. (1986). Organization development. In G. Germane (Ed.), *The executive course.* Reading, MA: Addison-Wesley.

Porras, J. I. (in press). Organization development. In M. D. Dunnette (Ed.), *Handbook of industrial and organizational psychology,* (2nd ed.) Chicago: Rand McNally.

Porras, J. I., & Berg, P. O. (1978). The impact of organization development. *Academy of Management Review, 3,* 249–266.

Porras, J. I., & Harkness, J. (1985). Managing planned change: A stream approach. In R. Tannenbaum, N. Margulies, & F. Massarik (Eds.), *Human systems development: New perspectives on people and organizations.* San Francisco: Jossey-Bass.

Porras, J. I., & Hoffer, S. (1986). Common behavioral changes in successful organization development. *Journal of Applied Behavioral Science, 22.*

Porras, J. I., & Patterson, K. (1979). Assessing planned change. *Group and Organization Studies, 4,* 39–58.

Porras, J. I., & Roberts, N. (1980). Toward a typology of organization development research. *Journal of Occupational Behaviour, 1,* 163–179.

Porras, J. I., & Wilkins, A. (1980). Organization development in a large system: An empirical assessment. *Journal of Applied Behavioral Science, 16,* 506–534.

Randolph, A. (1982). Planned organizational change and its measurement. *Personnel Psychology, 35,* 117–139.

Rogers, E. M. (1983). *Diffusion of innovations,* (3rd ed.) New York: Free Press.

Schein, E. H. (1964). The mechanisms of change. In W. G. Bennis, E. H. Schein, D. E. Berlew, & F. I. Steele (Eds.), *Interpersonal dynamics*. Homewood, IL: The Dorsey Press.

Schein, E. H. (1969). *Process consultation: Its role in organization development*. Reading, MA: Addison-Wesley.

Schmitt, N. (1982). The use of analysis of covariance structures to assess beta and gamma change. *Multivariate Behavioral Research, 17,* 343–358.

Slocum, J. (1978). Does cognitive style affect diagnosis and intervention strategies of change agents? *Group and Organization Studies, 3,* 199–210.

Steele, F. I. (1973). *Physical settings and organization development*. Reading, MA: Addison-Wesley.

Terborg, J. A., Howard, G. S., & Maxwell, S. E. (1980). Evaluating planned organizational change: A method for assessing alpha, beta, and gamma change. *Academy of Management Review, 5,* 109–121.

Tichy, N. M. (1975). How different types of change agents diagnose organizations. *Human Relations, 28,* 771–799.

Tichy, N. M. (1983). *Managing strategic change: Technical, political, and cultural dynamics*. New York: John Wiley and Sons.

Tichy, N. M., & Hornstein, H. A. (1976). Stand when your number is called: An empirical attempt to classify types of social change agents. *Human Relations, 29,* 945–967.

Walton, R. E. (1965). Two strategies of social change and their dilemmas. *Journal of Applied Behavioral Science, 1,* 167–179.

Walton, R. E. (1969). *Interpersonal peacemaking: Confrontations and third-party consultation*. Reading, MA: Addison-Wesley.

Weisbord, M. R. (1976). Organizational diagnosis: Six places to look for trouble with or without a theory. *Group and Organization Studies, 1,* 430–447.

Woodman, R. W., & Muse, W. V. (1982). Organization development in the profit sector: Lessons Learned. In J. O. Hammons (Ed.), *Organization development: Change strategies*. San Francisco: Jossey-Bass.

Woodman, R. W., & Sherwood, J. J. (1980). The role of team development in organizational effectiveness: A critical review. *Psychological Bulletin, 88,* 166–186.

Woodman, R. W., & Wayne, S. J. (1985). An investigation of positive-findings bias in evaluation of organization development interventions. *Academy of Management Journal, 28,* 889–913.

DEVELOPMENT ORGANIZATIONS AND ORGANIZATION DEVELOPMENT:

TOWARD AN EXPANDED PARADIGM FOR ORGANIZATION DEVELOPMENT

L. David Brown and Jane Gibson Covey

ABSTRACT

Shared assumptions about basic organizational metaphors, levels of analysis, interventions, and core values shape OD research and practice. But our work with organizations committed to social change and development identifies issues not easily explained or handled by the conventional OD paradigm: External events that drive internal dynamics, multiple internal realities, extremes of conflict escalation and avoidance, ideologies as central catalysts of organizational action, and successes that increase internal and external turbulence. We suggest an expansion of

Research in Organizational Change and Development, Vol. 1, pages 59–87.
ISBN: 0-89232-749-9

the OD paradigm on the basis of development organization experience that diversifies its basic metaphor, widens its analytic domain, broadens its range of intervention targets, recognizes the mutuality of action and research in social learning, and expands its vision to include interorganizational and societal change as possible impacts.

INTRODUCTION

For about a decade we have been working with organizations committed to various forms of social change and development. These development organizations (DOs) have included community development corporations, national advocacy organizations, private international development agencies, religiously based community empowerment organizations, and community mobilization agencies in the United States and several Third World countries. We began from conceptual and experiential bases in the organization development (OD) tradition of applied behavioral science. But our work has raised questions about several assumptions that are commonly held by OD practitioners.

This chapter explores implications of organization development work in development organizations for the "paradigm" that guides OD practice and research. We begin by describing some central premises of OD. We then briefly examine special characteristics of DOs and the consequences of those characteristics for planned organizational change. Finally we consider implications of the analysis for the OD paradigm, and we suggest the rudiments of an expanded framework for OD research and practice.

THE ORGANIZATION DEVELOPMENT PARADIGM

The scientific paradigms described by Kuhn (1970) provide worldviews that underpin the activities of communities of scholars. Paradigms define shared assumptions, methodologies for investigation, and interesting problems. They provide an intellectual backdrop against which scientific work can efficiently solve well-defined puzzles. Work within paradigms gradually produces anomalous results that raise questions about the paradigm itself. Eventually those anomalies may lead to paradigm shifts, in which central assumptions of the field are reformulated.

Social sciences by and large have less well-defined and generally-accepted worldviews than natural sciences (Lodahl & Gordon, 1972). The former may be characterized by multiple paradigms whose adherents compete with or ignore each other (Ritzer, 1975). Subcommunities within social science disciplines adopt quite different methodologies for investigating the same phenomena, and often operate in methodological and conceptual isolation from one another (Diesing, 1974).

Organization development has been a practice-oriented subfield of behavioral science for several decades. Although OD is often criticized for its lack of theoretical and conceptual integration (e.g., Kahn, 1974; Bowers et al., 1977), some elements of a shared paradigm can be identified. Educational programs have been created and textbooks have been written to train new practitioners. The premises of paradigms are often most visible in the materials used to socialize new members of the field. We have examined the contents of six OD texts to identify major paradigmatic assumptions of the field.

Texts of course are not gospel: Many would argue that texts do not cover critical elements of OD practice. We have preceded on the assumption that agreement about a premise across several texts offers at least a rough approximation of premises that shape OD practice. We have looked at four texts published in the last seven years: Beer's (1980) *Organizational Change and Development,* Burke's (1982) *Organization Development: Principles and Practices,* Huse and Cummings' (1984) *Organization Development and Change* (third edition), and French and Bell's (1985) *Organization Development* (third edition). We have also examined first editions of the last two texts, French and Bell (1973) and Huse (1975), to identify shifts in premises over the last decade. This examination yielded several assumptions that seem central to the OD paradigm.

All the texts agree on a core metaphor for describing and analyzing organizations. Such core metaphors shape how their users think about organizations in fundamental ways—the aspects that receive attention, the questions asked, and the dynamics expected.

ASSUMPTION 1:   *The OD paradigm conceives of organizations as open systems, organized around shared purposes.*

All the texts explicitly adopt the open systems perspective as a guide for organization development. The open system metaphor focuses analytic attention on the purposes around which systems are organized, on the processes by which inputs are transformed into outputs, on relations among subunits, and on the transactions between the system and its environment.

The texts also describe diagnostic procedures and levels of analysis appropriate to OD. Although the texts vary in their emphases, there is substantial agreement on the primary diagnostic importance of organizations and their component groups.

ASSUMPTION 2:   *The OD paradigm focuses on group and organizational analysis.*

Table 1 compares the number of chapters devoted to individual, group, organizational, and environmental analysis across newer (1980s) and older (1970s) texts. All the texts focus more than 75 percent of their diagnostic chapters on

Table 1.   Level of analysis in OD Texts

	1970s Texts			1980s Texts				
	French and Bell (1973)	Huse (1975)	Mean (1970s)	French and Bell (1985)	Huse and Cummings (1984)	Burke (1984)	Beer (1980)	Mean (1980s)
Individual	7%	25	16	6	10	17	14	12
Group	50	25	38	39	20	33	14	27
Organization	43	50	47	56	65	50	72	61
Environment	0	0	0	0	5	0	0	1
Total	100	100	101	101	100	100	100	101
Chapters	7	6	13	9	10	6	7	32

group and organizational analysis. Over the last decade the emphasis has apparently shifted to organizational analysis at the expense of individuals and groups. Environmental analysis receives little attention, then or now, even though the open systems metaphor suggests that organization-environment transactions are important.

A central component of OD technology is a variety of intervention strategies for solving problems and managing change in organizations. The texts describe many similar interventions, but they emphasize somewhat different targets.

ASSUMPTION 3:   *The OD paradigm emphasizes interventions to change people, processes, structures, and organizations as systems.*

Table 2 compares the distribution of intervention chapters among different change targets. Process interventions dominated both earlier and half of the newer texts. One newer text emphasizes structural interventions and one emphasizes systemic interventions. Diagnostic activities are treated by most texts as precursors to intervention rather than as interventions in themselves. In general the range of interventions considered seems to be expanding; systemic and structural interventions receive more attention in newer texts.

The texts emphasize the normative character of OD. Most discuss explicitly the importance of collaboration and participation in decisions, a spirit of inquiry and free exchange of information, and the value of realizing individual and organizational potentials. The field has strong roots in the human potential movement of the 1960s, though most newer texts emphasize special OD values less than the earlier ones.

In spite of the emphasis on a spirit of inquiry, the texts indicate that OD is more concerned with practice and intervention than with research and theory.

Table 2. Type of Intervention in OD Texts

	1970s Texts			1980s Texts				
	French and Bell (1973)	Huse (1975)	Mean (1970s)	French and Bell (1985)	Huse and Cummings (1984)	Burke (1984)	Beer (1980)	Mean (1980s)
People	20%	25	23	10	25	25	14	19
Process	80	50	65	60	25	50	14	37
Structure	0	25	13	20	38	0	14	18
Systemic	0	0	0	10	13	25	43	23
Diagnostic	0	0	0	0	0	0	14	4
Total	100	100	101	100	101	100	99	101
Chapters	5	6	11	6	8	4	7	25

The texts emphasize action, and research is valued primarily for evaluating interventions.

ASSUMPTION 4: *The OD paradigm values human and organizational growth, collaborative and participative processes, and a spirit of inquiry, but it emphasizes action over research.*

Table 3 compares chapters devoted to intervention and to research in the texts. Intervention far outweighs research as a chapter topic, when research appears at all. There is little discussion in these texts of research goals, procedures, and outcomes. OD is presented as an activity for improving organizational effectiveness, not as a process for developing knowledge, collecting data, or creating theory.

Finally, the impacts of OD are largely examined and described in terms of

Table 3. Research and Intervention in OD Texts

	1970s Texts			1980s Texts				
	French and Bell (1973)	Huse (1975)	Mean (1970s)	French and Bell (1985)	Huse and Cummings (1984)	Burke (1984)	Beer (1980)	Mean (1980s)
Intervention	6	7	6.5	7	7	5	11	7.5
Research	1	0	.5	2	.5	.5	0	.8
Ratio	6:1	7:0	13:1	7:2	14:1	10:1	11:0	10:1

their effects on the organization and its subunits. OD activities are intended to improve organizational performance, though interventions with individuals, teams, departments, or other subunits may be employed. OD can be distinguished from management development activity, since the latter is focused on individuals. Training or counseling may be used by OD practitioners, but they typically use it with organizational improvements in mind.

ASSUMPTION 5: *The OD paradigm focuses on improving the functioning of organizations and their subunits.*

In summary, the OD portrayed in texts defines a normatively-based, practice-oriented activity that conceives of organizations as open systems, focuses on group and organizational analysis, and intervenes with people, processes, structures and whole systems to improve organizational performance.

CHARACTERISTICS OF DEVELOPMENT ORGANIZATIONS

What are development organizations? And why are they relevant to the OD paradigm? In this section we briefly describe some DOs and the characteristics that distinguish them from other more familiar organizations. We will argue that these characteristics make DOs good analogs of future organizations, so we can learn much from them about OD work.

We will use examples drawn from work with a number of DOs in this and later sections. The following brief descriptions are intended to illustrate the variety and the similarities of DOs:

The Ghetto Community Development Corporation was formed to provide jobs and services in an urban black ghetto in the late 1960s. After a decade of success, it was threatened with defunding by a federal Administration more concerned with the profitability of its ventures than their capacity to provide jobs and services.

The Peace and Empowerment Coalition was organized to promote community action and peace education projects in a six-state region. The Coalition's traditional consensus decision making procedures were severely tested by their success in recruiting culturally and ethnically diverse staff and volunteers.

The International Relief and Development Agency used funds from First World donors to promote self-help projects in Third World countries and to challenge established development concepts in the First World. The Agency recruited staff strongly committed to its vision of a better world and ready to challenge oppression in all its forms.

The Urban Leadership Program brought together corporation executives, city councilmen, union officers, nonprofit administrators, neighborhood leaders, media personalities, and other urban leaders in a program designed to build awareness of regional problems and to encourage the evolution of new problem-solving networks.

The Equality in Education Program was created to press for more educational opportunities for women through organizing and advocacy. The Program faced a crisis when its initial leader moved on without having developed any individuals to take over in her place.

The Community Mobilization Association used adult education methods to help poor people in 75 Indian villages improve their lives. They developed a hugely successful method for the village leaders to organize for solving local problems.

These organizations vary considerably in missions and target populations, in technologies for accomplishing their tasks, in geographic locations, and in political and cultural positions. But they also display a number of common organizational characteristics that we believe are shared by a wide range of development organizations.

DO missions generally emphasize the creation of better (more equitable, more innovative, more productive, more healthy) communities and societies. They articulate and work for visions of a better world. Thus DO missions commit them to *changing their environments,* not just to producing a product or service sufficiently acceptable to insure their financial viability. The Ghetto Community Development Corporation, for example, was formed at federal government initiative after riots drew national attention to the lack of services, jobs, and opportunities for residents of black urban ghettoes (Brown, 1980; 1983). The Corporation used federal funds and help from local business leaders to launch local ventures to provide jobs and services for ghetto residents. Implicitly they sought to ameliorate generations of white economic and social exploitation of blacks. The center of DO concern is at their boundaries, at the points where they seek to influence their environments.

Visions of change and development are central to most DOs. One consequence of such visionary missions is that *values and ideologies are central* features of DO life. Shared values are sources of motivation and commitment for DO members, and organizational activity is often justified in value terms. Ideologies provide concepts and theories to underpin action by explaining linkages between what exists, what should be, and how changes can be accomplished (Beyer, 1981; Brown & Brown, 1983). The Peace and Empowerment Coalition was committed to promoting international peace and local empowerment of disadvantaged communities, especially those victimized by racism. Its staff and volunteers work long hours under hardships, against difficulties, and for rewards miniscule in comparison to those available elsewhere.

The emphasis on values and ideology often generalizes from external to internal settings: Staff sensitized to ideological issues in the environment are often concerned about those issues within the organization. The International Relief and Development Agency staff commitment to empowering oppressed peoples was applied internally as well as to the Third World. Agency staff were very sensitive to internal decisions that did not allow staff participation (Brown &

Brown, 1983). As one staff member put it, "Bolivian peasants get to participate in this organization's decisions more than I do!"

DO missions require that they deal with *many diverse external constituencies*. Many DOs bridge the gap between the rich and the poor, using resources from the former to enable the latter to act in their own interests. The Development Agency, for example, uses funds from private donors to launch small self-help projects in developing countries. The Agency must deal with wealthy donors in the First World, impoverished peasants in the Third World, and governments in both. Other DOs link diverse constituencies to solve social problems. The Urban Leadership Program, for example, brought together corporate executives, city councilmen, union leaders, educational administrators, neighborhood leaders, and representatives of different ethnic groups to learn about urban problems and build networks for future problem-solving (Brown & Detterman, in press). Many different organizations deal with diverse external agencies, but DOs are especially likely to face constituencies with interests that conflict.

The demands of diverse external constituencies encourage DO differentiation into *subunits linked to external constituencies*. As the Development Agency grew, for example, it created departments oriented to different constituencies: Fundraising handles donors; Projects works in the Third World; Development Education deals with the U.S. public; Public Relations works with the media; Policy Information lobbies the U.S. government; Administration handles internal matters. Different tasks combine with different training to create many kinds of diversity: Fundraisers dress more formally, take more moderate political positions, and manage less democratically than Project staff. Subunit differences are often interpreted in ideological and political terms (Brown & Brown, 1983).

Finally, DOs face complex tasks and situations that require flexibility and local discretion. Their members are often antagonistic to routine and bureaucratic procedures. So DOs are often very *loosely-organized*. Organizations regulate behavior with formal structures, informal expectations, technologies and physical arrangements, and leadership activity (Brown, 1980). DOs often depend primarily on informal expectations and leadership to guide behavior, and so are particularly vulnerable to questions about leadership succession or the legitimacy of important norms. DOs may be incapacitated by leadership transitions that would have little impact on organizations that use formal structures and procedures to regulate behavior. The Equality in Education Program was founded and developed by a charismatic leader, and almost foundered as she became less able to deal with new challenges. Loose organization allows innovation and local responsibility, but it also permits diffusion of energy, avoidance of critical issues, or escalation of conflict within DOs (Alderfer, 1976; 1979; Brown, 1980)

These characteristics—missions that require environmental change; the centrality of values and ideology; many diverse constituencies; subunits differentiated by constituency and ideology as well as tasks; loose organization—all distinguish DOs from the industrial organizations in which OD theories and technologies were initially evolved.

So what? If DOs are so different, isn't learning from them essentially irrelevant to most OD? We believe that OD in DO's is relevant precisely *because* of their differences, and that organizations of the future may be more like DOs than more familiar forms.

Consider the following trends. Service organizations increasingly dominate the economies of developed nations, and they—like ODs—must influence the external environment as they provide their services. Even industrial organizations are beginning to recognize the importance of shared values and ideologies for promoting high performance in Japanese (e.g., Pascale & Athos, 1981; Ouchi, 1981), U.S. (Peters & Waterman, 1983; Kanter, 1984), and European organizations (Pettigrew, 1986). The impact of diverse constituencies on the performance and viability of many organizations is increasingly recognized by strategic analysts (e.g., Freeman, 1984). As organizations seek to be "close to the customer" we can expect more subunit differentiation by constituency and ideology as in DOs. Finally, it has been recognized for some time that turbulent environments encourage looser internal organization for more flexible and rapid response (e.g., Burns & Stalker, 1961). In short, *the characteristics of DOs are likely to be common in successful organizations of the future.* So OD in DOs may be very relevant in the future of OD as a field.

ORGANIZATION DEVELOPMENT IN DEVELOPMENT ORGANIZATIONS

What are the implications of DO characteristics for OD? In this section we describe some features of planned change in DOs that are closely related to their special characteristics. If it is true that many other organizations will display similar characteristics in the future, then these special features will become important for OD.

External Explanations for Internal Events

DO missions require interaction with outside agencies. Empowering disadvantaged groups or solving social problems are tasks that cannot be accomplished inside the organization, unlike building automobiles or educating students. Much of our organization and management theory focuses on controlling and coordinating internal activities, and "buffering the technical core" from uncertainties and disruptions in the environment (Thompson, 1967). But the "core" activities of DOs are at organizational boundaries. The periphery for DOs is central; events outside are in many ways more important than the inside.

Often events in DOs cannot be understood without considering the external context. The Ghetto Community Development Corporation's performance difficulties are more easily understood given historical changes in outside agencies. The Johnson Administration wanted jobs and services in the ghetto, and literally overnight the Nixon Administration replaced that emphasis with concern for venture profitability. Even DO missions and goals may be altered by changes in external linkages.

Critical resource allocation decisions and authority relationships may also be located outside the DO. Wells (1984) argues that differences in internal dynamics and long-term viability between two very similar producer cooperatives can be traced to the powers conferred on them by organizing agencies. Federal authorities named a Ghetto Development Corporation President with little credibility in the ghetto community and no connections in local business circles, and so undermined Corporation capacity to work with its other "customers." Concern about federal decision-makers led Corporation staff to ignore other constituencies. External events often drive much internal DO activity.

DOs are often sensitive to external social issues that touch core values and ideologies. Corporation staff were very sensitive to societal histories of racism. That sensitivity affected relations among the multi-racial staff and between Corporation representatives, white businessmen and government officials, and predominantly black community members. The antagonism between Corporation staff and some businessmen, for example, drew as much on the historical context and mutual stereotyping as on actual interaction. OD may be caught up in such larger issues. The Corporation diagnostic team was also multi-racial, and gained access to aspects of Corporation problems that probably would not have otherwise been available (see Alderfer et al., 1980).

Many DOs do not recognize the ecological sources of internal dynamics. Corporation staff attributed tensions among individuals to incompetence, and they interpreted chief executive indecision under pressure from incompatible constituencies as "lack of leadership." Impersonal explanations for such phenomena can liberate energy and creativity previously locked up in rationalizations and self-protection. Ecological diagnoses can focus attention on both internal dynamics ("internal conflict suggests Corporation staff are working closely with diverse external constituencies") and critical external boundaries ("The Corporation ought to concentrate on projects where you have good external relations, like housing").

Multiple Internal Realities

DO subunits are differentiated by many forces: task specialization, external constituencies, occupational preferences, and real or perceived ideological differences. The variety of DO constituencies, their conflicts of interest, and their different constructions of reality often create major differences and discrepancies between subunit realities that pose special challenges to OD.

Access to different constituencies is not easily gained. When relations between subunits are strained, gaining access to one party may in itself undermine access to others. We were initially contacted by representatives of both management and staff points of view in the International Research and Development Agency. But significant tensions existed between races, genders, and departments as well. Developing credibility required multiple entry negotiations and repeated "credential checks" on a variety of issues. Staff members saw the initial diagnosis as a "management ploy" until we refused to continue without an affirmative Staff Association vote. The consulting team that diagnosed racism, sexism, and elitism problems included a black female and a white male, and so had initial credibility with many different groups. Different groups tested the team in different ways: Managers asked about intellectual credentials and consulting backgrounds; staff investigated political ideologies and biases for participative management; people of color checked sophistication and sensitivity on race relations. It is not easy to build credibility with so many diverse groups. Entry with the Agency constituencies required that we be explicit about our own values and biases, and that we demonstrate willingness to recognize the legitimacy of positions other than our own.

Different constituencies often have different perceptions, interpretations, and evaluations of the same events. OD accustomed to analyzing situations in which everyone agrees on major issues may find DO staffs bewilderingly inconsistent. A Development Agency effort at agency-wide participation in designing a new compensation plan was explained as "a management power-grab" (many staff), "a bureaucratic runaround" (other staff), or as "staff unwillingness to face differences or make decisions" (managers). Learning about multiple realities requires listening empathically to very different perspectives and interpretations. When DOs are severely conflicted, trust by one group may inhibit trust by other groups, and so subtly undermine the ability of outsiders to recognize and explore different perspectives. The diagnostic process itself is shaped by relations among internal and external constituencies.

The influence of multiple realities becomes painfully obvious as outsiders share their perceptions with insiders. OD depends on agreement about problem definitions and explanations as a basis for effective action planning. But different organizational stakeholders often define and explain problems quite differently. OD can be caught between multiple fires as each constituency presses for the ratification of its definition of the situation. The initial diagnostic report to the Development Agency evoked objections about pro-staff bias from management; the second draft drew similar criticisms from staff activists; the third and final version was grudgingly accepted as "balanced," albeit somewhat offensive to all parties.

The evolution of a shared organizational reality, or even the recognition of multiple realities, can be a powerful intervention. Most DOs do not have well developed organizational "memories." The combination of high turnover and rapid change often leaves subunits with little appreciation for either organizational history or the perspectives of other subunits. Building a commonly-accepted description of the organization and the historical roots of present tensions amounts to a "[re]creation of organizational history" that can underpin coordinated action by diverse subunits.

Extremes of Conflict Escalation or Avoidance

The multiple realities operating in DOs make differences of opinion among individuals and subunits quite common. Less familiar to analysts from industrial and business organizations are the intense feelings and the extreme dynamics generated by those differences.

Differences often result in escalating conflict or debilitating deadlocks. In the Peace and Empowerment Coalition, for example, successful affirmative action efforts increased ethnic and gender diversity of the staff without enhancing their capacity to deal with their differences. Differences about organizational goals and tactics combined with these differences to polarize staff and cripple organizational decision-making for months. The relatively loose organization of the Coalition provided little regulation of interactions on emotionally charged issues, and the conflict escalated to the point where no movement was possible until the leaders of both factions left the organization.

In other circumstances, subunit differences and ideological polarization produce systematic avoidance of issues that need to be discussed. In the International Relief and Development Agency, for example, the staff questioned the discrepancy between organizational commitment to equality and participation and a compensation structure that distinguished among levels. Although a task force spent a year collecting data and studying alternatives, many of the staff ultimately felt their views were not heard. The new salary plan was rejected by virtually everyone. In loosely-organized systems, conflict can be avoided, so that different interests and alternatives remain unexplored.

Intense conflicts often have major impacts on how decisions, particularly strategic decisions, are made in DOs. Sometimes decisions simply remain unmade. The deadlock over strategy in the Coalition in essence paralyzed decision-making for months. Sometimes decisions are delayed interminably. The compensation planning effort in the Development Agency infuriated its staff in part because it soaked up so much energy for so little tangible product—a year of meetings and analysis produced little but frustration.

When decisions are made, the pervasiveness of conflicts and ideological differences encourages decision-making processes different from the rational consideration of the issues often envisioned in the planning literature (e.g., Ansoff, 1975; MacMillan, 1982). Many DO staffs rely on a charismatic leader to deal with ambiguities or disagreements. The Equality in Education Program staff, for example, depended on the founder to handle complex policy decisions, and so were helpless when she became less able and willing to play that role.

When DO leaders have less legitimacy as charismatic figures, political maneuvering, side deals, and fiats may be used to create coalitions that make decisions without explicit discussion of major issues. Many of the Development Agency staff believed that strategic decisions were made by political bargaining with the Director. The compensation plan implemented after their year-long study was widely seen as imposed by Director fiat, in gross violation of the Agency's professed values for participative decision-making.

Finally, task ambiguities and conflicts among participants often encourage an extreme form of the "disjointed incrementalism" identified by Lindblom (1959; 1979). Negotiations over a limited set of alternatives relatively close to the current situation produce an iterative process that builds coalitions around limited objectives and generates new information in highly uncertain situations. The Ghetto Community Development Corporation developed projects as opportunities to link federal funds, local business interests, and ghetto community support appeared. Overreliance on this process can be costly, since it encourages short-term opportunism. The Corporation was unprepared for a predictable change in Administration priorities as Nixon took over from Johnson, and they almost went under as a result.

Since much conflict between DO subunits is driven by tensions among external constituencies, differences can be managed at several points. DOs that encourage subunits to identify closely with external constituencies experience intense internal conflict as subunits replicate environmental conflicts inside the organization. Fundraising and Projects in the Development Agency fought constantly because they were more closely identified with external constituencies than with each other.

On the other hand, differences may be expressed and handled at organizational boundaries. DOs are sometimes criticized for not being completely honest with their donors, or for not keeping close tabs on their beneficiaries (Smith, 1982). The lack of information may be interpreted as "constructive ignorance" that dampens internal tensions generated by close identification with diverse external constituencies. The Community Development Corporation, for example, preserved internal harmony and good relations with federal funders by reducing interaction with local business leaders and ghetto residents. In the long term, of course, overuse of this strategy severely curtailed their capacity to accomplish their purposes.

Learning Organizations and The Power of Ideas

Development work demands that DOs and their core staff be good learners. Development projects are seldom routine, and projects that involve clients in problem definition and analysis, action planning, and implementation inevitably require staff to invent or adapt to fit new situations. The values and ideologies of DOs often emphasize learning and innovation, and loose organization enables informal contacts and flexible use of resources. Subunit diversity and limited conflict encourage new ideas and innovative solutions. New ideas are very important in DOs, and many DO staff are skilled in conceptual and theoretical analysis. We have found that DO staff are fond of "philosophical" discussions that debate big issues, articulate value perspectives, and generate new perspectives.

DO biases in favor of ideas have several implications. DO staff are likely to be sophisticated analysts of values and ideologies—in contrast, for example, to the pragmatic, task-oriented staffs of manufacturing organizations. The values and ideologies that inspire many individuals to join DOs also influence their assessments of outsiders. We have been relentlessly quizzed about our values, ideologies, and ideas. Manufacturing personnel ask outsiders "Have you ever met a payroll or run a drill press?" DO staffs ask "What do you think about South Africa, Nicaragua, and race relations?"

Many DOs place a low value on standard operating procedures, well-defined jobs, formal hierarchies, and other "bureaucratic" mechanisms for organizing activity. They prefer shared values, informal norms, common theories and belief systems, and expectations negotiated in interaction as mechanisms for regulating behavior. New ideas are powerful interventions in systems organized by shared cultures. When the Ghetto Community Development Corporation reconceived its mission as promoting links among government, business, and community resources, staff attention was redirected from internal affairs to constituency relations. This change fundamentally altered member perceptions of their roles. The President, for example, decided that "politicking" with outside agencies was a core activity and became much more active in many outside settings in the next few months.

New concepts can touch off unexpected explosions of energy. The Peace and Empowerment Coalition waged a successful campaign to build a multi-racial staff and volunteer cadre. But the new internal diversity overtaxed their capacity to manage differences. People of color felt whites did not understand their concerns; whites felt misunderstood and guilty; everyone was frustrated by unproductive discussions of racism. In the course of an organization-wide planning process, the Coalition goal of "being non-racist" was reformulated as "becoming effectively multi-cultural." This apparently trivial relabelling has been very significant for some of the staff. The low energy, denial, and avoidance characteristic in discussions of racism do not dominate discussions of multiculturalism. For some, the discussions of multiculturalism actually generate active interest, high energy, and creativity.

In our experience, DOs may be almost transformed by ideas that reframe organizational difficulties or dilemmas. Hindsight suggests that ideas in idea-driven and learning-oriented organizations are like matches in a fireworks plant. But in fact, we have been startled and (sometimes unnerved) by how rapidly some ideas are understood, accepted as useful, adapted to fit the situation, and transformed into action. The power of ideas in DOs is impressive, if only partially predictable.

Societal Impacts and the Paradoxes of Success

DO missions emphasize changing their contexts. If DOs succeed, the consequences extend beyond better commercial products or services. Potentially DOs serve important functions for the larger society. They can mediate between individuals and impersonal social forces, and so make the growing complexity and impersonality of our institutions tolerable (Berger & Neuhaus, 1977). They can even the odds between powerful and powerless, rich and poor, elite and oppressed, and so reinforce the legitimacy of democratic political systems (Gricar & Brown, 1981). They can bring together the diverse stakeholders needed to solve complex social problems (Trist, 1979; 1983). Enhancing the capability of such agencies can have broad social consequences.

Sometimes the external consequences of DO activities are largely unplanned or unrecognized. The Community Mobilization Association in India experimented with an ''organization-building workshop'' to mobilize small farmers for self-reliant initiatives to improve village life. The workshop results electrified Association staff: Villager organizations undertook an unprecedented variety of problem-solving initiatives (Tandon & Brown, 1980), and the Association decided to apply the workshop ideas in scores of other villages. What began as a small OD intervention in the service of a dissertation project snowballed into impacts on many villages and DOs in India and other developing countries.

In other situations, external effects are planned from the beginning. The Urban Leadership Program, for example, was designed to expand awareness and increase cooperation between leaders from private and public sectors, management and labor, blacks and whites, corporations and communities, educators and politicians in a large metropolitan area (Brown & Detterman, in press). Program experiences encouraged shared perspectives on regional problems and interpersonal connections among participants. Analysis of later network contacts revealed that one new coalition united white businessmen against a populist Mayor and a later network combined neighborhoods and occupations for work on community problems. But precise prediction of environmental outcomes is not easy: We did intend to promote more community problem-solving networks, but we did not plan to strengthen the networks of white businessmen that already dominated the city.

When DOs are successful in altering their environments, with or without OD intervention, the outcomes frequently illustrate what we have come to call the "paradox of success." For most organizations success in achieving goals is associated with increased internal efficiency and external security. Because DO tasks focus on changing their environments and because their constituencies are often in conflict, success with some constituencies often makes their external position more precarious with others. The Community Mobilization Association's success in organizing villagers produced challenges from village elites infuriated by demands from newly-organized villagers, and the new organizations themselves wanted the Association to "join us in the struggle" (against oppressors who sometimes provided funds to the Association).

Effective links with outside constituencies in conflict can create unmanageable microcosms of those conflicts inside the organization. The Peace and Empowerment Coalition was so successful in their drive to recruit women and minorities that they overwhelmed their organizational capacity to manage differences, and so paralyzed its activities.

Sometimes success results in rapid growth that overloads the organization's capacity to absorb funds, train new staff, or manage activity. Organizational growth also encourages increased internal differentiation, and so can promote increased conflict among subunits. The International Relief and Development Agency was so successful in generating new funds that it grew tenfold in two years. The agency hired new staff and created several new departments, and found increased size and specialization was associated with more conflict between subunits and between levels. The resulting confusion undermined staff morale and the legitimacy of Agency leadership.

All of these successes taxed organizational capacities to learn from their experience, making OD activity at once more important and a more serious drain on already stretched resources. OD that enhances DO capacity to catalyze environmental change can have large multiplier effects in the larger society. Those effects are the joint product of DO action and contextual forces, so results are often quite distant from the actions of OD consultants. OD in DOs offers opportunities to influence events beyond the organizations, but eventually, results turn on the actions of many others—some immediately visible, some recognized later, and some always beyond recognition or influence.

TOWARD A REVISED PARADIGM FOR ORGANIZATION DEVELOPMENT

What are the implications of work with DOs for the OD paradigm? We have argued that some characteristics of DOs—externally oriented missions, concern with values and ideologies, multiple constituencies closely linked to organizational subunits, loose organization—are likely to be increasingly common in the future. Future OD activities can expect the dynamics we faced in DOs—internal events driven by external events, multiple internal realities, extremes of conflict escalation and avoidance, strong appetites for ideas and learning, and paradoxical consequences of success. If future organizations are like DOs, revision will be needed in fundamental premises of the OD paradigm. We found that some of our initial premises were incorrect or actively misleading as guides to work in DOs. In this section we return to the premises of OD identified in the first section. We believe each needs modification in the light of our experience.

Organizations as Multiple Overlapping Systems

OD texts define organizations as "open systems" and emphasize their organization around shared purposes. This single system metaphor is misleading in DOs, especially when diverse external constituencies and escalated internal conflict create dramatically different realities in organizational subunits. Subunits of the same DOs sometimes describe organizational purposes that are unrecognizable to each other, and they sometimes act as if they were parts of agencies in conflict. In such circumstances, the organization may be better understood as several partially overlapping systems whose members have different interests, goals and expectations. Fundraisers and Projects staff in the International Relief and Development Agency, for example, describe their goals as if they belonged to quite different organizations.

Organizational metaphors that imply a single set of goals and generally recognized organizational arrangements have been questioned in other settings. Students of planned organizational change in government agencies (Golembiewski, 1969; Warwick, 1975), public enterprises (Brown, 1984), universities (Cohen & March, 1972), and hospitals (Stoelwinder & Charns, 1981) have described complications introduced by multiple goals and constituencies. Many alternatives to the tightly-organized system premise dominant in the OD paradigm have been articulated: political coalitions (March, 1962; Pfeffer, 1981), "organized anarchies" (Cohen & March, 1972), "underorganized" or "underbounded" systems (Brown, 1980; Alderfer, 1979), or "loosely coupled systems " (Weick, 1976).

Viewing organizations as a multiple overlapping systems introduces several complications for OD inquiry and intervention. For example, multiple system organizations require *multiple entries and diagnoses*. In single systems, initial entry negotiations pave the way into many subunits that share common goals, authorities, and expectations. In multiple systems, entry and diagnosis begin again with each subunit, and previous entries may hamper rather than facilitate work with new subunits. Multiple systems require more investment in gaining access to and understanding the diverse perspectives of different subunits.

The logic of organizational analysis also varies across metaphors. Single system analysis focuses on an underlying organizational reality and converges diverse sources and measures on a common understanding. Multiple system analysis emphasizes finding and articulating diverse realities. Clarifying organizational characteristics and dynamics involves *divergent analyses* rather than convergence, dialectic more than consensus.

The multiple system metaphor also suggests alternative bases for organizational intervention. Single system interventions formulate consensus about problems as the basis for planned change. Multiple system interventions, in contrast, can emphasize *points of conflict* at which different perspectives must be articulated. The energy for change in multiple systems is often generated at interfaces between multiple realities. The President of the Ghetto Community Development Corporation, struggling to reconcile the conflicting expectations of community, government, and business leaders, became an important source of energy and ideas for change in both the Corporation and the city at large.

The nature of organizational improvement can vary with choice of organizational metaphor as well. Planned change efforts in tightly organized systems often focus on reducing gaps between goals and performance or releasing impacted information and energy. Multiple system metaphors focus attention on the need to *focus energy* constructively and to *hold together* diverse subunits (see Brown, 1980; Alderfer, 1979). Interventions that enable subunits to appreciate or to work with each other can unblock and channel organizational energies that might otherwise blow multiple systems apart. Thus reconceptualizing the Ghetto Development Corporation mission as linking diverse constitutencies enabled subunits to work together rather than squabble over priorities. The multiple system metaphor focuses attention on the management of differences as much as on the accomplishment of tasks.

The metaphor used to describe organizations shapes both analysis and influence activities. The multiple system metaphor emphasizes subunit diversity, diagnostic activities that recognize differences, and interventions that enable constructive use of conflicting perspectives.

Analysis of Organizational Ecologies

OD texts suggest that diagnosis should focus on groups and organizations, especially the latter. Environmental analysis has been largely neglected by OD texts, in spite of the importance of organization-environment transactions implicit in the open system metaphor. But experience with DOs suggests that some internal problems can be best understood in terms of external relations. The ecology within which the organization is embedded may be more important than group and organizational forces. That ecology includes other organizational actors and the historical context of economic, political, and cultural forces. Internal conflicts at the International Relief and Development Agency, for example, are hard to understand without reference to the demands of donors, clients, and external publics, or without recognizing their external event-driven growth.

Environmental analysis has received much attention from other branches of organization theory. Relations between organizations and environments has been an important growth area for some time (e.g., Lawrence & Lorsch, 1967; Aldrich & Pfeffer, 1975; Meyer et al., 1983). Some theorists have argued that organizations are largely controlled by environmental forces (e.g., Pfeffer & Salancik, 1978). Others have held that strategies for achieving environmental positions determine organizational structures and processes (e.g., Chandler, 1961; Miles et al., 1978; Galbraith & Nathanson, 1978).

Ecological analysis directs attention to actors and forces that might otherwise remain unrecognized. Expertise in job enrichment, process consultation, or organization design seldom sensitizes analysts to critical *external dependencies* on environmental actors or large scale social forces. So external causation of internal events may pass unnoticed: The Ghetto Development Corporation staff was largely unaware of the role played by external constituencies in its internal conflicts or the "indecisiveness" of its President, as were its external consultants.

Ecological analysis also focuses on *boundary spanning roles and mechanisms* by which organizations manage constituency relations. As the impacts of federal government demands and inattention to other external constituencies became clearer to the Corporation President, he became more aware of his own importance as an external representative of the organization. His choice to become a more active "politicker" with constituencies was an important influence on future internal events as well as on the Corporation's external relations. This implication of ecological analysis is very consistent with analyses of boundary spanning emerging in other areas of organization theory (e.g., Adams, 1976; Miles, 1980).

Another implication of the ecological perspective is the recognition of *societal microcosm effects* that sometimes replicate problems from the larger context inside the organizations (Brown & Brown, 1983). DOs often fight out larger social conflicts internally, even when outside observers see them as relatively "progressive" in their treatment of the issues. Struggles over decision-making and leadership at the International Relief and Development Agency reflected staff concerns with oppression, racism, and elitism, though by most standards the organization was relatively non-racist and non-elitist. Such microcosmic struggles can be extremely bitter because the staff feels seriously betrayed by DOs that do not live up to their own ideologies and values. In short, ecological analysis supplements group and organizational analysis with understanding of larger historical and environmental forces that shape internal events.

Ecological analyses emphasize the importance of *external relations strategies:* strategic maneuvering, internal design, interorganizational linkages, and intervention in the larger context (Kotter, 1979; Pfeffer & Salancik, 1978). Strategic changes can alter ecological pressures. The Peace and Empowerment Coalition has proposed a physical relocation of its headquarters to a multicultural environment that will encourage more learning about multicultural issues. Organizations can allocate internal resources to better manage external relations. The Development Corporation decided to emphasize housing projects to take advantage of their external reputation and connections. Developing linkages to other organizations or building an external reputation can also reduce external pressures. The Urban Leadership Program developed close ties with city government, national unions, local foundations, neighborhood organizations, and black leaders to supplement good relations with corporate leaders and ensure continued support.

The ecological perspective also raises the saliency of *longer-term social results* of organizational activities. Group or organizational perspectives often ignore other consequences of interventions (Nord, 1974). Ecological analysis highlights impacts on many stakeholders and on consequences that might otherwise be invisible. As the first farmer groups organized by the Community Mobilization Association decided to elect their own candidates to local government positions, it became very clear that present office holders would resist Association efforts to expand their activities. Ecological analysis places a premium on examining the longer-term consequences of organizational changes.

Ideas and Values as Interventions

The OD paradigm emphasizes interventions that improve group and organizational processes, redesign work and organization structures, and reshape the organization as a system. OD texts provide considerable detail on intervention techniques and procedures for changing people, processes and structures. Interventions have been focused on targets that are closely related to organizational tasks, so that organizational concerns with efficiency and effectiveness could be met in the course of OD activity. Consultants have often struggled to reconcile the values and ideas underlying OD with those of private sector clients (Tichy, 1974), and the field as a whole has focused on interventions less controversial than challenges to client values and ideologies.

In DOs, values and ideologies are central features of organizational life, inspiring both long hours for little reward and extremes of ideological conflict. Since their missions often require capacity to innovate and learn in new and complex situations, staff are often very interested in new perspectives. Our experience suggests that DO staffs respond dramatically to *new ideas*, especially ideas that reframe ideologies or values. The right concept, articulated in terms that make local sense, can liberate dammed resources of talent and energy. The notion of an organization-building as a village-level adult education intervention generated instant support and great excitement at the Community Mobilization Association. As the implications of the intervention for village activism unfolded, the organization almost overnight converted to the new approach.

Much research in organization theory has focused on organizational culture and its impact on performance (Pettigrew, 1979, 1986; Davis, 1985; Schein,

1985). Ironically, although many OD practitioners have conceived of their work in cultural terms (e.g., Harrison, 1971), they have not been central to the recent interest in organizational values and norms, beliefs and ideologies, myths, language systems and rituals. Some investigators have explored cultural interventions, such as mythmaking (e.g., Boje et al., 1982) or ideological negotiation (e.g., Brown & Brown, 1983), but OD has yet to develop much theory and practice explicitly focused on cultural change.

What would a paradigm shift that emphasizes values, ideologies, and ideas imply for OD? Developing locally meaningful ideas and perspectives requires more than superficial data collection and analysis. The capacity to recognize and analyze core organizational values and norms, to identify central beliefs, theories, and ideologies, or to describe the myths, rituals, and language systems that create meaning out of daily events depends on developing *sensitive methods of qualitative investigation and analysis.* "Thick description" and "local knowledge" of organizational events gained through participant observation (Geertz, 1973), holistic analysis of recurrent organizational patterns (Diesing, 1978), and group methods for building rich analyses of organizational culture (Schein, 1985) are more appropriate strategies of inquiry than the questionnaire and interview surveys common to most OD diagnoses.

As OD becomes more involved in analysis of values and ideologies, more *self-examination of practitioner values, beliefs, and aspirations* will become necessary. We found that DO clients actively challenged our values and beliefs. Their tests in part stemmed from organizational ideologies: At the Peace and Empowerment Coalition, for example, it was generally accepted that "Consultants are parasites." We were forced to be explicit about our own values and ideologies and to explain our work in terms consistent with Coalition concerns. Even when organizational values are not antagonistic to external consultants, cultural and ideological analysis encourages all involved to examine their positions.

We believe that values and ideologies are often important but seldom discussed in OD interventions. Interventions to transform ideologies and beliefs require *conceptual skills* for analyzing and developing alternatives, *symbolic sensitivity* for recognizing and formulating ideas appropriate to the stiuation, and *personal charisma* for articulating and enacting core concepts, new myths, or organizational sagas (Boje et al., 1982; Pettigrew, 1980). Interventions that reshape informal organization grow from informal interaction and "ideological negotiations" (Strauss, 1979; Brown & Brown, 1983), and so depend in large part on the personal characteristics of the individual. Credibility and personal charisma play important roles in such activities. It is our impression that many OD practitioners often use charismatic gifts, operate as behavioral models, and skillfully employ various types of informal influence skills. But those factors are difficult to analyze and measure, so they are often ignored in efforts to understand the OD process.

Learning as a Core Activity

The values expressed in OD texts emphasize collaborative and participative processes of work, the development of human and organizational potentials, and a spirit of inquiry. But the texts also indicate that the ultimate test is results in organizational terms, and they emphasize practice over research. The bias for action has been present from the start, and it reflects an Anglo-U.S. cultural base that emphasizes pragmatism and client concern with "bottom line" results (but see Faucheux et al., 1983).

But work with DOs once again suggests modifications of the dominant view. Development tasks compel concern with learning, both for DO clients who seek self-development and for DO staff who must regularly learn to effectively collaborate in new relationships with diverse clients. DO staff must learn with constituencies at the periphery, and then learn with their colleagues at the organizational center.

The relationship between action and research, intervention and inquiry, and various other approaches to learning and innovation are too complex for detailed exploration here. But it is worth noting that the connections between researchers and actors is often severely clouded by many issues. The gap between knowledge generation and knowledge use is all too often unbridgeable. Some analysts (e.g., Lindblom & Cohen, 1979) have argued that more attention to coordinating social problem-solving research with other sorts of knowledge could make it more usable. Others have suggested that overemphasis on scientific validity at the expense of relationships with policy-makers has undercut the impact of much rigorous policy research (van de Vall & Bolas, 1977). But it is also clear that in some circumstances inquiry has catalytic effects on action by both researchers and respondents (e.g., Brown & Tandon, 1978; Tandon & Brown, 1981). Clearly in DOs learning often leads to new action and vice versa.

What would be the implications of emphasizing learning as a core OD activity? First, in organizations like DOs the activity will necessarily be a *co-learning process,* in which the parties collaborate as equals with different resources. In many industrial organizations, people expect hierarchical differences and behave accordingly, acting like dependent (or counterdependent) research subjects to the high-status outside researcher-consultant. DO staffs place a high value on participation and equality and a low value on external consultants, and they expect a joint process in which they are teaching as well as learning. Members of the Peace and Empowerment Coalition, for example, doubted whether external consultants could understand or help their organization, and only agreed to try out the relationship after elaborate presentation and questioning of the consultants' theoretical and experiential base. Learning processes that emphasize participatory research and the empowerment of respondents are very important in such organizations.

The diversity of views and intensity of conflicts in DOs undermine learning strategies that emphasize consensus and convergence. When issues raise very different views, *dialectical learning processes* can clarify differences and generate new syntheses or compromises that recognize different interests. Lindblom (1959; 1979) has shown how learning and decision-making can continue in the absence of a consensus about either means or goals. OD practice could be expanded to facilitate such learning processes. Differences in perspective across blacks and whites, public and private leaders, and labor and management officials generated considerable conflict in the Urban Leadership Program. But third party facilitation and careful design of meetings permitted many participants to learn from their differences without ever requiring an unreachable homogeneity.

Behavior in all organizations is to some extent regulated by informally negotiated agreements among their members, "socially constructed" through repeated interactions. DOs in particular organize much member activity informally through shared expectations and values. Learning can *reshape the social architecture* in such organizations, and so alter members' behavior. New insights or reframed perspectives can lead to very rapid behavior changes. The President of the Community Development Corporation regarded external "politicking" as a vaguely immoral activity to be avoided by good administrators. When discussions of the Corporation effectiveness as a catalyst in the city suggested the necessity of more "politicking," he altered his behavior radically in the space of weeks.

Finally, in organizations like DOs whose core technology is learning, the staff often finds OD assumptions very congenial. The core values of many DOs are very similar in some respects to core values of OD. So work together can involve a *mutual influence* between DO staff and OD consultants. OD in its collaborative, participative, inquiring mode has much appeal to many DO staff. Activist, idealistic, democratic DO activities strike responsive chords for many OD consultants. We have remained in contact, professional and social, compensated and volunteer, with DO staff from years past. Our work with DOs has been dominated by learning for us, and we believe the same is true for our DO colleagues.

Societal as well as Organizational Development

OD has focused on influencing individuals, groups, and more recently, organizations. Comparing the texts of the 1970s and the 1980s reveals shifts in attention to organizational levels of analysis and to structural and systemic interventions. But, the emphasis remains inside the organization. The texts do not examine OD impacts on external environments (Nord, 1974).

For private sector manufacturing organizations, OD is expected to improve efficiency and effectiveness as measured by market performance. But, as OD is applied increasingly to organizations that are not primarily production-oriented—government agencies, hospitals, schools, and service organizations in general (Alderfer, 1974; Golembiewski, Proehl & Sink, 1982)—indicators beyond profitability become more important. More effective health organizations are expected to improve client health; more effective educational systems will produce more competent students; more effective government agencies provide better law enforcement, waste collection, or fire control. Increased effectiveness for such organizations must be measured in noncommercial terms.

Work with DOs is a good example: More effective DOs change their environments to reshape fundamental social arrangements. An effective Urban Leadership Program creates new networks for solving urban social problems. A more effective Equality in Education Program increases the quality of education available to deprived constituencies and potentially reshapes the distribution of social resources in the long run. OD that enhances DO capacity to achieve their goals promotes social change—macro-consequences from micro-interventions.

This possibility suggests that OD consultants need a *societal perspective* that recognizes external impacts and long-term consequences of their work. Without such a perspective, the consequences of success can be unpleasant surprises. The Community Mobilization Association was not prepared for challenges by village elites upset by the success of the newly-organized village farmer groups. Ecological analysis is important both for understanding internal events and for assessing the larger consequences of successful OD interventions in externally-focused organizations.

The potential for environmental impacts requires the articulation of *social values and aspirations* as well as values that guide intervention with organizations and individuals. Most OD consultants have examined values about interpersonal and organizational issues, but they often have less developed social philosophies or contextual analyses that illuminate the external impacts of their work. It was not clear initially to the Community Mobilization Association that successful farmer organizations might "destabilize" villages and create physical and social risks to farmer leaders and Association personnel in the process. OD activities with larger social consequences raise complex problems of values and tradeoffs to which present OD lore offers little guidance.

OD that influences larger contexts requires careful *analysis of preconditions* for environmental impacts and *strategic choices among clients* to be effective. Planned change in societal arrangements is even less easy to understand or control than change processes in large organizations. The initial intention of consultants to the Urban Leadership Program was to encourage the inclusion of women, minority groups, and neighborhood leaders in city decision-making networks. They were shocked to find that the first effect of the Program was a new network of white businessmen mobilized to combat a populist Mayor (Brown & Detterman, in press). Failure to understand the larger forces operating or work with the wrong client can produce perverse larger consequences. OD interventions may influence social change, but they will seldom control it. Pioneering efforts to understand interorganizational cooperation and partnerships among diverse organizations offer illustrations of applied behavioral science interventions that shape societal changes (e.g., Trist, 1978; Gricar & Brown, 1981; Gray, 1985). Much remains to be done, and OD with a societal perspective could make important contributions.

SUMMARY

This is a long and complex paper, and a brief summary of our argument may clarify its implications. We began by identifying premises of the present paradigm of OD. We reviewed some characteristics of DOs and the impacts of DO characteristics on our experience in OD. We argued that the current OD paradigm has deficiencies for some kinds of organizations and problems that may be expected to be common in the future.

Table 4 summarizes the present OD paradigm and the revisions we have proposed.

OD has been very successful in some spheres. There was evidence of constructive impacts more than a decade ago (Friedlander & Brown, 1974), and recent investigations suggest that OD outcomes are largely (though not universally) positive in both private and public organizations (Golembiewski, Proehl & Sink, 1982). It is less clear that OD theory and technology can be transferred across cultures (e.g., Faucheux et al., 1982). But the time is ripe for exploring how ideas developed in one sector and culture can be transformed to fit others.

Table 4. Present and Revised OD Paradigms

Issue	*Present Paradigm*	*Revised Paradigm*
Basic Metaphor	Organizations are open systems	Organizations are multiple overlapping systems
Level of Analysis	Groups and organizations are key to understanding events	Organizational ecology is also key to understanding events
Intervention Targets	People, processes, structures and systems are change levers	Ideas and values are as key as people, process, structure, and system change levers
Core Values	Collaboration, participation, growth, spirit of inquiry; action dominates research	Collaboration, participation in learning as a process for mutually-enhancing changes
Planned Change Impacts	Individual and group changes improve organization	Individual, group, and organization changes improve community and society

Expanding the paradigm of OD will require examining our own values and ideologies—the "governing variables" of our model (Argyris & Schon, 1978). What for example, does "development" mean? Private sector development has often been debated in terms of organizational "health" or "wealth"—human fulfillment or economic efficiency. But these terms are less relevant to organizations whose performance is not easily evaluated by market forces. Definitions of development have been hotly debated in the international arena. Some definitions emphasize economic productivity and efficiency; others emphasize equity and justice in the distribution of resources and power; some emphasize the promotion of self-reliance and local initiative; others stress liberation from external political and economic domination; still others focus on expanding options and choices available to individuals and groups (see Seers, 1969; 1977; de Kadt, 1985). As OD practitioners work with organizations focused on social service or social change, their values and ideologies will affect constituencies outside organizational boundaries. We need more dialogue about perspectives that potentially shape our societies.

We are proposing revisions in the OD paradigm that can have far-reaching effects. In essence we believe the paradigm should expand to embrace a more diversified basic metaphor, a larger analytic domain, a broader range of intervention targets, a recognition of the mutuality of action and research in learning, and an expanded vision of possible impacts. We want to see OD values, theories, and technologies operate on a larger stage. We know that OD consultants, researchers, and clients can jointly build better organizations. We believe an expanded OD can contribute to the creation of better societies. The world desperately needs social inventions that will enable us to go beyond the self-immolating contradictions of excessive reliance on either free markets or central planning, capitalism or socialism. We also need new forms of social inquiry that allow researchers and other participants to ask questions and seek answers in ways that generate new options for action and thought. An expanded paradigm of OD can contribute to all of these.

ACKNOWLEDGMENTS

We want to express our appreciation to Barbara Gray, Meryl Louis, and Philip Mirvis for comments on an earlier draft of this chapter.

REFERENCES

Adams, J. S. (1976). The structure and dynamics of behavior in organizational boundary roles. In M. Dunnette (Ed.), *Handbook of organizational and industrial psychology.* Chicago: Rand-McNally, 1175–1199.

Alderfer, C. P. (1976). Boundary relations and organizational diagnosis. In H. Meltzer and F. R. Wickert, *Humanizing organizational behavior.* Springfield, IL: Thomas.

Alderfer, C. P. (1977). Organization development. *Annual Review of Psychology, 28,* 197–224.

Alderfer, C. P. (1979). Consulting to underbounded systems. In C. P. Alderfer and C. Cooper, *Advances in Experiential Social Process,* Vol. 2. New York: Wiley.

Alderfer, C. P., Alderfer, C. J., Tucker, L. & Tucker, R. (1980). Diagnosing race relations in management. *Journal of Applied Behavioral Science, 16,* 135–166.

Aldrich, H. & Pfeffer, J. (1976). Environments of organizations. *Annual Review of Sociology, 2,* 79–106.

Ansoff, H. I. (1965). *Corporate strategy.* New York: McGraw-Hill.

Argyris, C. & Schon, D. (1978). *Organizational learning.* Reading, MA: Addison-Wesley.

Beer, M. (1980). *Organizational change and development: A systems view.* Santa Monica, CA: Goodyear.

Berger, P. L., & Neuhaus, R. J. (1977). *To empower people: The role of mediating structures in public policy.* Washington, D.C.: American Enterprise Institute for Public Policy Research.

Beyer, J. (1981). Ideologies, values and decision making in organizations. In P. Nystrom & W. Starbuck, *Handbook of organizational design, Vol. 2.* New York: Oxford University Press, 166–202.

Boje, D. M., Fedor, D. B. & Rowland, K. M. (1982). Mythmaking: A qualitative step in OD interventions. *Journal of Applied Behavioral Science, 18,* 17–28.

Bowers, D., Franklin, J. L., & Pecorella, P. A. (1977). Matching problems, precursors, and interventions in OD: A systemic approach. *Journal of Applied Behavioral Science, 11,* 391–409.

Brown, L. D. (1978). Toward a theory of power and intergroup relations. In C. A. Cooper & C. P. Alderfer, *Advances in Experiential Social Processes,* Vol. 1. London: Wiley.

Brown, L. D. (1980). Planned change in underorganized systems. In T. G. Cummings (Ed.), *Systems theory for organization development.* London: Wiley.

Brown, L. D. (1983). *Managing conflict at organizational interfaces.* Reading, MA: Addison-Wesley.

Brown, L. D. (1984). Effective change strategies for public enterprise: Lessons from turnaround cases. *Vikalpa,* April-June, 98–112.

Brown, L. D., & Brown, J. C. (1983). Organizational microcosms and ideological negotiation. In M. Bazerman & R. Lewicki, *Bargaining inside organizations.* Beverly Hills, CA: Sage.

Brown, L. D., & Detterman, L. (in press). Small interventions for large problems: Reshaping urban leadership networks. *Journal of Applied Behavioral Science.*

Brown, L. D., & Tandon, R. (1978). Interviews as catalysts in a community setting. *Journal of Applied Psychology, 63,* 197–205.

Brown, L. D., & Tandon, R. (1983). Ideology and political economy in inquiry: Action research and participatory research. *Journal of Applied Behavioral Science, 19,* 277–294.

Burke, W. W. (1982). *Organization development: Principles and practices.* Boston: Little, Brown & Co.

Burns, T., & Stalker, G. M. (1961). *The management of innovation.* London: Tavistock.

Chandler, A. (1962). *Strategy and structure.* Cambridge, MA: MIT Press.

Cohen, M. D., & March, J. G. (1972). *Leadership and ambiguity: The american college president.* New York: McGraw-Hill.

Davis, S. M. (1985). *Managing corporate culture.* Boston: Ballinger.

Diesing, P. (1971). *Patterns of discovery in the social sciences.* Chicago: Aldine-Atherton.

Faucheux, C., Amado, G., & Laurent, A. (1982). Organizational development and change. *Annual Review of Psychology, 33,* 343–370.

Freeman, R. E. (1984). *Strategic management: A stakeholder approach.* Boston, MA: Pitman.

French, W., & Bell, C. (1973). *Organization development.* Englewood Cliffs, NJ: Prentice-Hall. (First Edition).

French, W., & Bell, C. (1985). *Organization development.* Englewood Cliffs, NJ: Prentice-Hall. (Third Edition).

Friedlander, F., & Brown, L. D. (1974). Organization development. *Annual Reivew of Psychology*, *25*, 313–341.

Galbraith, J. R., & Nathanson, D. A. (1978). *Strategy implementation: The role of structure and process*. St. Paul: West.

Geertz, C. (1973). *The interpretation of culture*. New York: Basic Books.

Golembiewski, R. T. (1969). Organization development in public agencies: Perspectives on theory and practice. *Public Administration Review*, *29*, 366–377.

Golembiewski, R. T., Proehl, C. W., & Sink, B. (1982). Estimating success of OD applications. *Training and Development Journal*, April, 86–95.

Gray, B. (1985). Conditions facilitating interorganizational collaboration. *Human Relations*, *38*, 911–936.

Gricar, B. G., & Brown, L. D. (1981). Conflict, power and organization in a changing community. *Human Relations*, *34*, 877–893.

Harrison, R. (1972). Understanding your organization's character. *Harvard Business Review*, May-June, 119–128.

Huse, E. F. (1975). *Organization development and change*. St. Paul, West. (First Edition).

Huse, E. F., & Cummings, T. G. (1984). *Organization development and change*. St. Paul: West. (Third Edition).

de Kadt, E. (1985). Of markets, might and mullahs: A case for equity, pluralism, and tolerance in development. *World Development*, *13*, 449–556.

Kahn, R. L. (1974). Organization development: Some problems and proposals. *Journal of Applied Behavioral Science*, *10*, 485–502.

Kanter, R. M. (1983). *The changemasters: Innovation for productivity in the American corporation*. New York: Simon and Schuster.

Korten, D. (1980). Community organization and rural development: A learning process approach. *Public Administration Review*, *40*, 480–510.

Kotter, J. P. (1979). Managing external dependence. *Academy of Management Review*, *4*, 87–92.

Kuhn, T. S. (1970). *The structure of scientific revolutions* (2nd ed.). Chicago: University of Chicago Press.

Lawrence, P. R., & Lorsch, J. W. (1967). *Organization and environment*. Cambridge, MA: Harvard Business School.

Lindblom, C. E. (1959). The science of muddling through. *Public Administration Review*, *19*, 79–88.

Lindblom, C. E. (1979). Still muddling, not yet through. *Public Administration Review*, *39*, 517–526.

Lindblom, C. E., & Cohen, D. K. (1979). *Usable knowledge*. New Haven, CT: Yale.

Lodahl, A. B., & Gordon, G. (1972). The structure of scientific fields and the functioning of university graduate departments. *American Sociological Review*, *37*, 57–72.

MacMillan, I. C. (1982). Business strategy formulation. In D. Nadler, M. Tushman, & N. Hatvany (Eds.), *Managing organizations*. Boston: Little, Brown and Co.

March, J. (1962). The business firm as a political coalition. *Journal of Politics*, *24*, 662–678.

Meyer, J. W., & Scott, W. P. R. (1983). *Organizational environments: Ritual and rationality*. Beverly Hills, CA: Sage.

Miles, R. E., Snow, C. C., Meyer, A. D., & Coleman, H. J. (1978). Organizational strategy, structure, and process. *Academy of Management Review*, *3*, 546–562.

Miles, R. H. (1980). *Macro-organizational behavior*. Santa Monica: CA: Goodyear.

Nord, W. R. (1974). The failure of current applied behavioral science: A marxian perspective. *Journal of Applied Behavioral Science*, *10*, 557–578.

Ouchi, W. (1981). *Theory Z: How American business can meet the Japanese challenge*. Reading, MA: Addison-Wesley.

Pascale, R. P., & Athos, A. G. (1981). *The art of Japanese management*. New York: Simon and Schuster.

Peters, P. J., & Waterman, R. H. (1982). *In search of excellence: Lessons From America's best run companies.* New York: Warner Books.

Pettigrew, A. (1979). On studying organizational cultures. *Administrative Science Quarterly, 24,* 570–589.

Pettigrew, A. (1986). Limits to executive power in strategic changes. In S. Srivastva & Associates (Eds.), *Executive Power.* San Francisco, CA: Jossey-Bass.

Pfeffer, J. (1981). *Power in organizations.* Marshfield, MA: Pitman.

Pfeffer, J., & Salancik, G. (1978). *The external control of organizations.* New York: Harper and Row.

Ritzer, G. (1975). *Sociology, a multiple paradigm science.* Boston: Allyn and Bacon.

Schein, E. H. (1985). *Organizational culture and leadership.* San Francisco: Jossey-Bass.

Seers, D. (1969). The meaning of development. *International Development Review, 11.* 11, 4.

Seers, D. (1977). The new meaning of development. *International Development Review.* 19, 3.

Srivastva, S., & Associates (1986). *Executive power.* San Francisco: Jossey-Bass.

Strauss, A. (1979). *Negotiations.* San Francisco: Jossey-Bass.

Stoelwinder, J. U., & Charns, M. (1981). The task field model of organization analysis and design. *Human Relations, 34.*

Tandon, R., & Brown, L. D. (1981). Organization building for rural development: An experiment in India. *Journal of Applied Behavioral Science, 17,* 172–189.

Tichy, N. M. (1983). *Managing strategic change.* New York: Wiley.

Thompson, J. D. (1967). *Organizations in action.* New York: McGraw-Hill.

Trist, E. L. (1979). New directions of hope. *Human Futures, 2:*3, 176–185.

Trist, E. L. (1983). Referent organizations and the development of interorganizational domains. *Human Relations, 6,* 247–268.

van de Vall, M., & Bolas, C. (1977). Policy research as an agent of planned social intervention: An evaluation of methods, standards, data, and analytic techniques. *Sociological Practice, 2:* 2, 77–94.

Warwick, D. A. (1975). *A theory of public bureaucracy.* Cambridge, MA: Harvard University Press.

Weick, K. (1976). Educational organizations as loosely coupled systems. *Administrative Science Quarterly, 21,* 1–19.

Wells, M. J. (1982). Political mediation and agricultural cooperation: Strawberry farms in California. *Economic Development and Cultural Change, 30,* 413–32.

REASONING, ACTION STRATEGIES, AND DEFENSIVE ROUTINES

THE CASE OF OD PRACTITIONERS

Chris Argyris

ABSTRACT

The chapter examines defensive reasoning processes used by OD professionals. Model I and Model II theories-in-use, that underlie defensive or productive reasoning, are reviewed. Defensive reasoning by an OD professional is illustrated by an in-depth case analysis. Barriers to productive reasoning in OD and some consequences of defensive reasoning are explored. Finally, implications for theory and practice are discussed.

INTRODUCTION

The focus of this chapter is on a particularly thorny set of problems that OD practitioners face, usually with clients who have cooperated in the past but

Research in Organizational Change and Development, Vol. 1, pages 89–128.
Copyright © 1987 by JAI Press Inc.
All rights of reproduction in any form reserved.
ISBN: 0-89232-749-9

increasingly find it difficult to do so in the future. Their cooperation takes the form of going along with *and* resisting; adhering to *and* violating the values and assumptions of OD. I believe that much of the ambivalence of the clients is due largely to the actions that OD practitioners use to reduce or overcome the client ambivalence in the first place.

I hope to show that the OD professionals studied used defensive reasoning processes to design and implement their actions when dealing with difficult issues, yet they espoused and counseled their clients not to use such reasoning processes. The defensive reasoning and actions produced consequences that were counterproductive by the OD professionals' own criteria. This, in turn, led to the OD practitioners having decreasing credibility with their clients, which in turn reinforced the OD professionals' use of defensive reasoning.

The clients also used defensive reasoning. I focus on the OD professionals, because they are the ones who are supposed to help others use productive reasoning, and it is unlikely that they will do so unless they first learn these skills.

A Brief Description of the OD Group

An OD group in a very large high-tech organization sensed clues from their clients that their effectiveness and credibility with them was beginning to deteriorate. The deterioration was not severe, nor was it across all programs. Nevertheless, the OD professionals decided to examine their practice in order to make changes before the situation became more serious.

The story that I pieced together from what the OD professionals said is one that I have now heard in several organizations with a history of early commitment to the values of organizational development. In the early years, the major thrust of many OD programs was to emphasize such factors as involvement, participation, and ownership. The expression of feelings, the creation of trust, the reduction of defenses were high on their agendas. The early success of OD programs was related primarily to overcoming very difficult situations (e.g., highly authoritarian leadership, manipulative policies, and injustices such as the way minorities were dealt with).

As these programs succeeded, the support grew. The OD professionals were invited to redesign jobs, to redesign reward systems, and to redesign, or design from the beginning, new factories. As the scope of OD programs grew, the OD professionals began to confront traditional organizational dilemmas such as autonomy versus control, innovation versus no surprises, participation and ownership versus meeting deadlines, and job security versus excess employees, through job design. These dilemmas were there during the early years, but the programs did not face up to them because they took a back seat to authoritarian leadership, equal opportunities, and the like.

The OD professionals recalled the bewilderment they felt in dealing with these dilemmas. They were for involvement and ownership, and they knew how to produce these states of affairs. What they lacked was knowledge on how to deal with conditions where involvement and ownership were counterproductive, where unilateral control over employees was necessary, or where frustrating employee needs appeared necessary, or what to do when OD professionals designed programs that placed more demands on the employees than the employees expected. Too often they dealt with these dilemmas by bypassing them or by suggesting a short workshop to explore them.

Over time, the workshop strategy wore out its welcome. Line managers did not find the workshops helpful because most of them were designed with the assumption that line managers could solve these problems if they had an opportunity to think and discuss them. This assumption proved to be incorrect. The actions line managers took often expressed their bewilderment and ambivalence. For example, they would tighten up controls and hide their intentions by espousing the importance of increasing employee ownership. Others tried to give employees more influence, but kept to themselves that they would crack down if things got out of hand. In other words, when the OD programs ran up against these age-old dilemmas, the line management retrieved their old ways of exercising authority. Some OD practitioners reacted by confronting management for being two-faced. Others tried to work within the constraints by developing new concepts that could "organize people" and "energize efforts."

One frequently used concept in this organization was vision. If line management could only develop correct visions, they could manage these dilemmas more effectively. The different examples of visions that were found fell into two broad categories: one, visions of nonsense, back-to-the-basics approach that the OD people saw as regression to the old days; and two, visions of involvement and participation. When OD and line came up against the dilemmas described above, both "regressed" to the more traditional theories of unilateral control.

The Action Science Program to Help the OD Professionals

A program was designed that combined inquiry and re-education of the OD professionals. The first step was to obtain examples of nontrivial encounters and of how the OD professionals acted during them. They were asked to develop cases.

The case format is simple: first, a paragraph that describes the problem as they see it. This gives us insight into how they frame the problem. Next a paragraph or so as to how they would go about solving the problem if they had access to the people and systems they believe are relevant. This gives insight into the kinds of solutions they invent and the espoused theories of how to implement them.

Next they write a brief scenario of what they would say and expect others to say if the meeting they recommended actually took place. As they write the scenario, usually on the right-hand half of the page, they are asked to describe (on the left-hand half of the page) any thoughts and feelings that they would have but, for whatever reason, would not communicate. They write the scenario for two to three double-spaced, typewritten pages. The actual conversation plus the material on the left-hand side of the page provides the data needed to infer the theory-in-use.

These cases can be used to develop quantitative and qualitative data about the frames, the espoused theories, the theories-in-use, and the self-censoring mechanisms of the writers. The results from the individual cases can be aggregated to produce findings about such organizational phenomena as defensive routines and culture (Argyris, 1985).

The next step was to use the cases as vehicles for re-educating the OD professionals and their clients. For example, they were distributed to the OD professionals in a workshop. The task was to help each writer understand more completely the problems identified in his or her case and to design ways to overcome them. Typically, the participants' discussions included (1) the extent to which the writer produced the intended consequences, (2) the gaps and inconsistencies, and (3) patterns of undiscussable issues and the way they were covered up.

The discussions were tape recorded in order to study the reactions of the person being helped as well as the quality of help being given by the other participants. As the diagnoses became clear, the individuals turned to the third step which was to redesign their actions and to practice producing the new designs. These discussions produce additional knowledge about the organization and the OD professionals because the new insights were generated as people moved from discovering to inventing to producing or implementing their ideas.

The fourth step was for the OD practitioners to use their new ideas and skills in actual client situations. They formed subgroups to help each other out, and they met as a total group to compare experiences.

The Structure of the Chapter

First is a brief description of the theory that was used to design the action research and to intervene to help the OD professionals in order to increase their effectiveness. Second, the reasoning processes of Richard, an OD professional, are described in-depth. Third, a map is presented of the organizational defensive loops that the OD professionals agreed resulted from their actions and the actions of their clients. Fourth, there is a discussion of the implications of the research for theory and practice.

An Overview of the Perspective That Informed the Inquiry

The theory of action approach (Argyris & Schön, 1974, 1978; Argyris, 1976, 1980, 1982; Argyris, Putnam, & Smith, 1985) begins with a conception of human beings as designers of action. To see human behavior under the aspect of action is to see it as constituted by the meanings and intentions of agents. Agents design action to achieve intended consequences and monitor themselves to learn if their actions are effective. They make sense of their environment by constructing meanings to which they attend, and these constructions guide action. In monitoring the effectiveness of action, they also monitor the suitability of their construction of the environment.

Designing action requires that agents construct a simplified representation of the environment and a manageable set of causal theories that prescribe how to achieve intended consequences. It would be very inefficient to construct such representations and theories from scratch in each situation. Rather, agents learn a repertoire of concepts, schemas, and strategies, and they learn programs for drawing from their repertoire to design representations and action for unique situations. We speak of such design programs as *theories of action*. Theories of action determine all deliberate human behavior.

Espoused Theory and Theory-in-Use

There are two kinds of theories of action. Espoused theories are those that an individual claims to follow. Theories-in-use are those that can be inferred from action. For example, when asked how he would deal with a disagreement with a client, a management consultant said that he would first state what he understood to be the substance of the disagreement, and then negotiate what kind of data he and the client could agree would resolve it. This was his espoused theory. But when we examined a tape recording of what the consultant actually did in such a situation, we found that he advocated his own view and dismissed that of the client.

It is an old story that what people do often differs from the theories they espouse. We are saying, however, that there is a theory which is consistent with what they do; and this we call their theory-in-use. Our distinction is not between theory and action, but between two different theories of action: those that people espouse, and those that they use. One reason for insisting that what people do is consistent with the theory (in-use) they hold, albeit inconsistent with their espoused theories, is to emphasize that what people do is not accidental. They do not "just happen" to act that way. Rather, their action is designed; and as agents, they are responsible for the design.

The models we create in action science are shaped by our interest in helping human beings to make more informed choices in creating the worlds in which they are embedded. Because we are interested in helping human beings to design and implement action, our models should have the feature of being connectable to concrete situations. We seek both generalizability and attention to the individual case.

Modeling Theories-in-Use

Models of theories-in-use can be constructed in the schematic frame shown in Figure 1.

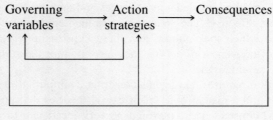

Figure 1

Governing variables are values that actors seek to satisfice. Each governing variable can be thought of as a continuum with a preferred range. Human beings live in a field of many governing variables. Any action can have an impact on many governing variables. Agents typically must trade off among governing variables, because actions that raise the value of one may lower the value of another.

Action strategies are sequences of moves used by actors in particular situations to satisfice among governing variables. Action strategies have intended consequences, which are those that the actor believes will result from the action and will satisfy governing variables. Consequences feed back to action strategies and governing variables. Consequences may also be unintended and counterproductive. Consequences which are unintended may nevertheless be designed, in the following sense: action intended to achieve particular consequences may, by virtue of its design, necessarily lead to consequences which are unintended. For example, the questioning strategy of easing-in typically creates the very defensiveness that it is intended to avoid, because the recipient typically understands that the actor is easing-in.

Single-loop and Double-loop Learning

When the consequences of an action strategy are as the agent intends, then there is a match between intention and outcome and the theory-in-use of the agent is confirmed. If the consequences are unintended, and especially if they are counterproductive, there is a mismatch or an error. The first response to error is typically to search for another action strategy that will satisfy the same governing variables. In such a case, when new action strategies are used in the service of the same governing variables, we speak of *single-loop learning*. We do so because the change is in action but not in governing variables.

Another possibility is to change the governing variables themselves. For example, rather than suppress conflict, the agent might choose to value open inquiry. The associated action strategy might be to initiate discussion of conflictual issues. In such cases we speak of *double-loop learning*.

MODEL I THEORY-IN-USE

Argyris and Schön (1974) developed a model, or an ideal type, which describes features of theories-in-use which inhibit double-loop learning. While espoused theories vary widely, research indicates that there is almost no variance in theory-in-use (Argyris, 1976, 1982). More precisely, the theories-in-use of virtually everyone we have studied are consistent with the master program called Model I, or with its mirror image, opposite Model I. There is considerable difference within Model I, in the weightings individuals give to particular governing variables, and in the particular strategies individuals favor; but these lower order variations appear to be governed by the Model I executive design program.

The four governing variables of Model I are (1) achieve the purpose as the actor defines it, (2) win, do not lose, (3) suppress negative feelings, and (4) emphasize rationality.

The primary behavioral strategies in Model I are to control unilaterally the relevant environment and tasks and to protect oneself and others unilaterally. The underlying behavioral strategy is unilateral control over others. Characteristic ways of implementing this strategy include making unillustrated attributions and evaluations, advocating in ways that discourage inquiry, treating one's own views as obviously correct, making covert attributions and evaluations, and face-saving.

The consequences of Model I strategies include defensive interpersonal and group relationships, low freedom of choice, and reduced production of valid information. There are negative consequences for learning, because there is little public testing of ideas. The hypotheses that people generate tend to become self-sealing. What learning does occur remains within the bounds of what is acceptable. Double-loop learning does not tend to occur. As a result, error escalates and effectiveness in problem solving and in execution of action tends to decrease.

In claiming that human beings are programmed with Model I theory-in-use, we are making predictions about the kinds of strategies they will and will not use, and the kinds of consequences that will and will not occur. These predictions have been tested in dozens of client groups including thousands of individuals, and to date they have not been disconfirmed (see Argyris, 1982, Chapter 3 for a recent review). Most people hold espoused theories inconsistent with Model I, and when confronted with our predictions seek to demonstrate that they are not valid. At best, they are able to produce strategies consistent with opposite Model I.

The governing variables of opposite Model I are (1) participation of everyone in defining purposes, (2) everyone wins, no one loses, (3) express feelings, and (4) suppress the cognitive intellective aspects of action. The associated behavioral strategies include inquiry and minimizing unilateral control (Argyris & Schön, 1974).

Figure 2. Model I Theory-in-Use

Governing variables	Action strategies	Consequences for the behavioral world	Consequences for learning	Effectiveness
1. Define goals and try to achieve them.	1. Design and manage the environment unilaterally (be persuasive, appeal to larger goals).	1. Actor seen as defensive, inconsistent, incongruent, competitive, controlling, fearful of being vulnerable, manipulative, withholding of feelings, overly concerned about self and others or underconcerned about others.	1. Self-sealing.	Decreased effectiveness
2. Maximize winning and minimize losing.	2. Own and control the task (claim ownership of the task, be guardian of definition and execution of task).	2. Defensive interpersonal and group relationship (dependence upon actor, little additivity, little helping others).	2. Single-loop learning.	

3. Minimize generating or expressing negative feelings.

4. Be rational.

3. *Unilaterally protect yourself* (speak with inferred categories accompanied by little or no directly observable behavior, be blind to impact on others and to the incongruity between rhetoric and behavior, reduce incongruity by defensive actions such as blaming, stereotyping, suppressing feelings, intellectualizing).

4. *Unilaterally protect others from being hurt* (withhold information, create rules to censor information and behavior, hold private meetings).

3. Defensive norms (mistrust, lack of risk-taking, conformity, external commitment, emphasis on diplomacy, power-centered competition, and rivalry).

4. Low freedom of choice, internal commitment, and risk-taking.

3. Little testing of theories publicly. Much testing of theories privately.

97

Model O-I: The Behavioral World

The consequences of Model I theory-in-use, as we have described, include defensiveness, low freedom of choice, and self-sealing processes. If it is the case that Model I identifies features of theories-in-use that are common to virtually everyone, it follows that the behavioral worlds of groups, families, and organizations will have features that correspond to Model I. The interaction of people programmed with Model I theories-in-use generates pattern-building forces that create a characteristic behavioral world.

Argyris and Schön (1978) created a model of the behavioral world that is congruent with Model I theory-in-use. Model O-I ("O" signifies "organization") is a model of a *limited learning system.* The model states that when individuals programmed with Model I theory-in-use deal with difficult and threatening problems, they create primary inhibiting loops. That is, they create conditions of undiscussability, self-fulfilling prophecies, self-sealing processes, and escalating error, and they remain unaware of their responsibility for these conditions. Primary inhibiting loops lead to win-lose group dynamics, conformity, polarization between groups, and organizational games of deception. These secondary inhibiting loops reinforce primary inhibiting loops; together they lead people to despair of double-loop learning in organizations.

In a recent publication, these defensive loops have been called defensive routines. A defensive routine is any action or policy that prevents experiencing embarrassment or threat *and simultaneously* prevents reducing the causes of the embarrassment or threat (Argyris, 1985).

MODEL II THEORY-IN-USE

The action scientist is an interventionist, seeking to help members of client systems to reflect on the world they create and to learn to change it in ways more congruent with the values and theories they espouse. The normative perspective that guides the action scientist is described by a model of an alternative theory-in-use, Model II (Argyris & Schön, 1974). Model II as an espoused theory is not new; indeed most people readily espouse it. But as a theory-in-use it is rare. The action scientist intends to produce action consistent with Model II, because it is by so doing that the counter-productive features of Models I and O–I can be interrupted. Just as action consistent with Models I and O–I creates threats to validity and inhibits learning, action consistent with Models II and O-II is hypothesized to enhance validity and learning. Model II provides an image of the theory-in-use that the action scientist as interventionist seeks to help clients learn.

The governing variables of Model II (Figure 3) include (1) valid information, (2) free and informed choice, and (3) internal commitment. These are the features of the alternative worlds that action science seeks to create (Argyris, 1980). Creating conditions in which these values are realized is the primary task of the interventionist (Argyris, 1970).

The behavioral strategies of Model II involve sharing control with those who have competence and who are relevant to designing or implementing the action. Rather than unilateral advocacy (Model I) or inquiry that conceals the agent's own views (opposite Model I), in Model II the agent combines advocacy and inquiry. Attributions and evaluations are illustrated with relatively directly observable data and the surfacing of conflicting views is encouraged in order to facilitate public testing.

The consequences of Model II action strategies should include minimally defensive interpersonal and group relationships, high freedom of choice, and high risk taking. The likelihood of double-loop learning is enhanced, and effectiveness should increase over time. Model O-II describes the behavioral world created by individuals interacting with Model II theory-in-use. Instead of creating primary inhibiting loops, when members of organizations deal with difficult and threatening problems using Model II theory-in-use they engage in Model II inquiry. Previously undiscussable issues will be surfaced, assumptions will be tested and corrected, and self-sealing processes will be interrupted. Both single-loop and double-loop learning can occur. Dysfunctional group and intergroup dynamics should decrease, and there should be less need for camouflage and games of deception.

At the espoused level, Models II and O-II sound like motherhood and apple pie. The trick is to produce them in the real world. This is quite difficult, both because people have been socialized to produce Model I and because the world continues to operate largely according to Model I even when some people try to act according to Model II.

Finally, Model I theory-in-use encourages the use of defensive reasoning (Figure 4) and the O-I learning system culturally reinforces its use. Model II theory-in-use encourages also the use of productive reasoning (Figure 5) and the O-II learning system culturally reinforces its use. Reasoning processes include all the "mind" activities that are used to produce premises, make inferences, and draw conclusions about any type of problem. The fundamental assumption is that individuals programmed with Model I and embedded in an O-I learning system will use defensive reasoning for problems that are difficult and potentially embarrassing to them or to others. It is the defensive reasoning that leads to ideas or feelings that are counterproductive to learning and effective action. Let us turn to examining several cases written by OD professionals who were trying to learn how to minimize creating defensive routines while interacting with their clients.

Figure 3. Model II Theory-In-Use

Governing variables	Action strategies	Consequences for the behavioral world	Consequences for learning	Consequences for quality of life	Effectiveness
1. Valid information.	1. *Design situations or environments where participants can be origins and can experience high personal causation (psychological success, confirmation, essentiality).*	1. *Actor experienced as minimally defensive (facilitator, collaborator, choice creator).*	1. Disconfirmable processes.	1. *Quality of life will be more positive than negative (high authenticity and high freedom of choice).*	Increased long-run effectiveness.
2. Free and informed choice.	2. *Tasks are controlled jointly.*	2. *Minimally defensive interpersonal relations and group dynamics.*	2. Double-loop learning.	2. *Effectiveness of problem solving and decision making will be great, especially for difficult problems.*	

100

3. Internal commitment to the choice and constant monitoring of its implementation.

3. *Protection of self is a joint enterprise and oriented toward growth* (speak in directly observable categories, seek to reduce blindness about own inconsistency and incongruity).

4. *Bilateral protection of others.*

3. *Learning-oriented norms* (trust, individuality, open confrontation on difficult issues).

3. Public testing of theories.

101

Figure 4.   Defensive Reasoning

Its Characteristics are:
- The use of soft data (i.e., difficult to accept as valid descriptions of reality by individuals with contradictory views).
- Inferences are tacit and private.
- Conclusions are not publicly testable.

Behind Defensive Reasoning
- A tacit theory of dealing with threat.
- a set of concepts that are tacitly interrelated.
- a set of tacit rules of how to use these concepts to make permissable inferences, reach private conclusions, and private criteria to judge the validity of the test.

The Case of Richard[1]

Richard wrote a case to describe some difficulties he had with a line manager who liked the idea of using a vision to manage employees, but whose views of an effective vision were quite different from Richard's. The dialogue material is taken from a transcript of Richard's discussion with his fellow OD practitioners on how to deal with the problem.

The reasoning processes Richard used were similar to those I observed his colleagues using when they were dealing with difficult but different issues. Therefore, I could have selected any of the other 11 cases and illustrated the same underlying reasoning processes. Indeed, these results were replicated in discussions with another OD practitioner's group in the United States (a group of twenty) and two groups in Europe (of twenty-four each).

Figure 5.   Productive Reasoning

Its Characteristics are:
- The use of hard data (i.e., easily acceptable as valid descriptions of reality by individuals with contradictory views).
- premises are explicit.
- inferences are explicit.
- conclusions are publicly testable.

Behind Productive Reasoning
- An explicit or tacit theory of strategy formulation.
- a set of interrelated concepts.
- a set of explicit rules of how to use these concepts to make permissable inferences, reach testable conclusions, and criteria to judge the validity of the test.

Conversation[2]	Inferences I made during the conversation about Richard's action strategies and reasoning

Q: "How certain were you by the time the session finished that you had explicit commitment (from your client)?"

Richard: "I think I had a commitment, but not an explicit one."

"He is fairly indirect in terms of making expectations explicit. Lots of politeness. Easing-in. He is a master at it."

Richard did not test this attribution about client commitment with the client. Richard appears to explain the reasoning behind not testing his attribution by creating another, namely that the clients prefer to ease-in.

Making the easing-in attribution about the client and acting consistently with it is itself an act of easing-in. Thus the attribution Richard makes about his client may be also made about him. Richard appears unaware of this possibility. How does he know the easing-in he is attributing to the client is not partially caused by his own easing-in?

At another level of inquiry, how much of the attribution made by Richard is a projection? Why not test?

(later)

Q: "What was your reaction to his intended use of the video?"

Richard: "I am opposed to using a video in order to hook people into a vision in which they were not intimately involved (in creating)."

How does he know the client intends to use the video tape to hook people in?

How does he know that the use of a video tape must necessarily hook people in? Why cannot it be designed to get genuine involvement?

If he thinks a video can be used in a way that is constructive, what prevented Richard from pointing out the difficulties with the client's views and how they could be corrected?

Again, Richard appears to be making attributions about the client's intentions that he does not test.

Q: "Do you have ideas as to how to construct a good tape?"

Richard: "I've never done this before so I do not know what a good tape would look like. I do not even know how his would look like."

How can he then be so certain that a video tape will be harmful?

"What I do know is that if we have the right tape, everything will happen."

How would he know what is the right tape if he does not know what a good video tape would look like?

"The tape must communicate the correct vision. I believe in the importance of having the right vision. I feel it in my bones and in my cells, but I do not know how to deliver it."

He believes strongly in the right vision. What leads him to believe so strongly? He feels it but is equally clear that he could not produce the right vision.

What is the nature of his knowing? What prevents him from communicating it to his client?

Q: "Have you told the client that you oppose video tape as an exclusive media?"
Richard: "I think I've said it to him perhaps not in so many words. I do not know whether he buys that idea."
"I'm not sure that he would not be happy if we produced a tape that his staff could use to indoctrinate lots of people."

What prevented him from testing the attribution with the client?

Again, what prevented him from testing the attribution?

Richard's Reasoning: Reflection I

Richard makes attributions about the clients' intentions which he does not test.

Richard is unable to present the data in order to illustrate, nor is he able to make explicit the chain of reasoning that has led to his attributions about the client.

Many of the attributions Richard makes about the client can be made about Richard.

Richard believes that having the "right" vision is key to success. Yet he cannot define the features of the right vision to his own satisfaction.

Richard judges the client's ideas about video tape as counterproductive yet he neither can state what makes them counterproductive nor does he discuss this with the client.

Richard has little hard data with which to develop his premises about the importance and the practical value of having a vision. He is unable to make explicit his reasoning that leads him to conclude that he has the better or the more complete vision.

We may conclude that Richard's conversation so far was characterized by several patterns.

1.   Untested and untestable attributions about the client. Yet the validity of his conversation and help were dependent on the attributions being valid.

2.   Inconsistencies and gaps. Richard questions the effectiveness of easing-in yet does it himself. He laments client's unawareness yet he is also unaware.

3.   Strategies of persuasion through ideology and faith. For example, Richard is sure that it is possible to produce an effective video tape yet he cannot describe its characteristics nor has he ever seen one. Richard asks the client to have faith that with genuine participative problem solving, a solution will be produced.

Richard's automatic reactions to the inconsistencies and gaps pointed out by his peers was a surprise. Instead of inquiring into the basis for his unawareness, Richard asserted that the problem would be resolved if the client and he engaged in a mutually productive problem-solving process.

The responses by Richard to his peers included untested attributions, distancing himself from his own unawareness, and trying to persuade his peers to have faith that the problems could be solved by a genuine joint problem-solving process; a process that he has not yet been able to produce with the client. Richard dealt with his peers with the same type of defensive reasoning he used with his client. Moreover, until now, he acted as if this was not a problem about which he or they should be concerned.

Back to the discussion.   As the discussion continues, Richard's peers begin to question more actively the reasoning behind and the validity of his attributions. For example, one asked him what he meant when he wrote, in his case, about the client "That's what I was afraid of (about him)."

Richard: Yes, (but notice that I realized that my doubts may be unfair). "You know why should I expect a left-brain analytically trained manager to have this (my) notion of vision and to be able to pick up on it like that quick in a conversation."

Richard "explains" the client's "inability to understand" Richard's view of vision by saying that the client was educated as an engineer and is left-brain dominated.

Note that Richard has presented no data that the client has an inability to understand; no data that this particular engineer was dominated by the left brain; nor any data that all engineers who are left-brain

"I mean I really believe that. It took me a year and I still cannot articulate it well."

dominated cannot understand his notion of vision.

Richard makes private attributions about the client's inabilities to understand his view of vision yet Richard does not understand it well enough to articulate it to his own satisfaction.

It is at least a plausible hypothesis that Richard's inarticulateness could be causally relevant in the client not understanding.

Richard's reasoning excludes him as a causal variable in the problem that he identifies and focuses on the client in ways difficult to test: he is left-brain dominated.

One of his peers questioned Richard about some features of the reasoning that were identified above.

Q: "It sounds like you're saying, well okay, this left-brained-trained manager doesn't know any better . . . so you chose to teach him . . . about what is a vision."

Richard: "Well, in a way, I was trying to back off and not be judgemental and kind of accept him where he is and you know I was there too not too long ago."

Instead of Richard exploring the possibility that he has prejudged the client as needing education, Richard "explains" his action to educate the client as an act of acceptance and tolerance. He will educate the uneducated.

"By backing off (I meant) that I realized that it was maybe unfair for him to understand it so quickly. Recognizing my own struggle to understand this concept, I realize that it is going to take some time."

Note phrases "in a way" and "kind of accept him" The question arises, "In what way?" "What kind of acceptance?" I believe if Richard explained their meaning, he might begin to get insight into the gaps in his reasoning.

Richard implies that he understands the meaning of vision enough to communicate it and/or teach it to clients. So far, he has not illustrated this capacity with the client nor with his peers.

Richard: "We're gonna have to work together for us to understand our meanings of the word (vision) and then to be able to engage in some kind of a mutual process

Richard expects that through a mutual problem-solving process the client can be helped to see what he now does not see.

around how are we going to do it together
in this context.''

Richard's Reasoning: Reflection II

Richard continues all the defensive reasoning processes described in Reflection I and adds a few more.

Richard explains the client's difficulties to understand Richard's meaning of vision by (1) attributing that he has difficulties, and (2) attributing the cause of the difficulties to the "fact" that the client was educated as an engineer and is therefore left-brain dominated. Richard now assigns full causal responsibility to the client.

Richard explains his attempt to educate the client in Richard's meaning of vision as an act of tolerance and patience with the client's limits.

Two additional patterns in Richard's reasoning appear in this episode:

1. Richard reacted to the client's questioning of Richard's beliefs by seeing the doubts expressed as signs of the client's limitations.
2. Richard acted as if the vague language that he used to explain his actions (e.g., "kind of accept him") was clear. If Richard's language is vague and if he believes it is clear, then he must be unaware of its vagueness.

If we combine the first three patterns with these two, Richard's conversation intended to help the client contained: (1) untested attributions, (2) inconsistencies and gaps, (3) reliance on ideology and faith, (4) deflecting client questions by blaming him for his "ignorance," and (5) by using language that was vague.

Richard was not aware of these features while he was producing them with the client. His automatic reactions to his peers as they pointed out these problems was to use the same five defensive reasoning and action strategies just described. However, as we shall see below, when his peers were able to present further data and were able to discuss the consequences of these five defensive reasoning and action strategies, Richard began to see what his peers were trying to help him to learn.

There is a theory of intervention embedded in the five defensive reasoning and action strategies which is itself inconsistent and highly unlikely to be effective. For example, Richard is, in effect, maintaining:

1. Although I (Richard) cannot articulate my meaning of vision, I will educate the client in my meaning of vision by engaging with him in a mutual problem-solving process.
2. It is possible for me to create a mutual problem-solving process with a client who I consider to be unable to understand my meaning of vision, who has

had an education that causes important blind spots, and with whom I have never tested my attributions and indeed kept them secret.

3. It is possible for me to hide my untested negative attributions from the client so that they do not inhibit creating a mutual problem-solving process.

Back to the discussion.   When Richard denied his peers' attributions that he was communicating to the client that his (Richard's) vision was better, several of his peers questioned him closely by referring to the dialogue Richard wrote in his case. Richard finally said:

> *Richard:*   "I guess I did back off when I said okay, you've got one meaning for the term vision. But you haven't got the one that I want you to get."
>
> "(Your understanding) is the commonly accepted meaning of the term. It is, however, *wrong*" (emphasis his).

Richard was surprised by what he identified as a slip. There was a silence. The silence was broken by laughter. Then he said "It's the unenlightened term" and laughed. His peers joined in the laughter and added terms like "The unwashed version," "the left-lane definition," each accompanied by heavy laughter.

> *Richard:*   "I realize that I may come across (that my version is better than his) but I really do believe that we need both."
>
> *Chris:*   "Could you illustrate in the case where you say this?"

Richard scans his case and nods his head negatively.
At one point in the conversation, I roleplayed a supportive client interacting with Richard.

> *Chris:*   "Richard, it sounds to me as if you believe that if this company had the right vision, if it understood it, a hell of a lot of good things would follow."
>
> *Richard:*   "That is essentially correct. Yes."
>
> *Chris:*   "Could you tell me what is that vision."
>
> *Richard:*   "No I can't. Because I do not know the vision for what the company ought to do."
>
> "I do not believe there is one vision. (Visions vary at different levels of the organization.)"
>
> (later)
>
> *Richard:*   "Once we are clear about the vision then I can help you find the appropriate people to discuss it and implement it."
>
> *Chris:*   "And what is it that they will tell me?"
>
> *Richard:*   "A way of getting people involved in developing your vision."

I then turned to his peers and asked, "What is your reaction?"

•   I wouldn't let you (Richard) operate on me.

- I think you know more than you're telling me. If you read these (outsider's stuff) then you must have some idea of what they would bring to the table.
- Why do I need you? Are you the middle man in this relationship?

(later)

Richard: "I have a very clear concept of what a vision is as a concept and as an outcome. I've seen visions work for individuals."

"What I have never seen or been part of is how do you do this with an organization. I've seen it work beautifully for individuals. I *know* it will work for organizations."

Chris: "In what way?"

Richard: "It will provide a sense of purpose, a sense of clarity, a sense of direction, a sense of excitement, a sense of moving in a positive direction."

Richard's Reasoning: Reflection III

As I listened to Richard, the following questions came into my mind. What is Richard's view of when he knows when he knows something? How does he know he knows what a vision is if he cannot produce it? How does he know it will work for organizations as it does for individuals when he has never seen that work?

Richard assigns to the successful use of a successful concept of vision all the outcomes that he wishes he could help produce in the organization. The reasoning behind what he is saying is instructive. I (Richard) conclude that all the good outcomes I promise will occur although I have never seen nor produced these outcomes. All I need to know is what is a successful concept of vision and a successful process to produce it. Yet, I do not know either. The logic appears more consistent with magic than with mutual problem solving.

What prevents Richard from admitting the gaps in his knowledge and therefore, problem solving with the client? If we recall the early discussion of Richard's case, he acted toward the client as if he knew what the correct vision is and how to produce it.

Back to the discussion.   We now enter a new phase where his peers are more openly critical of Richard's intervention as illustrated in his case. The comments included the following evaluations:

- You focus on what client is missing and not on what he is saying.
- You identify gaps in client's thinking and then you back off.
- You focus heavily on making sure the client would succeed by making sure he understood your view that you never got around to problem solving a solution that was acceptable to both.
- You create, right from the beginning, a win/lose situation.

Each of these comments focused on Richard's behavior and was easily illustrated by the speakers. In all cases Richard agreed. He stopped the group to say that he was finding the feedback difficult to hear but very helpful. "I see now that I made quite a few misses."

> *Chris:* "Would you identify the misses that you have heard so far?"

Richard responded that he missed the following: (1) he did not understand his own meaning of vision; (2) he tried to coerce the client to buy into his (Richard's) version of vision; (3) he persisted that his meaning of vision was better, and (4) he did not help the client to clarify his vision.

Richard then repeated his gratitude by saying, "This dialogue has been very helpful. It has helped me to clarify where the mismatches are right now between the client and myself." He then reflected further.

Richard's Reflections	Comments on Richard's Reasoning
"(I now remember) that the client talked about the importance of visions before I did."	This provides some data that contradicts Richard's assertion that the client, being educated as a left-brain engineer would naturally be uncomfortable with the concept of a vision.
"My axe with the client was that he was using vision in a rather manipulative way to sell his ideas."	Richard used his concept of vision to manipulate the client. For example:
	"In a sense, I can now see that I am manipulating the client. I'm trying to parley his notion of a vision into something bigger which I believe would be more beneficial to the organization."

Reflection on Gaps in the Help Being Given to Richard

Richard reported the discussion was very productive. He reported that he learned because he was helped to identify inconsistencies and gaps in his behavior. Neither he nor his peers, however, took the next step of exploring the reasoning behind his blindness. For example, during the conversations with Richard, none of his peers explored the questions raised about his reasoning on the right-hand columns. It is as if their view of help was equivalent to helping Richard become aware of his blind spots, gaps, and inconsistencies.

These are important and necessary learnings, but they are not sufficient. The argument for these not being sufficient has been made elsewhere and can be summarized as follows (Argyris & Schön, 1974, 1978; Argyris, 1982, 1985):

1. All diagnoses of reality and actions are designed. We are responsible for the designs that we produce. We cannot knowingly kid ourselves. As the Greek

philosophers pointed out, it is not possible to knowingly lie to ourselves. To say to myself I am lying is to tell the truth.

Similarly it is also not possible to knowingly produce mismatches or errors. If I say I intend to produce an error and do so that is a match.

2.   However, it is obvious that people produce errors all the time. One way to explain the puzzle is to say that the individuals were unaware that they were producing errors while doing so.

But if unawareness is action and all actions are designed then unawareness must be designed. This means that human beings have designs that keep them unaware of their errors and they are unaware of these designs. Although they cannot produce errors they can produce the designs that keep them unaware of their errors when they make them.

3.   Productive reasoning requires that that part of the theory being used, the inferences made, and the conclusions produced be tested for validity.

It is highly unlikely that defensive reasoning will lead to anything except defensive consequences. Unfortunately, the predisposition to use defensive reasoning under conditions of threat is widespread in most organizations. Hence when productive reasoning is most needed it is rarely found. One of the basic tasks of organizational development professionals is to help individuals and systems to use productive reasoning in their actions and policies, especially those related to threat.

4.   How can individuals be unaware of the programs in their heads that keep them unaware? First, the unawareness could be due to the fact that the actions are highly skilled and therefore automatic. The very fact that they are skilled makes them tacit. Second, the program that keeps people unaware may be related to the way they reason. The key to their unawareness is the reasoning that informed their actions. For example, if Richard were asked the questions about his reasoning processes that are described in the right-hand columns above, he would probably conclude that his reasoning was consistent with defensive reasoning. Defensive reasoning does not tend to encourage public testing nor confrontation by others. The key to becoming aware of the defensive reasoning is to create a dialectic in order to question one's reasoning. This is unlikely because defensive reasoning acts to reduce the creation of a dialectic mode of inquiry. Third, as in this example, Richard is in a world where help includes identifying the gaps and inconsistencies but not the reasoning behind the gaps nor the consequences that flow from the gaps.

Back to the discussion.   Returning to the discussion one of Richard's peers advised him to go back to the client and create the mutual problem-solving process that he had mentioned. I asked, given the analysis that we have made so far, what are the data and the reasoning that would lead her to believe that Richard could create such a problem-solving process.

Richard: "Yes, well I think that is part of the dilemma. I don't think I know how to define vision well enough (that I can help the clients see the gaps in their views).

"Yet, I also feel this is a great opportunity (for us OD people). It is an opportunity to really address a real void (in line's thinking and action.)"

Richard now introduces another important variable. The OD practitioners need to fill in voids in management's thinking and action. Thus, part of his pressuring the client may be related to the organizational requirement to show management how to perform more effectively. Yet, if the analysis above is correct, Richard will have difficulty in being effective because he is not able to bring to the helping relationship such critical features as knowing his concept of vision, being aware when he is evaluating and attributing, being aware of his self-fulfilling prophecies and self-sealing processes. Before this new organizational role dimension could be explored, another peer asked:

Q: "I was touched by your willingness to acknowledge that you do not know how (to define your wider view of vision)."

"But I also wonder if you are not angry at the clients who do not have a vision?"

Richard: "The word hostility doesn't feel right for me. Frustration maybe."

> Is Richard suggesting that the criterion for validity of the question is whether it feels right? How can his ideas then be genuinely disconfirmed?

Chris: "You may be correct. Is there a way that we can test the different views?"

Richard: "Test? What is there to test?"

Chris: "To test the extent to which anger may be relevant."

Richard: "Well do we need to test it. I mean there is a lot of frustration for me around the topic. I have a lot of frustration about where our company is and where we are going to come out."

> What is the reasoning processes that lead Richard to say that there is no need for the test and at the same time admit that he feels highly frustrated? Could not his feelings of frustration lead to distortions?

Chris: "Yes, and?"

Richard: "I think our ability to succeed has a lot to do with the ability of people who are in key leadership positions to be conceptual . . . around complex situations."

> Richard believes his success is dependent upon line executives to be skilled at conceptualizing complex situations.

Richard (continued): "What frustrates me is the way the line managers handle complex, difficult situations. They analyze it and give it a quick and dirty, one, two, three answer."

"For example, I sent a memo (describes situation). I received a typical (simplistic) answer. That's not really a good answer. I don't like it. I expect more from them."

Yet he does not appear, so far, to have such reasoning skills himself. For example abstractions that are to be productive must be comprehensive yet explicitly connectable to a given situation. Richard cannot do it with his concept of vision.

We may now formulate the following diagnosis based on Richard's comments.

- I believe that our company and OD people are in trouble if we do not become better conceptualizers of complexity.
- I cannot meet this standard in my own work.
- I do not seem to be able to create mutual problem-solving situations where we can produce new solutions.
- I get upset when the line sends me simplistic responses.
- I do not explore these responses with line because it may upset them and I could get rejected.
- I try as diplomatically as I can to get them to see the gaps in their thinking and action but, being left-brain dominated, they are unable to understand me.

This formulation provides a reasonable explanation for Richard's frustration. He is unlikely to be effective under these conditions. It is reasonable to expect frustration under these conditions.

One explanation is that Richard's reasoning leads him to place the primary responsibility for possible failure on the client. It is the client who is closed. But, it is also the client who has power. Therefore, Richard has to be careful and diplomatic with these people lest they reject him.

The moment Richard takes on these protective actions he is violating his own theory of interpersonal openness and trust. Moreover, in his mind, he has to collude to do things that he believes are simplistic in order to get "good press" with the line, in order to have credibility to remain as an interventionist.

One source of the anger could be that Richard sees himself as forced to be supportive and cooperative with line executives who value and act differently but who have power over him. The support and cooperation take the form of saying and doing things that he (and others) call "shitty details."

But, note that there is no evidence that the reasoning described above is valid. We do not know if the engineers are closed. We do not know if their view of vision is wrong. We do not know that they will fire Richard if he does not cooperate.

All of these fears could be valid or invalid. Richard never tests them. Moreover, they could be valid because Richard has in part made them so. That is, the line management may have come to believe that Richard holds concepts such as vision that he cannot define and that they do not feel are implementable. They could believe that Richard is closed to having his reasoning confronted and hence believe that they better ease-in and be gentle with him. Under these conditions they may ask Richard for help, but only to the extent that they can control him. In their view, this unilateral control is the only way they can protect themselves from Richard's use of unilateral control.

What unilateral control does Richard use? After all, he is against using such control. There are several levels at which the line could experience Richard as using unilateral control.

First, Richard creates win/lose situations and acts as if he does not. He asserts that his view of vision is better than his client's without saying what leads him to think so. Richard prejudges the line with evaluations and attributions which he does not test and acts if none of this is happening. Third, Richard insists that they should use his more encompassing view of vision which he cannot define and they therefore cannot independently reject. Fourth, Richard asks for mutual problem solving when he does little of it himself. Fifth, the only way the clients can continue to work with him is to act as if none of this is happening. It is as if they are controlled by the intention they attribute to Richard, which is if they believe any of the above is valid, they will, for his sake, not discuss it.

The clients are now in a double bind. If they discuss these issues, they could upset Richard and make it less likely that they can protect him organizationally. After all, why pay OD people who cannot perform by their own standards. On the other hand, if they do not discuss these issues, they have to collude in a game that makes it less likely that they or Richard will be as effective as they are capable of being.

Back to the discussion.   Returning to the dialogue, several peers began to discuss their feelings of anger with clients. For example:

- I can identify with that. I do not know if that speaks to you or not. But the job that needs to be done is so much greater than the tools that I have to do it.
- Yes, I agree with that. A lot of my anger comes after working with an issue for a while and not making progress. And then I get angry at *them!*
- The issue is that we do not know how to deliver what we are selling. I want to understand that better.

We now add a new issue to explore. It may be that the OD professionals are aware of the gaps in their skills between what they wish to deliver and what they are able to deliver. Indeed as one of them said, she did not even know how to conceptualize what it is that they are delivering. The anger that they express about the client could then be as much related to their inability to deal with client defenses. But client defenses are basically defensive reasoning.

It is unlikely that these OD professionals are going to help clients examine their defensive reasoning if they are not able to examine their own. In order to examine defensive reasoning, the individuals must use productive reasoning under the conditions where they automatically use defensive reasoning.

Unless these OD professionals can learn to use productive reasoning they may eventually create a set of self-fulfilling, self-sealing processes that would mean the slow but sure disintegration with their clients.

BARRIERS TO PRODUCTIVE REASONING IN OD

The defensive reasoning illustrated in Richard's case was also the predominant reasoning used by Richard's peers in their cases. This was true even though the nature of the problems reported in the cases varied widely, the location in the hierarchy at which they were working varied widely, and the degree of commitment of the clients varied widely.

Although the actions used by the OD professionals in the cases varied widely, the action strategies varied minimally and the reasoning almost not at all. The behavioral strategies were consistent with Model I or the opposite of Model I. The reasoning was defensive.

For example:

- The OD professional was impatient with his client who kept seeing failure of performance by a manager as an individual problem. The cure, in the manager's mind, was therefore to fire or transfer the manager and bring in someone who can produce.
- The OD professional wanted to introduce systemic thinking. The failure of managerial performance is more accurately attributable to system variables than to individual ones.
- The way the OD professional dealt with his client and the way the client reacted (as recalled by the OD professional) created a problem at the level that he asserted was not important. For example, as the OD professional expressed his impatience, the client felt misunderstood, unfairly judged and under attack. The client interpreted this as an individual, not a systemic, problem. The OD professional in the client's eyes, was creating the causal conditions that he was downplaying.

There is a puzzle embedded in the issue of individual and system. If systemic variables are causes of actions, then as long as individuals are acting as the agents of the system, they will experience advice or pressure by the OD professionals to change as a deeply individual, personal risk. One OD professional, for example, identified the following organizational rule that informed line managers' behavior: "Success in production schedules is always the priority. You can break any commitment to make the operations successful (short term)." The result, according to the OD professional, was a system which, "had almost no integrity and so you're dealing with a shifting pile of sand."

The OD professional did not appear to appreciate the client's dilemma. The client was acting consistently within the rules of the system. The client realized that to violate the rules would bring down the wrath of the system. The client was being told that he was not thinking systemically when in fact he was. As the OD professional pointed out, the rules that the client followed were systemic.

To compound the problem, the OD professional explained the client's willingness to follow the systemic rules as "short-term oriented." Strictly speaking this is not true. The client was acting in his long-term interest when he was conforming to systemic rules.

The OD professionals considered the systemic rules as short-term oriented. They also considered themselves more long-term oriented. But to change the manager's orientation from short-term to their view of long-term, it would be their responsibility to help the client move toward the long-term perspective. In order for the client to do so, the OD professional would have to help the entire system change to a new state of affairs. But, by the OD professionals' own views, they did not know how to help systems move from where they are to where (the OD professionals) believed they should be.

> In another case the dilemma identified by the interventionist was "how to help the clients take more responsibility for their future without forcing them to create the future of our choice."
>
> Again, the reasoning processes were defensive. The case began with the clients describing their situation much more positively than the OD professional thought was true. She noted, in the column designated thoughts and feelings not expressed, that "We've really got a problem here of ownership." The attribution was never tested publicly with the clients.
>
> The OD professional then attempted to help the clients see the error of their ways by using easing-in and other diplomatic strategies. The clients apparently sensed the covert negative evaluations. They responded by rejecting them, diplomatically of course. They kept insisting, "We're doing nicely right now."
>
> As the dialogue continued, the OD professional wrote, "I'm so sick of this stuff." A couple of pages later, she asked, "What are you telling me? That you are perfect and do not need change?"
>
> The clients denied that this was their message, a denial that could be accurate. For example, they could have been saying that they did not trust the validity or the implementability of the future world that the OD professional was suggesting.
>
> Interestingly, the clients agreed to be influenced by the OD professional in "accepting" that they may be wrong. Hence the clients ended up appearing to buy the future promulgated by the OD professional. This was the very consequence the OD professional wished to avoid.

> Client A was having problems with Client B. The OD professional concluded that Client A was afraid to be open and frank with B. For reasons described in the case, the OD professional felt that she had to be careful in how she communicated the (not tested) attributions.

Soon Client A was blaming Client B. The OD professional tried to help Client A see that blaming others was not the way to solve the problem. Unfortunately she acted in ways that blamed Client A. In trying to help Client A, the OD professional used the behavior that she was recommending that Client A stop using.

A word about the apparent unawareness of the OD professionals. "Looking backwards everything seems obvious, embarrassingly so," was the comment made by one OD professional. If there are readers who may be somewhat bewildered by the unawareness and inconsistency of the OD professionals, they may wish to keep in mind that in every case that I have experienced to-date where such individuals have expressed surprise, they have turned out to be equally inconsistent and unaware in their own practice.

A question that arises is what prevents the OD professionals from being more reflective of their practice while they are practicing? What prevents them from being on-line researchers or reflective practitioners? I believe that there are several important factors. First, defensive reasoning is anti-reflection for the purpose of discovering an error and correcting it. It is even less likely to encourage the kind of dialectical inquiry that is required for such learning (Argyris & Schön, 1978; Schön, 1983). Second, the OD professionals studied so far have used a Model I theory-in-use or the opposite of Model I theory-in-use. Neither of these theories of action will lead to the reflective inquiry required to learn to detect and correct error in an on-line manner. The defensive reasoning and the two theories-in-use combine to create inconsistency and unawareness as well as the unawareness of the program in their heads to keep them unaware.

There is also a systemic factor that is a very powerful causal agent of the inconsistency and unawareness. Elsewhere, we have shown that Model I or the opposite of Model I theories-in-use will lead to a learning system in organizations that does not encourage reflective practice, especially of the kind that reexamines governing values. We have called this double-loop learning (Argyris & Schön, 1974, 1980).

I should now like to turn to the map of the organizational learning system that existed in the heads of the OD professionals and the line managers that describes the organizational learning system created while the OD professionals were trying to make the company more humane and more productive. The map was developed by analyzing the tape recordings. It was then fed back to the OD professionals to check it for validity. I will discuss the issue of the validity of the map in a concluding section below.

TWO ORIENTATIONS IN OD PRACTICE

All the OD professionals agreed that they were operating within an organization where the company was experiencing increased competition. This has resulted in pressures for meeting increased customer demands including quality and delivery schedules.

Pressures also have increased for the organization to become more cost conscious and to integrate many interfaces among departments that had hitherto not existed.

According to the cases and discussions with the OD professionals, I concluded that there were two dominant orientations to dealing with these contextual pressures. The control orientation was the most prominent and assigned largely to the line management. The learning orientation was the one advocated by the OD professionals and a few line executives who had been converted. These two orientations are shown in Figure 6.

The Control Orientation

The control orientation had at least six major components. First there was the commitment to respond to short-term rewards—"Get the product out." The second component was to respond to crises. This led individuals to create crises in order to get individuals to pay attention. Understandably the greater the organizational status and power of the creator of the crisis, the more attention would be paid to that crisis. The third component was to seek diagnoses that could be dealt with by "quick fix." Motion and action were key strategies to keep superiors off subordinates' backs. A going metaphor was "apparent motion." As long as someone was seen as being in action, then the anxieties of the top would be reduced almost regardless of the relevance of that action (at least in the early stages of a crisis).

A fourth component was the tendency of superiors to evaluate performance of subordinates privately and covertly. Performance evaluation was one of those public secrets while it was going on. After the superior has amassed the evidence and decided upon action, the fifth component, the implementation was as swift and with as much face-saving as possible.

The sixth component was the key criteria for the success orientation; the technology, the quality of the product, and the immediate performance.

The Learning Orientation

The OD professionals acknowledged the importance of such criteria as technology, the quality of the product, and immediate performance—such as shipment on time. They believed that it was possible to involve the employees in such a way that they would take on more causal responsibility to make sure that the criteria were achieved.

In order to accomplish the integration of people and organizations, the OD professionals strove to help reduce the self-inflicted crises created by line. They attempted to make the more long-term rewards as powerful as the short-term rewards.

The OD professionals believed that a fundamental shift must occur from individual to systemic. It was simplistic to assume that major errors were made by individuals. Major errors were systemic. Hence, if major errors were to be corrected, the focus should be on the system. The focus on the system was not initiated to exhonerate the individuals. On the contrary, the OD professionals sought a more just distribution of responsibility for errors and for their correction.

The OD professionals sought to create a certain type of technological system that focused on excellence in quality, on timeliness of shipment, and on generating a sense of internal commitment among employees to continually monitor their performance in order to maintain the high standards that they had set.

The Tension Between the Two Orientations

It is not difficult to see that there are built-in tensions between these approaches. The degree of tension could vary widely with the problem, the individuals involved, the competitive pressures, and so on.

The point of this map is not to identify ahead of time the degree of each individual tension. That is a matter of empirical research. The point is to identify a pattern of variables that accounts for how the OD and line people dealt with the tensions, especially the more difficult ones. Once the pattern is identified, it too is subject to test.

The first response of the line was to maintain vigilance and pressure. In other words, they reinforced their control orientation. Second, they were willing to support experiments in creating learning orientations at the lower levels where "things can't get out of control."

Whenever the experiments were not producing the intended consequences, alterations were made in favor of the control orientation. The changes were justified in terms of competition and costs (the two governing variables identified in the first column). The result was that commitment to this system was ambivalent and often the ambivalence was covert and not discussable.

Like the line, the OD professionals' reactions were to continue to espouse their learning orientation. However, as the line appeared to be ambivalent or to resist, as we saw in the cases, the OD professionals reverted to selling or persuading through the use of metaphors such as "vision," "purposing," "ownership," and "energy."

Those metaphors made sense to the line managers. The line managers interpreted these metaphors differently than the OD professionals. The line wanted purposing, ownership, and energy to be produced in ways that were consistent with the control orientation which, in turn, violated the OD professionals' views.

Another strategy the OD professionals used was to develop technological instruments for selling the systems. For example, the OD professionals developed a systematic and thorough review of variance analysis that would be the envy of every production engineer. The OD professionals hoped to create em-

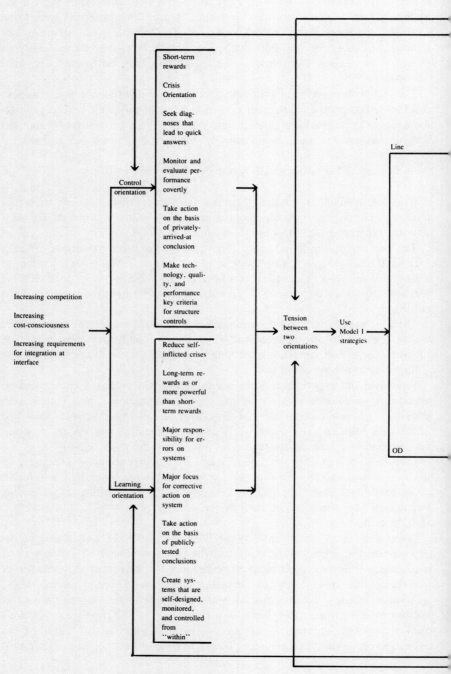

Figure 6.   Strategies and Defensive Routines by OD and Line

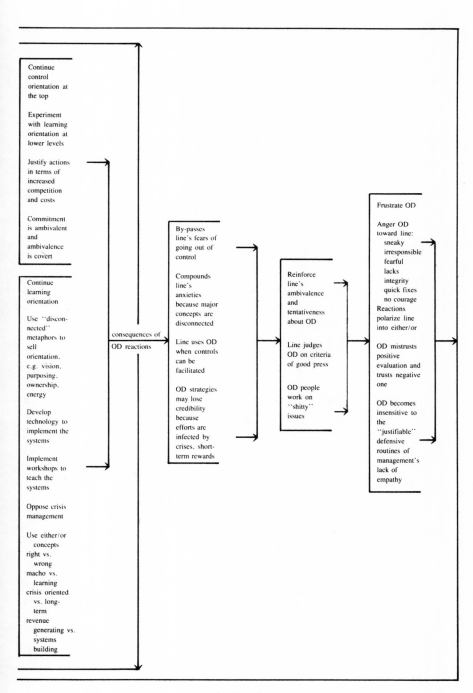

(continued)

ployee involvement in designing and producing the variance analysis. More often than the OD professionals preferred, they found themselves selling and pressuring employees into using the new instruments.

The OD professionals also opposed the use of crisis management. They often found themselves in a win/lose combative relationship with management where issues were polarized in terms of wrong versus right, macho versus learning, and so on.

To sum up, the line and the OD professionals tended to deal with the tensions by using their respective Model I theories-in-use and defensive reasoning. This would feed back to reinforce the tensions which, in turn, would feed back to reinforce and polarize more the control and learning orientations.

CONSEQUENCES OF OD REACTIONS

The four major consequences of the OD professionals' reactions, as identified and confirmed by them, were unintended and counterproductive. First, the OD professionals tended to bypass dealing with the line's fears of things getting out of control. The OD professionals would attempt to assure the line that they were in favor of control. They simply wanted the control to be more self-control, embedded in every employee. The problem, according to the line, was that they doubted this self-control was produceable, and that the OD professionals and employees often behaved in ways to make the doubt a self-fulfilling prophecy.

The line's anxiety about the systems was whether they were produceable and whether the OD people could help the organization produce them. The more the OD professionals attempted to assure the line by using metaphors such as vision and purposing in ways that were disconnected from reality, the more the line became anxious.

Not surprisingly, the line dealt with their anxieties by reverting to and reinforcing their control orientation. They "bought" the systems only to the extent that they could control them. The OD professionals, in order to implement the systems, reluctantly accepted these constraints. Unfortunately, they tended to make the theory behind these systems less credible in the eyes of the employees. As the line continued its crisis and short-term orientation, it reduced the validity and credibility of the learning orientation.

Consequences of the Consequences

The result of the previous consequences was to reinforce the line's ambivalence about OD and about the systems. They sought to have their ambivalence reduced by seeking examples where the systems and OD professionals were to be trusted. This led OD people to act in ways that gave them "good press." Good press meant showing that their systems could operate under short-term rewards and meet immediate performance goals. Often the OD professionals helped the employees accomplish "good press" results by feeding upon or even creating their own crises.

These actions angered the OD professionals. "My personal sense of integrity is an issue. I want to do something significant. I do not want to get trapped in another petty issue."

Further Consequences

The consequences of previous consequences was OD frustration. The frustration was followed by anger. As one OD professional stated it, "My anger comes after having worked at an issue for a while, and not having made any progress."

The anger led the OD professionals to develop attributions about the line which came to the fore when they were reflecting on their frustration and anger. They described line managers, when under stress, as sneaky, irresponsible, fearful, lacking integrity, quick fixers, and lacking courage. It is interesting to note that the OD professionals found that they could make the same attributions about themselves when they were under pressure. Moreover, the attributions they made about the line managers that they believed they kept hidden actually came through in the reasoning they used to design and implement their interventions.

Under these conditions, it was difficult for the OD professionals to trust the positive evaluations made by line. It was easier to trust the negative ones. It was also more likely to exaggerate the negative and deemphasize the positive evaluations.

The frustration, anger, and mistrust could combine to make it less likely that the OD professionals would be understanding of the line managements' defensive routines. I do not mean understanding in the sense of identifying the defensive routines. OD professionals were, as we have seen, quite competent at identifying the defensive routines. The lack of understanding is akin to a lack of empathy. It is illustrated by the inability of the OD professionals to have their "buttons pushed" by line defensive routines.

Finally, all the consequences reinforced each other and fed back to reinforce the tensions described earlier in the model. We now have a self-maintaining system that makes it less likely that errors will be detected and corrected and more likely that mutual trust will slowly deteriorate.

We can now see how the learning system encourages Model I theories-in-use and defensive reasoning. We can now hypothesize that some of the anger that the OD professionals built up against the line could be related to the fact that the system of relationships that they helped to create caused them to behave inconsistently with their learning orientation while, at the same time, espousing that orientation as the preferred one. Not only were they being inconsistent but that inconsistency could lead to a deterioration in their credibility.

In a world locked in to these counterproductive consequences, it is reasonable to expect the consequences described in the cases. It is also reasonable to predict the sense of deterioration between line and OD professionals. To the credit of the latter, they decided to explore these issues rather than ignore them.

Mutual Problem Solving, Gap Filling, Ownership, and Energy

Richard, we may recall, provided explanations for clients' actions by making attributions. He did not test these attributions because he believed they were correct or he believed that testing them could upset the client. The latter was, in effect, a second attribution to make it unnecessary to test the first one. If we were to conceive of untested attributions as gaps in valid knowledge, then one primary pattern of Richard's reasoning is the creation of gaps, of further gaps to support the first one, and of still further gaps to support the second ones.

A second pattern is to produce inconsistencies that he does not recognize as inconsistencies. For example, he judged the client's view of the video tape as incorrect, yet he admitted he neither knew the client's view of the video tape, nor did he have one of his own, nor did he know how to create it. These inconsistencies occurred almost one after the other in the same conversation.

There is another order of inconsistency that Richard produced. It became apparent as Richard interacted with the client over time. After making one untested attribution after another he then explained some of his behavior as his attempt to be nonjudgemental. It is as if he had not seen or kept track of the series of unilateral judgements that he had made. He seemed to have no sense of the patterns of history that he was creating.

Richard had two reactions to these patterns. The first was that he wanted to learn how to reduce them. The second was that he held the faith that if the client wanted to engage in genuine mutual problem solving, the negative consequences of his reasoning and actions could be reduced.

This reaction is one that I observed throughout these seminars as well as others. I suggest that one of the most fundamental working assumptions of current OD practice is the importance of mutual problem solving to close gaps, to identify and to correct errors such as inconsistencies. Moreover, an effective problem-solving process will lead to a sense of ownership on the part of the clients to monitor the implementation of their decisions. Closely allied with ownership is the idea of energy for work. The assumption is that ownership causes the clients to have more energy to work the problem and to follow through.

Richard depends heavily on this working assumption in his dealings with the clients. Recall that Richard knew he did not know what was an appropriate vision for his client, he knew his client had the wrong one, and he believed if they could sit down and problem solve they would find a solution to the problem. The solution could include bringing in outside consulting professionals who knew how to produce effective visions.

From what we knew of Richard's reasoning and action strategies and from the contextual forces acting upon him and the clients, what can we say ahead of time about the likelihood that an effective mutual problem-solving process can be established? We do not know the answer for the routine, simple problems but let us assume that the probability is high that he could help to create an effective mutual problem-solving process. We do know, however, that the probability is quite low for creating a mutually satisfying problem-solving process to deal with issues that contain threat to Richard or his clients. How do we arrive at this conclusion?

First, a word about the clients' states of mind. Many of them believed that the values underlying these concepts made good sense. Richard and the clients espoused some of the same values. Second, few of them realized how difficult it would be to design and implement a world consistent with their values. Their commitment was so high, however, that they not only invested thousands of dollars in the exercise, but they took major risks such as to delay the opening of new plants until the employees were adequately educated in the new theory of management and organization. Third, few of them realized the changes that would be necessary, not so much in their espoused values but in the values in their theories-in-use. Indeed few realized there would be much inconsistency. The degree of inconsistency they uncovered troubled and embarrassed them. Nevertheless, the clients persisted in their endeavors to learn. The conclusion is that the OD professionals were interacting with clients who were supportive of the changes to be made and the designs to be implemented. Thus the clients would probably come to the challenge of creating an effective mutual problem-solving process with a good deal of concern and trepidation but a willingness to learn.

If the analysis above is correct, however, the clients are likely to frustrate the OD professionals leading the latter to reason and act in ways that will frustrate the clients and be unaware that this is happening. For example:

The OD Professionals	What the Clients Can Conclude
1. Tell the clients that the ultimate test of knowing is to be able to produce whatever ideas they espouse.	1. The OD professionals violate their own epistemology of knowledge.
and	
1. Tell the clients that they know what their key concepts such as vision, ownership, energy mean but they have great difficulty in producing them.	
2. Define their key concepts by listing the outcomes they prefer to occur if the clients followed their advice.	2. OD professionals use reasoning that is bewildering. They define their concepts by their outcomes but they cannot define how to produce the outcomes.

3. Become impatient and angry with clients when they are seen as resisting yet the resistance is predictable either from the attribution the OD professionals make or from the theory of action as described herein.

4. Make attributions about the clients that place the primary responsibility for lack of progress onto the clients.

3. The OD professionals are unfair. How can they get angry at us because we are acting consistently with their attributions?

4. We are dealing with OD professionals who hold us responsible for slow progress. This will make it less likely that they will explore their responsibility with us. They are asking us to take ownership but they are not taking it themselves in certain crucial areas.

5. Deal with persistent "resistance" on the part of the clients by either:

a. backing off which, upon reflection by the OD colleagues, is seen as putting down and pressuring.

b. Openly put down and pressure.

a. Our OD professionals are unaware of important inconsistencies in their actions, at least while they are producing them.

b. When OD professionals are under stress and pressure, they act by creating the same kinds of defensive routines that they are telling us not to use.

To the extent the above is valid, the clients may develop a second-order set of inferences. They are:

1. The OD professionals do not deal well with the inner contradictions in their theory in management and organization.
2. The OD professionals are unfair because they deal with us in the very ways they ask us not to use.
3. The OD professionals appear to be unaware of the first- and second-order consequences when they are producing them. They vary widely in their willingness to reflect on their errors after some time has passed.

If we examine these first- and second-order consequences in light of current OD practice, I believe we would have to conclude that the odds are low that these OD professionals can create a mutual problem-solving process that is consistent with their own standards when dealing with threat.

It is important to add that this particular group came to this conclusion early in the seminars. They decided to learn the additional skills and knowledge required to begin to turn this around. Those with whom we are working have shown a great deal of progress. This will be the subject of another report. The point is that these defensive routines and loops can be interrupted and altered while the professionals are going about their practice.

IMPLICATIONS

More empirical research is needed to assess the extent to which the findings described above are applicable in other situations. To the extent that the findings are applicable, then OD professionals should find it helpful to focus on the issues below.

Espoused theories, actions, and theories-in-use are key factors in the effectiveness of OD practice. OD professionals should identify the degree to which they produce inconsistencies and gaps among these three factors and the conditions under which they occur. A key feature of this inquiry should be the reasoning processes the OD professionals use to understand their world and to act in it. More empirical research, in turn, is needed to understand the relationship between defensive reasoning and organizational defensive routines.

OD professionals should learn how to develop maps of the behavioral worlds that they tend to create. The maps should especially focus on the organizational defensive routines and how they create organizational self-reinforcing, nonlearning patterns. Again, more research is needed on what the features of action maps are, how are they constructed, and how can they be used to inform OD practice and simultaneously test their theories.

More research is needed on why human beings appear to use a different set of reasoning processes when inventing solutions from those used to produce the solutions. What are the factors that cause the unawarenesses of the inconsistencies and gaps among espoused theories, theories-in-use, and action? What are the organizational processes by which the behavioral worlds feed back to reinforce defensive reasoning? What interventions can be used to reduce the limited learning features of the behavioral worlds in organizations?

What impact can structural factors have on producing double-loop learning? For example, what would be the features of management information systems or reward systems that could facilitate the use of productive reasoning when dealing with difficult issues, be they at the individual, group, intergroup, or organizational level? Can work be redesigned so that it encourages productive reasoning?

If management information systems, reward systems, and work can be designed to encourage productive reasoning, how will the existing defensive reasoning be overcome? Are individuals able to overcome their skilled defensive reasoning and use productive reasoning because the organization expects and rewards them for doing so?

ACKNOWLEDGMENTS

I would like to express my thanks for the help received from Dianne Argyris, Victor Friedman, Philip McArthur, Robert Putnam, Peter Raymond, Diana Smith, and Professor Donald Schön. I also wish to express my gratitude to the OD consultants who, given commitments of anonymity, cannot be identified by name.

NOTES

1. All names except the author's are pseudonyms.
2. All questions not otherwise identified are by peers or the author.

REFERENCES

Argyris, C. (1970). *Intervention theory and method*. Reading, MA: Addison-Wesley.

Argyris, C. (1976). *Increasing leadership effectiveness*. New York: Wiley-Interscience.

Argyris, C. (1980). *Inner contradictions of rigorous research*. New York: Academic Press.

Argyris, C. (1982). *Reasoning, learning, and action: Individual and organizational*. San Francisco: Jossey-Bass.

Argyris, C. (1985). *Strategy, change, and defensive routines*. Boston: Pitman.

Argyris, C. & Schön, D. (1974). *Theory in practice*. San Francisco: Jossey-Bass.

Argyris, C. & Schön, D. (1978). *Organizational learning*. Reading, MA: Addison-Wesley.

Argyris, C. Putnam, R. & Smith, D. M. (1985). *Action science*. San Francisco: Jossey-Bass.

Schön, D. (1983). *The reflective practitioner*. New York: Basic Books.

APPRECIATIVE INQUIRY IN
ORGANIZATIONAL LIFE

David L. Cooperrider and Suresh Srivastva

ABSTRACT

This chapter presents a conceptual refiguration of action-research based on a "so-ciorationalist" view of science. The position that is developed can be summarized as follows: For action-research to reach its potential as a vehicle for social innovation it needs to begin advancing theoretical knowledge of consequence; that good theory may be one of the best means human beings have for affecting change in a postindustrial world; that the discipline's steadfast commitment to a problem-solving view of the world acts as a primary constraint on its imagination and contribution to knowledge; that *appreciative inquiry* represents a viable complement to conventional forms of action-research; and finally, that through our assumptions and choice of method we largely create the world we later discover.

Research in Organizational Change and Development, Vol. 1, pages 129–169.
Copyright © 1987 by JAI Press Inc.
All rights of reproduction in any form reserved.
ISBN: 0-89232-749-9

We are sometime truly to see our life as positive, not negative, as made up of continuous willing, not of constraints and prohibition.

Mary Parker Follett

We are steadily forgetting how to dream; in historical terms, the mathematicist and technicist dimensions of Platonism have conquered the poetical, mythical, and rhetorical context of analysis. We are forgetting how to be reasonable in nonmathematical dialects.

Stanley Rosen

INTRODUCTION

This chapter presents a conceptual reconfiguration of action research.[1] In it we shall argue for a multidimensional view of action-research which seeks to both generate theory and develop organizations. The chapter begins with the observation that action-research has become increasingly rationalized and enculturated to the point where it risks becoming little more than a crude empiricism imprisoned in a deficiency mode of thought. In its conventional *unidimensional* form action-research has largely failed as an instrument for advancing social knowledge of consequence and has not, therefore, achieved its potential as a vehicle for human development and social-organizational transformation. While the literature consistently signals the worth of action-research as a managerial tool for problem solving ("first-order" incremental change), it is conspicuously quiet concerning reports of discontinuous change of the "second order" where organizational paradigms, norms, ideologies, or values are transformed in fundamental ways (Watzlawick, et al., 1974).

In the course of this chapter we shall touch broadly upon a number of interrelated concerns—scientific, metaphysical, normative, and pragmatic. Linking these streams is an underlying conviction that action-research has the potential to be to the postindustrial era what "scientific management" was to the industrial. Just as scientific management provided the philosophical and methodological legitimacy required to support the bureaucratic organizational form (Clegg & Dunkerly, 1980; Braverman, 1974), action-research may yet provide the intellectual rationale and reflexive methodology required to support the emergence of a more egalitarian "postbureaucratic" form of organization. Unlike scientific management however, which provided the means for a technorational science of administration, action-research holds unique and essential promise in the sociorational realm of human affairs. It has the potential to become the paradigmatic basis of a truly significant—a humanly significant—generative science of administration.

In the first part of the essay it is suggested that the primary barrier limiting the potential of action-research has been its romance with "action" at the expense of "theory." This tendency has led many in the discipline to seriously underestimate the power of theory as a means for social-organizational reconstruction. Drawing largely on the work of Kenneth Gergen (1978; 1982), we re-examine the character of theoretical knowledge and its role in social transformation, and then appeal for a redefinition of the scientific aims of action-research that will dynamically reunite theory and practice. The aim of science is not the detached discovery and verification of social laws allowing for prediction and control. Highlighted here instead, is an alternative understanding that defines social and behavioral science in terms of its "generative capacity," that is, its "capacity to challenge the guiding assumptions of the culture, to raise fundamental questions regarding contemporary social life, to foster reconsideration of that which is 'taken for granted' and thereby furnish new alternatives for social actions" (Gergen, 1978, p. 1346).

Assuming that generative theory is a legitimate product of scientific work and is, in fact, capable of provoking debate, stimulating normative dialogue, and furnishing conceptual alternatives needed for social transformation, then why has action-research till now so largely downplayed creative theorizing in its work with organizations? Here we will move to the heart of the chapter and argue that the generative incapacity of contemporary action-research derives from the discipline's unquestioned commitment to a secularized problem-oriented view of the world and thus to the subsequent loss of our capacity as researchers and participants to marvel, and in marvelling to embrace, the miracle and mystery of social organization. If we acknowledge Abraham Maslow's (1968) admonition that true science begins and ends in wonder, then we immediately shed light on why action-research has failed to produce innovative theory capable of inspiring the imagination, commitment, and passionate dialogue required for the consensual re-ordering of social conduct.

Appreciative inquiry is presented here as a mode of action-research that meets the criteria of science as spelled out in generative-theoretical terms. Going beyond questions of epistemology, appreciative inquiry has as its basis a metaphysical concern: it posits that social existence as such is a miracle that can never be fully comprehended (Quinney, 1982; Marcel, 1963). Proceeding from this level of understanding we begin to explore the uniqueness of the appreciative mode. More than a method or technique, the appreciative mode of inquiry is a way of living with, being with, and directly paticipating in the varieties of social organization we are compelled to study. Serious consideration and reflection on the ultimate mystery of being engenders a reverence for life that draws the researcher to inquire beyond superficial appearances to deeper levels of the life-generating essentials and potentials of social existence. That is, the action-researcher is drawn to affirm, and thereby illuminate, the factors and forces involved in organizing that serve to nourish the human spirit. Thus, this chapter seeks to enrich our conception of administrative behavior by introducing a "second dimension" of action-research that goes beyond merely a secularized problem-solving frame.

The proposal that appreciative inquiry represents a distinctive complement to traditional action-research will be unfolded in the following way: First, the role of theory as an enabling agent of social transformation will be considered; such consideration can help to eliminate the artificial dualism separating theory from practice. Second, we will challenge the problem-oriented view of organizing inherent in traditional definitions of action-research, and describe an affirmative form of inquiry uniquely suited for discovering generative theory. Finally, these insights will be brought together in a general model of the conceptual underpinnings of appreciative inquiry.

TOWARD GENERATIVE THEORY IN ACTION-RESEARCH

The current decade has witnessed a confluence of thinking concerning the paradigmatic refiguration of social thought. As Geertz (1980) notes, there is now even a "blurring of genres" as many social scientists have abandoned—without apology—the misdirected quest to mimic the "more mature" physical sciences. Turning away from a Newtonian laws-and-instances-type explanation rooted in logical empiricist philosophy, many social theorists have instead opted for an interpretive form of inquiry that connects organized action to its contextually embedded set of meanings, "looking less for the sorts of things that connect planets and pendulums and more for the sorts that connect chrysanthemums and swords" (Geertz, 1980, p. 165).

In the administrative sciences, in particular, this recent development has been translated into observable movement away from mechanistic research designs intended objectively to establish universal causal linkages between variables, such as organizational size and level of centralization, or between technology, environment, and organizational structure. Indeed, prominent researchers in the field have publicly given up the logical positivist idea of "certainty through science" and are now embarking on approaches to research that grant preeminence to the historically situated and ever-changing "interpretive schemes" used by members of a given group to give life and meaning to their actions and decisions (Bartunek, 1984). Indicative of the shift away from the logical positivist frame, researchers are converging around what has been termed the "sociorationalist" metatheory of science (Gergen, 1982). Recognizing the symbolic nature of the human universe, we now find a flurry of innovative work supporting the thesis that there is little about human development or organizational behavior that is "preprogrammed" or stimulus-bound in any direct physical or biological way. In this sense, the social universe is open to indefinite revision, change, and self-propelled development. And, this recognition is crucial because to the extent to which social existence *is* situated in a symbolic realm, beyond deterministic forces, then to that extent the logical positivist foundation of social science is negated and its concept of knowledge rendered illusionary.

Nowhere is this better evidenced than in the variety of works concerned with such topics as organizational paradigms (Brown, 1978; McHugh, 1970); beliefs and master scripts (Sproull, 1981; Beyer, 1981); idea management and the executive mind (Srivastva, 1983; 1985); theories of action and presumptions of logic (Argyris & Schon, 1980; Weick, 1983); consciousness and awareness (Harrison, 1982; Lukes, 1974); and, of course, an array of work associated with the concept of organizational or corporate culture (Ouchi & Johnson, 1978; Schein, 1983; Van Maanen, 1982; Deal & Kennedy, 1982; Sathe, 1983; Hofsteede, 1980). As Ellwood prophetically suggested almost half a century ago, "This is the cultural view of human society that is [or will be] revolutionizing the social sciences" (Ellwood, 1938, p. 561).

This developing consensus on the importance of the symbolic realm—on the power of ideas—by such independent sources embracing such diverse objectives reflects the reality of organized life in the modern world. However reluctantly, even the most traditional social thinkers are now recognizing the distinctiveness of the postindustrial world for what truly is—an unfolding drama of human interaction whose potential seems limited or enhanced primarily by our symbolic capacities for constructing meaningful agreements that allow for the committed enactment of collective life.

Never before in history have ideas, information, and beliefs—or theory—been so central in the formulation of reality itself. Social existence, of course, has always depended on some kind of idea system for its meaningful sustenance. The difference now, however, is that what was once background has become foreground. Today, the very fact that society continues to exist at all is experienced not so much mechanistically (an extension of machines) or even naturalistically (a by-product of fateful nature) but more and more humanistically as a social construction of interacting minds—"a game between persons" (Bell, 1973). And under these conditions—as a part of the change from an agrarian society to a goods-producing society at first and then to an information society—ideas and meaning systems take on a whole new life and character. Ideas are thrust center stage as the prime unit of relational exchange governing the creation or obliteration of social existence.

This line of argument applies no less potently to current conceptions of social science. To the extent that the primary product of science is systematically refined idea systems—or theory—science too must be recognized as a powerful agent in the enhancement or destruction of human life. And while this presents an unresolvable dilemma for a logical empiricist conception of science, it spells real opportunity (and responsibility) for a social science that wishes to be of creative significance to society. Put most simply, the theoretical contributions of science may be among the most powerful resources human beings have for contributing to change and development in the groups and organizations in which they live. This is precisely the meaning of Kurt Lewin's early view of action-science when he proposed: "There is nothing so practical as good theory" (1951, p. 169).

Ironically, the discipline of action-research continues to insist on a sharp separation of theory and practice, and to underrate the role of theory in social reconstruction. The irony is that it does so precisely at a time when the cultural view of organizing is reaching toward paradigmatic status. The sad and perhaps tragic commentary on action-research is that it is becoming increasingly inconsequential just as its opportunity to contribute is on the rise (Argyris, 1983).

Observers such as Rappaport (1970) and Bartunek (1983) have lamented the fact that action-researchers have come to subordinate research aims to action interests. Levinson (1972) has gone even further by branding the discipline "atheoretical." And, Friedlander and Brown (1974) have noted that the definition of action-research in classic texts give virtually no mention to theory-building as an integral and necessary component of the research/diagnostic process, or the process of organizational change. Whenever theory is mentioned, it is almost always referred to as a springboard for research or diagnosis, not the other way around. Bartunek (1983, p. 3–4) concludes that "even the most recent papers that describe action-research strategies tend to focus primarily on the process of action-research and only secondarily on the specific theoretical contributions of the outcomes of such research" (e.g., Frohman, Sashkin, & Kavanaugh, 1976; Shani & Pasmore, 1982; Susman and Evered, 1978; see Pasmore and Friedlander, 1982, for an exception). For those of us trained in the field this conclusion is not surprising. Indeed, few educational programs in organizational behavior even consider theory-building as a formal part of their curriculum, and even fewer place a real premium on the development of the theoretical mind and imagination of their students.

According to Argyris (1983), this lack of useful theorizing is attributable to two major factors. On the one hand practice-oriented scholars have tended to become so client-centered that they fail to question their clients' own definition of a problem and thereby to build testable propositions and theories that are embedded in everyday life. Academics, on the other hand, who are trained to be more scientific in their bent, also undercut the development of useful theory by their very insistence on the criteria of "normal" science and research—detachment, rigor, unilateral control, and operational precision. In a word, creative theorizing has literally been assaulted on all fronts by practitioners and academic scientists alike. It must also be noted that implicit in this critique by Argyris (1983), and others (e.g., Friedlander & Brown, 1974), is an underlying assumption that action-research has built into it certain natural conflicts that are likely to lead either to "action" (consulting) or "research" (diagnosis or the development of organizational theory), but not to both.

The situation is summed up by Friedlander and Brown (1974) in their comprehensive review of the field:

> We believe that research will either play a far more crucial role in the advancement of this field, or become an increasingly irrevelant appendage to it . . . . We have generally failed to produce a theory of change which emerges from the change process itself. We need a way of enriching our understanding and action synergistically rather than at one or the other's expense—to become a science in which knowledge-getting and knowledge-giving are an integrated process, and one that is valuable to all parties involved (p. 319).

Friedlander and Brown concluded with a plea for a metatheoretical revision of science that will integrate theory and practice. But in another review over a decade later, Friedlander (1984) observed little progress coming from top scholars in the discipline. He then put words to a mounting frustration over what appears as a recurring problem:

> They pointed to the shortcomings of traditional research and called for emancipation from it; but they did not indicate a destination. There is as yet no new paradigm that integrates research and practice, or even optimizes useful knowledge for organizations . . . . I'm impatient. Let's get on with it. Let's not talk it, write it, analyze it, conceptualize it, research it. Instead let's actively engage and experiment with new designs for producing knowledge that is, in fact, used by organizations (p. 647).

This recurrent problem is the price we pay for continuing to talk about theory and practice in dualistic terms. In a later section in this chapter another hypothesis will be advanced on why there is this lack of creative theorizing, specifically as it relates to action-research. But first we need to look more closely at the claim that social theory and social practice are, indeed, part of a synthetic whole. We need to elaborate on the idea that scientific theory is a means for both understanding *and* improving social practice. We need to examine exactly what it means to merge the idea and the act, the symbolic and the sociobehavioral, into a powerful and integral unity.

The Sociorationalist Alternative

As the end of the twentieth century nears, thinkers in organizational behavior are beginning to see, without hesitation, why an administrative science based on a physical science model is simply not adequate as a means for understanding or contributing in relevant ways to the workings of complex, organized human systems (see, for example, Susman and Evered, 1978; Beyer & Trice, 1982). Kurt Lewin had understood this almost half a century earlier but his progressive vision of an action science fell short of offering a clear metatheoretical alternative to conventional conceptions of science (Peters & Robinson, 1984). Indeed, the epistemological ambiguity inherent in Lewin's writing has been cited as perhaps the critical shortcoming of all his work. And yet, in hindsight, it can be argued that the ambiguity was intentional and perhaps part of Lewin's social sensitivity and genius. As Gergen (1982) suggests, the metatheoretical ambiguity in Lewin's work might well have been a protective measure, an attempt to shield his fresh vision of an action science from the fully dominant logical positivist temper of his time. In any event, whether planned or not, Lewin walked a tightrope between two fundamentally opposed views of science and never did make clear how theory could be used as both an interpretive and a creative element. This achievement, as we might guess, would have to wait for a change in the intellectual ethos of social science.

That change, as we earlier indicated, is now taking place. Increasingly the literature signals a disenchantment with theories of science that grant priority to the external world in the generation of human knowledge. Instead there is growing movement toward granting preeminence to the cognitive processes of mind and the symbolic processes of social construction. In *Toward Transformation in Social Knowledge* (1982), Kenneth Gergen synthesizes the essential whole of this movement and takes it one crucial step beyond disenchantment to a bold, yet workable conception of science that firmly unites theory with practice—and thereby elevates the status of theoretical-scientific work. From a historical perspective there is no question that this is a major achievement; it brings to completion the work abruptly halted by Lewin's untimely death. But more than that, what Gergen offers, albeit indirectly, is a desperately needed clue to how we can revitalize an action-research discipline that has never reached its potential. While a complete statement of the emerging sociorationalist metatheory is beyond the scope of this chapter, it is important at least to outline the general logic of the perspective, including its basic assumptions.

At the heart of sociorationalism is the assumption of impermanence—the fundamental instability of social order. No matter what the durability to date, virtually any pattern of social action is open to infinite revision. Accepting for a moment the argument of the social constructionists that social reality, at any given point, is a product of broad social agreement (shared meanings), and further granting a linkage between the conceptual schemes of a culture and its other patterns of action, we must seriously consider the idea that alterations in conceptual practices, in ways of symbolizing the world, hold tremendous potential for guiding changes in the social order. To understand the importance of these assumptions and their meaning for social science, let us quote Gergen (1982) at length:

> Is not the range of cognitive heuristics that may be employed in solving problems of adaptation limited only by the human imagination?
>
> One must finally consider the possibility that human biology not only presents to the scientist an organism whose actions may vary in an infinity of ways, but it may ensure as well that novel patterns are continuously emerging . . . variations in human activity may importantly be traced to the capacities of the organism for symbolic restructuring. As it is commonly said, one's actions appear to be vitally linked to the manner in which one understands or construes the world of experience. The stimulus world does not elicit behavior in an automatic, reflex-like fashion. Rather, the symbolic translation of one's experiences virtually

transforms their implications and thereby alters the range of one's potential reactions. Interestingly, while formulations of this variety are widely shared within the scientific community, very little attention has been paid to their ramifications for a theory of science. As is clear, without such regularities the prediction of behavior is largely obviated . . . to the extent that the individual is capable of transforming the meaning of stimulus conditions in an indeterminate number of ways, existing regularities must be considered historically contingent—dependent on the prevailing meaning systems of conceptual structure of the times. In effect, from this perspective the scientist's capacity to locate predictable patterns of interaction depends importantly on the extent to which the population is both homogeneous and stable in its conceptual constructions (pp. 16–17).

While this type of reasoning is consistent with the thinking of many social scientists, the ramifications are rarely taken to their logical conclusion: "Virtually unexamined by the field is the potential of science to shape the meaning systems of the society and thus the common activities of the culture" (Gergen, 1978, p. 1349). Virtually unexamined is the important role that science can—and does—play in the scientific construction of social reality.

One implication of this line of thought is that to the extent the social science conceives its role in the logical positivist sense, with its goals being prediction and control, it not only serves the interests of the status quo (you can't have "good science" without stable replication and verification of hypotheses) but it also seriously underestimates the power and usefulness of its most important product, namely theory; it underestimates the constructive role science can have in the *development* of the groups and organizations that make up our cultural world. According to Gergen, realization of this fact furnishes the opportunity to refashion a social science of vital significance to society. To do this, we need a bold shift in attention whereby theoretical accounts are no longer judged in terms of their predictive capacity, but instead are judged in terms of their generative capacity—their ability to foster dialogue about that which is taken for granted and their capacity for generating fresh alternatives for social action. Instead of asking, "Does this theory correspond with the observable facts?" the emphasis for evaluating good theory becomes, "To what extent does this theory present provocative new possibilities for social action, and to what extent does it stimulate normative dialogue about how we can and should organize ourselves?" The complete logic for such a proposal may be summarized in the following ten points:

1. The social order at any given point is viewed as the product of broad social agreement, whether tacit or explicit.
2. Patterns of social-organizational action are not fixed by nature in any direct biological or physical way; the vast share of social conduct is potentially stimulus-free, capable of infinite conceptual variation.
3. From an observational point of view, all social action is open to multiple interpretations, no one of which is superior in any objective sense. The in-

terpretations (for example, "whites are superior to blacks") favored in one historical setting may be replaced in the next.

4. Historically embedded conventions govern what is taken to be true or valid, and to a large extent govern what we, as scientists and lay persons, are able to see. All observation, therefore, is theory-laden and filtered through conventional belief systems and theoretical lenses.[2]

5. To the extent that action is predicated on ideas, beliefs, meanings, intentions, or theory, people are free to seek transformations in conventional conduct by changing conventional codes (idea systems).

6. The most powerful vehicle communities have for transforming their conventions—their agreements on norms, values, policies, purposes, and ideologies—is through the act of dialogue made possible by language. Alterations in linguistic practices, therefore, hold profound implications for changes in social practice.

7. Social theory can be viewed as a highly refined language with a specialized grammar all its own. As a powerful linguistic tool created by trained linguistic experts (scientists), theory may enter the conceptual meaning system of culture and in doing so alter patterns of social action.

8. Whether intended or not, all theory is normative and has the potential to influence the social order—even if reactions to it are simply boredom, rebellion, laughter, or full acceptance.

9. Because of this, all social theory is morally relevant; it has the potential to affect the way people live their ordinary lives in relation to one another. This point is a critical one because there is no such thing as a detached/ technical/scientific mode for judging the ultimate worth of value claims.

10. Valid knowledge or social theory is therefore a communal creation. Social knowledge is not "out there" in nature to be discovered through detached, value-free, observational methods (logical empiricism); nor can it be relegated to the subjective minds of isolated individuals (solipsism). Social knowledge resides in the interactive collectivity; it is created, maintained, and put to use by the human group. Dialogue, free from constraint or distortion, is necessary to determine the "nature of things" (sociorationalism).

In Table 1 the metatheory of sociorationalism is both summarized and contrasted to the commonly held assumptions of the logical empiricist view of science. Especially important to note is the transformed role of the scientist when social inquiry is viewed from the perspective of sociorationalism. Instead of attempting to present oneself as an impartial bystander or dispassionate spectator of the inevitable, the social scientist conceives of himself or herself as an active agent, an invested participant whose work might well become a powerful source of change in the way people see and enact their worlds. Driven by a desire to "break the hammerlock" of what appears as given in human nature, the scientist attempts to build theories that can expand the realm of what is conventionally

Table 1.   Comparison of Logical Empiricist and Socio-Rationalist
Conceptions of Social Science

Dimension for Comparison	Logical Empiricism	Socio-Rationalism
1. Primary Function of Science	Enhance goals of understanding, prediction, and control by discerning general laws or principles governing the relationship among units of observable phenomena.	Enhance understanding in the sense of assigning meaning to something, thus creating its status through the use of concepts. Science is a means for expanding flexibility and choice in cultural evolution.
2. Theory of Knowledge and Mind	Exogenic—grants priority to the external world in the generation of human knowledge (i.e., the preeminence of objective fact). Mind is a mirror.	Endogenic—holds the processes of mind and symbolic interaction as pre-eminent source of human knowledge. Mind is both a mirror and a lamp.
3. Perspective on Time	Assumption of temporal irrelevance: searches for transhistorical principles.	Assumption of historically and contextually relevant meanings; existing regularities in social order are contingent on prevailing meaning systems.
4. Assuming Stability of Social Patterns	Social phenomena are sufficiently stable, enduring, reliable and replicable to allow for lawful principles.	Social order is fundamentally unstable. Social phenomena are guided by cognitive heuristics, limited only by the human imagination: the social order is a subject matter capable of infinite variation through the linkage of ideas and action
5. Value Stance	Separation of fact and values. Possibility of objective knowledge through behavioral observation.	Social sciences are fundamentally nonobjective. Any behavioral event is open to virtually any interpretative explanation. All interpretation is filtered through prevailing values of a culture. "There is no description without prescription."

(continued)

Table 1. (*Cont.*)

Dimension for Comparison	Logical Empiricism	Socio-Rationalism
6. Features of "Good" Theory	Discovery of transhistorically valid principles; a theory's correspondence with fact.	Degree to which theory furnishes alternatives for social innovation and thereby opens vistas for action; expansion of "the realm of the possible."
7. Criteria for Confirmation or Verification (Life of a Theory)	Logical consistency and empirical prediction; subject to falsification.	Persuasive appeal, impact, and overall generative capacity; subject to community agreement; truth is a product of a community of truth makers.
8. Role of Scientist	Impartial bystander and dispassionate spectator of the inevitable; content to accept that which seems given.	Active agent and co-participant who is primarily a source of linguistic activity (theoretial language) which serves as input into common meaning systems. Interested in "breaking the hammerlock" of what appears as given in human nature.
9. Chief Product of Research	Cumulation of objective knowledge through the production of empirically disconfirmable hypothesis.	Continued improvement in theory building capacity; improvement in the capacity to create generative-theoretical language.
10. Emphasis in the Education of Future Social Science Professionals	Rigorous experimental methods and statistical analysis; a premium is placed on method (training in theory construction is a rarity).	Hermenuetic interpretation and catalytic theorizing; a premium is placed on the theoretical imagination. Sociorationalism invites the student toward *intellectual expression* in the service of his or her vision of the good.

understood as possible. In this sense the core impact of sociorationalist metatheory is that it invites, encourages, and requires that students of social life rigorously exercise their theoretical imagination in the service of their vision of the good. Instead of denial it is an invitation to fully accept and exercise those qualities of mind and action that make us uniquely human.

Now we turn to a question raised earlier: How does theory achieve its capacity to affect social practice, and what are some of the specific characteristics of generative theory?

The Power of Theory in Understanding Organizational Life

The sociorationalist vision of science is of such far-reaching importance that no student, organizational scientist, manager, educator, or *action-researcher* can afford to ignore it. Good theory, as we have suggested, is one of the most powerful means we have for helping social systems evolve, adapt, and creatively alter their patterns over time. Building further on this metatheoretical perspective we can talk about five ways by which theory achieves its exceptional potency:

1. Establishing a conceptual and contextual frame;
2. Providing presumptions of logic;
3. Transmitting a system of values;
4. Creating a group-building language;
5. Extending visions of possibility or constraint.

1. Establishing a Perceptual and Contextual Frame

To the extent that theory is the conceptual imposition of order upon an otherwise "booming, bustling, confusion that is the realm of experience" (Dubin, 1978), the theorist's first order of business is to specify what is there to be seen, to provide an "ontological education" (Gergen, 1982). The very act of theoretical articulation, therefore, highlights not only the parameters of the topic or subject matter, but becomes an active agent as a cueing device, a device that subtly focuses attention on particular phenomena or meanings while obscuring others. In the manner of a telescope or lens, a new theory allows one to see the world in a way perhaps never before imagined.

For example, when American eugenicists used the lens of biological determinism to attribute diseases of poverty to the inferior genetic construction of poor people, they literally could see no systematic remedy other than sterilization of the poor. In contrast, when Joseph Goldberg theorized that pellegra was not genetically determined but culturally caused (as a result of vitamin deficiency and the eating habits of the poor), he could discover a way to cure it (Gould, 1981). Similarly, theories about the "survival of the fittest" might well help executives locate "predators," "hostile enrironments," and a world where self-interest reigns, where it is a case of "eat or be eaten." Likewise, theories of leadership have been known quickly to facilitate the discovery of Theory X and Theory Y interaction. Whatever the theory, it provides a potential means for members of a culture to navigate in an otherwise neutral, meaningless, or chaotic sea of people, interactions and events. By providing an "ontological education" with respect to what is there, a theory furnishes an important cultural input that affects people's cognitive set. In this sense "the world is not so constituted until the lens is employed. With each new distinction the groundwork is laid for alterations in existing patterns of conduct" (Gergen, 1982, p. 23).

As the reader may already surmise, an important moral issue begins to emerge here. Part of the reason that theory is, in fact, powerful is that it shapes perceptions, cognitions, and preferences often at a preconscious level, much like subliminal communications or even hypnosis. Haley (1973) talks about how Milton Erickson has made this a central feature of this psycho-therapeutic work. But Lukes (1974) cautions that such thought control may be "the supreme and most insidious exercise of power," especially when it prevents people from challenging their role in the existing order of things and when it operates contrary to their real interests.

2. Providing Presumptions of Logic

Theories are also powerful to the extent to which they help shape common expectations of causality, sequence, and relational importance of phenomena within a theoretical equation. Consider, for example, the simple logic underlying almost every formal performance-appraisal system. Stripped to essentials, the theoretical underpinnings run something like this: "If you want to evaluate performance (P), then you must evaluate the individual employee (E); in other words, 'P = E'." Armed with this theory, many managers have entered the performance-appraisal meeting shaking with the thought of having to pass god-like judgment on some employee. Similarly, the employee arrives at the meeting with an arsenal of defenses, designed to protect his or her hard-won self-esteem. Little genuine communication occurs during the meeting and virtually no problem-solving takes place. The paperwork is mechanically completed, then filed away in the personnel office until the next year. So powerful is this subtle P = E equation that any alternative goes virtually unnoticed, for example the Lewinian theory that behavior (performance) is a function of the person *and* the environment (in this case the organizational situation, the "OS" in which the employee works). Following this Lewinian line, the theory underlying performance appraisal would now have to be expanded to read P = E × OS. That is, P ≠ E. To adequately assess performance there must be an assessment of the individual *in relation to* the organizational setting in which he or she works and vice-versa. What would happen to the performance-appraisal process if this more complete theory were used as a basis for re-designing appraisal systems in organizations throughout the corporate world? Isn't it possible that such a theory could help shift the attribution process away from the person-blame to systems analysis?[3]

By attributing causality, theories have the potential to create the very phenomena they propose to explain. Karl Weick, in a recent article examining managerial thought in the context of action, contends that thought and action are part and parcel of one another; thinking is best viewed as a kind of activity, and activity as the ground of thought. For him, managerial theories gain their power by helping people overlook disorder and presume orderlinesss. Theory *energizes* action by providing a *presumption of logic* that enables people to act with certainty, attention, care, and control. Even where it is originally inadequate as a description of current reality, a forceful theory may provoke action that brings into the world a new reality that then confirms the original theory. Weick (1983) explains:

> Once the action is linked with an explanation, it becomes more forceful, and the situation is thereby transformed into something that supports the presumed underlying pattern. Presumptions [theories] enable actions to be tied to specific explanations that consolidate those actions into deterministic events. . . .
>
> The underlying explanation need *not* be objectively "correct." In a crude sense any old explanation will due. This is so because explanation serves mostly to organize and focus the action. The focused action then modifies the situation in ways that confirm the explanation, whatever it is.
>
> Thus, the adequacy of any explanation is determined by the intensity and structure it adds to potentially self-validating actions. More forcefulness leads to more validation and more perceived adequacy. Accuracy is subordinate to intensity. Since situations can support a variety of meanings, their actual content and meaning are dependent on the degree to which they are arranged in sensible, coherent configurations. More forcefulness imposes more coherence. Thus, those explanations that induce greater forcefulness become more valid, not because they are more accurate, but because they have a higher potential for self-validation . . . the underlying explanations they unfold (for example, "This is war") have great potential to intensify whatever action is underway (1983, pp. 230–232).

Thus, theories are generative to the extent that they are forceful (e.g., Marx), logically coherent (e.g., Piaget), and bold in their assertions and consistency (e.g., Freud, Weber). By providing a basis for focused action, a logic for attributing causality, and a sequence specification that grounds expectations for action and reaction, a theory goes a long way toward forming the common expectations for the future. "And with the alteration of expectation, the stage is set for modification of action" (Gergen, 1982, p. 24).

3. *Transmitting a System of Values*

Beyond abstract logic, it is often the affective core of social theory that provides its true force and appeal, allowing it to direct perception and guide behavior. From the tradition of logical positivism, good "objective" theory is to be value-free, yet upon closer inspection we find that social theory is infused with values and domain assumptions throughout. As Gouldner (1970) so aptly put it, "Every social theory facilitates the pursuit of some, but not all, courses of action and thus, encourages us to change or accept the world as it is, to say yea or nay to it. In a way, every theory is a discrete obituary or celebration of some social system."

Nowhere is this better exemplified—negatively—than in the role scientific theory played in the arguments for slavery, colonialism, and belief in the genetic superiority of certain races. The scientific theory in this case was, again, the theory of biological determinism, the belief that social and economic differences between human beings and groups—differences in rank, status, political privilege, education privilege—arise from inherited natural endowments, and that existing social arrangements accurately reflect biological limits. So powerful was this theory during the 1800s that it led a number of America's highest-ranking scientific researchers unconsciously to miscalculate "objective" data in what has been brilliantly described by naturalist Steven Jay Gould (1981, p. 54) as a "patchwork of fudging and finagling in the clear interest of controlling a priori convictions". Before dismissing this harsh judgment as simple rhetoric, we need to look closely at how it was determined. One example will suffice.

When Samual Morton, a scientist with two medical degrees, died in 1851, the *New York Tribune* paid tribute saying, "Probably no scientific man in America enjoyed a higher reputation among scholars throughout the world than Dr. Morton" (in Gould, 1981, p. 51). Morton gained this reputation as a scientist who set out to rank racial groups by "objectively" measuring the size of the cranial cavity of the human skull which he regarded as a measure of brain size. He had a beautiful collection of skulls from races throughout the world, probably the largest such collection in existence. His hypothesis was a simple one: The mental and moral worth of human races can be arrived at objectively by measuring physical characteristics of the brain; by filling skull cavities with mustard seed or lead shot, accurate measurement of brain size is possible. Morton published three major works which were reprinted repeatedly as providing objective, "hard" data on the mental worth of races. Gould comments:

> Needless to say, they matched every good Yankee's prejudices—whites on top, Indians in the middle, and blacks on the bottom; and among whites, Tuetons and Anglo-Saxons on top, Jews in the middle, and Hindus on the bottom. . . . Status and access to power in Morton's America faithfully reflected biological merit (p. 54).

Morton's work was undoubtedly influential. When he died, the South's leading medical journal proclaimed: "We of the South should consider him as our benefactor, for aiding most materially in giving the Negro his true position as an inferior race" (in Gould, 1981, p. 69). Indeed Morton did much more than only give "the Negro his true position," as the following remarks by Morton himself convey:

> Negroes were numerous in Egypt, but their social position in ancient times was the same as it is now, that of servants and slaves.

> The benevolent mind may regret the inaptitude of the Indian civilization . . . [but values must not yield to fact]. The structure of his mind appears to be different from that of the white man, or can the two harmonize in social relations except on the most limited scale. [Indians] are not only averse to restraints of education, but for the most part are incapable of a continued process of reasoning on abstract subjects (in Gould, 1981, p. 53).

The problem with these conclusions—as well as the numerical data which supported them—was that they were based not on "fact" but purely and simply on cultural fiction, on Morton's belief in biological determinism. As Gould meticulously shows, all of Morton's data was wrong. Having reworked it completely, Gould concludes:

> Morton's summaries are a patchwork of fudging and finagling in the clear interst of controlling a priori convictions. Yet—and this is the most intriguing aspect of the case—I find no evidence of conscious fraud; indeed, had Morton been a conscious fudger, he would not have published his data so openly.
>
> Conscious fraud is probably rare in science. . . . The prevalence of *unconscious* finagling, on the other hand, suggests the general conclusion about the social context of science . . . prior prejudice may be found anywhere, even in the basics of measuring bones and totaling sums (pp. 55–56).

Morton represents a telling example of the power of theory. Theory is not only a shaper of expectations and perceptions. Under the guise of "dispassionate inquiry" it can also be a peddler of values, typecasting arbitrary value as scientific "fact." Along with Gould, we believe that we would be better off to abandon the myth of "value-free" science and that theoretical work "must be understood as a social phenomenon, a gutsy, human enterprise, not the work of robots programmed to collect pure information" (Gould, 1981, p. 21). Even if Morton's data were correct, his work still could not be counted as value-free. His data and theories were not only shaped by the setting in which he worked; they were also used to support broad social policy. This is akin to making nature the source of cultural values, which of course it never can be ("What is" does not equal "what should be").

4.   Creating a Group-Building Language

The sociorationalist perspective is more than a pessimistic epitaph for a strictly logical positivist philosophy. It is an invitation to inquiry that raises the status of theory from mere appendage of scientific method to an actual shaper of society. Once we acknowledge that a primary product of science—theory—is a key resource for the creation of groups, the stage is set for theory-building activity intended for the use and development of human society, for the creation of human options.

Students of human behavior have been aware of the group as the foundation of society since the earliest periods of classical thought. Aristotle, for example, discussed the importance of bands and families. But it was not until the middle of the present century that scientific interest in the subject exploded in a flurry of general inquiry and systematic interdisciplinary research (for a sample review of this literature see Hare, 1976). Among the conclusions of this recent work is the crucial insight that:

The face-to-face group working on a problem is the meeting ground of individual personality and society. It is in the group that personality is modified and socialized; and it is through the workings of groups that society is changed and adapted to its times (Thelen, 1954, p. vi).

Similarly, in the field of organization development, Srivastva, Obert, and Neilsen (1977) have shown that the historical development of the discipline has paralleled advances in group theory. And this, they contend, is no accident because:

Emphasis on the small group is responsive to the realities of social change in large complex organizations. It is through group life that individuals learn, practice, develop, and modify their roles in the larger organization. To enter programmatically at the group level is both to confront and potentially co-opt an important natural source of change and development in these systems (p. 83).

It is well established that groups are formed around common ideas that are expressed in and through some kind of shared language which makes communicative interaction possible. What is less clear, though, is the exact role that science plays in shaping group life through the medium of language. However, the fact that science frequently does have an impact is rarely questioned. Andre Gorz (1973) offers an explosive example of this point.

In the early 1960s a British professor of sociology by the name of Goldthorpe was brought in from a nearby university to make a study of the Vauxhall automobile workers in Luton, England. At the time, management at the factory was worried because workers in other organizations throughout the United Kingdom were showing great unrest over working conditions, pay, and management. Many strikes were being waged, most of them wildcat strikes called by the factory stewards, not by the unions themselves. Goldthorpe was called in to study the situation at Vauxhall, to find out for management if there was anything to worry about at their factory. At the time of the study there were at Vauxhall no strikes, no disruptions, and no challenges by workers. Management wanted to know why. What were the chances that acute conflict would break out in the "well-managed" and "advanced" big factory?

After two full years of research, the professor drew his conclusions. Management, he said, had little to worry about. According to the study, the workers were completely socialized into the system, they were satisfied with their wages and neither liked or disliked their work—in fact, they were indifferent to it, viewing it as boring but inevitable. Because their job was not intrinsically rewarding, most people did it just to be done with it—so they could go home and work on other more worthwhile projects and be with their family. Work was marginal and instrumental. It was a means to support other interests outside the factory, where "real life" began. Based then on his observations, Goldthorpe theorized that management had nothing to worry about: Workers were passively apathetic and well integrated into the system. They behaved according to middle-class patterns and showed no signs of strength as a group (no class-consciousness). Furthermore, most conflict with management belonged to the past.

The sociologist's report was still at the printer's when some employees got hold of a summary of his findings. They had the conclusions copied and distributed reports to hundreds of co-workers. Also at around this time, a report of Vauxhall's profits was being circulated, profits that were not shared with the employees. The next day something happened. It was reported by the *London Times* in detail:

> Wild rioting has broken out at the Vauxhall car factories in Luton. Thousands of workers streamed out of the shops and gathered in the factory yard. They besieged the management offices, calling for managers to come out, singing the 'Red Flag,' and shouting, 'String them up!' Groups attempted to storm the offices and battled police which had been called to protect them (quoted in Gorz, 1973).

The rioting lasted for two days.

All of this happened, then, in an advanced factory where systematic research showed workers to be apathetic, weak as a group, and resigned to accept the system. What does it all mean? Had the researchers simply misread the data?

To the contrary. Goldthorpe knew his data well. He articulated the conclusions accurately, concisely, and with force. In fact, what happened was that the report gave the workers a *language* with which to begin talking to one another about their plight. It brought them into interaction and, as they discussed things, they discovered that Goldthorpe was right. They felt alike, apathetic but frustrated; and they were apathetic because they felt as individuals working in isolated jobs, that no one could do anything to change things. But the report gave them a way to discuss the situation. As they talked, things changed. People were no longer alone in their feelings, and they did not want things to continue as they were. As an emergent group, they now had a means to convert apathy into action, noninvolvement into involvement, and individual powerlessness into collective strength. "In other words," analyzes Gorz, "the very investigation of Mr. Goldthorpe about the lack of class-consciousness helped tear down the barriers of silence and isolation that rendered the workers apathetic" (p. 334).

The Vauxhall case is an important one for a number of reasons. At a general level it demonstrates that knowledge in the social sciences differs in quality and kind from knowledge generated in the physical sciences. For instance, our knowledge of the periodic chart does not change the elements, and our knowledge of the moon's orbit does not change its path. But our knowledge of a social system is different. It can be used by the system to change itself, thus invalidating or disconfirming the findings immediately or at some later time. Thus the human group differs from objects in an important way: Human beings have the capacity for symbolic interaction and, through language, they have the ability to collaborate in the investigation of their own world. Because of our human capacity for symbolic interaction, the introduction of new knowledge concerning aspects of our world carries with it the strong likelihood of changing that world itself.

Gergen (1982) refers to this as the "enlightenment effect" of scientifc work, meaning that once the formulations of scientific work are made public, human beings may act autonomously either to disconfirm or to validate the propositions. According to logical positivist philosophy, potential enlightenment effects must be reduced or—ideally-eliminated through experimental controls. In social psychology, for example, deception plays a crucial role in doing research; enlightenment effects are viewed as contaminants to good scientific work. Yet there is an alternative way to look at the reactive nature of social research: it is precisely because of the enlightenment effect that theory can and does play an important role in the positive construction of society. In this sense, the enlightenment effect—which is made possible through language—is an essential ingredient making scientific work worthwhile, meaningful, and applicable. It constitutes an invitation to each and every theorist to actively participate in the creation of his or her world by generating compelling theories of what is good, and just, and desirable in social existence.

5.   Extending Visions of Possibility

The position taken by the sociorationalist philosophy of science is that the conduct of inquiry cannot be separated from the everyday negotiation of reality. Social-organizational research is, therefore, a continuing moral concern, a concern of social reconstruction and direction. The choice of what to study, how to study it, and what to report each implies some degree of responsibility. Science, therefore, instead of being considered an endpoint, is viewed as one means of helping humanity create itself. Science in this sense exists for one singular overarching purpose. As Albion Small (1905) proposed almost a century ago, a generative science must aim at "the most thorough, intense, persistent, and systematic effort to make human life all that it is capable of becoming" (pp. 36–37).

Theories gain their generative capacity by extending visions that expand to the realm of the possible. As a general proposition it might be said that theories designed to empower organized social systems will tend to have a greater enlightenment effect than theories of human constraint. This proposition is grounded in a simple but important consideration which we should like to raise as it relates to the unity of theory and practice: Is it not possible that scientific theory gains its capacity to affect cultural practices in very much the same way that powerful leaders inspire people to new heights? Recent research on the functioning of the executive mind (Srivastva, 1983; 1985) raises a set of intriguing parallels between the possibilities of a generative science and the workings of the executive mind.

The essential parallel is seen in the primary role that ideas or ideals play in the mobilization of diverse groups in the common construction of a desired future. Three major themes from the research stand out in this regard:

a.   *Vision:* The executive mind works largely from the present and extends itself out to the longer-term future. It is powerful to the extent that it is able to envision a desired future state which challenges perceptions of what is possible and what can be realized. The executive mind operates beyond the frontier of conventional practice without losing sight of either necessity or possibility.

b.   *Passion:* The executive mind is simultaneously rational and intuitive, which allows it to tap into the sentiments, values, and dreams of the social collectivity. Executive vision becomes "common vision" to the extent that it ignites the imaginations, hopes, and passions of others—and it does so through the articulation of self-transcending ideals which lend meaning and significance to everyday life.

c.   *Integrity:* The executive mind is the mental muscle that moves a system from the present state to a new and different future. As such, this muscle gains strength to the extent that it is founded upon an integrity able to withstand contrary pressures. There are three dimensions to executive integrity. The first, *system integrity,* refers to the fact that the executive mind perceives the world (the organization, group, or society) as a unified whole, not as a collection of individual parts. The second type of integrity is *moral integrity.* Common-vision leadership is largely an act of caring. It follows the "path of the heart," which is the source of moral and ethical standards. Finally, *integrity of vision* refers to consistency, coherence, and focus. Executive vision—to the extent to which it is compelling—is focused and unwavering, even in the midst of obstacles, critics, and conflicting alternatives.

Interestingly, these thematic dimensions of the executive mind have their counterparts in recent observations concerning the utilization of organizational research. According to Beyer and Trice (1982), the "affective bonding" that takes place during the research largely determines the attractiveness of its results and generates commitment to utilize their implications. For example, Henshel (1975) suggests that research containing predictions of an appealing future will be utilized and preferred over research that points to a negative or repelling future: "People will work for predicted states they approve of and against those they detest" (p. 103). Similarly, Weiss and Bucavalas (1980) report that results which challenge the status quo are most attractive to high-level executives because they are the persons expected to make new things happen, at least on the level of policy. And, with respect to passion and integrity, Mitroff (1980) urges social scientists to become caring advocates of their ideas, not only to diffuse their theories but also to challenge others to prove them wrong and thus pursue those ideas which have integrity in action.

This section has explored a number of ways in which social theory becomes a powerful resource for change and development in social practice. The argument is simple. Theory is agential in character and has unbounded potential to affect patterns of social action—whether desired or not. As we have seen, theories are not mere explanations of an external world lying "out there" waiting to be objectively recorded. Theories, like powerful ideas, are formative. By establishing perceptual cues and frames, by providing presumptions of logic, by transmitting subtle values, by creating new language, and by extending compelling visions of possibility or constraint—in all these ways social theory becomes a powerful means whereby norms, beliefs, and cultural practices may be altered.

REAWAKENING THE SPIRIT OF ACTION-RESEARCH

The key point is this: Instinctively, intuitively, and tacitly we all know that important ideas can, in a flash, profoundly alter the way we see ourselves, view reality, and conduct our lives. Experience shows that a simple economic forecast, political poll, or technical discovery (like the atomic bomb) can forever change the course of human history. Thus one cannot help but be disturbed and puzzled by the discipline of action-research in its wide-ranging indifference to theory. Not only does it continue to underrate the role of theory as a means for organizational development (Friedlander & Brown, 1974; Bartunek, 1983; Argyris, 1983) but it appears also to have become locked within an assumptive base that systematically distorts our view of organizational reality and inadvertantly helps reinforce and perfect the status quo (Brimm, 1972).

Why is there this lack of generative theorizing in action-research? And, more importantly, what can be done to rekindle the spirit, excitement and passion required of a science that wishes to be of vital significance to organizations? Earlier we talked about a philosophy of science congenial to the task. Sociorationalism, it was argued, represents an epistemological point of view conducive to catalytic theorizing. Ironically though, it can be argued that most action-researchers *already do* subscribe to this or a similar view of science (Susman & Evered, 1978). Assuming this to be the case, it becomes an even greater puzzle why contemporary action-research continues to disregard theory-building as an integral and necessary component of the craft. In this section we shall broaden our discussion by taking a look at some of the metaphysical assumptions embedded in our conventional definitions of action-research—assumptions that can be shown to govern our thought and work in ways inimical to present interests.

Paradigm I: Organizing As A Problem to be Solved

The intellectual and spiritual origins of action-research can be traced to Kurt Lewin, a social psychologist of German origin who coined the term *action-research* in 1944. The thrust of Lewin's work cenetered on the need to bridge the gap between science and the realm of practical affairs. Science, he said, should be used to inform and educate social practice, and subsequent action would then inform science: "We should consider action, research, and training as a triangle that should be kept together" (Lewin, 1948, p. 211). The twofold promise of an action science, according to Lewin, was to simultaneously contribute to the development of scientific knowledge (propositions of an if/then variety) and use such knowledge for bettering the human condition.

The immense influence of Lewin is a complete puzzle if we look only to his writings. The fact of the matter is that Lewin published only 2 papers—a mere 22 pages—concerned directly with the idea of action-research (Peters & Robinson, 1984). Indeed, it has been argued that his enduring influence is attributable not to these writings but to the sheer force and presence of the man himself. According to biographer Alfred Marrow (1968), Lewin was a passionate and creative thinker, continuously knocking at the door of the unknown, studying "topics that had been believed to be psychologically unapproachable." Lewin's character was marked by a spirit of inquiry that burned incessantly and affected all who came in contact with him, especially his students. The intensity of his presence was fueled further by the belief that inquiry itself could be used to construct a more democratic and dignified future. At least this was his hope and dream, for Lewin had *not* forgotten his experience as a refugee from facism in the late 1930s. Understanding this background, then, it is clear why he revolted so strongly against a detached ivory-tower view of science, a science that is immersed in trivial matters, tranquilized by its standardized methods, and limited in its field of inquiry. Thus, the picture we have of Lewin shows him to have been a committed social scientist pioneering uncharted territory for the purpose of creating new knowledge about groups and societies that might advance the democratic ideal (see, for example, Lewin, 1952). It was this spirit—a relentless curiosity coupled with a conviction of the need for knowledge-guided societal development—that marked Lewin's creative impact on both his students and the field.

Much of this spirit is now gone from action-research. What is left is a series of assumptions about the world which exhibits little, if any, resemblance to the process of inquiry as Lewin lived it. While many of the words are the same, they have been taken too literally and in their translation over the years have been bloated into a set of metaphysical principles—assumptions about the essence of social existence—that directly undermine the intellectual and speculative spirit. Put bluntly, under current norms, action-research has largely failed as an instrument for advancing social knowledge of consequence and now risks being (mis)understood as little more than a crude empiricism imprisoned in a deficiency mode of thought. A quick sketch of six sets of assumptions embedded in the conventional view of action-research will show exactly what we are talking about while also answering our question about the discipline's lack of contribution to generative theory:

Research equals problem-solving; to do good research is to solve "real problems." So ingrained is this assumption that it scarcely needs documentation. Virtually every definition found in leading texts and articles equates action-research with problem solving—as if "real" problem solving is virtually the essence of the discipline. For example, as French and Bell (1978) define it, "Action-research is both *an approach to problem solving*—a model or paradigm, and a *problem-solving process*—a series of activities and events" (p. 88)[4] Or in terms of the Bradford, Gibb, and Benne (1964) definition, "It is an application of scientific methodology in *the clarification* and *solution of practical problems*" (p. 33). Similarly, Frohman, Sashkin, and Kavanaugh (1976) state: "Action researach describes a particular process model whereby behavioral science knowledge is applied to help a client (usually a group or social system) *solve real problems and not incidentally learn the process involved in problem solving*" (p. 203). Echoing this theme, that research equals problem solving, researchers at the University of Michigan's Institute in Social Research state,

> "Three factors need to be taken into account in an organization development [action-research] effort: The behaviors that are problematic, the conditions that create those behaviors, and the interventions or activities that will correct the conditions creating the problems. What is it that people are doing or not doing, that is a problem? Why are they doing or not doing these particular things? Which of a large number of possible interventions or activities would be most likely to solve the problems by focusing on why problems exist?" (Hausser, Pecorella & Wissler, 1977, p. 2).

Here it is unmistakeably clear that the primary focus of the action-research approach to organizational analysis is the ongoing array of concrete problems an organization faces. Of course, there are a number of differences in the discipline as to the overall definition and meaning of the emerging action-research paradigm. But this basic assumption—that research equals problem solving—is not one of them. In a recent review intended to discover elements of metatheoretical agreement within the discipline, Peters and Robinson (1984) discovered that out of 15 different dimensions of action-research studied, only 2 had unanimous support among leaders in the field. What were these two elements of agreement? Exactly as the definitions above suggest: Social science should be "action-oriented" and "problem focused."

Inquiry, in action-research terms, is a matter of following the standardized rules of problem solving; knowledge is the result of good method. "In essence," write Blake and Mouton (1976), "it is a method of empirical data gathering that is *comprised of a set of rather standardized steps:* diagnosis, information gathering, feedback, and action planning" (pp. 101–102). By following this ritual list, they contend that virtually any organization can be studied in a manner that will lead to usable knowledge. As Chiles (1983) puts it, "The virtue of the model lies in the sequential process. . . . Any other sequence renders the model meaningless" (p. 318). The basic idea behind the model is that "in management, events proceed as planned unless some force, not provided against by the plan, acts upon events to produce an outcome not contemplated in the plan" (Kepner & Tregoe, 1973, p. 3). Thus, a problem is a deviation from some standard, and without precise diagnosis (step one) any attempt to resolve the problem will likely fail as a result of not penetrating the surface symptoms to discover the true causes. Hence, like a liturgical refrain which is seldom questioned or thought about, Cohen, Fink et al. (1984) tell the new student that *knowledge is the offspring of processing information through a distinct series of problem-solving stages:*

> Action-research begins with an identified problem. Data are then gathered in a way that allows a diagnosis which can produce a tentative solution, which is then implemented with the assumption that it is likely to cause new or unforeseen problems that will, in turn, need to be evaluated, diagnosed, and so forth. *This action-research method assumes a constantly evolving interplay between solutions, results, and new solutions. . . . This model is a general one applicable to solving any kind of problem in an ongoing organization* (pp. 359–360).

Action-research is utilitarian or technical; that is, it should be initiated and designed to meet a need in an area specified by the organization, usually by "top management." The search is controlled by the "felt need" or object of inquiry; everything that is not related to this object should be dismissed as irrelevant. As we are beginning to see, action-research conventionally understood does not really refer to research per se but rather to a highly focused and defined *type* of research called problem solving. Taken almost directly from the medical model, the disease orientation guides the process of inquiry in a highly programmed way. According to Levinson (1972), diagnostic action-research, "like a therapeutic or teaching relationship should be an alliance of both parties to discover and resolve these problems. . . . [The researcher] *should look for experiences which appear stressful to people. What kinds of occurrences disrupt or disorganize people"* (p. 37). Hence in a systematically limiting fashion, the general topic of research is largely prescribed—before inquiry even begins. As we would guess:

> Typical questions in [action-research] data gathering or "problem sensing" would include: *What problems* do you see in your group, including problems between people that are interfering with getting the job done the way you would like to see it done? And *what problems* do you see in the broader organization? Such open-ended questions provide latitude on the part of respondents and encourage a *reporting of problems* as the individual sees them (French, 1969, pp. 183–185).

In problem solving it is assumed that something is broken, fragmented, not whole, and that it needs to be fixed. Thus the function of problem solving is to integrate, stabilize, and help raise to its full potential the workings of the status quo. By definition, a problem implies that one already has knowledge of what "should be"; thus one's *re*search is guided by an instrumental purpose tied to what is already known. In this sense, problem solving tends to be inherently conservative; as a form of research it tends to produce and reproduce a universe of knowledge that remains sealed. As Staw (1984) points out in his review of the field, most organizational research is biased to serve managerial interests rather than exploring broader human and/or social purposes. But even more important, he argues, the field has not even served managerial interests well since research has taken a short-term problem focus rather than having formulated logics of new forms of organization that do not exist. It is as if the discipline's *concept of social-system development* means only clearing up distortions in current functioning (horizontal development) and does not include any conception of a stage-based movement toward an altogether new or transformed reality (vertical development or second-order change).

Action-research should not inquire into phenomena that transcend the competence of human reason. Questions that cannot be answered should not be asked and issues that cannot be acted upon should not be explored (i.e., action-research is not a branch of political philosophy, poetry, or theology). This proposition is a "smuggled-in" corollary to the preceding assumptions. It would appear that once one agrees with the ground rules of a pragmatic problem-solving science, the universe for inquiry is largely predetermined, defined, and delimited in scope. Specifically, what one agrees to a secularized view of a human universe that is predictable, controllable, and rational, one that is sequentially ordered into a series of causes and effects. As both a credit and a weakness, the problem-solving mode narrows our gaze in much the same manner that a blinder over one eye narrows the field of vision and distorts one's perception of depth. As a part of a long-term movement evidenced in social sciences, contemporary action-research embodies the trend toward metaphysical skepticism and denial (Quinney, 1982). That is, it operates out of a sacred void that cuts off virtually any inquiry into the vital forces of life. Indeed, the whole promise of modern science was that it would finally banish illusion, mystery, and uncertainty from the world. An inquiry process of immediate utility (problem solving), therefore, requires an anti-religious, secular spirit that will limit the realm of study to the sphere of the known. And because of the recognition that the formulation of a problem depends largely on one's views of what constitutes a solution, it is not surprising to find that *research on the utilization of research* shows a propensity for social scientists and organizations to agree on studying only those variables that can be manipulated (Beyer & Trice, 1982). As one might imagine, such a view has crippling implications for generative theorizing. For example, as typically practiced, action-research does little in the way of theorizing about or bringing beauty into organizational life. Does this mean that there is no beauty in organizing? Does this mean that the realm of the esthetic has little or nothing to do with organizational dynamics?

The tidy imagery of the problem-solving view is related to what Sigmund Koch (1981) has called, in his presidential address to the APA, the syndrome of "ameaningful thinking." One element of this syndrome is the perpetuation of the scientistic myth which uses the rhetoric of prediction and control to reassure people that their lives are not that complex, their situations not all that uncertain— and that their problems are indeed manageable through causal analysis. In the process, however, science tends to trivialize, and even evade, a whole class of issues that "transcend the competence of human reason" yet are clearly meaningful in the course of human experience. One way in which the field of inquiry is restricted, according to Koch, has to do with one's choice of methodology:

> There are times and circumstances in which able individuals, committed to inquiry, tend almost obsessively to frustrate the objectives of inquiry. It is as if uncertainty, mootness, ambiguity, cognitive infinitude were the most unbearable of the existential anguishes. . . . *Ameaningful* thought or inquiry regards knowledge as the result of "processing" rather than discovery. It presumes that knowledge is an almost automatic result of a gimmickry, an assembly line, a "metholology" . . . . So strongly does it see knowledge under such aspects that it sometimes seems to suppose the object of inquiry to be an ungainly and annoying irrevelance (1981, p. 259).

To be sure, this is not to argue that all action-research is "ameaningful" or automatically tied to a standardized problem-solving method. Likewise, much of the success achieved by action-research until now may be attributed to its restricted focus on that which is "solvable." However, it is important to recognize that the problem-solving method of organizational inquiry quite systematically paints a picture of organizational life in which a whole series of colors are considered untouchable. In this way the totality of being is obviously obscured, leading to a narrowed conception of human nature and cultural possibility.

Problems are "out there" to be studied and solved. The ideal product of action-research is a mirror-like reflection of the organization's problems and causes. As "objective third party," there is little role for passion and speculation. The action-researcher should be neither a passionate advocate nor an inspired dreamer (utopian thinker). One of the laudable and indeed significant values associated with action-research has been its insistence upon a collaborative form of inquiry. But unfortunately, from a generative-theory perspective, the term *collaboration* has become virtually synonomous with an idealized image of the researcher as a facilitator and mirror, rather than an active and fully engaged social participant. As facilitator of the problem-solving process, the action-researcher has three generally agreed-upon "primary intervention tasks": to help generate valid organizational data; to enable others to make free and informed choices on the basis of the data; and to help the organization generate internal commitment to their choices. Elaborating further, Argyris (1970) states:

> One condition that seems so basic as to be defined as axiomatic is the generation of *valid information*. . . . *Valid information is that which describes the factors, plus their interrelationships, that create the problem (pp. 16–17).*

Furthermore, it is also assumed that for data to be useful there must be a claim to neutrality. The data should represent an accurate reflection of the observed facts. As French and Bell (1978) describe it, it is important for the action-researcher to stress the objective, fact-finding features: "A key value inculcated in organizational members is a belief in the validity, desirability, and usefulness

of the data" (p. 79). Then through feedback that "refers to activities and processes that 'reflect' or 'mirror' an objective picture of the real world" (p. 111),
the action-researcher facilitates the process of priortizing problems and helps
others make choices for action. And because the overarching objective is to help
the organization develop its own internal resources, the action-researcher should
not play an active role or take an advocate stance that might in the long run foster
an unhealthy dependency. As French and Bell (1978) again explain, an active
role "tends to negate a collaborative, developmental approach to improving
organizational processes" (p. 203).

As must be evident, every one of these injunctions associated with the problem-solving view of action-research serves directly to diminish the likelihood of
imaginative, passionate, creative theory. To the extent that generative theory
represents an inspired theoretical articulation of a new and different future, it
appears that action-research would have nothing to do with it. According to
French and Bell (1978) "Even the presenting of options can be overdone. If the
[action-researcher's] ideas become the focal point for prolonged discussion and
debate, the consultant has clearly shifted away from the facilitator role" (p.
206).

At issue here is something even more important. The fundamental attitude
embodied in the problem-solving view is separationist. It views the world as
something external to our consciousness of it, something "out there." As such it
tends to identify problems not here but "over there": Problems are not ours, but
yours; not a condition common to all, but a condition belonging to this person,
their group, or that nation (witness the acid-rain issue). Thus, the action-researcher is content to facilitate *their problem solving* because he or she is not part
of that world. To this extent, the problem-solving view dissects reality and
parcels it out into fragmented groups, families, tribes, or countries. In both form
and substance it denies the wholeness of a dynamic and interconnected social
universe. And once the unity of the world is broken, passionless, mindless,
mirror-like inquiry comes to make logical sense precisely because the inquirer
has no ownership or stake in a world that is not his or hers to begin with.

*Organizational life is problematic. Organizing is best understood as a histor-
ically situated sequence of problems, causes, and solutions among people,
events, and things. Thus, the ultimate aim and product of action-research is the
production of institutions that have a high capacity to perceive, formulate, and
solve an endless stream of problems.*

The way we conceive of the social world is of consequence to the kind of
world we discover and even, through our reconstructions, helps to create it.
Action-researchers, like scientists in other areas, approach their work from a
framework based on taken-for-granted assumptions. To the extent that these
assumptions are found useful, and are affirmed by colleagues, they remain
unquestioned as a habitual springboard for one's work. In time the conventional
view becomes so solidly embedded that it assumes the status of being "real,"

without alternative (Morgan, 1980; Mennhiem, 1936). As human beings we are constantly in symbolic interaction, attempting to develop conceptions that will allow us to make sense of and give meaning to experience through the use of language, ideas, signs, theories, and names. As many have recently shown, the use of metaphor is a basic mode under which symbolism works and exerts an influence on the development of language, science, and cognitive growth (Morgan, 1980; Ortony, 1979; Black, 1962; Keely, 1980). Metaphor works by asserting that A equals B or is very much like B. We use metaphors constantly to open our eyes and sensitize us to phenomenal realities that otherwise might go unnoticed. Pepper (1942) argues that all science proceeds from specifiable "world hypotheses" and behind every world hypothesis rests the boldest of "root metaphors."

Within what we are calling Paradigm I action-research, there lies a guiding metaphor which has a power impact on the theory-building activity of the discipline. When organizations are approached from the deficiency perspective of Paradigm I, all the properties and modes of organizing are scrutinized for their dysfunctional but potentially solvable problems. It is all too clear then that the root metaphor of the conventional view is that *organizing is a problem.* This image focuses the researcher's eye on a visible but narrow realm of reality that resides "out there" and is causally determined, deficient by some preexisting standard—on problems that are probably both understandable and solvable. Through analysis, diagnosis, treatment, and follow-up evaluation the sequential world of organizing can be kept on its steady and productive course. And because social existence is at its base a problem to be solved, real living equals problem solving, and living better is an adaptive learning process whereby we acquire new and more effective means for tackling tough problems. The good life, this image informs, depends on solving problems in such a way that problems of utility are identified and solutions of high quality are found and carried out with full commitment. As one leading theorist describes:

> For many scholars who study organizations and management, the central characteristic of organizations is that they *are* problem-solving systems whose success is measured by how efficiently they solve problems associated with accomplishing their primary mission and how effectively they respond to emergent problems. Kilmann's approach (1979, pp. 214–215) is representative of this perspective: "One might even define the essence of management as problem defining and problem solving, whether the problems are well-structured, ill-structured, technical, human, or environmental. . . . " In this view, the core task of the executive is problem management. Although experience, personality, and specific technical expertise are important, the primary skill of the successful executive is the ability to manage the problem-solving process in such a way that important problems are identified and solutions of high quality are found and carried out with the full commitment of organizational members (Kolb, 1983, pp. 109–110).

From here it is just a short conceptual jump to the idealized aim of Paradigm I research:

Action-research tends to build into the client system an institutionalized pattern for continuously collecting data and examining the system's processes, as well as for the continuous
review of *known* problem areas. *Problem solving becomes very much a way of organizational
life* (Marguiles and Raia, 1972, p. 29).

I have tried in these few pages to highlight the almost obvious point that the
deficiency/problem orientation is pervasive and holds a subtle but powerful
grasp on the discipline's imagination and focus. It can be argued that the generative incapacity of contemporary action-research is securely linked with the
discipline's guiding metaphor of social-organizational existence. As noted by
many scholars, the theoretical output of the discipline is virtually nonexistent,
and what theory there is is largely problem-focused (theories of turnover, intergroup conflict, processes of dehumanization. See Staw, 1984 for an excellent
review). Thus, our theories, like windsocks, continue to blow steadily onward in
the direction of our conventional gaze. Seeing the world as a problem has
become "very much a way of organizational life."

It is our feeling that the discipline has reached a level of fatigue arising from
repetitive use of its standardized model. Fatigue, as Whitehead (1929) so aptly
surmised, arises from an act of excluding the impulse toward novelty which is
the antithesis of the life of the mind and of speculative reason. To be sure, there
can be great adventure in the process of inquiry. Yet not many action-researchers
today return from their explorations refreshed and revitalized, like pioneers
returning home, with news of lands unknown but most certainly there. Perhaps
there is a different root metaphor from which to work.

Proposal for a Second Dimension

Our effort here is but one in a small yet growing attempt to generate new
perspectives on the conduct of organizational research, perspectives that can
yield the kind of knowledge necessary for both understanding and transforming
complex social-organizational systems (Torbert, 1983; Van Maanen et al., 1982;
Mitroff & Kilmann, 1978; Smirchich, 1983; Forester, 1983; Argyris, 1970;
Friedlander, 1977). It is apparent that among the diverse views currently emerging there is frequently great tension. Often the differences become the bat-
tleground for fierce debate about theories of truth, the meaning of "facts,"
political agendas, and personal assertions of will. But, more fruitfully, what can
be seen emerging is a heightened sensitivity to and interdisciplinary recognition
of the fact that, based on "the structure of knowledge" (Kolb, 1984), there may
be multiple ways of knowing, each of them valid in its own realm when judged
according to its own set of essential assumptions and purposes. In this sense there
are many different ways of studying the same phenomenon, and the insights
generated by one approach are, at best, partial and incomplete. According to
Jürgen Habermas (1971) different perspectives can be evaluated only in terms of

their specified "human interests," which can broadly be differentiated into the realm of practical rationality and the realm of technical rationality. In more straightforward language Morgan (1983) states:

> The selection of method implies some view of the situation being studied, for any decision on *how* to study a phenomenon carries with it certain assumptions or explicit answers to the question, *"What is being studied?"* Just as we select a tennis racquet rather than a golf club to play tennis because we have a prior conception as to what the game of tennis involves, so too, in relation to the process of social research, we select or favor particular kinds of methodology because we have implicit or explicit conceptions as to what we are trying to do with our research (p. 19).

Thus, in adopting one mode over another the researcher directly influences what he or she will finally discover and accomplish.

It is the contention of this chapter that advances in generative theorizing will come about for action-research when the discipline decides to expand its universe of exploration, seeks to discover new questions, and rekindles a fresh perception of the extra ordinary in everyday organizational life. In this final section we now describe the assumptions and philosophy of an applied administrative science that seeks to embody these suggestions in a form of organization study we call appreciative inquiry. In distinction to conventional action-research, the knowledge-interest of appreciative inquiry lies not so much in problem solving as in social innovation. Appreciative inquiry refers to a research perspective that is uniquely intended for discovering, understanding, and fostering innovations in social-organizational arrangements and processes.[5] Its purpose is to contribute to the generative-theoretical aims of social science and to use such knowledge to promote egalitarian dialogue leading to social-system effectiveness and integrity. Whatever else it may be, social-system effectiveness is defined here quite specifically as a congruence between social-organizational values (the ever-changing normative set of values, ideas, or interests that system members hold concerning the question, "How should we organize ourselves?") and everyday social-organizational practices (cf. Torbert, 1983). Thus, appreciative inquiry refers to both a search for knowledge and a theory of intentional collective action which are designed to help evolve the normative vision and will of a group, organization, or society as a whole. It is an inquiry process that affirms our symbolic capacities of imagination and mind as well as our social capacity for conscious choice and cultural evolution. As a holistic form of inquiry, it asks a series of questions not found in either a logical-positivist conception of science or a strictly pragmatic, problem-solving mode of action-research. Yet as shown in Figure 1, its aims are both scientific (in a sociorationalist sense) and pragmatic (in a social-innovation sense) as well as metaphysical and normative (in the sense of attempting ethically to affirm all that social existence really is and should become). As a way of talking about the framework as it is actually practiced, we shall first examine four guiding principles that have directed our work in the area to date:

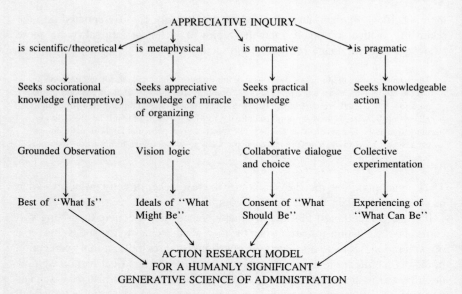

Figure 1. Dimensions of Appreciative Inquiry

Principle 1: Research into the social (innovation) potential of organizational life should begin with appreciation. This basic principle assumes that every social system "works" to some degree—that it is not in a complete state of entropy—and that a primary task of research is to discover, describe, and explain those social innovations, however small, which serve to give "life" to the system and activate members' competencies and energies as more fully functioning participants in the formation and transformation of organizational realities. That is, the appreciative approach takes its inspiration from the current state of "what is" and seeks a comprehensive understanding of the factors and forces of organizing (ideological, techno-structural, cultural) that serve to heighten the total potential of an organization in ideal-type human and social terms.

Principle 2: Research into the social potential of organizational life should be applicable. To be significant in a human sense, an applied science of administration should lead to the generation of theoretical knowledge that can be used, applied, and thereby validated in action. Thus, an applicable inquiry process is neither utopian in the sense of generating knowledge about "no place" (Sargent, 1982) nor should it be confined to academic circles and presented in ways that have little relevance to the everyday language and symbolism of those for whom the findings might be applicable.

Principle 3: Research into the social potential of organizational life should be provocative. Here it is considered axiomatic that an organization is, in fact, an open-ended indeterminate system capable of (1) becoming more than it is at any given moment, and (2) learning how to actively take part in guiding its own evolution. Hence, appreciative knowledge of *what is* (in terms of "peak" social innovations in organizing) is suggestive of what *might be* and such knowledge can be used to generate images of realistic developmental opportunities that can be experimented with on a wider scale. In this sense, appreciative inquiry can be both pragmatic and visionary. It becomes provocative to the extent that the abstracted findings of a study take on normative value for members of an organization, and this can happen only through their own critical deliberation and choice ("We feel that this particular finding is [or not] important for us to envision as an ideal to be striving for in practice on a wider scale"). It is in this way then, that appreciative inquiry allows us to put intuitive, visionary logic on a firm empirical footing and to use systematic research to help the organization's members shape the social world according to their own imaginative and moral purposes.

Principle 4: Research into the social potential of organizational life should be collaborative. This overarching principle points to the assumed existence of an inseparable relationship between the process of inquiry and its content. A collaborative relationship between the researcher and members of an organization is, therefore, deemed essential on the basis of both epistemological (Susman & Evered, 1978) and practical/ethical grounds (Habermas, 1971; Argyris, 1970). Simply put, a unilateral approach to the study of social innovation (bringing something new into the social world) is a direct negation of the phenomenon itself.

The spirit behind each of these four principles of appreciative inquiry is to be found in one of the most ancient archetypes or metaphorical symbols of hope and inspiration that humankind has ever known—the miracle and mystery of being. Throughout history, people have recognized the intimate relationship between being seized by the unfathomable and the process of appreciative knowing or thought (Marcel, 1963; Quinney, 1982; Jung, 1933; Maslow, 1968; Ghandi, 1958). According to Albert Schweitzer (1969), for example, it is recognition of the ultimate mystery that elevates our perception beyond the world of ordinary objects, igniting the life of the mind and a "reverence for life":

> In all respects the universe remains mysterious to man. . . . As soon as man does not take his existence for granted, but beholds it as something unfathomably mysterious, thought begins. This phenomenon has been repeated time and time again in the history of the human race. Ethical affirmation of life is the intellectual act by which man ceases simply to live at random. . . . [Such] thought has a dual task to accomplish: to lead us out of a naive and into a profounder affirmation of life and the universe; and to help us progress from ethical impulses to a rational system of ethics (p. 33).

For those of us breastfed by an industrial giant that stripped the world of its wonder and awe, it feels, to put it bluntly, like an irrelevant, absurd, and even distracting interruption to pause, reflect deeply, and then humbly accept the depth of what we can never know—and to consider the ultimate reality of living for which there are no coordinates or certainties, only questions. Medicine cannot tell me, for example, what it means that my newborn son has life and motion and soul, anymore than the modern physicist can tell me what "nothingness" is, which, they say, makes up over 99 percent of the universe. In fact, if there is anything we have learned from a great physicist of our time is that the promise of certainty is a lie (Hiesenberg, 1958), and by living this lie as scientistic doctrine, we short-circuit the gift of complementarity—the capacity for dialectically opposed modes of knowing, which adds richness, depth, and beauty to our lives (Bohr, 1958). Drugged by the products of our industrial machine we lose sight of and connection with the invisible mystery at the heart of creation, an ultimate power beyond rational understanding.

In the same way that birth of a living, breathing, loving, thinking human being is an inexplicable mystery, so too it can be said in no uncertain terms that *organizing is a miracle* of cooperative human interaction, of which there can never be final explanation. In fact, to the extent that organizations are indeed born and re-created through dialogue, they truly are unknowable as long as such creative dialogue remains. At this point in time there simply are no organizational theories that can account for the life-giving essence of cooperative existence, especially if one delves deeply enough. But, somehow we forget all this. We become lulled by our simplistic diagnostic boxes. The dilemma faced by our discipline in terms of its creative contribution to knowledge is summed up perfectly in the title of a well known article by one of the major advocates of action-research. The title by Marv Wiesbord (1976), has proven prophetic: "Organizational diagnosis: six places to look for trouble, with or without a theory." Content to transfer our conceptual curiosity over to "experts" who finally must know, our creative instincts lie pitifully dormant. Instead of explorers we become mechanics.

This, according to Koch (1981), is the source of "ameaningful" thinking. As Kierkegaard (1954) suggests, it is the essence of a certain dull-minded routine called "philistinism":

> Devoid of imagination, as the Philistine always is, he lives in a certain trivial province of experience as to how things go, what is possible. . . . Philistinism tranquilizes itself in the trivial (pp. 174–175).

As we know, a miracle is something that is beyond all possible verification, yet is experienced as real. As a symbol, the word *miracle* represents unification of the sacred and secular into a realm of totality that is at once terrifying and beautiful, inspiring and threatening. Quinney (1982) has suggested with respect to the rejuvenation of social theory, that such a unified viewpoint is altogether necessary, that it can have a powerful impact on the discipline precisely because in a world that is at once sacred and secular there is no place, knowledge, or phenomenon that is without mystery. The "miracle" then is pragmatic in its effect when sincerely apprehended by a mind that has chosen not to become "tranquilized in the trivial." In this sense, the metaphor "life is a miracle" is not so much an idea as it is—or can be—a central feature of experience enveloping (1) our perceptual consciousness; (2) our way of relation to others, the world, and our own research; and (3) our way of knowing. Each of these points can be highlighted by a diverse literature.

In terms of the first, scholars have suggested that the power of what we call the miracle lies in its capacity to advance one's perceptual capacity what Maslow (1968) has called a B-cognition or a growth-vs-deficiency orientation, or what Kolb (1984) has termed integrative consciousness. Kolb writes:

> The transendental quality of integrative consciousness is precisely that, a "climbing out of". . . . This state of consciousness is not reserved for the monastary, but it is a necessary ingredient for creativity in any field. Albert Einstein once said, "The most beautiful and profound emotion one can feel is a sense of the mystical. . . . It is the dower of all true science" (p. 158).

Second, as Gabriel Marcel (1963) explained in his William James lectures at Harvard on *The Mystery of Being,* the central conviction of life as a mystery creates for us a distinctly different relationship to the world than the conviction of life as a problem to be solved:

> A problem is something met which bars my passage. It is before me in its entirety. A mystery on the other hand is something I find *myself* caught up in, and whose essence is therefore not before me in its entirety. It is though in this province the distinction between "in me" and "before me" loses its meaning (p. 80).

Berman's (1981) recent analysis comes to a similar conclusion. The re-enchantment of the world gives rise to a "participatory consciousness" where there is a sense of personal stake, ownership, and partnership with the universe:

> The view of nature which predominated the West down to the eve of the Scientific Revolution was that of an enchanted world. Rocks, trees, rivers, and clouds were all seen as wondrous, alive, and human beings felt at home in this environment. The cosmos, in short, was a place of *belonging.* A member of this cosmos was not an alienated observer of it but a direct participant in its drama. His personal destiny was bound up with its destiny, and this relationship gave meaning to his life.

Third, as so many artists and poets have shown, there is a relationship between what the Greeks called *thaumazein*—an experience which lies on the borderline between wonderment and admiration—and a type of intuitive apprehension or knowing that we call appreciative. For Keats, the purpose of his work was:

> to accept things as I saw them, to enjoy the beauty I perceived for its own sake, without regard to ultimate truth or falsity, and to make a description of it the end and purpose of my appreciations.

Similarly for Shelley:

> Poetry thus makes immortal all that is best and most beautiful in the world . . . it exalts the
> beauty of that which is most beautiful . . . it strips the veil of familiarity from the world, and
> lays bare the naked and sleeping beauty, which is in the spirit of its forms.

And in strikingly similar words, learning theorist David Kolb (1984) analyzes the
structure of the knowing mind and reports:

> Finally, appreciation is a process of affirmation. Unlike criticism, which is based on skep-
> ticism and doubt (compare Polanyi, 1968, pp. 269ff.), appreciation is based on belief, trust,
> and conviction. And from this affirmative embrace flows a deeper fullness and richness of
> experience. This act of affirmation forms the foundation from which vital comprehension can
> develop. . . . Appreciative apprehension and critical comprehension are thus fundamentally
> different processes of knowing. Appreciation of immediate experience is an act of attention,
> valuing, and affirmation, whereas critical comprehension of symbols is based on objectivity
> (which involves a priori controls of attention, as in double-blind controlled experiments),
> dispassionate analysis, and skepticism (pp. 104–105).

We have cited these various thinkers in detail for several reasons: first, to
underscore the fact that the powerful images of problem and miracle (in)form
qualitatively distinct modes of inquiry which then shape our awareness, relations, and knowledge; and second, to highlight the conviction that the renewal of
generative theory requires that we enter into the realm of the metaphysical. The
chief characteristic of the modern mind has been the banishment of mystery from
the world, and along with it an ethical affirmation of life that has served history
as a leading source of values, hope, and normative bonding among people. In
historical terms, we have steadily forgotten how to dream.

In contrast to a type of research that is lived without a sense of mystery, the
appreciative mode awakens the desire to create and discover new social possibilities that can enrich our existence and give it meaning. In this sense, appreciative inquiry seeks an imaginative and fresh perception of organizations as
"ordinary magic," as if seen for the first time—or perhaps the last time (Hayward, 1984). The appreciative mode, in exploration of ordinary magic, is an
inquiry process that takes nothing for granted, searching to apprehend the basis
of organizational life and working to articulate those possibilities giving witness
to a better existence.

The metaphysical dimension of appreciative inquiry is important not so much
as a way of finding answers but is important insofar as it heightens the living
experience of awe and wonder which leads us to the wellspring of new questions—much like a wide-eyed explorer without final destination. Only by raising
innovative questions will innovations in theory and practice be found. As far as
action-research is concerned, this appears to have been the source of Lewin's
original and catalytic genius. We too can re-awaken this spirit. Because the
questions we ask largely determine what we find, we should place a premium on

that which informs our curiosity and thought. The metaphysical question of what makes social existence possible will never go away. The generative-theoretical question of compelling new possibilities will never go away. The normative question of what kind of social-organizational order is best, most dignified, and just, will never go away, nor will the pragmatic question of how to move closer to the ideal.

In its pragmatic form appreciative inquiry represents a data-based theory-building methodology for evolving and putting into practice the collective will of a group or organization. It has one and only one aim—to provide a generative-theoretical springboard for normative dialogue that is conducive to self-directed experimentation in social innovation. It must be noted, however, that the conceptual world which appreciative inquiry creates remains—despite its empirical content—an illusion. This is important to recognize because it is precisely because of its visionary content, placed in juxtaposition to grounded examples of the extraordinary, that appreciative inquiry opens the status quo to possible transformations in collective action. It appreciates the best of "what is" to ignite intuition of the possible and then firmly unites the two logically, caringly, and passionately into a theoretical hypothesis of an envisioned future. By raising ever new questions of an appreciative, applicable, and provocative nature, the researcher collaborates in the scientific construction of his or her world.[6]

CONCLUSION

What we have tried to do with this chapter is present conceptual refiguration of action-research; to present a proposal arguing for an enriched multidimensional view of action-research which seeks to be both theoretically generative and progressive in a broad human sense. In short, the argument is a simple one stating that there is a need to re-awaken the imaginative spirit of action-research and that to do this we need a fundamentally different perspective toward our organizational world, one that admits to its uncertainties, ambiguities, mysteries, and unexplicable, miraculous nature. But now we must admit, with a certain sense of limited capability and failure, that the viewpoint articulated here is simply not possible to define and is very difficult to speak of in technological, step-by-step terms. From the perspective of rational thought, the miraculous is impossible. From that of problem solving it is nonsense. And from that of empirical science, it is categorically denied (Reeves, 1984). Just as we cannot prove the proposition that organizing is a problem to be solved, so, too, we cannot prove in any rational, analytical, or empirical way that organizing is a miracle to be embraced. Each stance represents a commitment—a core conviction so to speak—which is given to each of us as a choice. We do, however, think that through discipline and training the appreciative eye can be developed to see the ordinary magic, beauty, and real possibilitiy in organizational life; but we are not sure we can so easily transform our central convictions.

In sum, the position we have been developing here is that for action-research to reach its potential as a vehicle for social innovation, it needs to begin advancing theoretical knowledge of consequence; that good theory may be one of the most powerful means human beings have for producing change in a post-industrial world; that the discipline's steadfast commitment to a problem-solving view of the world is a primary restraint on its imagination, passion, and positive contribution; that appreciative inquiry represents a viable complement to conventional forms of action-research, one uniquely suited for social innovation instead of problem solving; and that through our assumptions and choice of method we largely create the world we later discover.

NOTES

1.   While we draw most of our examples from the Organization Development (OD) school of action-research, the argument presented here should be relevant to other applications as well. As noted by Peters and Robinson (1984), the discipline of action-research has been prevalent in the literature of community action, education and educational system change, and organization change, as well as discussions of the social sciences in general.

2.   As physicist Jeremy Hayward (1984) has put it, "I'll see it when I believe it," or oppositely, "I won't see it because I don't believe it." The point is that all observation is filtered through belief systems which act as our personal theories of the world. Thus, what *counts* as "fact" depends largely on beliefs associated with theory and therefore, on the community of scientists espousing this belief system.

3.   A group of colleagues and we are engaged in a two-year study of a major industrial plant where introduction of this simple theory has led to changes in job design, work relations, training programs, motivational climate, and hierarchical ideology. For an introduction to this work see Pasmore, Cooperrider, Kaplan and Morris, 1983.

4.   Emphasis in this and the following definitions are ours, intended to underscore the points being made. Earlier we noted the importance of language as a subtle cueing device. Keeping this in mind, the reader is asked to pay special attention to the language of problem solving, and perhaps even count the sheer number of times the word problem is used in relation to definitions of action research.

5.   Following Whyte (1982), a social innovation will be defined as: (1) a new element in organizational structure or interorganizational relations; (2) innovative sets of procedures, reward systems, or interaction and activity and the relations of human beings to the natural and social environment; (3) a new administrative policy in actual use; (4) new role or sets of roles; and (5) new belief systems of ideologies transforming basic modes of relating.

6.   For an example of the type of theory generated through appreciative inquiry, see "The Emergence of the Egalitarian Organization" (Srivastva and Cooperrider, 1986).

REFERENCES

Argyris, C. (1973). Action science and intervention. *The Journal of Applied Behavioral Science, 19,* 115–140.

Argyris, C. (1970). *Intervention theory and methods.* Reading, MA: Addison-Wesley.

Argyris, C. & Schon, D. (1978). *Organizational learning: A theory of action perspective.* Reading, MA: Addison-Wesley.

Bartunek, J. (1983). How organization development can develop organizational theory. *Group and Organization Studies, 8,* 303–318.

Bartunek, J. (1984). Changing interpretive schemes and organizational restructuring: The example of a religious order. *Administrative Science Quarterly, 27,* 355–372.

Bell, D. (1973). *The coming of the post-industrial society.* New York: Basic Books.

Beyer, J. (1981). Ideologies, values and decision making in organizations. In P. C. Nystrom and W. H. Starbuck (Eds.), *Handbook of organizational design, Vol. 2.* Oxford University Press.

Beyer, J. & Trice, H. (1982). Utilization process: Conceptual framework and synthesis of findings. *Administrative Science Quarterly, 22,* 591–622.

Blake, R. & Mouton, J. (1976). *Consultation.* Reading, MA: Addison-Wesley.

Bohr, N. (1958). *Atomic theory and human knowledge.* New York: John Wiley.

Bradford, L. P., Gibb, J. R., & Benne, K. (1964). *T-group theory and laboratory method.* New York: John Wiley.

Braverman, H. (1974). *Labor and monopoly capital.* New York: Monthly Review Press.

Brimm, M. (1972). When is change not a change? *Journal of Applied Behavioral Science, 1,* 102–107.

Brown, R. H. (1978). *Leadership.* New York: Harper & Row.

Chiles, C. (1983). Comments on "design guidelines for social problem solving interventions." *The Journal of Applied Behavioral Science, 19,* 189–191.

Clegg, S. & Dunkerley, D. (1980). *Organization, class, and control.* Boston: Routledge and Kegan Paul.

Cohen, A. R., Fink, S. L., Gadon, H., & Willits, R. D. (1984). *Effective behavior in organizations.* Homewood, IL: Irwin.

Cooperrider, D. (1986). *Appreciative inquiry: Toward a methodology for understanding and enhancing organizational innovation.* Unpublished Ph.D. dissertation, Case Western Reserve University, Cleveland, OH.

Deal, T. E. & Kennedy, A. A. (1982). *Corporate cultures.* Reading, Mass.: Addison-Wesley.

Dubin, R. (1978). *Theory building.* New York: The Free Press.

Ellwood, C. (1938). *A history of social philosophy.* New York: Prentice-Hall.

Forester, John (1983). Critical theory and organizational analysis. In G. Morgan (Ed.), *Beyond method.* Beverly Hills, CA: Sage Publications.

French, W. L. (1969). Organization development objectives, assumptions, and strategies. *California Management Review, 12*(2), 23–34.

French, W. L. & Bell, C. H. (1978). *Organization development.* New Jersey: Prentice-Hall.

Friedlander, F. (1984). Producing useful knowledge for organizations. *Administrative Science Quarterly, 29,* 646–648.

Friedlander, F. (1977). Alternative modes of inquiry. Presented at APA Convention, San Francisco, Ca.

Friedlander, F. & Brown, L. D. (1974). Organization development. *Annual Review of Psychology, 25,* 313–341.

Frohman, M., Sashkin, M., and Kavanaugh, M. (1976). Action-research as applied to organization development. *Organization and Administrative Sciences, 1,* 129–161.

Geertz, C. (1980). Blurred genres: The refiguration of social thought. *American Scholar, 49,* 165–179.

Gergen, K. (1982). *Toward transformation in social knowledge.* New York: Springer-Verlag.

Gergen, K. (1978). Toward generative theory. *Journal of Personality and Social Psychology, 36,* 1344–1360.

Ghandi, M. (1958). *All men are brothers.* New York: Columbia University Press.

Gorz, A. (1973). Workers' control is more than just that. In Hunnius, Garson, and Case (Eds.), *Workers control.* New York: Vintage Books.

Gould, S. J. (1981). *The mismeasure of man.* New York: Norton and Company.

Gouldner, A. (1970). *The coming crisis of Western sociology.* New York: Basic Books.

Habermas, J. (1971). *Knowledge and human interests.* Boston: Beacon Press.

Haley, J. *Uncommon therapy.* New York: W. W. Norton, 1973.

Hare, P. H. (1976). *Handbook of small group research.* New York: The Free Press.

Harrison, R. (1982). *Leadership and strategy for a new age: Lessons from "conscious evolution."* Menlo Park, CA: Values and Lifestyles Program.

Hausser, D., Pecorella, P., & Wissler, A. (1977). *Survey-guided development II.* LaJolla, Calif.: University Associates.

Hayward, J. (1984). *Perceiving ordinary magic.* Gouldner: New Science Library.

Hiesenberg, W. (1958). *Physics and philosophy: The revolution in modern science.* London: Allen and Urwig.

Henshel, R. (1975). Effects of disciplinary prestige on predictive accuracy. *Futures, 7,* 92–106.

Hofsteede, G. (1980). *Culture's consequences.* Beverly Hills, CA: Sage.

Jung, C. (1933). *Modern man in search of a soul.* New York: Harcourt, Brace & Company.

Keeley, M. (1980). Organizational analogy: Comparison of orgasmic and social contract models. *Administrative Science Quarterly, 25,* 337–362.

Kepner, C. & Trego, B. (1973). *Executive problem analysis and decision making.* Princeton, NJ.

Kierkegaard, S. (1954). *The sickness unto death.* New York: Anchor Books. Translated by Walter Lowrie.

Kilmann, R. (1979). Problem management: A behavioral science approach. In G. Zaltman (Ed.), *Management principles for non-profit agencies and organizations.* New York: American Management Association.

Koch, S. (1981). The nature and limits of psychological knowledge. *American Psychologist, 36,* 257–269.

Kolb, D. A. (1984). *Experiential learning.* Englewood Cliffs, NJ: Prentice-Hall.

Kolb, D. A. (1983). Problem management: Learning from experience. In S. Srivastva (Ed.), *The executive mind.* San Francisco: Jossey-Bass.

Levinson, H. (1972) The clinical psychologist as organizational diagnostician. *Professional Psychology, 10,* 485–502.

Levinson, H. (1972). *Organizational diagnosis.* Cambridge, MA: Harvard University Press.

Lewin, K. (1948). Action research and minority problems. In G. W. Lewin (Ed.), *Resolving social conflicts.* New York: Harper & Row.

Lewin, K. (1951). *Field theory in social science.* New York: Harper & Row.

Lukes, S. (1974). *Power: A radical view.* London: Macmillan.

Mannheim, K. (1936). *Ideology and utopia.* New York: Harcourt, Brace & World.

Marcel, G. (1963). *The existential background of human dignity.* Cambridge: Harvard University Press.

Margulies, N. & Raia, A. P. (1972). *Organization development: Values, process and technology.* New York: McGraw Hill.

Marrow, A. (1968). *The practical theorist.* New York: Basic Books.

Maslow, A. (1968). *Toward a psychology of being.* New York: Van Nostrand Reinhold Co.

McHugh, P. (1970). On the failure of positivism. In J. Douglas (Ed.), *Understanding everyday life.* Chicago: Aldine.

Mitroff, I. (1980). Reality as a scientific strategy: Revising our concepts of science. *Academy of Management Review, 5,* 513–515.

Mitroff, I. & Kilmann, R. (1978). *Methodological approaches to social sciences.* San Francisco: Jossey-Bass.

Morgan, G. (1983). *Beyond method.* Beverly Hills: Sage Publications.

Morgan, G. (1980). Paradigms, metaphors, and puzzle solving in organization theory. *Administrative Science Quarterly, 24,* 605–622.

Ortony, A. (Ed.) (1979). *Metaphor and thought.* Cambridge: Cambridge University Press.

Ouchi, W. G. & Johnson, J. B. (1978). Types of organizational control and their relationship to emotional well-being. *Administrative Science Quarterly, 23,* 293–317.

Pasmore, W., Cooperrider, D., Kaplan, M. & Morris, B. (1983). Introducing managers to performance development. In *The ecology of work*. Proceedings of the Sixth NTL Ecology of Work Conference, Cleveland, Ohio.

Pasmore, W. & Friedlander, F. (1982). An action-research program for increasing employee involvement in problem solving. *Administrative Science Quarterly, 27,* 343–362.

Pepper, S. C. (1942). *World hypothesis*. Berkeley, CA: University of California Press.

Peters, M. & Robinson, V. (1984). The origins and status of action research. *Journal of Applied Behavioral Science, 20,* 113–124.

Quinney, R. (1982). *Social existence: Metaphysics, Marxism, and the social sciences*. Beverly Hills, CA: Sage Publications.

Rappaport, R. W. (1970). Three dilemmas of action-research. *Human Relations, 23,* 499–513.

Reeves, G. (1984). The idea of mystery in the philosophy of Gabriel Marcel. In J. Schlipp, & L. Hahn, (Eds.), *The philosophy of Gabriel Marcel*. LaSalle, IL: Open Court.

Sargent, L. T. (1982). Authority and utopia: Utopianisms in political thought. *Polity, 4,* 565–584.

Sathe, V. J. (1983). Implications of corporate culture. *Organizational Dynamics,* Autumn, 5–23.

Schein, E. (1983). The role of the founder in creating organizational culture. *Organizational Dynamics,* Summer, 12–28.

Schweitzer, A. (1969). *The teaching of reverence for life*. New York: Holt, Rinehart and Winston.

Small, A. (1905). *General sociology: An exposition of the main development in sociological theory from Spencer to Ratzenhofer*. Chicago: University of Chicago Press.

Smirchich, L. (1983). Studying organizations as cultures. In G. Morgan (Ed.), *Beyond method*. Beverly Hills, CA: Sage Publications.

Sproull, L. S. (1981). Beliefs in organizations. In P. C. Nystrom & W. H. Starbuck (Eds.), *Handbook of organizational design*, Vol. 2. New York: Oxford University Press.

Srivastva, S. (1985). *Executive power*. San Francisco: Jossey-Bass Publishers.

Srivastva, S. (1983). *The executive mind*. San Francisco: Jossey-Bass Publishers.

Srivastva, S. & Cooperrider, D. (1986). The emergence of the egalitarian organization. *Human Relations,* London: Tavistock.

Srivastva, S., Obert, S. & Neilsen, E. (1977). Organizational analysis through group process: A theoretical perspective for organization development. In C. Cooper (Ed.) *Organization development in the U.K. and U.S.A.* New York: The Macmillan Press.

Staw, B. (1984). Organizational behavior: A review and reformulation of the field's outcome variables. *Annual Review of Psychology, 35,* 626–666.

Susman, G. & Evered, R. (1978). An assessment of the scientific merits of action-research. *Administrative Science Quarterly, 23,* 582–603.

Thelen, H. (1954). *Dynamics of groups at work*. Chicago: University of Chicago Press.

Torbert, W. (1983). Initiating collaborative inquiry. In G. Morgan (Ed.), *Beyond method*. Beverly Hills, CA: Sage Publications.

Van Maanen, J., Dabbs, J. M., & Faulkner, R. R. (1982). *Varieties of qualitative research*. Beverly Hills, Calif.: Sage Publications.

Watzlawick, P., Weakland, J., & Fish, R. (1974). *Change: Principles of problem formation and problem resolution*. New York: Horton.

Weick, K. E. (1983). Managerial thought in the context of action. In S. Srivastva (Ed.), *The executive mind*. San Francisco: Jossey-Bass.

Wiesbord, M. (1976). Organization diagnosis: Six places to look for trouble with or without a theory. *Group and Organization Studies, 1,* 430–447.

Weiss, C. H. & Bucuvalas, M. (1980). The challenge of social research to decision making. In C. H. Weiss (Ed.), *Using social research in public policy making*. Lexington, MA: Lexington Books.

Whitehead, A. N. (1929). *The function of reason*. Boston: Beacon Press.

Whyte, W. F. (1982). Social inventions for solving human problems. *American Sociological Review, 47,* 1–13.

THE CASE META-ANALYSIS
METHOD FOR OD

R. J. Bullock and Mark E. Tubbs

ABSTRACT

This chapter describes a new approach to OD research called case meta-analysis. Case meta-analysis combines features of the case study, the simplest complete unit of analysis in OD, with features of meta-analysis, which attempts to understand the pattern of results across a series of studies. Rather than use effect sizes, case meta-analysis relies on coded variables for independent and dependent variables, with rigorous criteria established for developing the most reliable, valid, and replicable measures. The method is illustrated through an extended example of case meta-analysis applied to gainsharing. The rationale supporting case meta-analysis and the successful application of the method suggest that case meta-analysis is potentially a major tool for advancing OD knowledge. The chapter presents case meta-analysis as a research advance in resolving basic philosophy of science issues facing the field of OD. The chapter details the nine steps of case meta-analysis, and resolves many practical problems encountered in applying the method successfully.

Research in Organizational Change and Development, Vol. 1, pages 171–228.
Copyright © 1987 by JAI Press Inc.
All rights of reproduction in any form reserved.
ISBN: 0-89232-479-9

INTRODUCTION

The purpose of this chapter is to describe a new approach to OD research that we think has significant potential for advancing OD knowledge. We call the method case meta-analysis because it combines features of the case study research method with the meta-analysis research method.

In OD research, the simplest possible complete unit of analysis is a case study. The most basic piece of OD research is not a laboratory study, or even a field study comparing two groups of people, but a single organization in a system-wide change effort. OD is concerned with the entire social system, so even when the direct intervention target is an individual or a group, the effects on the entire organization are paramount. Because of that natural reliance on whole, intact organizations, most OD learning has come from implementing case studies of OD principles.

Unfortunately, case studies are regarded as nonscientific by traditional thinking in the social sciences. Campbell and Stanley (1966) asserted that case studies "have such a total absence of control as to be of almost no scientific value" (p. 6), reflecting the widely held belief that nothing can be learned from an n of 1. As a piece of scientific research, case studies are generally viewed as virtually worthless. They may be interesting, fun to read, even insightful—but not scientific.

Since case studies are regarded as nonscientific by traditional standards, they have been almost totally ignored in attempts to advance OD knowledge. Literature reviews consistently omit OD case studies because they do not fit classical criteria for research design rigor. These reviews normally come to the conclusion that more rigorous research is needed in OD and call upon the OD research community to provide more examples of the direct application of traditional research principles.

Such a straight-forward application is not possible. Bullock (in press) concluded that a true experiment in OD can never be done. The problem is not the practical difficulty of random assignment, but the logical impossibility of using random selection and random assignment to study the OD process. The OD process is collaborative and diagnosis-based, and is fundamentally incompatible with the unilateral control and random process required for rigorous experiments. You can randomly assign individuals, groups, and organizations to OD techniques, but random assignment to OD techniques is not studying the OD process. Since random assignment is necessary for a true experiment in the classical sense of experimental design, it follows—for better or worse—that there will never be a true experiment of the OD process.

A gap has thus developed between the calls for more rigorous research and the actual practice of OD. On the one hand, methodologists and reviewers call for more experimental controls, random assignment, and true experimental design.

On the other hand, OD practice relies on multiple case study applications, learning from the experiences of those individual case studies.

This gap is getting wider. OD practice continues to expand rapidly and the research literature has not kept pace. As the gap widens, OD practitioners are forced to learn more from their personal experiences and professional contacts than from the research literature.

What is needed is a bridge between rigor rules and reality. Case meta-analysis is, we think, such a bridge because case meta-analysis method relies on individual case study applications of OD in an attempt to learn from the pattern of those case studies. The process is systematic and involves testing OD hypotheses by coding process and result variables in the OD case study. Certain patterns are expected to emerge across OD cases as a result of OD theories, and the case meta-analysis process provides one way of assessing these relationships.

Consider team-building, for instance. Team-building has historically been an important OD intervention. In the past 25 years, thousands of groups have undergone OD team-building processes. Some of these team building interventions have worked very well, some have worked not as well, and some not at all. Many variables differ from site to site, so how does one make sense of the varied results of a series of partially related, yet unique and separate, applications of the OD team-building process?

Case meta-analysis is one answer. It gives the OD researcher a handle for understanding the pattern of a complex series of variables for very different OD projects. The process could be team-building, quality of worklife projects, survey feedback, socio-technical systems, job redesign, or any other class of OD interventions. By defining a class of OD interventions and identifying in advance the key ideas to be tested across the case studies, the case meta-analysis researcher can code process and result variables to determine patterns that support or do not support hypotheses about how OD works.

For example, consider that an OD practitioner of team-building believes the size of the team affects the success of the team-building process. In one situation a larger group may be more effective than another smaller group, but in general, we would probably expect that large groups would be less effective than smaller groups in the OD team-building process. This basic idea of the relationship between group size and team-building results cannot be tested in a true experiment in the laboratory or in the field, nor can this question be answered with a single OD case study. You can, however, answer the question using case meta-analysis. If there is a general relationship between group size and team-building results, it should become apparent when we study the pattern of team-building case studies across a wide variety of organizations, situations, and OD practitioners.

As occurs in most applications of case meta-analysis, theoretical work is necessary in advance of the coding steps. Much work remains to be done on converting basic OD concepts and principles to testable hypotheses. Using the team-building example, do we expect that team-building is more effective in smaller groups than in larger groups? How small? How large? Is the small-large dichotomy the issue, or is effectiveness a continuous function of size? Or, is it curvilinear, so that there is an optimum size around 8–10, with less impact for groups smaller than 8 or larger than 10? Just how strong an impact does size make? Do we expect it to be relatively minor so that large but committed groups can overcome the negative impact of their size, or is the size effect so significant that team-building for groups larger than, say, 12 or 15 would have such a low probability of success that they will not be practical?

At this point, the reader can see the potential interplay between case meta-analysis research and practice. Case meta-analysis relies on practitioners for ideas, conjectures, principles, theoretical inspiration, and insight to the key variables of process and results. In turn, practitioners benefit from understanding how these variables operate singly and jointly across a variety of situations. Such information can be used to diagnose a situation, to estimate the chances of success for a given technique in a given situation, and to guide implementation decisions.

The development of an inventive case meta-analysis method comes at a time when traditional scientific standards are coming under close scrutiny. Developing a more important role for case studies in OD research parallels case study development in other areas of social science and is a part of our rethinking of the way social science research could be conducted (see Yin, 1984). In considering this broader context of OD case studies and the changing focus of social science research, it may be useful to reconsider what Kuhn (1962, 1970) said regarding the components of scientific paradigms. A paradigm is defined by its disciplinary matrix, the constellation of concepts, beliefs, and values that all members of the paradigm share. Part of this disciplinary matrix is what Kuhn calls shared exemplars, which are essentially those research methods deemed appropriate for investigating the sort of problems the paradigm is concerned with. These research methods are not only used consistently within the paradigm, but are taught in graduate schools as the only way in which research issues can be validly addressed.

We should recognize that there are substantial differences between the commitments and exemplars shared by OD researchers and those held by traditional social scientists, just as the social sciences need a different paradigm from the natural sciences. Some components of the disciplinary matrix are similar, but the subject matter is different enough to justify breaking away from the traditional exemplars and moving toward a new set of methods where OD research knowledge can be accumulated and presented with an acceptable degree of rigor. The next major section of this chapter gives a background of some of the issues in this changing philosophy of science. This background explains the broader context of OD case study research.

BACKGROUND OF THE CASE META-ANALYSIS METHOD

This section is devoted to identifying and discussing three sets of issues that provide the reader with a context for case meta-analysis. The first set of issues relates to the search for new methods in OD. OD researchers are dissatisfied with traditional methods and, in the search for better methods, case meta-analysis is a potential solution.

The second set of issues relates to the use of case studies. Case studies are rapidly becoming an important research tool, although historically they have been denigrated as unscientific and have been virtually ignored in the empirical literature. Understanding this new perspective on case studies is an important foundation for a full appreciation of the case meta-analysis method.

The third set of issues relates to the meta-analysis process. Meta-analysis has quickly earned a solid place in the empirical literature as a technique for integrating knowledge across studies. Applications of the meta-analysis method are increasing, and it is important for the reader to understand some basic ideas of meta-analysis method to understand the adaptations required for case meta-analysis.

Issues About New Methods

We have a major problem in OD research. The problem is not the relevance of the field to society, nor a lack of interested researchers and practitioners, nor even a lack of OD applications. The problem is that generally traditional social science research methods do not apply to OD research. Some traditional tools for conducting research are applicable and relevant to OD, but many are not.

This is not a new problem. Dissatisfaction with social science research methods has been documented in the OD literature for over 20 years. Argyris (1968, 1970) explained how the conduct of rigorous research had dysfunctional consequences for the research conclusions, for the participants in the research, and for the scientific field and society in general. The unintended consequences of rigorous research include physical and psychological withdrawal and overt or covert hostility. These consequences occur when a person becomes a "subject," being manipulated, controlled, and deceived as the researcher sees fit. Argyris pointed out that the type of social system created by rigorous experiments was the same as that designed for organizations by scientific management, with the same consequences. He compared this mechanistic research process with organic research and suggested that organic research process was more appropriate.

This concern for the applicability and impact of traditional research methods has been a consistent theme for many years. Nowhere is the application of the positivist approach to science more strained than in OD. Susman and Evered (1978) contrasted the positivist approach to science, which characterizes virtually all organizational research, with the action research approach. Positivist science attempts to use value-neutral methods with the researcher as a detached spectator observing "subjects." Epistemologically, positivist research attempts to predict and control events from a series of propositions arranged hierarchically from a set of general laws to more specific laws. Action research was viewed by Susman and Evered (1978) as a correction to the deficiencies of a positivist science. Action research, originally proposed and developed by Collier (1945), Lewin (1946), Rapoport (1970), and others, is future-oriented, collaborative, and builds theory grounded in action. The action research process is a spiral of steps of diagnosing, planning, taking action, evaluating the action, and learning from the findings.

Action research has legitimacy and philosophical traditions different from, but equal to, positivist traditions. Action research fails to meet the critical tests for a positivist science, but as Susman and Evered (1978) noted, positivist criteria for science are inappropriate for action research. The dissatisfaction in OD with traditional research methods then can be viewed as a special case of a more fundamental problem that philosophers of science have with the traditional positivist school of thought.

A more recent example of the stream of literature articulating problems with traditional research methods when applied to OD is Bullock (in press), who compared the social processes that define the field of OD with those required of random selection and assignment and concluded that it was logically impossible to study the OD process with random assignment.

The basic problem then is the inapplicability of traditional experimental methods to the field of OD. The problem can be viewed in terms of the dysfunctional social systems created by traditional research methods, epistemological flaws in the underlying philosophy of science of logical positivism, or a detailed consideration of the incompatibility of particular research methods with OD processes. Whatever the approach, the fundamental issue remains that many of the tools and techniques that have been so valuable to other fields do not readily apply to OD.

Our current problem, however, goes further than this. We have no shortage of critiques of traditional methods, for OD in particular, or for social science in general; but we do have a lack of replacements. At this point, the dissatisfaction with traditional methods is clear, but the alternatives are not. Not only must the problems with traditional research methods be clearly articulated and documented, but newer and better methods must be found. Critics of traditional research methods have been more articulate in documenting problems of traditional methods than in finding better replacements. Such a dynamic is reasonable, since it is important to identify a problem before attempting to solve it. Articulating the problems with traditional methods is, however, only one step, and much work remains to be done to identify equally rigorous, but more relevant research methods.

The study of OD research methods can learn here from OD practice. We use in practice a fundamental model where change depends on two preconditions: (1) dissatisfaction with the status quo, and (2) availability of a better alternative. It is not enough to be dissatisfied with the current situation—change only occurs if people are dissatisfied *and* they have an image of a new possibility. These two conditions are not predictors of change—they are necessary conditions for change—and, without them, planned change does not occur. Dissatisfaction with the current situation often leads to a search for better alternatives, but without better alternatives, dissatisfaction leads to frustration without change. If we wish to change the situation, we must not only identify clearly the inadequacies of past research methods, but must also develop better ones. Case meta-analysis is one such attempt to develop a better way of learning about organizational change and is proposed here in the spirit of improving OD research. We hope the approach benefits OD researchers and encourages any feedback that readers or appliers of the method might have.

Issues About Case Studies

Historically the traditional scientific view held that case studies were only one cut above journalism—nothing can be learned from an n of one because the statistical methods that have come to define social science cannot be applied. This view, which historically has dominated psychological research and organizational research, is changing. Interest is increasing in the development of case study research designs and case study interpretation. The important but undervalued role that case studies have played in the development of OD has also been true of other areas of social science. Yin (1984), in his book on *Case Study Research,* presented the case study as a legitimate, potentially rigorous research strategy. He documented dozens of classic case studies in a variety of social sciences and pointed out that although case study methods have been harshly criticized, many well-respected researchers have conducted classics of the case study method, including Whyte (1943), Liebow (1967), Kaufman (1960), Allison (1971), Selznick (1949), and many others. The development in OD of an increased role of case studies parallels improvements in case study methodology in other research. Our conclusion is that the case study will be an increasingly viable method for conducting research in OD, as well as in other areas of the social sciences.

There is no shortage of OD case studies at this point. Proehl (1980) documented 574 case studies of organization development in the literature. No doubt scores or even hundreds more could be added to that list. Case studies have not been undervalued by practitioners and those who live with the intervention, so case studies continue to be implemented and documented at a rapid pace.

The key problem with OD case studies, however, is that they have been undervalued and underutilized by the scientific literature. A significant amount of informal learning has occurred, not only from the implementers of the intervention and those who have lived with the intervention, but also in the professional community through the informal networks of the OD Network, the OD Institute, the OD Division of the American Society for Training Development, and the OD Division of the Academy of Management. In many cases, this learning has not been translated to the empirical scientific literature because the case study method of learning has not been deemed rigorous by traditional standards.

Thus, our orientation to case meta-analysis is to develop a technique to more effectively utilize a resource that already exists, that will become increasingly important in the future, and for which a more important role is being carved out in social science research methods and in the underlying philosophy of science.

Issues About Meta-Analysis

The integration of knowledge across studies is a critical element in the scientific process. Historically, this integration has been accomplished through reviews of the literature. Serious problems have, however, arisen in the conduct of literature reviews. The analyses of social science reviews (e.g., Jackson, 1978) have identified many fundamental problems, including an emphasis on verbal summaries (which might be called the "one paragraph per study" approach), use of a biased subset of potential studies for review, much subjectivity throughout the review process, inability to integrate large literatures, inconsistent results between reviewers of the same literature, and little or no documentation of how conclusions were obtained. Some have concluded that literature reviews in the social sciences are largely the results of "private judgment . . . and personal style" (Glass, McGaw, & Smith, 1981, p. 14).

The serious deficiencies of current literature reviews have led to a search for new and better ways to accomplish the important task of knowledge accumulation through research integration. One approach is a statistical method known as "meta-analysis," a term coined by Glass (1976). Broadly speaking, meta-analysis is "a study of studies." Meta-analysis involves the systematic collection of documented studies relevant to some research question, conversion of the findings and characteristics of the studies to measured variables through some coding scheme, and the analysis of these variables using the best statistical procedures available. In effect, meta-analysis treats prior studies as individual data points in a statistical analysis. The pattern of results in the literature are statistically analyzed to see how differences in the way studies were conducted affected the findings. By using statistical formulas, one can determine estimates of the population parameters and summarize findings of a wide literature.

Several approaches to meta-analysis have been developed. The first and most basic has been described by Glass et al. (1981). A special form of meta-analysis known as validity generalization has been used successfully in industrial psychology for employment selection issues (Callender & Osburn, 1980; Schmidt & Hunter, 1977; Schmidt, Hunter, Pearlman, & Shane, 1979). Hunter, Schmidt, and Jackson (1982) proposed an integration of Glass' approach and the validity generalization approach based on the strong features of both. A fourth approach has developed from aggregation of studies based on probability values (Rosenthal, 1978). Several other approaches use still different statistics (Rosenthal, 1984), that differ in the statistics and procedures used for aggregation, role of theory, and points of emphasis (see Hunter et al., 1982). Variations in application techniques (with and without the label meta-analysis) have created some problems, and a series of explicit criteria have been proposed for evaluating the quality of meta-analysis research, regardless of the approach used (Bullock & Svyantek, 1985).

This chapter describes a new approach to meta-analysis that has potential utility for the field of OD. This approach was developed specifically for the analysis of OD case studies, but may be applicable to other fields using case studies. Since OD interventions are accomplished on a case-by-case basis, case studies have been widely used in OD, although they are harshly criticized because little can be gained from them using statistical principles of research. The approach described here is directly applicable to knowledge integration from individual case studies and thus has the potential for integrating information already available in the OD literature but inaccessible by other methods.

The meta-analysis approach described here is not standard meta-analysis in the sense that it does not strictly involve the statistical analysis of prior statistical results. The current approach does, however, involve the systematic accumulation and statistical analysis of independent research efforts, which is the primary aim of meta-analysis. The key difference between the meta-analysis method described here and prior methods of meta-analysis is the treatment of the dependent variable. Standard meta-analysis methods have used probability values (Rosenthal's approach), effect sizes (Glass' approach), and correlations (Schmidt & Hunter's approach), and developed special methods to accumulate previous findings using these three statistics. None of these statistics are regularly available for case studies, so some adaptation of meta-analysis is necessary. The adaptation here is to use coded dependent variables (i.e., effects) for the meta-analysis (i.e., study characteristics). The measurement quality of these coded effect variables is determined in the same ways that reliability and validity are assessed for study characteristics. Thus, the primary adaptation of this approach to meta-analysis is an extension of the measurement approach used to assess study characteristics to effect variables as well. The emphasis here on coded variables leads us to several conclusions that differ from past approaches to meta-analysis; we explain these conclusions in the sections that follow. Because our approach is based on coded variables rather than aggregated statistics, formula corrections for sampling error, attentuation, etc. are often not applicable even though they may be relatively important to other meta-analysis approaches. To distinguish the approach of this paper from past approaches to meta-analysis, and to avoid implications that this method is something it is not, we use the label "case meta-analysis" to refer to the approach detailed in this paper (Macy et al., 1986).

THE CASE META-ANALYSIS METHOD

The nine steps. To explain the case meta-analysis process, in this section a logical progression of steps in the research process is used: (1) developing research questions, (2) setting criteria for study collection, (3) collecting studies, (4) developing decision rules for coding variables, (5) coding studies, (6) computing reliability, estimates of coding quality, (7) resolving rating discrepancies, (8) analyzing the consensus data matrix, and (9) reporting the results. It may be difficult to fully understand these steps when explained in general terms. To help the reader appreciate and resolve the issues involved in case meta-analysis, several examples throughout the explanation are used although some of these examples are hypothetical while others are real. Elsewhere (Bullock & Tubbs, 1983), we have applied case meta-analysis to the literature on gainsharing. To provide continuity throughout the chapter we used this extended example, labeled "Gainsharing Application," in each step to show the practical problems encountered in applying the method and how we chose to resolve them. This extended example of case meta-analysis demonstrates that it is practical and useful to apply the method, and the results can be theoretically meaningful as well as practically useful.

A short-cut for the reader. We have written this chapter to be as specific as possible to guide those who wish to apply the method to a given literature. The chapter is written with sufficient detail so that experienced or inexperienced researchers can apply the method directly. Not all readers desire the level of detail we provide in this chapter, particularly on their first reading. To accommodate the reader who wishes to have a relatively quick overview of the method, we have provided a paragraph summary at the end of each step of the process. Readers who wish a brief overview of the method can read the background section, the summary at the end of each step, and the discussion section at the end of the chapter. This will provide an overview of the basic process used to analyze OD case studies and we hope will entice the reader to delve more deeply into this new research method. Another summary of the method has been provided by Bullock (1986).

Step 1. Develop the Research Questions

The first logical step in any research effort is developing research questions. The creative process of developing innovative, high quality research questions is not well understood, but some speculative literature is available here.

Defining quality research questions.   The first issue is to determine what high quality research questions are. Kerlinger (1973) proposed that good research questions should express a relationship, should be stated unambiguously, and should imply empirical testing. Stating research questions in this way allows the researcher to identify the potential target population where these research questions are relevant and hypotheses predicted to be true. Kerlinger (1973) also pointed out that the researcher should avoid extremely narrow questions, since their lack of generality dramatically reduces their value.

Problems in defining research questions.   Campbell, Daft, and Hulin (1982) identified major problems in research questions as currently used in organizational research. First, research methods too often determine the research question (e.g., "I just learned about path analysis, now what can I do with it?"). Second, too many research questions are based on faddish topics. Third, the research questions often involve specific methodologies and instrumentation, so that findings have little external validity or practical value. Fourth, the pressure of publishing exerts too much influence on the choice of research questions, as researchers cater to journal publication policies. Finally, the research questions are often based on some available data set, rather than on its conceptual importance. Campbell et al. (1982) believed that these problems have led to a situation where the importance of much research is questionable.

Improving quality of research questions.   Several strategies are available for improving the quality of research questions. Campbell et al. (1982) interviewed a sample of organizational researchers to find out what personal strategies they had used in research later evaluated as important or unimportant. Six recommendations emerged. First, high quality research comes from active involvement in real organizations. Second, significant research results from investigator interest, resolve, and efforts, rather than expedience or profit. Third, significant research projects were chosen based on intuition, not logic or certainty of publication. Fourth, important research begins with confusion and ambiguity, risk taking, and communication with others about the issue. Logic and certainty are the result of high quality research, not precursors. Fifth, quality organizational research focuses on real problems with practical utility. Sixth, most "milestones" of organizational research have developed from substantive theory originating outside the field of organizational psychology so researchers with links to other knowledge areas are in a position to make major contributions.

Specific practical suggestions for improving quality of research questions have also been developed. Researchers can expand the knowledge base through teaching a course, writing a proposal, or preparing a review paper on a given topic. The variety of one's experience can also be increased by attending conferences and conventions, maintaining interdisciplinary contact, being involved in projects in real organizations, or during an exploratory case study. Individual and group strategies for improving creativity of research questions include brainstorming, nominal groups, Delphi technique, Synectics, creative confrontation, etc., all techniques of common use in OD but rarely applied to the process of generating research questions.

Facet analysis. A strategy of potential value in improving the conceptual rigor of research questions is facet analysis (Foa, 1965; Guttman, 1954; Runkel & McGrath, 1972). Facet analysis structures a conceptual domain and allows the generation of research questions based on that simplified conceptual structure. White and Mitchell (1976) have provided a preliminary facet analysis of OD and although they did not use this facet analysis for generating research questions, they used it to organize OD research. Determining the facets, or dimensions, of a construct allows the researcher to divide the facet into mutually exclusive categories for classifying objects in a domain. It also provides a basis for determining the logical relations among elements of the facet and among the facets so that a conceptual structure is developed.

Facet analysis may be particularly valuable to case meta-analysis. First, facet analysis is an organizing strategy useful in situations where a varied combination of things with mixed properties exist, as occurs in the case study of team-building literature, for example. Second, facet analysis goes beyond its organization function to specify relationships between facets and between categories within facets, which may be of direct value in developing testable research questions for case meta-analysis research. Third, a well-done facet analysis provides a basis later for a rigorous coding scheme to test the hypotheses. The reader is referred to the general literature on facet analysis (Foa, 1958; Foa, 1965; Foa, 1966; Guttman, 1954; Runkel & McGrath, 1972; McGrath, 1967) and to specific examples of facet analysis (Mudd, 1985; Payne, Fineman, & Wall, 1976; White & Mitchell, 1976) for direct assistance in accomplishing a facet analysis.

White and Mitchell's (1976) facet analysis identified three facets subdivided into elements: The recipient of change (individual, group, organization), level of expected change (conceptual, behavioral, procedural, structural), and relationships involved in change (intrapersonal, interpersonal, intragroup, intergroup, organizational). Both authors independently applied these facets and elements to the OD literature, using discussion to resolve disagreements. The initial interrater reliability (percent agreement) ranged from 90.3 percent to 96.0 percent. The facet classification scheme was used to describe the OD literature and to criticize OD research design, but basic relationship tests between the independent variables and success outcome variables were not accomplished, although the facet classification scheme was applied to both independent and dependent variables.

Bullock and Lawler (1985) model. Bullock and Lawler (1985) provided a conceptual framework that has been directly used to generate research questions for meta-analysis of OD cases. They proposed that the outcomes of an OD intervention could be understood in terms of three sets of factors. Structural factors, answering the question "What was done?" include committees formed, workshops and development experiences used, specific changes in reward structures, meetings, and special events. Implementation factors, answering the question "How was it done?" include the use of OD consultants, the model of intervention, the target of the intervention, the length of planning and development time, and the amount of employee involvement in design. Situational factors, answering the question "In what situation was this done?" include such factors as size of the organization, union status, business climate, and type of technology. These three sets of factors can be directly translated to testable hypotheses using case meta-analysis.

Home-grown models. Rudimentary theories of OD are already available for understanding the pattern of results across case studies. These models exist in the minds of practitioners who expect certain outcomes from their work. One way to develop a theory of a particular intervention is an in-depth interview of someone who has worked with the intervention for several years. Their implicit models of what process leads to what results can be uncovered by the repetitive childlike, "Why?" Implicit models are also frequently mentioned when interpreting the data from a given case study documentation. Again, there is potential for significant researcher-practitioner interaction in developing concepts and hypotheses, conjectures and theories of OD processes.

Gainsharing application of Step 1. To apply case meta-analysis to the gainsharing literature we used the Bullock and Lawler (1985) framework because this particular approach to research questions had a dual emphasis on theory and practice. In our experience, there has been an over-emphasis in OD research on "what" and inadequate emphasis on "how." The literature on OD practice consistently emphasizes the importance of the process, even to the point of defining the OD field in terms of the process, but the research has consistently ignored process factors. In the gainsharing situation, since we needed models that would direct both theory and practice, we chose the framework that allowed the analysis of structural and situational factors as well as factors of implementation process. The facet analysis application also has great potential for OD because of its consistent simplification of a wide body of literature into a relatively small number of testable facets and would encourage future users of the case meta-analysis method to strongly consider the facet analysis approach. For one example of the application of the facet analysis approach to developing an OD method in education, see Mudd (1985).

Summary of Step 1. The first step of case meta-analysis is the most important. All future steps rely on the adequacy of this first critical step. Rather than code convenience variables, we suggest that case meta-analysis researchers develop testable hypotheses that are part of an overall model of the change process for that given intervention. To do so, one can use facet analysis, grounded theories of the OD process, or even interviews with OD practitioners, but in each case the hypothesis should be specific, should propose a relationship between two or more variables, and should be testable. Although theory development has been under-emphasized in past meta-analysis research, as well as in most social science research, we think it is an area of utmost importance to the future success of the case meta-analysis method and to developing cumulative knowledge in OD.

Step 2. Set Criteria for Study Inclusion

The criteria used to determine the set of studies used in a meta-analysis are very similar to the criteria used in traditional literature reviews, with some important exceptions. In OD, literature reviewers have been unusually explicit about the criteria used to select studies for their review. The reader is referred to these reviews for specific examples (see DeMeuse & Liebowitz, 1981, p. 359–60; Margulies, Wright, & Scholl, 1977; p. 431; Porras & Berg, 1978, p. 153–55; Woodman & Sherwood, 1980, p. 169).

The primary problem of setting criteria for study selection is determining the theoretical domains within which the research hypotheses are theorized to be true. Using all studies that fit a well defined conceptual domain allows the researcher to draw conclusions about research questions that apply to that entire domain. In OD, the domain may range from the entire field of OD (e.g., Golembiewski, Proehl, & Sink, 1982) to particular types of organizations (e.g., Golembiewski, Proehl, & Sink, 1981), to particular dependent variables (e.g., Nicholas, 1982), to a particular type of OD intervention (e.g., Bullock & Tubbs, 1983; DeMeuse & Liebowitz, 1981; Woodman & Sherwood, 1980), or to a class of interventions such as human processual interventions (e.g., Porras & Berg, 1978). The important concern is that the domain within which the research questions are to be tested be clearly defined. Researchers should be acutely aware that strictly speaking, any generalizations are limited to this domain.

Three criteria are explicitly excluded from meta-analysis, although they are often used in literature reviews. First, methodological rigor criteria are not used. Literature reviews are often limited to research studies fitting the reviewer's subjective criteria of what constitutes rigorous research. The operating assumption is that sound knowledge can only come from good research, so poor research should be exempted from reviews. Meta-analysis research does not accept this assumption a priori and includes all studies, regardless of whether or not they meet subjective or objective criteria of methodological rigor, so long as they fit within a well-defined conceptual domain. Any presumption by the reviewer that rigor and results are associated is converted to coded variables and tested statistically (e.g., Bullock & Svyantek, 1985; Woodman & Wayne, 1985).

Second, publication status criteria are not used. This assumption is compatible with the rigor criterion assumption and is rejected for the same reason. The operating assumption, compatible with the rigor assumption above is that ''The best studies get published anyway, so including unpublished studies is basically a waste of time.'' Literature reviews usually exclude dissertations and unpublished studies, but in meta-analysis, systematic efforts are made to secure all documented studies in the domain, including dissertations and unpublished studies. Again, any assumption that publication status affects results should be subjected to explicit testing within the meta-analysis.

Third, time is not a relevant criterion for selected studies. Some literature reviews exclude older studies, based on the operating assumption that the research area is making progress, so that recent research is the best research upon which to base conclusions. Again, meta-analysis includes all studies within a content domain, regardless of the year they were done or published, and any assumption that recency affects results is explicitly tested. A meta-analysis of the relationship between class size and educational achievement, for example, spanned a literature of about 100 years (Smith & Glass, 1977).

The primary purpose of carefully defining the theoretical domain is to provide explicit criteria for inclusion or exclusion of a given study in the research. If these criteria are not explicitly stated, then the sample used to determine the results comes under serious question (see Bullock & Svyantek, 1983). In OD, explicitly defining the criteria for study inclusion may be difficult. DeMeuse and Liebowitz (1981), for example, developed an operating definition of team-building for their research and excluded some studies that did not fit this content domain, even though the studies used the label of team-building (p. 358–360). Such an approach is an important step toward defining content domains within OD based on theoretical considerations rather than based on the use of a common label with or without common meaning.

Gainsharing application for Step 2. In applying the method to the gainsharing case literature, Step 2 was not as obvious as it would first seem. Our experience for the gainsharing literature was similar to that found by reviewers of team building, survey feedback, etc. The OD literature has not emphasized the strict use and interpretation of key concepts, so terms are used inconsistently in the literature. We expect readers to encounter the same situation we did and would propose a similar solution: define carefully in advance exactly what is considered as the intervention. This requires a clear definition of the intervention concept and a comparative definition so that closely related concepts can be distinguished. In the case of gainsharing, we were familiar with the literature and able to distinguish gainsharing plans from incentive plans, simple profit-sharing plans, suggestion systems, employee involvement programs, management bonus schemes, and the like. This step of the process is most helpful in clarifying to the researcher, and potentially to the field, exactly what the intervention is and is not. To decide what is and is not team-building, gainsharing, and survey feedback, one must define specific criteria that must be met for the intervention to be considered as part of that particular class of interventions. This theoretical and systematic definition is relatively difficult for many interventions.

Readers have help here from the several typologies of organization development (see Miles & Schmuck, 1983; Blake & Mouton, 1969). Although many typologies of organization development have defined the intervention classes, they are often not defined in such a way as to allow an exclusive assignment of a given case of OD to one category. It is certainly appropriate for a given case to, for example, have both team building and survey feedback, so it is not necessary that cases be assigned to mutually exclusive categories. It is necessary, however, for the assignment of a given case to a given class of interventions be made in an unambiguous way.

The integrity of the definition gives a foundation for developing a theoretical model of the effects of gainsharing, or of team building, etc. Case meta-analysis studies should research a theoretical domain, *not* a group of studies that used the same label.

It is important to remember in interpreting results that generalizations are limited to this theoretical domain. We expect the precision to make for more powerful hypotheses and more powerful results, and to clarify the extent of the generalizability of the findings. This is a key step, by no means obvious, and worth the additional effort required to define the intervention precisely and to distinguish it from similar interventions.

Summary of Step 2.   Research questions are tested within a defined domain. In case meta-analysis, the definition of the content domain is converted to a set of specific criteria for selecting studies. The domain may be a particular class of interventions or a particular example of an intervention, particular types of organizations, or even particular dependent variables. The important issue here is that the domain within which the research questions are tested be clearly defined, so that interpretations of results can be limited to this domain. In setting the domain it is important to select studies based on criteria rather than the use of a common label, since everything that is labeled "team-building" does not fall within specified criteria of an OD team building process. Similarly, it is important to not include criteria for the age of the study, the methodological rigor of the study, or the publication status of the study. Rather than limiting the case meta-analysis research to good studies, recent studies, or published studies, available studies are collected and any hypothesis within which rigor or age affects the pattern of results is converted to specific codes and tested through the case meta-analysis method.

Step 3.   Collect Relevant Studies

Once the specific inclusion criteria have been defined and documented the studies must be collected. There is a wide literature in OD, so the collection process is sometimes time-consuming. The sources are the same as for traditional literature reviews: bibliographies, books, computer-based and manual searches of relevant journals, computer indexes, cross-referencing of reference lists, and interpersonal communication. Porras and Berg (1978) provided detailed documentation regarding their search procedures and included many relevant references for bibliographies, etc., in OD. By contrast, Nicholas (1982) provided no documentation. In meta-analysis, it is important that the search procedures be well documented. Hunter et al. (1982, p. 146–154) have given several suggestions regarding the use of computer indexes and the use of personal queries and the reader is referred to this discussion.

Reviewers of past research become acutely aware of the inadequacies of the reporting standards, yet often fail to fully report their own work. It is critical that careful descriptions of the literature search process be documented and published (Hunter et al., 1982, p. 153). Not only does such a process allow readers to judge the representativeness of the studies included, but it also provides the strongest possible base upon which future analysis can work.

The most important resource by far for OD cases is the set of 574 cases analyzed by Golembiewski, Proehl, and Sink (1981, 1982) and documented in Proehl (1980). The comprehensive search extended from 1945–1980 and included seven specialized bibliographies, computer searches, review of 88 journals, over 100 books, and personal letters to 50 change agents requesting case information. Case meta-analysis researchers can use this extenstive data base to good advantage, since it refers to case studies and sources of case studies such as OD bibliographies.

Gainsharing application of Step 3.   This step was more difficult than it normally should have been because much of the gainsharing literature has not been incorporated into the mainstream of the OD literature, so that most cases found had never been referenced in OD bibliographies or journals. In our study, we relied extensively on the use of a professional network of contacts, who were both authors and implementers of the gainsharing process. Since the first author had implemented gainsharing plans, many internal documents, gainsharing plan booklets, and the like were acquired that would not normally be available to people outside the company. Table 1 shows the final list of our sources for gainsharing case studies. This list may cover a wider range than many other OD interventions and we suggest that other case meta-analysis researchers similarly report the sources of their case study information.

In several cases the companies requested anonymity for their site, even though they were happy to share the results of their experiences with us. Our recommendation is for the case meta-analysis researcher to systematically contact other professionals in the field, including those who had implemented the intervention, and people at the case study organizations. In our experiences, managers in OD case studies are more responsive to requests if the researcher has demonstrated

Table 1.   Examples of Information Sources for Case Meta-
Analysis from Gainsharing Application

Type of Information Source for OD Case Studies	Number	Percentage
Articles from journals, serials, etc.	29	20.1
Book and monograph chapters, sections, appendices, etc.	30	20.8
Collections of case study descriptions	26	18.1
Internal company documents	24	16.7
Theses and dissertations	18	12.5
Speeches and presentations	12	8.3
Newspaper articles	5	3.5
Total	144[a]	100.0

Note:

[a]Data are from the case meta-analysis example of Bullock and Tubbs (1983), which studied 33
cases of gainsharing application. The number of information sources is greater than the number of
cases because some well-known cases had been reported in more than one source.

some involvement in the field and is willing to share the results of the past work
as well as any results that may come from the study.

To illustrate some of the difficulties one can encounter in collecting literature,
consider the following. In one article, a series of Master's theses and Ph.D.
dissertations at MIT were referenced. Although recent theses and dissertations
are normally available through University Microfilm, these particular theses and
dissertations were not available. To acquire them, the first author had to travel to
Boston and spend a day in the warehouses of MIT, sorting through archives to
physically find volumes over 30 years old. These volumes provided a rich source
of information accessible only through diligence. We would expect that future
applications of the case meta-analysis method will be able to use Proehl's (1980)
dissertation documenting the OD literature through 1980.

Another practical suggestion that emerged from our gainsharing application
relates to the final tally of cases included in the dataset. In our application, we
encountered two separate instances where organizations we had coded as separate organizations were in fact the same as anonymous organizations reported
elsewhere. We determined this based on idiosyncratic details in the case descriptions and close familiarity with some of the gainsharing cases. Avoiding double-
counting is important since it biases the results, and in our experience, although
the amount of bias is small, it is important to preserve the independence of the
cases to allow for strict interpretation of the statistical results. Thus, the case
meta-analysis researcher should handle anonymous cases carefully. This careful
handling also relates to the results, since vicarious identification of an anony-

mous case prevents the publication of data for an organization that wished to remain anonymous.

Summary of Step 3. After the domain criteria have been clarified, the case studies can be located. In addition to the traditional use of computer indexes, bibliographies, and reference lists, case meta-analysis researchers should use the informal college of researchers, convention presentations, and personal correspondence via phone or letter. An important resource is Proehl (1980), who documented 574 case studies of OD. Case meta-analysis researchers can supplement case studies gained through the traditional publication outlets by collecting internal company documents, practitioner reports, in-house memos, etc. In calculating the number of independent case studies done, researchers need to confirm as well as possible that anonymous cases are not duplicates of other anonymous cases or duplicates of other identified cases. This can be done through the informal college network and by extensive cross-checking of idiosyncratic characteristics of the case study.

Step 4. Develop a Coding Scheme

Once the studies have been collected and any ambiguities in applying the inclusion criteria resolved, the studies must be converted to variables for analysis. To do this requires a coding scheme. In essence, a coding scheme is a transformation process of converting some reality (such as a research literature) to a set of numbers. This transformation process invariably involves a loss of meaning. The better the coding scheme, the less the loss of meaning. Thus, it is critical in meta-analysis that the coding scheme be developed carefully.

General principles. A coding scheme is a set of decision rules. These decision rules explicitly define for a rater how to convert some information to a variable code. In our experiences with coding schemes, we have found two general principles to apply. First, simpler is better. Three clearly defined coding categories are vastly superior theoretically and empirically to 5 or 10 vague categories. Not only are they more meaningful theoretically, but they also provide better results in terms of reliability and more powerful tests of the hypotheses. In general, we have found ourselves forced to use simpler coding schemes rather than more complex schemes. Therefore, we strongly recommend that meta-analysis researchers begin with simple schemes and only make them complex if the research studies support finer discriminations. If raters can reliably and validly discriminate only three levels of some variable (for example, "intensity of an intervention") no more valid information will be obtained by adding more categories.

Second, explicit written documentation is necessary. The coding schemes should be simple but the documentation should be thorough. There is a strong tendency among coding scheme developers to attempt to use relatively simple rules without regard for the ambiguities that arise. Raters become frustrated from attempting to provide a reliable and valid code for an ambiguous situation that does not fit the simple decision rule. Explicit criteria are, therefore, needed to enable raters to apply the coding scheme in many special situations that arise. These ambiguities arise from the variety of approaches used in any research, particularly OD, and because there are vast differences in reporting style and thoroughness.

These decision rules should be documented and available for those attempting to understand and/or replicate the research in the future. Terpstra (1981), for example, used a very simple coding scheme for coding the methodological rigor of OD studies, yet when Bullock and Svyantek (1983) applied the coding scheme dozens of ambiguities were found. Woodman and Wayne (1985) reported similar coding difficulties. In light of these conflicting results, decision rules should state as specifically as possible what rating should be used for what situation.

Facet analysis. Facet analysis is one potential technique for developing coding schemes. Facet analysis helps to determine the conceptually distinct categories of individual codes. These categories are then translated directly into numerical codes. The contribution of facet analysis is in the conceptual rigor it imposes on the researcher to define carefully and systematically what the theoretical dimensions are and what the distinct levels on this dimension are. Thus facet analysis can be helpful in avoiding the rather typical situation where a quick and dirty rating scheme is used, only to find poor reliability and poor results.

Insufficient information. It is important to include a potential rating of "insufficient information" for every variable. This code means that the rater has analyzed the documentation and reached the conclusion that insufficient information exists for the application of the decision rules. Such a code is not a missing data code in a traditional sense that no judgment was made, as occurs when a survey respondent skips a question. Since case meta-analysis relies on documented case evidence, there should never be a situation involving missing data as a lack of judgment (as when a rater simply omits a variable), although there may be frequent cases where the rater makes a judgment that insufficient information exists in the documentation for applying the decision rules. The differentiation of these two types of missing data has important implications for the calculation of reliability as discussed in a later section. Our experience indicates that the number of cases where insufficient information exists can be reduced by developing special decision rules for cases of partial information and for cases where reasonable estimates can be generated given information in the documentation (see Glass et al., 1981, Appendix B, for an example of the use of estimation procedures in meta-analysis). If nonjudgment missing data exist in a case meta-analysis situation, it is simple and necessary to complete the omission, since the documentation and decision rules are readily available.

Gainsharing application of Step 4.   Our application of this step was straight-forward. We were coding a variety of journalistic styles, ranging from newspaper articles to speeches to theses to full case study descriptions to in-house booklets and memos and documents, so we decided to use the simplest possible scheme unless we were fully confident that the finer levels of discrimination could be validly and reliably applied. A full list of our coding levels and our coding measures is shown in Table 2.

Consider, for example, coding a variable called "labor-management rela-

Table 2.   Examples of Coding Rules for Case Meta-Analysis
from Gainsharing Application

Variables	Codes	Decision Rules
Structural Variables		
Involvement structure	0	No formal employee involvement system used.
	1	Used a formal employee involvement system.
	9	Insufficient data for coding.
		Additional decision rules for special cases:
		1. Organizations using only a communication system for reporting financial results were coded as 0 for no formal system, since employee involvement here was interpreted as involvement in decision-making.
Payout period	0	Used a period longer than a month, including quarterly, semiannually, or annually, as basis for calculating and distributing financial gains.
	1	Used a month period for calculating and distributing financial gains.
	9	Insufficient data for coding.
		Additional decision rules for special cases:
		1. Organizations that used both monthly and annual payouts (through a reserve) were coded a 1 since the payout period was interpreted here as the frequency of getting performance information rewarded through a cash bonus.
Implementation Variables		
Employee involvement in design	0	No employee involvement in design. (That is, designed by outsider and/or by top management.)
	1	Used employee involvement in design process.
	9	Insufficient information for coding.
		Additional decision rules for coding special cases:
		1. Organizations that allowed employees to approve the plan through an all-employee vote prior to implementation were coded as 1 since employees were an integral part of the decision process.

(*continued*)

Table 2.   (Cont.)

Variables	Codes	Decision Rules
Use of outside facilitator	0	No outside facilitator used during design and implementation.
	1	Used an outside facilitator during design and implementation.
	9	Insufficient information for coding. Additional decision rules for coding special cases: 1. Organizations that consulted with an outside expert during the initial exploration only were coded as 0 since the interpretation here was that the process of design and implementation are important independently of the content knowledge.
Situational Variables		
Managerial Style	0	Autocratic management style.
	1	Paternalistic or participative style.
	9	Insufficient information for coding. Additional decision rules for special cases: 1. Management style indicated in case study anecdotes was coded only if the anecdote was described as representative.
Union status	0	Workforce was not unionized.
	1	Workforce was unionized.
	9	Insufficient information for coding. Additional decision rules for special cases: 1. If the workforce was partially unionized, the organization was coded as 1, since the issues around union approval, bargaining and arbitration occur independently of the proportion of the workforce represented by the union.
Success Outcomes		
Program retention	0	Program was discontinued as of most recent documentation.
	1	Program was being continued as of most recent documentation.
	9	Insufficient information for coding.
Program impact	0–5	This variable was not a simple coded variable. It was the sum of five other coded variables, each an area of potential impact coded 0–1.
	9	Insufficient information for coding.

tions.'' We believed that gainsharing implementations will be more likely to be successful in situations where labor-management relations were collaborative. Many detailed measures are available for assessing labor-management relations (see Bullock, Macy, & Mirvis, 1983), but we chose to begin with the simple codes of collaborative or not collaborative. Even then, one can encounter many special cases: an article may report one critical incident only tangentially related to labor-management relations. For example, the articles may report a mixed picture, such as a long strike plus survey data indicating cooperation, or there may be a situation where cooperative labor-management relations deteriorate into competitive dynamics. A case could show labor-management relations are collaborative most of the time, but competitive around negotiation, or there may be two unions involved, one of which is collaborative, and the other competitive. Or, in some cases, labor-management in one department are cooperative and another area of the plant is not. We did not encounter all these special cases in the application, but include them here to indicate the importance of clear, specific decision rules in applying the coding scheme. These coding schemes should be determined in advance as far as it is possible, but it is impossible to anticipate all the special cases that arise. When the special cases arise, additional decision rules are necessary (see Bullock & Svyantek, 1985) so that the coders, readers, and future researchers can validate the coding scheme.

Summary of Step 4.   Once the research questions have been identified, the study inclusion criteria specified, and the studies collected, the studies can then be coded. Developing an adequate coding scheme is an important link in the case meta-analysis chain. Coding schemes have been used in a variety of research methods in the past, often in an unrigorous and unsystematic way. We recommend the use of simple coding schemes with explicit documentation on the decision rules. We also recommend the inclusion of an "insufficient information" rating as part of the coding scheme. This is not missing data in the traditional sense, but allows the computation of the proportion of case studies that do not provide adequate information, which can be useful for improving future case study documentation.

In developing a coding scheme, the basic principle is to keep it simple. Our experience in assessing various coding schemes indicates that coding scheme reliability is more a function of the quality of the decision rules than the quality of the raters. We discuss measurement quality in terms of "interrater reliability" but in actuality, we are assessing "decision rule reliability," that is, the quality of the decision rules. Our experience indicates that if the coding scheme is carefully prepared and thoroughly documented through decision rules, trained raters will make the same judgments given the same documentation. The quality problem is not in the raters (see the next step), but in the decision rule documentation. Rigorous coding schemes are not only important for the validity of the case meta-analysis results, but are also the basis for insuring replicability of any results obtained. In general, we recommend keeping the category simple and the documentation thorough.

Step 5.   Code the Studies

Training and practice.   Once the decision rules have been formulated, the actual coding can commence. Each rater should have a general working knowledge of the literature (so that jargon and commonly used procedures are understood). Before beginning the rating process, the raters should be trained in the use of the decision rules, and each rater should receive a copy of the written documentation of all decision rules. Training and practice are important. The rating process can be frustrating and time-consuming and raters need to be prepared with patience and diligence. Too often, frustrated raters begin minimizing time spent on coding and the researchers pay the price in terms of inaccurate ratings, low reliability estimates, and no findings, or even worse—invalid findings. Careful reading of all available documentation and adherence to the decision rules is necessary for validity of the ratings and reproducibility of the results, a key aspect of the meta-analysis process. The greater the clarity of the decision rules, the less training and practice are needed before raters become comfortable with the coding schemes. By rating a case excluded from, but similar to, the final sample, raters can gain experience in applying the decision rules without affecting ultimate reliability of the actual sample. Coders can do this individually and then compare their results with other raters as a way of gaining confidence in themselves and the coding scheme and clarifying any ambiguous instructions in the coding scheme.

Number of raters.   How many raters to use is an issue worth mentioning. It is not possible to assess the reliability of ratings using traditional psychometric procedures without multiple raters, so at least two raters are needed for most meta-analyses. The normal practice is to use two or three raters. Traditional psychometric principles imply that the greater the number of raters, the higher the quality of the pooled ratings. In our experience, this is frequently not the case, and many raters are not needed if the coding scheme is carefully developed. We have encountered situations where users of coding schemes have attempted to use multiple raters as a way of compensating for poorly defined decision rules, and we propose that this should be avoided. A major logistical problem of multiple raters arises since ratings are time-consuming; therefore, the use of more than three raters is seldom if ever, necessary for meta-analysis. In fact, if the decision rules are well documented at the beginning, two raters are probably adequate. If only two raters are used, we recommend that a third person be used to assist the process of resolving rater discrepancies, as described in a later section.

To code the studies, each rater should have a coding sheet with all variables. An example of a coding sheet is given in Cooper (1984, p. 33–34). The coding sheet should, in our opinion, contain only those variables that are to be used to test the hypotheses in the study. We disagree with Cooper's (1984) recommendation that "If the number of studies involved in the research review is small, it may not be necessary for the reviewer to have a well-formulated idea about what information to extract from reports before the literature search begins" (p. 30–31). We think the need for theory exists independently of the size of the literature. Rather than reading and re-reading the studies without prespecification of the hypotheses to be tested, as Cooper suggested for integrative research reviewers, case meta-analysis researchers should emphasize clear hypotheses and solid theory. This avoids the dynamic of searching for "interesting findings" without theoretical significance or relevance. It also avoids the major problem of post hoc selection of variables to report, which introduces significant but unknown bias into the results. This selection and reporting bias is discussed in the ninth step of the case meta-analysis process in this chapter.

Gainsharing application of Step 5. We did not encounter any special problems in coding the studies, beyond the issue of clarifying the decision rules for ambiguous cases discussed in the prior step. We used three raters, but found that three were not better than two. Our experience with this and other applications indicated that using multiple raters and averaging them did not clarify the decision rules for the measurement system and produced worse measures than having two or three coders with documentation for each code and a discussion resolving the discrepancies between each code.

One logistical note may be useful to some readers. We found it worthwhile to provide each rater with a complete set of all references organized into 3-hole binders. As we entered the numerical value in the coding sheet, we marked passages in the text that served as the basis of the rater's code. By checking, highlighting, etc., these passages with a quick abbreviation of the variable we were able to document the data actually used in the coding process, rather than relying on a "gut feeling" of the case. This ensured that the raters were rating specific passages in the available documentation rather than using an intuitive guess. We found that this process increased the accuracy of the rating process and greatly facilitated the verification of proper codes and the resolution of rating discrepancies later, since each rater was able to quickly reconstruct the passage upon which their rating was based. We also found this process to be highly superior to the typical method of having three, four, or more different people rate without documentation and using the average of the raters.

Summary of Step 5. In rating the studies with a prespecified coding scheme, trained raters should be used after practicing the coding scheme on studies not included in the final dataset. Because of the use of consensus coding resolution as discussed in the next section, we do not recommend that case meta-analysis researchers use multiple raters and simply take the average of the raters, but rather use two or three raters that are well-trained and carefully document the process of their decision. In our experience, if the decision rules are carefully developed, two well-trained raters are adequate.

Step 6. Assess Coding Quality

Whenever judgments are made by two or more raters, it is important to assess interrater reliability. Unfortunately, the pursuit of high reliability coefficients could become a dysfunctional end in itself for many research efforts (see Harris,

1963). Meta-analysis researchers should realize that obtaining adequate reliability is a necessary but not sufficient step in the process of producing a valid and meaningful data set. Other important steps in the process include developing specific decision rules for variable codes, and resolving the rating discrepancies that do occur, as we discuss in other sections.

Meta-analysis research relies on the reproducibility of ratings and results. This confirmation can be obtained by using multiple raters in the same study and by future researchers applying the same coding scheme. Measures of this reproducibility are thus very important in meta-analysis research. Unfortunately, the statistical literature on computing and interpreting interrater reliability is often confusing and inconsistent. To provide meta-analysis researchers with assistance in handling reliability issues, this section reviews (1) the key questions to answer in selecting the most appropriate reliability statistic, (2) interpretation of reliability statistics for categorical variables, (3) interpretation of reliability statistics for continuous variables, and (4) the handling of insufficient information codes and missing data.

Selection factors. The three most important factors to consider in choosing reliability coefficients are variable type, amount of variance in the data, and type of indicator needed. First, is the variable categorical or continuous? Categorical variables are assessed using statistics for discrete codes, while continuous variables are assessed using statistics that consider codes to be points on an underlying dimension. Second, how much variance is there in the analyzed data? If there is little variance among the possible codes, then statistics that adjust for chance will tend to underestimate the reliability of the ratings. Third, does the researcher desire a measure of agreement or a measure of covariance? Agreement statistics measure the extent to which raters use identical codes, while covariance statistics measure the extent to which the pattern of ratings is similar. For example, if one meta-analysis rater assessed the success of three OD interventions as 3, 4, and 5 on a scale of 1–5, while a second more skeptical rater rated the same interventions' success as 2, 3, and 4, respectively, there would be perfect disagreement, but perfect covariance. In the discussion that follows, we explain how the meta-analysis researcher can use these three factors to select the most appropriate statistic. Since the most crucial factor is the type of variable, we consider categorical variables separately from continuous variables.

Categorical variables. If the variable is coded into discrete categories, the three generally recommended reliability statistics are percent agreement, kappa, and weighted kappa (Burton, 1981; Cohen, 1968; Jones, Johnson, Butler, & Main, 1983). Percent agreement, the simple percentage of cases for which all raters used identical codes, is an intuitively appealing indicator of reliability for categorical variables, but it does have drawbacks. Percent of agreement can either over-estimate or under-estimate the reliability of the ratings (Jones et al., 1983). Overestimation can occur because there is no adjustment for chance agreements, which can occur when there are only a few categories and when ratings are concentrated in relatively few of the available categories. Underestimation can also occur for variables with many rating categories, since as the number of categories increases, there is a greater a priori chance for disagreement (Burton, 1981, p. 961).

Kappa (Cohen, 1960) and weighted kappa (Cohen, 1968) were developed to correct these problems. These two statistics adjust for chance agreement by utilizing the information in the marginals of the contingency table to calculate the expected or chance level of agreement. Kappa equals the percent agreement after possible agreement due to chance is eliminated (Cohen, 1968, p. 214). Weighted kappa makes the same adjustment, but also allows the researcher to indicate the degree of similarity between categories and weigh disagreements accordingly (Cohen, 1968, p. 215). For example, in assessing the technology of an organization implementing an OD program, the meta-analysis researcher using Marsh and Mannari's (1981) technology scale might weigh inconsistent ratings (for one organization) of custom technology and mass-production technology more heavily than inconsistent rating of large-batch and small-batch manufacturing technologies.

When three or more raters are used, special methods for using kappa are necessary, as discussed by Conger (1980) who reviewed procedures developed by Light (1971) and Fleiss (1971). Light's formulation is equivalent to the average pairwise kappa, while the exact Fleiss procedure adjusts the average pairwise kappas for pairwise chance agreements. If the covariance between the pairwise kappas and the pairwise chance agreement is zero, these two indices will be equivalent. In practice, Conger asserted that the two procedures will produce "nearly equivalent values" (p. 328). Uebersax (1982) pointed out that the exact Fleiss procedure would not be correct if each pair of raters did not rate the same number of objects, and suggested a more general method to deal with this issue. However, since all raters would be rating the same sample of cases in a meta-analysis, this would not pose a problem. Alternatively, as Hubert (1977) suggested, these formulations would be altered to represent, for example, true three-way agreement, rather than averaged pairwise agreement. We think the most generally appropriate and interpretable procedure is Light's (1971) formulation. As it reduces to the average kappa, it would be easily comparable across situations involving two or more raters.

Both kappa and weighted kappa have their problems as well. Both assume that each rating is done independently of all other ratings, (Jones et al., 1983) and that enough variance exists in the data that observations are equally spread across the available categories (Burton, 1981, p. 957). Kappa becomes increasingly undependable in situations where coding (correct or not) is concentrated in a few categories. In these situations, percent agreement can be very high, with kappa near zero. Overall (1980) stated that this problem can reduce the meaningfulness of kappa to the point that it is useless. Thus, a zero kappa does not indicate unreliability. In the gainsharing example, we assessed the reliability of rating 34 case studies for the use of an outside interventionist and 32 of the ratings agreed there was an outside interventionist with disagreement on the two cases, so the percent agreement would be 94 percent, but kappa equaled .00. Jones et al. (1983) and Burton (1981) both concluded that in such cases, percent agreement is the only accurate measure available.

Since there are no clear guidelines in the literature on what constitutes "too little variance" or "too few" categories for properly using kappa, it is not possible to precisely specify when kappa (or weighted kappa) should be used and when percent agreement should be used. We recommend that meta-analysis researchers compute both percent agreement and kappa (or weighted kappa, if appropriate) and interpret them carefully, keeping in mind the number of possible categories and the amount of variance across the categories. Since most meta-analysis research uses relatively simple coding schemes with two or three possible codes, and since conventional wisdom in the field may lead to nonrandom patterns across the codes (such as 90 percent of OD cases using outside interventionists instead of the 50/50 pattern that would happen randomly), we expect that percent agreement will usually be the most appropriate statistic in assessing the reliability of categorical variables in meta-analysis research. Percent agreement also provides action-relevant information to the meta-analysis researcher, since each instance of disagreement should be discussed and resolved.

In our experience, trained raters should be able to generate identical codes in at least three-quarters of the cases they jointly analyze, if the decision rules are clearly specified. Thus we suggest a general rule of thumb of 75 percent interrater agreement as indicating a reasonably precise initial set of decision rules. Failure to achieve at least 75 percent interrater agreement does not mean that the variables should be discarded, but rather that thinking should be clarified and the decision rules for coding the documentation should be made more precise. This allows hypothesis testing using variable codes that are both meaningful and reproducible.

Continuous variables.   For continuous variables, the most widely used reliability procedures are the average pairwise correlation, calculated using Fisher's r to z transformation (Hays, 1973), and the intraclass correlation coefficient, or ICC (Ebel, 1951; Shrout & Fleiss, 1979). Although the average pairwise correlation has historically been the most popular means of assessing interrater reliability for continuous variables, it has some drawbacks, as does a reliability measure based on the average correlation—Cronbach's coefficient alpha (Cronbach, 1951). First, they are measures of covariation and not of agreement (Jones et al., 1983), which means that the average correlation, and thus alpha, will be high if the ratings have a similar pattern even if the ratings are not the same. For case meta-analysis research, this is a serious problem since the process of converging on the most valid and replicable data-matrix requires identifying all discrepancies in ratings, not just computing pattern similarities. In case meta-analysis research, measures of agreement are more important and useful than measures of covariance.

The intra-class correlation coefficient can be such a measure of agreement. The ICC calculation, which is based on an ANOVA table, is done somewhat differently depending on three factors (Shrout & Fleiss, 1979): (1) whether all raters rate all cases or whether raters rate different cases, (2) whether mean differences between raters are important, (which means that raters would be considered as a random effect), and (3) whether individual or average ratings are used. For meta-analysis, we recommend that all raters rate all cases, that mean differences be considered important, and that the raters' individual rating be used. This combination means that the form of ICC labled ICC (2,1) in Shrout and Fleiss (1979, p. 423) be used. This version of the ICC is a measure of agreement. Some other versions, for example ICC (3,1) and ICC (3,k), are measures of covariation. In its (3,k) form, the ICC is equivalent to coefficient alpha. These latter versions of the ICC assume that judges are a fixed effect.

By designating raters as a random effect, discrepancies between raters (between-rater variance) are treated as error in calculating the ICC (Ebel, 1951, p. 411; Jones et al., 1983; Shrout & Fleiss, 1979, p. 423). This is an important point, since treating raters as a random effect means that the experimenter views the raters as a random sample from the population of potential raters. The alternative would be that raters was a fixed effect, as in ICC (3,k), meaning that the raters used were the only ones of interest. Since we are concerned with generating the most valid set of ratings possible, and would hope that the obtained ratings would generalize to another set of raters, we are clearly assuming that raters are a random factor. This highlights another advantage of ICC (2,1) over measures of covariance: in calculating the average correlation coefficient or coefficient alpha, the researcher does not have the option of including the between-rater variance in the error term, thus a fixed effect model is implicitly assumed.

A lack of variance across the variable codes adversely affects these coefficients, as it did kappa and weighted kappa. If a correlational measure is used, the researcher can correct for restriction of range following Guilford (1965). Some researchers have treated continuous measures as though they were categorical (e.g., Jenkins, Nadler, Lawler, & Cammann, 1975) and computed percent agreement. Bartko (1976) believed that covariation measures are never appropriate for computing the reliability of raters.

For those wishing to use an ICC statistic for computing interrater reliability for continuous variables, we recommend ICC (2,1). If this reliability statistic is used, it should be supplemented with percent agreement, which reports the proportion of discrepant codes and which is most useful in improving reliability through the decision rules. Percent agreement is the key reliability statistic because it is the acid test of the extent to which different raters generated the same ratings given the same documentation and decision rules.

Missing data. When calculating reliability estimates for a variable, researchers often exclude cases for which one or more raters coded a missing value. We think this practice should not be followed in case meta-analysis. Typically, a missing value indicates that a subject did not respond to a question or a stimulus, and thus no information is available for analysis. Excluding such a case from the reliability analysis of an attitude scale might be justifiable; however, when estimating categorical interrater reliability of documented case studies, indicating that sufficient information is not available is as important a judgment as is any other code. There should be no missing data in meta-analysis, at least in the traditional sense that missing data means no data. That is, "insufficient information" is a legitimate code for a rater to use, and thus one code of "insufficient information" and another of "yes" is no more or less of a rating discrepancy than would be codes of "yes" and "no." Properly done, a meta-analysis variable should never have missing data although it may often be the case that insufficient information exists. A missing data code means that a rater did not make a judgment (i.e., no rating exists), while an insufficient information code indicates that a judgment was made. This is not a trivial difference, since it means that all cases should be used in assessing coefficients of reliability. This will usually produce lower reliability estimates than if missing cases are excluded, but we believe that a more realistic estimate of rater agreement will be obtained. This means, for example, that if all raters coded a set of cases as insufficient information, then perfect agreement would exist, and interrater reliability would be 1.0 for these cases on this variable. In our view, the primary purpose of these analyses is to determine the amount of interrater agreement as a basis for assessing measurement quality and resolving discrepancies. Table 3 shows that the extent of insufficient information in our gainsharing example was usually in the 10–20 percent range. One exception to this pattern was managerial style, which was not documented most of the time.

When computing a reliability estimate for a continuous measure, missing values must be treated differently. There is no way to quantify a missing value so that it can be used in the reliability analyses except when using percent agreement. Therefore, cases for which missing data exists have to be excluded from ICC or other reliability computations. However, the researcher should acknowledge that if any cases are excluded from the analyses for this reason, the resulting coefficient will be an overestimate of the true reliability for that measure (since some raters' disagreements are effectively being ignored). Thus we suggest that percent agreement be used as the primary reliability index for all case meta-analysis ratings.

Table 3. Examples of Distributions and Extent of Insufficient Information in Gainsharing Application of Case Meta-Analysis

	Coded 0		Coded 1		Coded 9	
Variable and Short Form of Codes[a]	*n*	*%*	*n*	*%*	*n*	*%*
Structural Factors						
Involvement structure (0 = no, 1 = yes)	3	9	24	73	6	18
Payout period (0 = longer than month, 1 = month)	2	6	28	85	3	9
Implementation Factors						
Employee involvement in design (0 = no, 1 = yes)	4	12	22	67	7	21
Use of outside facilitator (0 = no, 1 = yes)	3	9	24	73	6	18
Situational Factors						
Managerial style (0 = autocratic, 1 = participative)	8	24	3	9	22	67
Union status (0 = nonunion, 1 = union)	6	18	22	67	5	15
Success Outcomes						
Program retention (0 = discontinued, 1 = continued)	11	33	22	67	0	0
Program impact (0 = no impact, 1-5 = amount of impact)	0	0	33[b]	100[b]	0	0

Notes:

[a]A short form of the code is used here as a mnemonic. The reader is referred to Table 2 for a full description. For all variables, codes of 9 meant insufficient information.

[b]This entry includes all cases with a sum of 1–5, indicating that the case study description reported improvement in at least one of the five impact dimensions.

Gainsharing application of Step 6. Our gainsharing application of case meta-analysis had both categorical and continuous variables. For the categorical variables, like union-nonunion status, we calculated and reported both kappa and percent agreement, but used percent agreement in our decision-making regarding the reliability of the decision rule documentation. For continuous variables like size (number of employees), we calculated and reported percent agreement and ICC (2,1) and again relied on percent agreement in making reliability decisions.

Table 4 shows initial coding reliability of the example variables in our gainsharing case meta-analysis. The consensus process described in the next step was followed with our final interrater reliability of 100 percent agreement, so Table 4 shows initial coding reliability, not the reliability of the measures used in the actual data analysis. Noting the differences between initial and final reliability is important since some meta-analysis procedures use formulas that adjust final results for attenuation (lack of reliability). We found that more explicit documentation was necessary for each variable, particularly for the process variables that we coded. Process variables (like employee involvement in design) were not as simple as stating union-nonunion status or number of employees but involved a summary judgment based on several bits of information about how the process unfolded. Another factor hurting our initial reliability was the use of multiple

Table 4.   Examples of Coding Reliability found in
Gainsharing Application of Case Meta-Analysis

Variables	Percent Agreement[a]	Kappa
Structural Factors		
Involvement structure	83.3	.70
Payout period	70.0	.73
Implementation Factors		
Employee involvement in design	56.7	.54
Use of outside facilitator	66.7	.45
Situational Factors		
Managerial style	73.3	.68
Union status	83.3	.81
Success Outcomes		
Program retention	90.0	.86
Program impact	NA[b]	NA[b]

Notes:
[a]Percentage of the 33 gainsharing cases where all three coders agreed on the initial assessment. After application of special cases decision rules, there was 100% percent agreement on all variables on all cases, because of consensus process used. See text for explanation.
[b]Since program impact was a sum, percent agreement and kappa cannot be calculated.

reports of the case, such as in-house company documents, newspaper articles, and conference presentations, which often gave slightly discrepant information.

Summary of Step 6.   The assessment of measurement reliability has been emphasized in psychological research and there is an extensive statistical literature on measuring interrater reliability. In the final analysis, we think the most useful index of interrater reliability is the percent agreement. Since discrepant codes are resolved in the next step of the case meta-analysis process, the use of percent agreement not only assesses interrater reliability but also provides a basis for resolving inconsistencies. Using kappa or ICC (2,1) is another alternative to assessing case meta-analysis reliability, but they hide inconsistencies because they assess covariance rather than agreement. In instances where unequal distribution of categories occur, kappa tends to grossly underestimate the reliability of the measures, particularly given that nonchance processes are operating in assigning numerical codes.

Step 7.   Resolve Rating Discrepancies

Once reliability analyses are completed, the raters should resolve each rating discrepancy. Three techniques can be used for resolving discrepancies: (1) use the average or modal score, (2) use the ratings of one rater (e.g., Golembiewski, Proehl, & Sink, 1981), and (3) develop a consensus rating (e.g., Bullock & Svyantek, 1983, 1985; Woodman & Wayne, 1985). All three techniques can meet reliability standards, but they differ in validity and reproducibility, which we believe are more important than reliability in case meta-analysis. Though average, modal, or single expert ratings are frequently used, we recommend the consensus approach because the data are readily available to improve the potential validity and reliability. One key to quality of meta-analysis research is developing unambiguous decision rules for coding OD studies. If the decision rules are clear and can be objectively applied, then it should be possible for multiple raters to develop the same ratings; if not, then the decision rules need to be improved. By clarifying and documenting the applications of the decision rules, validity and reproducibility of the measures are maximized.

To use the consensus approach, all raters need to meet as a group to identify and reconcile discrepancies. Four types of rating discrepancies occur: (1) clerical errors (i.e., a rater located the proper information, but miscoded it by transposing a number, etc.), (2) omission errors (i.e., a rater did not locate the information in the references and thus coded it as "insufficient information"), (3) inconsistency errors (i.e., raters rely on conflicting pieces of information), and (4) interpretation errors (i.e., raters made differing judgments based on the same information). Clerical and omission errors can usually be resolved with little difficulty. If the raters followed our recommendations and noted (by underlining, checking, highlighting, etc.) the coded passage, then resolution consists of finding the coded passage and clarifying the clerical error or omission.

Inconsistency errors sometimes occur in meta-analyses of OD case studies, since a given case can be reported in multiple references. Such an error does not typically occur in a traditional meta-analysis, as there is usually a single reference for each research study and most studies are internally consistent. Researchers using case meta-analysis, however, must accumulate as many relevant references as possible and use them as a set to make the best possible rating of that study. Bullock and Tubbs (1983) found as many as nine references for a given case study, indicating that the number of retrievable references per study will vary. The quality of these references vary as well, since case reports include research articles, books, magazine articles, and company documents. It is not surprising that conflicting data emerges. Specific decision rules are needed to clarify the appropriate rating strategy, which can be: (1) use the most frequent value reported, (2) use the value reported by the highest quality information source (e.g., empirical article vs. newspaper account), or (3) contact the organizations and/or researcher to clarify the real value.

Interpretation errors usually occur when the only information relevant to a variable is ambiguous, anecdotal, or both. This often occurs in case meta-analysis, since authors of case study references vary widely in orientation and discuss the events or reactions salient to them. For example, where coding a variable such as "employee involvement in the design of an intervention," some authors may find it unimportant to discuss (or even acknowledge) the employees' role, while others may not mention the design phase of the intervention at all.

This results in the raters attempting to fit together bits and pieces of an incomplete puzzle and then making the best rating possible, and sometimes having discrepant ratings. The discrepancies should be investigated in the same way as other disagreements: review the passages in the literature upon which the ratings were based and come to a consensus based upon the a priori decision rule.

In some instances these a priori decision rules may be inadequate. The factors that would best distinguish coding categories may not become obvious until after the references have been thoroughly examined. If this is the case, the decision rule should be altered to more adequately distinguish among cases. Great care must be taken in developing such post hoc decision rules, since experimenter bias is a possibility. The possibility for bias is lessened by our recommendation that the decision rules be publicly available; logically flawed or obviously biased decision rules will not pass the test of public scrutiny. The revised decision rule should be applied to all studies, thus also helping avoid experimenter bias. Another technique for avoiding bias is to have a neutral party to assess and clarify the logical adequacy of the decisions without knowing about any given case.

The effect of these supplemental decision rules was reported in Bullock and Svyantek (1985). They attempted to replicate the decision rules published in earlier research. After coding the first half of the studies, the two coders resolved discrepancies by developing more exclusive decision rules. With the exception of the sampling strategy variable, the use of these specific decision rules increased the interrater agreement from a range of 69–86 percent to a range of 85–94 percent. For example, the original success-outcome variable, codes as "uniformly positive, uniformly negative," and "mixed or non-significant" produced an interrater agreement of only 75 percent. In resolving the discrepancies, it became clear that different raters interpreted the words "uniformly" and "mixed" differently. In each application of coding schemes, we have encountered these instances where relatively vague words are used. The greater ambiguity of the words used in the coding scheme, the lower the interrater agreement in application. To avoid unnecessary time in resolving rating discrepancies in coding schemes after the fact, we encourage case meta-analysis researchers to be as precise as possible in specifying their decision rules in advance.

Gainsharing application of Step 7.   We found the emphasis on resolving rater discrepancies rather than simply taking the average of inconsistent codes to be an important one for clarifying our thinking about the meaning and interpretation of the variables, for improving the quality of the data matrix, and for improving the validity of the interpretation of relations found from those codes. The process of developing consensus ratings for inconsistent codes required significant time, but the improvements in clarity were, in our opinion, well worth the trouble. We have been encouraged to find similar researchers in OD to be equally willing to go the extra research mile to improve the quality of the data analyzed (see Woodman & Wayne, 1985).

Often the clarification of discrepant codes involved developing supplemental decision rules. These supplemental decision rules, which apply not only to a special case that prompted their development but to all other cases in the dataset as well, converted judgments about interpretation to documented decision processes. In some cases, because of the vagueness of the documentation, the supplemental decision rule was how to handle the variable codes given incomplete data. For example, when coding the variable "employee involvement in the design of the gainsharing plan," we encountered difficulties in determining whether or not employees were involved and how much. For some cases employee involvement in design was clearly documented, while for others it was unclear whether there was no involvement or whether the authors merely did not document the involvement or the lack of involvement. With the assistance of an additional OD practitioner who was not a rater, we adopted the following decision rule: (1) If employee involvement in design was documented, code the variable "1" to indicate involvement. (2) If the design process of the gainsharing plan was described and no mention was made of employees participating in the process, code the variable as "0" to indicate no involvement. (3) If the design phase of the intervention was not described, code the variable as "9" for insufficient information. The consensus ratings for this variable were easily obtained once the references were re-examined and this decision rule was uniformly applied to all cases.

This example from the gainsharing application demonstrates a basic principle in making consensus ratings based on ambiguous information. The goal should be to make the most valid, objective, replicable judgment about the case study given the references available without reading into the source more than can be justified for replication. By requiring the coding of specific passages, it is possible to minimize the amount of projection by the reader into the case study documentation. If, because of limited information, the consensus decision discussion results in a "hung jury," then a more explicit decision rule needs to be developed and uniformly applied. In this way, not only will the most valid and reproducible set of ratings be obtained, but any inadequacies or biases in judgments will be immediately obvious in the decision rule documentation.

Summary of Step 7.   The best way to resolve discrepancies in rating is to develop a consensus rating among all raters. Discrepancies arise from clerical errors, failure of one rater to locate information in the case study documentation, and errors that arrive from inconsistent documentation or inconsistent interpretations from the same documentation. In most cases, our experience indicates that for most cases the resolution of rating discrepancies can be accomplished directly by cross-checking the documentation and developing a consensus interpretation among the raters. In some cases, it is necessary to develop more explicit rules for applying the coding scheme to the documentation. Developing supplemental decision rules is critical for validity and reproducibility. Further, case meta-analysis researchers can often use to good advantage an additional rater or process facilitator to help in the resolution of difficult interpretations.

Step 8.   Analyze the Data

Data analysis in case meta-analysis is treated the same as other statistical research. In case meta-analysis, however, emphasis for early research will be simple bivariate tests—for example, test of the effects of some intervention factor on success. As basic bivariate relationships become established and case study literature grows, it will be possible to study multivariate relationships more adequately. Since research in the near future will probably focus on fundamental bivariate relationships, this section examines the array of bivariate statistics that are available and makes specific recommendations concerning their usage in case meta-analysis.

The reader may ask, and rightly so, why an extended treatment of basic bivariate statistics is needed in this context. There are four reasons. First, no single source is currently available that reviews all available bivariate statistics and issues of importance in their selection and interpretation. Statistical literature is often incomplete (only a few statistics are even mentioned) or biased (only one side of an issue is discussed). Second, the research literature, partially as a result of the first reason, is very inconsistent in usage and interpretation so that researchers cannot rely on common practice or accepted convention. Third, because of the inconsistencies in the statistical and empirical literature, researchers can spend much time unnecessarily (as we have done) attempting to locate unbiased discussions of available statistics so they can be used and interpreted properly. The discussion here is designed to simplify and clarify the analysis task of the meta-analysis researcher. Fourth, it is quite possible (and common) to naively use inappropriate statistics and arrive at incorrect conclusions, which would destroy the statistical conclusion validity of the meta-analysis. The OD literature has been consistently criticized for the inadequacy of its statistics, and it is important to pay more attention to correcting this problem.

Type of measures.   In a meta-analysis of OD case studies, four basic types of measures can be obtained: natural dichotomies, forced dichotomies, continuous measures, and categorical measures. A natural dichotomy is a variable with only two naturally occurring outcomes and thus, an assumed binomial distribution (e.g., interventionist or not, union or nonunion). A forced dichotomy is a variable that is naturally continuous and is thus assumed to have an underlying normal distribution, but is measured as a dichotomy for convenience or necessity (e.g., favorable environment, intervention success). A continuous measure is assumed to have an underlying normal distribution and in practice is represented by ratio, interval, or ordinal scales (e.g., size, payout percentage). A categorical variable (e.g., type of technology, type of formula) is assumed to have several mutually exclusive and exhaustive categories and therefore an underlying multinomial distribution.

Types of combinations. Any one of these four types of measures could potentially serve as a predictor variable or criterion variable in a meta-analysis of OD cases. It is unlikely, however, that a categorical variable would be used as a criterion measure; in most cases some form of ordered outcome measure of success and results would be obtainable and desirable. After dropping categorical criterion measures there are 12 likely combinations of variable types. Different combinations of these measures require different statistics; the nature of the variable pair in question determines the statistic appropriate for that particular instance.

Special problems. For most variable-type combinations the statistical literature consistently prescribed a particular statistic, but we found inconsistencies in three cases. The first difficulty arose when the variables of interest were both forced dichotomies (e.g., favorable environment versus organizational effectiveness improvement). Many sources advise the use of the tetrachoric correlation coefficient in such a case (e.g., McNemar, 1969; Dick & Hagerty, 1971). Nunnally (1967), however, advises against the use of such coefficients. As he points out, the tetrachoric correlation serves to estimate the strength of the relationship between continuous variables which were forced into a dichotomy prior to analysis. He believes it is misleading to make such estimates since they misrepresent the "size of correlations obtainable from existing data" (p. 123). The fact that an underlying normal distribution is being assumed causes a further problem (Nunnally, 1967; Andrews et al., 1974). As the sampling distribution becomes increasingly skewed, the standard error increases dramatically, rendering large coefficients nonsignificant. Meta-analysis researchers will probably find that tetrachorics consistently overestimate relationships in the data and also estimate the relationship with less statistical power. Thus, we recommend against the use of tetrachorics in OD case meta-analysis.

The second problem combination occurs with a continuous measure versus a forced dichotomy (e.g., payout percentage versus organizational effectiveness improvement). Many sources recommend the biserial correlation coefficient as the appropriate statistic (e.g., McNemar, 1969; Dick & Hagerty, 1971). It estimates what the relationship would have been had the dichotomized variable actually been continuous, much as the tetrachoric correlation does. The problems described above in using the tetrachoric correlation coefficient are problems for the biserial correlation coefficient as well (overestimation, large standard errors, weak significance, and invalid assumptions). For those reasons, the point-biserial correlation is recommended for meta-analysis of OD cases involving combinations of continuous and forced dichotomy variables.

The final problem combination involves the analysis of a natural dichotomy versus a forced dichotomy (e.g., unionization versus organization effectiveness improvement). This situation requires a statistic that could reasonably estimate the relationship between two dichotomous measures that are assumed to have underlying binomial and normal distributions respectively. In no statistical source we examined was there any mention of such a statistic. In fact, there was never even an acknowledgment that such an analytic situation could arise. Since Nunnally (1967) and others recommend the use of phi coefficients for both natural dichotomy pairs and forced dichotomy pairs (which necessitates the treatment of a forced dichotomy as though it was a naturally-occurring one), it logically follows that a researcher should also use a phi coefficient for the case in which one variable is a forced dichotomy and the other is a natural dichotomy. On this basis we recommend the phi coefficient for use in such instances and also for all dichotomous pairs, whether they are natural or forced dichotomies.

A major advantage in using the recommended phi and point-biserial coefficients is that, unlike the tetrachoric and biserial, they can be directly interpreted as product-moment correlations. While the tetrachoric and biserial coefficients are used to estimate a relationship that would exist if the product-moment coefficient were used under special circumstances, the phi and point-biserial coefficients *are* product-moment correlations and can be interpreted as such. The formulas typically given for phi and point-biserial coefficients are simply short-cut versions of the product-moment formula, applicable when either one or both of the variables are dichotomous. This simplifies matters greatly, as one computer program can be used to calculate these two statistics, as well as product-moment correlations.

There are drawbacks to using phi and point-biserial coefficients. Point-biserials can occasionally exceed unity causing interpretation problems. Phi has a maximum value (i.e., "phi-max") less than unity if the two sets of marginals are not equivalent. However, we felt that the advantages of using these statistics outweighed these disadvantages.

Table 5 presents all 12 probable variable combinations, with examples of each, recommended statistics, and alternative statistics. This section of the paper explains the rationale for the recommended statistics and the alternatives, which other researchers can use if they find our recommendations less than compelling. The statistic actually chosen in a given situation will generally depend not only on data characteristics and the researcher's preferences for certain modes of analysis, but also on the data analysis approach, since there are occasions when a variable can legitimately be regarded in different ways (e.g., a dichotomy can be treated as nominal, ordinal or interval).

The approach to our recommendations in Table 5 tended to be based on some version of the product-moment correlation coefficient, for seven reasons. First, there is a legitimate statistical rationale for its use in each case. Second, it simplifies interpretation of the results across variable types, allowing the re-

Table 5. Recommended Statistics for Basic Variable Combinations in Case Meta-Analysis

Variable Combinations	Gainsharing Application Example	Possible Statistics to Use Recommended Alternatives
1. Natural dich. vs. natural dich.	Involv. struc. vs. program retention	Phi
2. Natural dich. vs. forced dich.	Involv. struc. vs. org. effect.	Phi[a]
3. Natural disch. vs. continuous var.	Involv. struc. vs. program impact	Pt. biserial
4. Forced dich. vs. natural dich.	Costs incl. vs. program retention	Phi[a]
5. Forced dich. vs. forced dich.	Costs incl. vs. org. effect.	Phi
6. Forced dich. vs. continuous dich.	Costs incl. vs. program impact	Pt. biserial
7. Continuous vs. natural dich.	Payout % vs. program retention	Pt. biserial
8. Continuous vs. forced dich.	Payout % vs. org. effect.	Pt. biserial
9. Continuous vs. continuous var.	Payout % vs. program impact	r
10. Categorical vs. natural dich.	Technology vs. program retention	r or R $\quad$ Omega^2, epsilon^2, eta^2, ICC, Freeman's theta, C, V
11. Categorical vs. forced dich.	Technology vs. org. effect.	r or R $\quad$ Omega^2, epsilon^2, eta^2, ICC, Freeman's theta, C, V
12. Categorical vs. continuous var.	Technology vs. program impact	r or R $\quad$ Omega^2, epsilon^2, eta^2, ICC

Note:
[a]See text for a discussion on how to handle this special situation.

searcher to avoid difficulties of making relative statements about relationships when several different statistics are used. Since all of the recommended statistics in Table 5 are some version of Pearson product-moment correlations, such relative statements can be easily and meaningfully made. Third, with the correlation, the meta-analysis researcher can avoid interpretation problems due to sample in contrasting the strength of various relationships. Fourth, statements regarding proportions of variance explained can easily be made (using r^2 or R^2); this cannot easily be done for many of the alternate statistics. Fifth, correlational statistics can also be used in multivariate analysis, as when a meta-analysis researcher wishes to understand the individual and collective impact of a set of structural factors on OD outcomes. Sixth, the use of correlations in a study simplifies the accumulation of effect sizes across studies (see Hunter, Schmidt, & Jackson, 1982). Finally, the product-moment correlation is *the* most widely used and understood statistic for describing relationships in the social sciences.

Combinations #1, #2, #4, and #5.   Whenever two dichotomies are involved (combinations #1, #2, #4, and #5 in Table 5) we recommend the use of the phi coefficient. Note that the tetrachoric r could be used if both variables are forced dichotomies (combination #5). We located several other alternative statistics which would be appropriate if the two dichotomies were not viewed as interval scales. Some of these procedures were not expressly developed with dichotomies in mind, and computational simplicity may be sacrificed, but they could legitimately be used in such instances. If both variables were classified as nominal, gamma (Hays, 1973) could be used, as well as phi. Gamma is based on the relative numbers of concordant and disconcordant pairs of cases in the sample, with no correction being made for "ties" on one or both variables. It can take on values from -1 to $+1$, but these extreme values can be obtained in situations other than when all data lies on a diagonal. It should be noted that in a 2×2 situation such as this, gamma is equivalent to Yule's Q (Yule & Kendall, 1957). If both variables are ordinal, Spearman's Rho (Siegel, 1956), Kendall's 3 tau coefficients: a, b and c (Kendall, 1970), Kim's d (Kim, 1971), and gamma would be suitable. All of these statistics transform the data to a set of ranks and, excepting gamma, make corrections for ties. If one wants to treat those ranks as an interval scale, rho can be used. Otherwise, tau, gamma, or d are appropriate. In a 2×2 table tau b equals phi, and is generally better for square (e.g., 3×3, $\times 4$) tables than is tau c, which corrects for table size. When ties are present in the data, gamma will be largest (due to its handling of ties) tau the smallest, and the others somewhere in between. When there are no ties, all five measures produce the same results. All of these statistics can vary from $+1$ to -1. Jaspen's coefficient of multiserial correlation (Freeman, 1965) was developed for use with one ordinal and one interval variable, while Somers' d (Somers, 1962) can be used with one ordinal and one nominal variable. Jaspen's coefficient normalizes the ordinal variable; it is a product-moment correlation of an internal variable and the normalized ordinal variable and can thus range from +1 to −1. The assumption of normality is a very strict one in this case (Andrews et al., 1974). Somers' d takes ties into consideration, but does so differently than other statistics. Both an asymmetric (i.e., one variable being dependent) and a symmetric version are available. If the predictor was nominal and the criterion was interval, a researcher could choose to perform a two-sample t-test or use one of several F-related statistics of effect size: Eta-squared (Hays, 1973), Omega-squared (Hays, 1973), the Intraclass correlation coefficient (Shrout & Fleiss, 1979; Hays, 1973), or Kelley's epsilon-squared (Kelley, 1935; Glass & Hakstian, 1969). Eta-squared is used to describe the sample relationship, while the others serve to estimate the population parameter. Omega-squared and epsilon-squared are used for fixed effects models while the Intraclass correlation can be used with either fixed or random effects models. In most case meta-analyses, a fixed effects model would be appropriate.

Combinations #3, #6, #7, and #8.   In situations involving one dichotomy and one continuous measure (combinations #3, #6, #7, and #8) the point-biserial correlation coefficient is recommended. Of course, the biserial r could also be used if the dichotomy is forced (combination #8). If the dichotomous measure is not treated as interval, making this a combination of an interval and either a nominal or an ordinal measure, then alternatives already suggested for such instances could be calculated.

Combination #9.   Combination #9, with two continuous measures, can easily be analyzed with a Pearson r. Any other reasonable method would require some form of data reduction.

Combinations #10, #11, and #12.   In combinations of categorical predictors and either continuous or dichotomous criteria (combinations #10, #11, and #12) the multiple correlation (R) is recommended. This would involve dummy-coding category membership and entering these new variables on the predictor side of a multiple regression equation. Alternate measures would include the other F-related statistics offered for use with nominal predictors and interval criteria. In combinations #10 and #11, the criterion could be treated as either nominal or ordinal. If treated as nominal, Cramer's V and the contingency coefficient (c) would be appropriate, while Freeman's coefficient of differentiation could be used if the criterion is judged to be ordinal. Cramer's V is a modified version of phi which adjusts for the number of rows and columns; phi has no upper limit when calculated for tables which are not 2×2. Cramer's V can take on values from 0 to +1. C, on the other hand, makes no such correction and thus has a maximum which is dependent on table size. This maximum can only equal +1 with an infinite number of categories. It should thus only be used to compare tables of the same size.

Calculation and software.   Nearly all of these statistics can be easily calculated with computer packages. Researchers interested in using Kim's d, Jaspen's coefficient, Freeman's coefficient, Omega-squared or the Intraclass correlation coefficient should consult the cited references for procedures to calculate these statistics. All other measures (with corresponding significance tests), save for the tetrachoric r, epsilon-squared, and eta-squared, can be calculated using any of the three major statistical packages: SPSS (Nie et al., 1975), BMDP (Dixon & Brown, 1979), and SAS (Ray, 1982). Only SPSS can calculate eta-squared and epsilon-squared, while the tetrachoric r and its significance test are calculated solely by BMDP. If BMDP is not available, one's options for calculating tetrachorics are limited; the formulas are quite cumbersome, and only the most adventurous researchers should attempt to make use of them. Chesire, Saffir and Thurstone (1933) prepared a set of diagrams to approximate the tetrachoric r, due to the complexity of hand calculation, but tests for significance are not included.

To capture the interplay of multiple variables and their effects on the results of the OD process, higher-level statistical analyses can be used. The one most commonly used in some form of multiple regression. The use of multiple regression requires a significant number of cases for even a relatively small number of independent variables. One rule of thumb is to use multiple regression only when the number of cases is at least 10 times the number of variables, with a minimum of 50 cases regardless of the number of variables. If the case meta-analysis researcher is limited to two or three dozen cases, it will be statistically impractical to apply multiple regression to the results. Given the hundreds of OD case studies available and the possibility of applying case meta-analysis techniques to the group level (as with team-building, survey feedback, socio-technical systems, etc.), this limitation can be overcome in many instances. By identifying the hypotheses and specifying the data needed to confirm the hypotheses, case meta-analysis will pave the way for OD case study reports to more adequately portray their case study and to provide information necessary for building a systematic body of knowledge about the OD process.

Gainsharing application of Step 8.   In applying case meta-analysis to the gainsharing literature, we found that the product-moment correlation was vastly more useful than the specialized statistics proposed as alternatives. As shown in Table 5, our data set included instances of all 12 variable combinations. In no case did we find any of the alternative statistics to be superior to a product-moment correlation.

Our experience with the use of tetrachorics was congruent with Nunnally's analysis. We calculated tetrachoric and phi for 30 combinations of two forced dichotomies, shown as combination #5 in Table 5. The tetrachorics were larger in 27 of 30 instances, but only 1 tetrachoric was statistically significant. Although the coefficients were consistently smaller, 8 phi coefficients were statistically significant at the .05 level. For instance, in assessing the relationship between payout period and individual quality of work life outcomes, phi = .47 and was statistically significant at the .01 level, while tetrachoric equalled .75 and was not statistically significant at the .01 level. We visually studied the array of data, and the .47 phi seemed to be a more reasonable assessment of the scatterplot than the .75 tetrachoric. Based on our experience, we would expect case meta-analysis researchers to probably find that tetrachorics consistently estimate the relationship with less statistical power, which is why we recommend against the use of tetrachoric for case meta-analysis.

The gainsharing correlation results are shown in Table 6. The table shows that researchers can expect some moderate correlations for independent variable-dependent variable relationships. Unlike experimental research, where correlations are often very low, we would expect case meta-analysis correlations to be in the range of .20 to .40 and possibly even higher for some dramatic effects. In comparison to most experimental research, case meta-analysis research probably has less random error, so that convergence on results should be expected more rapidly. It is here that the additional energy lost in handling organizational cases is repaid, since the relationships should be clearer. In our experience, this same pattern of somewhat higher correlations is typically found in meta-analysis research because the highly random individual errors are washed out in aggregating to the study level: correlations between groups on two variables are often higher than correlations within groups on the same variables.

Another key advantage of the correlation coefficient, which we were unable to use for the current dataset was its full use in multiple regression. As the documentation of gainsharing cases grows, this potential of the correlation coefficient will become much more significant.

Table 6. Examples of Correlations Found in the Gainsharing Application of Case Meta-analysis

Variable	n	Program Retention	Program Impact
Structural Factors			
Involvement structure	27	.29*	.48***
Payout period	30	.39*	.58***
Implementation Factors			
Employee involvement in design	26	.32*	.36**
Use of outside facilitator	27	.25	.39**
Situational Factors			
Managerial style	11	.67**	.39
Union status	28	− .03	− .01

Notes:
*p<.10
**p<.05
***p<.01

Summary of Step 8. There is a large but inconsistent amount of statistical literature on the assessment of bivariate relationships with different types of measures. After extensively considering the statistical options, our resolution is that all special cases of variable combinations found in case meta-analysis reduce to the simple product-moment correlation. In all examples, the correlation coefficient can be meaningfully applied and interpreted and its statistical properties are known. We have encountered all possible variable combinations in practice and in each instance have found the product-moment correlation coefficient to be the superior statistic to use in assessing bivariate relations. We document the alternatives to the product-moment correlation coefficient in this section and Table 6 so that future case meta-analysis researchers can make an informed choice as to how best to assess bivariate relations they study.

Step 9.   Report Results

Research reporting is a major problem in the social sciences. Nowhere are the inadequacies of past research reporting more obvious than when doing a meta-analysis of the research. Three problems are encountered: incomplete reports, biased discussions of results, and unclear writing styles. The pressures of compacting research reports into minimal space, researcher bias (see Bass, 1983), and the norms of poor communication among academic researchers combine to limit the effectiveness of journal reports of organizational research. Since meta-analysis is one answer to the analysis and reporting problems of traditional literature reviews, it is of utmost importance that high standards of reporting accuracy and completeness be maintained. Failure to do so will seriously undermine the potential contribution of meta-analysis research, particularly case meta-analysis.

Bullock and Svyantek (1985) made some specific recommendations for reporting standards for meta-analysis research; those standards also apply here. First, the list of studies used should be published or made available (e.g., Nicholas, 1982, p. 534) or made directly available (e.g., Porras & Berg, 1978, p. 156). Second, detailed documentation on the coding scheme and the manner in which discrepancies were resolved should also be reported or made directly available (e.g., Glass et al., 1981, pp. 255–256). By using the same set of studies and detailed documentation on the application of coding schemes, any researcher should be able to replicate the results of the meta-analysis, a feature which sets it apart from most social science research (see Woodman & Wayne, 1985).

Third, reporters of case meta-analysis should provide descriptive summaries of the sample. Meta-analysis methodologists differ on this recommendation with Glass et al. (1981) always reporting study characteristics summaries because of convenience (without theory), and Hunter et al. (1982) arguing that study characteristics should only be coded and investigated in the unusual case when a generalized validity is not obtained. We agree with Glass et al. (1981), but for a different reason: meta-analysis is done within a carefully defined conceptual domain, which serves as the boundaries for generalizing the results. To know how much the results can be generalized, it is essential to know the characteristics of the sample actually obtained. Terpstra (1981), for example, analyzed four OD interventions, and generalized the findings to the entire field of OD. A later report on the data (Terpstra, 1982) indicated that although the domain allowed the inclusion of four types of interventions, the vast majority of studies were only one type and the other three were represented by only a handful of studies. Not only can the results not be generalized to the entire field of OD, but they cannot even be safely made to the four types of interventions because of sample bias. It is not possible to know the limits of generality unless researchers systematically report the characteristics of the studies included in the sample, so Bullock and Svyantek (1985) recommended that study characteristics always be analyzed and reported.

Fourth, copies of the data set should be available for re-analysis. Surprisingly few researchers allow their data sets to be re-analyzed so replication and re-analysis are often impossible, even though both are critical elements in the scientific method. We recommend that meta-analysis researchers prepare for public distribution a copy of their data, including explanations of format and copies of computer analyses. Small data sets can often be summarized on index cards or keypunch cards, while large data sets may require a short computer tape for most efficient distribution.

Gainsharing application of Step 9. In applying the recommendations for reporting standards for case meta-analysis two special issues arose that may be relevant for other applications. The first issue is the tension between brevity and completeness in reporting meta-analysis results. Some research journals focus on brevity, following the unstated decision rule that to improve any article for publication, it should be cut in half. These journals tend to focus on relatively short research articles in the interest of publishing more articles. Given that the cost of publishing the journal article, extra tables, appendices, descriptions of the full data matrix, publication of all decision rules, etc., can be lengthy and expensive, case meta-analysis researchers should expect some journals to prefer briefer, more incomplete reports. This requires making available the data matrix, copies of the data analyses, and other pieces of supplemental information that enable future researchers to completely replicate the data matrix and judgements used in coding. In those instances where publication of all supplemental information is not possible or cost effective, we suggest that authors make the data available to interested researchers through personal correspondence.

The second issue relates to identifying the cases. In many instances, OD case studies are anonymous. One traditional argument for anonymity is that it can potentially increase the quality of the reporting since the public reputation of the company is not being compromised by discussing negative information about the case example. Rather than the case being viewed as advertising for the company, good public relations, or even a recruitment for innovative managers, anonymous OD case studies are useful in focusing on the theory and processes of the case study and not on particular characteristics of that particular site. Just as we report experimental research on 30 individuals, rather than John Williams, Sue Johnson, Mary Smith, George Campbell, etc., we think it will be more functional in the long term to allow anonymity for whatever sites choose to maintain that anonymity.

In the past, several organizations pursuing OD have had negative experiences as a result of openly sharing information about their case studies. Misrepresentation in the media, grossly distorted reports by those with a strong bias, incomplete reports by students or young researchers eager for publication, etc., have, in many instances, led organizations to close their doors to outsiders requesting information. In the gainsharing example, we encountered several organizations that had originally openly shared information about their story, but had become tight-lipped because of the perceived abuses by those who had used the information. Our access to the information came based on our personal reputations and commitment to the field and professional behavior in handling the data.

In some instances of anonymous cases, we were referred to a master thesis, doctoral dissertation, senior honors thesis, unpublished technical report, etc., where a student or professor from the local college or university "had come out and written us up." These research representations of the case study were usually anonymous, but because of our personal contact with the site, we were able to link anonymous case study documentation with the specific site. Since we were committed to respecting the choice of anonymity by the site, this prevented linking the full list of anonymous case studies with identified case studies. Confidential information reported in the anonymous case study would no longer be confidential because cross-referencing the identified and anonymous cases would remove the curtain of anonymity from the anonymously reported case. The resolution we use and suggest for similar instances in future case meta-analysis research is to report the fullest possible documentation within the limits of confidentiality and anonymity requested by the site.

Summary of Step 9. To overcome the major problems of research reporting in the social sciences, the case meta-analysis process follows the high reporting standards proposed for meta-analysis research. This includes publication or direct availability of the list of studies used to code the case studies, detailed documentation on the application of the coding schemes and the resolution of discrepancies, copies of the analysis, and full reporting of measures selected. Case meta-analysis researchers will probably encounter some special cases where special steps need to be taken to protect the confidentiality of anonymous cases, but in general, it should be possible to provide enough documentation to allow replication of case meta-analysis results. Because the case meta-analysis process is cumulative, it is important that case meta-analysis results be reproducible so that future collections of case studies can be used to extend the results with greater statistical power.

SUMMARY

This paper describes case meta-analysis in terms of nine logical steps of the research process. In developing research questions, researchers should express testable relationships unambiguously. By specifying precisely the domain within which these research questions are to be tested, it is possible to prepare written criteria for including or excluding a study, regardless of the label used to describe the intervention. This helps build toward focus areas of OD based on content considerations rather than on the use of common labels. The documentation of these case studies is converted to numerical codes using coding schemes based on simple, maximally discriminable categories with a compulsive regard for documenting the decision rules used to handle the many special cases encountered in OD. This feature allows for replication and confirmation of results. Coders should have training and practice, but work independently in applying the scheme. After computing and reporting the interrater reliability of all ratings, a consensus rating is then developed by discussing all examples of disagreement. This consensus data matrix is then analyzed, emphasizing bivariate relationships and correlations at this early stage. Finally, several aspects of the meta-analysis are especially important to report or make directly available, including domain criteria, the list of studies analyzed, research questions, detailed documentation on the coding scheme and decision rules for handling special cases, and copies of the dataset and computer analyses.

Key Characteristics

Now that we have documented the philosophical background of the case meta-analysis method and detailed the steps to the method, we can more effectively review the three key characteristics of case meta-analysis.

Hypothesis testing, not data snooping. Case meta-analysis is theory-driven and is used to test a specific hypothesis. It is not data snooping, nor is it exploratory data analysis. Much social science research has traditionally been method-driven rather than theory-driven. Even in the application of standard meta-analysis procedures, there has been a tendency for researchers to code variables based on convenience and ease of measurement, rather than based on prespecified hypotheses. The problem is pervasive with Cooper (1984) instructing reviewers: "The first rule in constructing a review coding sheet is that any information that might have the remotest possibility of being considered relevant to the research review should be retrieved from the studies" (p. 31).

Such a perspective has hindered scientific progress, in our opinion. If we are to make progress in OD or any other field, knowledge accumulation needs to be theory-based. Case meta-analysis supports a theory base by developing and specifying the hypotheses in advance of the coding, then coding only those variables involved in testing an OD hypothesis.

Rigorous coding. The second key characteristic of case meta-analysis is the emphasis in the method on rigorous and replicable variable codes. Coding rigor is a fundamental part of standard meta-analysis methods and is even more important in case meta-analysis because not only are study characteristics coded, but also outcome variables are coded as well. The historical approach to coding variables is to use multiple raters to assess the studies and compute the average, with the belief that biases and poor judgments will tend to cancel each other out and make the average rating more reliable.

We think such a process is inadequate, and propose an alternative process for case meta-analysis. The emphasis in case meta-analysis is on rigorous decision rules, trained raters, and replicable, not just reliable, codes. The reliability and replicability of any coding scheme relies on the clarity and specificity of decision rules. In most coding methods, the reliability is usually interpreted as interrater reliability, but we think it can be more adequately construed as decision-rule reliability. The case meta-analysis method emphasizes the total replication of the data matrix through the specification of decision rules and the resolution of all discrepant codes. Discrepant codes are resolved by correcting clerical errors in the coding process and resolving different interpretations. The resolution is reached by developing a specific decision rule as to the proper judgment involved in such instances and applying the revised, documented decision rule uniformly. If there are any biases or improper judgments being made in the coding process, it is not hidden in the lack of documented decision rules, nor are we left to chance with the hope that the average ratings will somehow filter out these imperfections. Instead, any inadequacies of the rating process are easily discovered by simply reading the set of decision rules used to code the studies. Given these decision rules and the documentation used to apply them, any future researcher should be able to perfectly replicate the data matrix used in the case meta-analysis. Such a method would overcome the vague yet serious charges of bias and distortion that have characterized criticisms of OD research in the past (Terpstra, 1981; Bullock & Svyantek, 1983, 1985).

Reporting standards. The reporting of social science research has been grossly inadequate. Wolin (1962) documented that a majority of authors of published articles refused to share their data matrix and had a disproportionately high percentage of data lost in fires. Because case meta-analysis relies on documentation of real OD case studies, the analysis in reporting of results follows high standards of completeness and public availability. No missing data are allowed in the method. Authors are encouraged to publish the entire data matrix, as was done by Woodman and Wayne (1985). Not only should the studies be available, but also the decision rule documentation should be available. These and other standards of public availability are the heart of the case meta-analysis method and are the basis for providing a consensus interpretation of the results.

Strengths of Case Meta-Analysis

As with any tool, case meta-analysis has strengths and limitations. We think understanding these strengths and limitations is important, since deciding on a particular method inevitably involves trade-offs.

Relies on organic research. One key strength is the reliance on organic research as the unit of analysis. In the past, OD researchers have often been forced to choose between (1) the rigorous application of well-known statistical methods to OD techniques artificially applied in the laboratory and (2) adapting experimental design techniques to field work in real organizations while sacrificing rigor according to conventional standards. Case meta-analysis is one possible solution to this no-win situation. The case meta-analysis process is based on the integrity of an OD intervention in an intact organization, adapting and changing as necessary, applying the cyclical action research process. The case meta-analysis process does not give the researcher direct control over the independent variables in a real organization, which we and others consider to be inappropriate (Argyris, 1968; Bullock & Svyantek, in press), but the method does allow researchers to understand general patterns of processes and results that occur when organizations systematically apply OD principles.

Builds knowledge cumulatively. The traditional model of science is that knowledge is cumulative through a series of independent studies. Supposedly, by allowing independent researchers to conduct separate experiments and report them independently, the development of knowledge occurs by combining the results across these studies. Unfortunately, social science research is predominantly fragmented, idiosyncratic, and not directly comparable, so that systematic accumulation of knowledge is not possible. The brick-laying model of doing experimental studies is not congruent with the reality and dynamics of modern social science research. A series of partially related studies, each with their own idiosyncrasies of concepts, measures, and analyses, is no more a body of knowledge than a pile of bricks is a wall.

The case meta-analysis process is cumulative. By reporting the data matrix in the case meta-analysis report, future researchers can extend and replicate the results by simply adding additional case studies and replicating the analyses. Through this approach, 20 case studies in 1987 may expand to 40 case studies in 1997, and hopefully more useful data are reported in the second 20 than in the first 20 because of the case meta-analysis research done with the first 20. Since case study data are converted to codes and made public, case meta-analysis helps build knowledge that is much more systematic, programmatic, and cumulative than our current framework.

Our view that the experimental literature has not been cumulative and that case meta-analysis is cumulative contrasts sharply with the traditional view that "the experiment . . . [is] the only way of establishing a cumulative tradition in which improvements can be introduced" (Campbell & Stanley, 1966). If this statement were true, a "cumulative tradition" in OD would be impossible, since a true experiment of the OD process is impossible (Bullock, in press).

Allows use of conventional statistics.   Organic research typically relies on qualitative methods for which traditional statistics are not applicable (Van Maanen et al., 1983). This is an advantage for those researchers who wish to be freed from the limitations imposed by statistical methods, but it impedes communication with those who are familiar with and committed to conventional statistics. New methods are desperately needed, but it still behooves the OD researcher to use more conventional methods when appropriate to improve diffusion of OD knowledge. Reporting a statistically significant correlation at the .05 level between the use of an outside facilitator and success of an OD effort has more impact on many researchers than an anecdotal report, however valid, from a manager in a single organization stating "we could not have done it without them." The opposite is true for nonstatisticians, so we must use different ways of communicating results to the multiple audiences interested in OD. The case meta-analysis method allows the valid reporting of statistically based conclusions to an audience accustomed to empirical studies and traditional hypothesis testing.

Encourages researcher-practitioner interaction.   One characteristic of most alternatives to positivist social science is a closer interaction of the researcher with the data. Historically, most research has been conducted by detached researchers who do not experience first-hand the processes they attempt to describe. This has consistently led to a situation where the researcher's interpretation and results are not relevant to the experience of the people in the research.

This type of situation could occur in case meta-analysis, but the tools are available to prevent such an occurrence. First, case meta-analysis researchers should have some direct experience of the intervention to build a sound theory of what OD processes lead to what results for that particular type of intervention. It would be difficult to develop an adequate case meta-analysis study of team-building, for example, if one had never been part of an OD team-building project.

Further, case meta-analysis researchers should not consider the limitations of published documentation to be a dead-end alley. In the past, literature reviewers and most meta-analysis researchers have been content with the published data and not tried to get additional information because of the time and trouble involved. We encourage case meta-analysis researchers to overcome this barrier by directly contacting the authors, practitioners, and employees involved to resolve discrepancies in coding, to clarify ambiguous information in the case study documentation, to collect further follow-up data, and in general, to discuss the experience of the intervention. In our experience, those who implement and live with the intervention are more than happy to discuss their experiences with someone whom they trust to use the information in a professional way. Not only does this improve the completeness and accuracy of the data matrix, but also helps build a network of researchers and practitioners who can benefit from each other. These communication and cooperation benefits of the case meta-analysis process is a key advantage of the method.

Uses current resources. Because of the natural reliance on the case research, case studies have been the major reporting method for OD researchers. Although they have been ignored by literature reviewers, the case study literature has continued to grow. Proehl (1980) documented no less than 574 OD case studies, the vast majority of which were successful, and since that time, hundreds more have been implemented and documented.

In OD practice, we emphasize more effective utilization of human resources. In OD research, we need to emphasize the more effective utilization of our case study resources. Case meta-analysis allows us to make more effective use of the hundreds of important case studies already available. Like our human resources, these case studies are under-utilized and have had far less impact than their potential warrants. In using these resources more effectively, case meta-analysis takes an OD case study from the realm of an interesting story to a key position as a building block in empirically understanding processes of organizational change.

Limitations of Case Meta-analysis

Case meta-analysis also has limitations. By recognizing these limitations, we can find improvements in the method.

Information availability. First, case meta-analysis is limited by the available data. To paraphrase a methodological truism: "limited information in, limited information out." Many OD case studies are written to convey the experience of the case study rather than to include all pertinent data about the case study. A complete treatment of a longitudinal OD case study requires a book, and in fact several books have been written about individual case studies which can be used to good advantage in case meta-analysis research. For example, a series of case studies is available on Quality of Work Life programs.

Most OD case studies, however, will be article-length treatments and presentations. The case meta-analysis researcher should expect to encounter limitations in information availability. This limitation can be overcome in many instances by contacting the researcher and the organization involved. Often internal documents, company booklets, materials assembled for visitors, presentations to corporate management, and the like are available from the site, particularly if the case meta-analysis researcher has a solid background in the field and is committed to helping the client organizations.

Number of cases.   The second frequent limitation of applying the case meta-analysis method is the limited number of case study organizations for which adequate information is available. In the gainsharing application, we could only find documented case studies on 33 organizations that were reported in adequate detail to allow for coding although there have been hundreds of applications of the gainsharing process (Bullock & Tubbs, 1983).

A reasonable sample for case meta-analysis is 20 organizations or more. A case meta-analysis based on less than 10 organizations would probably not have adequate statistical power to pursue. With most OD interventions, however, we think it should certainly be possible to find at least a dozen examples of case study applications. For small samples, the results need to be interpreted cautiously, but given the impact of many OD interventions, we would expect patterns to begin emerging in as few as 10 cases. Case meta-analyses done on relatively limited samples can have important benefits, not only for identifying preliminary patterns of results, but also for identifying the type of data that case study reporters should include in future documentation.

The number of cases may limit the types of statistical analyses that can be done. The algorithms used for many higher-order statistical tests (such as least squares regression, factor analysis, and structural equation analysis) have a strong tendency to capitalize on chance variations. This has consistently produced the situation where researchers report significant results that are not replicated. Case meta-analysis researchers can avoid this major problem by using statistics like the product-moment correlation, which is not only cumulative over studies (by weighted averaging), but is also less sensitive to the chance variations in a given dataset. For most early case meta-analysis studies, tested hypotheses will probably be constrained to bivariate relationships. The use of conventional multivariate tests must await the accumulation of samples of 50 or more cases. For popular interventions such as survey feedback, team-building, Quality Circles, and sociotechnical systems, such a sample could be developed either now or in the immediate future. Sources such as Proehl's (1980) listing of 574 OD cases should be instrumental in developing such a dataset.

Coding limitations.   The measurement process involves assignment of a number to some phenomenon based on a prescribed set of rules. In case meta-analysis, the measurement process is a coding system by raters where the phenomenon is assessed through documentation. The coding process often involves assignment of relatively simple coding schemes, such as 0–1 codes, to relatively complex processes. For example, we would expect the characteristics of labor-management relations to have significant impact on the results of many OD interventions. The simple distinction of collaborative versus competitive relations captures some important variance in labor-management relations, but it by no means captures the full dynamic involved. Because of the limitations of representing relatively complex organizational dynamics in a simplified code, case meta-analysis researchers need to avoid interpreting their results more strongly than their coding schemes would allow.

This limitation can be overcome by developing more extensive documentation on the case studies and then applying more sophisticated coding schemes. Some of these complex codes are already available. In the labor-management relations example, more sophisticated measures are available (see Bullock, Macy, & Mirvis, 1983), while for others, such as the "intensity of the intervention," more extensive coding schemes still need to be developed. Case meta-analysis researchers can make a significant contribution by pointing out those areas where theory and results warrant more extensive assessment.

CONCLUSION

Case meta-analysis is a method; it is a tool—no more, no less. If used appropriately, we believe it can help us make an important step toward understanding organizational change in real social systems.

Perhaps the most important contribution of the case meta-analysis method is to provide a bridge between methodologies that have been increasingly split apart. Rather than splitting schools of thought into opposing camps, case meta-analysis provides a link between two important approaches. One approach to social science research, labeled the "positivist school," emphasizes observable data, rigorous experiments, statistical inferences, and the search for causal laws. Another approach, often labeled the "humanist school" or other similar labels, emphasizes understanding the whole person or the whole organization, learning from real situations, collaboration between researcher and participants in the research, qualitative data, longitudinal change, and individual case studies. Supporters of the positivist approach have charged that the humanist approach is not rigorous by scientific standards. Supporters of the humanist approach have charged that positivism is irrelevant, socially counter-productive, and is not useful in practice.

Bridging these contrasting approaches is case meta-analysis. An OD case is a single, organic piece of research. It is collaborative and nonmanipulative. It operates in real organizations on real problems. It uses methods that develop human systems and human potential. And it produces guides for actions. At the same time, we can learn from experiences through these cases. Is OD usually successful? How often does it work? What types of results can one expect from a given intervention? These and other basic questions about the impact of OD can be answered by applying basic statistical concepts to coded variables collected across case studies. By using individual OD case studies as independent units in a statistical analysis, we can use to good advantage many statistical tools that are already developed. It is both possible and practical to apply these statistical techniques to individual case studies, following ideas and hypotheses developed from OD theory.

In short, case meta-analysis is a "have your pie and eat it too" solution. It allows processes that are necessary for OD research: diagnosis, collaboration, nonrandom assignment, joint roles of researcher and change agent, consensus decision making, iterative data collection and action planning, and adaptation to changing environmental conditions. At the same time, case meta-analysis allows the use of many statistical tools that are well-known and well respected. Case meta-analysis takes an OD case study from the realm of "an interesting story" to a key position as a building block for understanding system change.

We need new methods and new techniques to better study the OD process. The case meta-analysis method detailed here is one proposed solution to the problem. We think case meta-analysis can help us take an important step forward in synthesizing information across individual OD case studies, each with its own conceptual and practical integrity, into a body of literature that is both rigorous and relevant.

ACKNOWLEDGMENTS

The authors contributed equally to this chapter and the order of authorship is shown alphabetically. The authors are very grateful to Marshall Sashkin, Virginia Welfare, Chuck DeBettignies, and Richard Perlow for their helpful comments on earlier drafts of this chapter.

NOTE

1. The dissertation is available on microfilm for $10.00 (catalog number 8029147) through University Microfilms International, 300 N. Zeeb Road, Ann Arbor, Michigan 48106 (phone: (800) 521–0600).

REFERENCES

Allison, G. T. (1971). *Essence of decision-making: Explaining the Cuban missile crisis*. Boston: Little, Brown.
Andrews, F. M., Klem, L., Davidson, T. N., O'Malley, P. M., & Rodgers, W. L. (1974). *A guide for selecting statistical techniques for analyzing social science data*. Ann Arbor, MI: Institute for Social Research, University of Michigan.
Argyris, C. (1968). Some unintended consequences of rigorous research. *Psychological Bulletin, 70,* 185–197.
Argyris, C. (1970). *Intervention theory and method*. Reading, MA: Addison-Wesley.
Bartko, J. J. (1976). On various intraclass correlation reliability coefficients. *Psychological Bulletin, 83,* 762–765.
Bass, B. M. (1983). Issues involved in relations between methodological rigor and reported out-

comes in evaluations of organization development. *Journal of Applied Psychology, 68,* 179–199.

Blake, R. R., & Mouton, J. S. (1969). *Building a dynamic corporation through grid organization development.* Reading, MA: Addison-Wesley.

Bullock, R. J. (1986). A meta-analysis method for OD case studies. *Group & Organization Studies, 11,* 33–48.

Bullock, R. J. (in press). The effects of a quality of work life program on job attitudes: A field experiment. *International Journal of Management.*

Bullock, R. J., & Lawler, E. E., III. (1980). Incentives and gainsharing: Stimuli for productivity. In J. D. Hogan and A. M. Craig (Eds.), *Dimensions of productivity research* (vol. 1, pp. 453–466). Houston: American Productivity Center.

Bullock, R. J., & Lawler, E. E., III. (1984). Gainsharing: A few questions, and fewer answers. *Human Resource Management, 23,* 23–40.

Bullock, R. J., Macy, B. A., & Mirvis, P. H. (1983). Assessing unions and union-management collaboration in organizational change. In S. E. Seashore, E. E. Lawler, P. H. Mirvis, & C. Cammann (Eds.), *Assessing organizational change: A guide to methods, measures, and practices* (pp. 389–415). New York: Wiley.

Bullock, R. J., & Svyantek, D. J. (1983). Positive-findings bias in positive-findings bias research: An unsuccessful replication. In K. H. Chang (Ed.), *Academy of Management Proceedings '83* (pp. 221–224). Dallas: Academy of Management.

Bullock, R. J., & Svyantek, D. J. (1985). Analyzing meta-analysis: Potential problems, an unsuccessful replication, and evaluation criteria. *Journal of Applied Psychology, 70,* 108–115.

Bullock, R. J., & Svyantek, D. J. (in press). On the impossibility of using random strategies to study the OD process. *Journal of Applied Behavioral Science.*

Bullock, R. J., & Tubbs, M. (August 17, 1983). *A meta-analysis of gainsharing plans as OD interventions.* Paper presented at the meeting of the OD Division of the Academy of Management, Dallas, TX.

Burton, N. (1981). Estimating scorer agreement for nominal categorization systems. *Educational and Psychological Measurement, 41,* 953–962.

Callender, J. C., & Osburn, H. G. (1980). Development and test of a new model for validity generalization. *Journal of Applied Psychology, 65,* 543–558.

Campbell, J. P., Daft, R. L., & Hulin, C. L. (1982). *What to study: Generating and developing research questions.* Beverly Hills, CA: Sage.

Campbell, D. T., & Stanley, J. C. (1966). *Experimental and quasi-experimental designs for research.* Chicago: Rand-McNally.

Chesire, L., Saffir, M., & Thurstone, L. L. (1933). *Computing diagrams for the tetrachoric correlation coefficient.* Chicago, IL: The University of Chicago.

Cohen, J. (1960). A coefficient of agreement for nominal scale. *Educational and Psychological Measurement, 20,* 37–46.

Cohen, J. (1968). Weighted kappa: Nominal scale agreement with provision for scaled disagreement or partial credit. *Psychological Bulletin, 70,* 213–220.

Cohen, J., & Cohen, P. (1975). *Applied multiple regression/correlation analysis for the behavioral sciences.* Hillsdale, NJ: Lawrence Erlbaum.

Collier, J. (1945). United States Indian administration as a laboratory of ethnic relations. *Social Research, 12,* 275–276.

Conger, A. J. (1980). Integration and generalization of kappas for multiple raters. *Psychological Bulletin, 88,* 322–328.

Cooper, H. M. (1984). *The integrative research review: A systematic approach.* Beverly Hills, CA: Sage.

Cronbach, L. J. (1951). Coefficient alpha and the internal structure of tests. *Psychometrika, 16,* 297–334.

DeMeuse, K. P., & Liebowitz, S. J. (1981). An empirical analysis of team-building research. *Group & Organization Studies, 6,* 357–378.

Dick, W., & Hagerty, N. (1971). *Topics in measurement: Reliability and validity.* New York: McGraw-Hill.

Dixon, W. J., & Brown, M. B. (Eds.). (1979). *BMDP-79.* Los Angeles, CA: University of California Press.

Ebel, R. L. (1951). Estimation of the reliability of ratings. *Psychometrika, 16,* 407–421.

Fleiss, J. L. (1971). Measuring nominal scale agreement among many raters. *Psychological Bulletin, 76,* 378–382.

Foa, U. G. (1958). The contiguity principle in the structure of interpersonal relations. *Human Relations, 11,* 229–238.

Foa, U. G. (1965). New developments in facet design and analysis. *Psychological Review, 72,* 262–274.

Foa, U. G. (1966). Perception of behavior in reciprocal roles: The ringex model. *Psychological Monographs: General and Applied, 80*(15, Whole No. 623).

Freeman, L. C. (1965). *Elementary applied statistics for students in behavioral science.* New York: Wiley.

Glass, G. V. (1976). Primary, secondary and meta-analysis of research. *Educational Researcher, 5,* 3–8.

Glass, G. V., & Hakstian, A. R. (1969). Measures of association in comparative experiments: Their development and interpretation. *American Educational Research Journal, 6,* 403–414.

Glass, G. V., McGaw, B., & Smith, M. L. (1981). *Meta-analysis in social research.* Beverly Hills, CA: Sage.

Golembieski, R. T., Proehl, C. W., & Sink, D. (1981). Success of OD applications in the public sector: Toting up the score for a decade, more or less. *Public Administration Review, 41,* 679–682.

Golembieski, R. T., Proehl, C. W., & Sink, D. (1982). Estimating the success of OD applications, *Training and Development Journal, 72,* 86–95.

Guilford, J. P. (1965). *Fundamental statistics in psychology and education* (4th ed.). New York: McGraw Hill.

Guttman, L. (1954). A new approach to factor analysis: The radex. In P. F. Lazarsfeld (Ed.), *Mathematical thinking in the social sciences.* New York: Free Press.

Harris, C. W. (Ed.). (1963). *Problems in measuring change.* Madison: University of Wisconsin Press.

Harris, R. J. (1975). *A primer of multivariate statistics.* New York: Academic Press.

Hays, W. L. (1973). *Statistics for the social sciences.* New York: Holt, Rinehart, & Winston.

Hubert, L. (1977). Kappa revisited. *Psychological Bulletin, 84,* 289–297.

Hunter, J. E., Schmidt, F. L., & Jackson, G. B. (1982). *Meta-analysis cumulating research findings across studies.* Beverly Hills: Sage.

Jackson, G. B. (1978). *Methos for reviewing and integrating research in the social sciences.* Final report to the National Science Foundation for Grant No. DIS 76-20309. Washington, DC: Social Research Group, George Washington University, April.

Jenkins, G. D., Nadler, D. A., Lawler, E. E., III, & Cammann, C. (1975). Standardized observations: An approach to measuring the nature of jobs. *Journal of Applied Psychology, 61,* 642–651.

Jones, A.P., Johnson, L. A., Butler, M. C., & Main, D. S. (1983). Apples and oranges: An empirical comparison of commonly used indices and interrater agreement. *Academy of Management Journal, 26,* 507–519.

Kaufman, H. (1960). *The forest ranger: A study in administrative behavior.* Baltimore, MD: Johns Hopkins University Press.

Kelley, T. L. (1935). An unbiased correlation ratio measure. *Proceeding of the National Academy of Sciences, 21,* 554–559.

Kendall, M. G. (1970). *Rank correlation methods.* (4th ed.). London: Griffin.

Kerlinger, F. N. (1973). *Foundations of behavioral research* (2nd ed.). New York: Holt, Rinehart, and Winston.

Kim, J. (1971). Predictive measures of ordinal association. *American Journal of Sociology, 76,* 891–907.

Kuhn, T. S. (1962). *The structure of scientific revolutions.* Chicago, IL: University of Chicago Press.

Kuhn, T. S. (1970). *The structure of scientific revolutions,* (2nd ed.) Chicago, IL: University of Chicago Press.

Lewin, K. (1946). Action research and minority problems. *Journal of Social Issues, 2,* 34–46.

Liebow, E. (1967). *Tally's corner.* Boston: Little, Brown.

Light, R. J. (1971). Measures of response agreement for qualitative data: Some generalizations and alternatives. *Psychological Bulletin, 76,* 365–377.

Macy, B. A., Hurts, C. C. M., Norton, L. W., Izumi, H., & Smith, R. R. (August, 1986). *Meta-analysis of empirical work improvement and organizational change experiments: Methodology and preliminary results.* Paper presented at the meeting of the Academy of Management Organization Development Division, Chicago, IL.

Margulies, N., Wright, P. L., & Scholl, R. W. (1977). Organization development techniques: Their impact on change. *Group & Organization Studies, 2,* 428–448.

Marsh, R. M., & Mannari, H. (1981). Technology and size as determinants of the organizational structure of Japanese factories. *Administrative Science Quarterly, 26,* 33–57.

McGrath, J. E. (1967). A multi-facet approach to classification of individual, group, and organizational concepts. In B. Indik and K. Berrien (Eds.), *People, groups, and organizations: An effective integration* (pp. 191–215). New York: Teachers College Press.

McNemar, Q. (1969). *Psychological statistics* (4th ed.). New York: John Wiley & Sons.

Miles, J. B., & Schmuck, R. A. (1983). The nature of organization development. In W. L. French, C. H. Bell, & R. A. Zawacki (Eds.), *Organization development: Theory, Practice, Research.* Plano, TX: Business Publications, Inc.

Mudd, R. M. (1984). Organization development intervention: A theoretical model for the implementation of a process for educational leadership assessment and development (PELAD). (Doctoral dissertation, University of Houston, 1981).

Nicholas, J. M. (1982). The comparative impact of organization development interventions on hard criteria measures. *Academy of Management Review, 7,* 531–542.

Nie, N. H., Hull, C. H., Steinbrenner, K., & Bent, D. H. (1975). *Statistical packages for the social sciences* (2nd ed.). New York: McGraw-Hill.

Nunnally, J. C. (1967). *Psychometric theory.* New York: McGraw-Hill.

Overall, J. E. (1980). Power of chi-squared test for 2×2 contingency tables with small expected frequencies. *Psychological Bulletin, 87,* 132–135.

Payne, R. L., Fineman, S., & Wall, T. D. (1976). Organizational climate and job satisfaction: A conceptual synthesis. *Organizational Behavior and Human Performance, 16,* 45–62.

Porras, J. I., & Berg, P. O. (1978). Evaluation methodology in organization development: Analysis and critique. *Journal of Applied Behavioral Science, 14,* 151–174.

Proehl, C. W. (1980). *Planned organizational change.* Unpublished doctoral dissertation, University of Georgia.

Rapoport, R. N. (1970). Three dilemmas of action research. *Human Relations, 23,* 499–513.

Ray, A. A. (Ed.). (1982). *SAS user's guide: Statistics.* Cary, NC: SAS Institute.

Rosenthal, R. (1978). Combining results of independent studies. *Psychological Bulletin, 85,* 185–193.

Rosenthal, R. (1984). *Meta-analysis procedures for social research.* Beverly Hills, CA: Sage.

Runkel, P. J., & McGrath, J. E. (1972). *Research on human behavior: A systematic guide to method.* New York: Holt, Rinehart, and Winston.

Schmidt, F. L., & Hunter, J. E. (1977). Development of a general solution to the problem of validity generalization. *Journal of Applied Psychology, 62,* 529–540.

Schmidt, F. L., Hunter, J. E., Pearlman, K., & Shane, G. S. (1979). Further tests of the Schmidt-Hunter Bayesian validity generalization procedure. *Personnel Psychology, 32,* 257–281.

Selznick, P. (1949). *TVA and the grass roots: A study of politics and organization.* Berkeley: University of California Press.

Shrout, P. E., & Fleiss, J. L. (1979). Intraclass correlation: Uses in assessing rater reliability. *Psychological Bulletin, 86,* 420–428.

Siegel, S. (1956). *Nonparametric statistics for the behavioral sciences.* New York: McGraw-Hill.

Smith, M. L., & Glass, G. V. (1977). Meta-analysis of psychotherapy outcome studies. *American Psychologist, 32,* 752–760.

Somers, R. H. (1962). A new asymmetric measure of association for ordinal variables. *American Sociological Review, 27,* 799–811.

Susman, G. I., & Evered, R. D. (1978). An assessment of the scientific merits of action research. *Administrative Science Quarterly, 23,* 582–603.

Terpstra, D. E. (1981). Relationship between methodological rigor and reported outcomes in organization development evaluation research. *Journal of Applied Psychology, 66,* 541–543.

Terpstra, D. E. (1982). Evaluating selected organization development interventions: The state of the art. *Group & Organization Studies, 7,* 402–417.

Uebersax, J. S. (1982). A generalized kappa coefficient. *Educational and Psychological Measurement, 42,* 181–183.

Van Mannen, J., Dabbs, J. M., & Faulkner, R. R. (1982). *Varieties of qualitative research.* Beverly Hills, CA: Sage.

White, S. E., & Mitchell, T. R. (1976). Organization development: A review of research content and research design. *Academy of Management Review,* April, *1,* 57–73.

Whyte, W. F. (1955, 1943). *Street corner society: The social structure of an Italian slum.* Chicago: University of Chicago Press.

Winer, B. J. (1971). *Statistical principles in experimental design* (2nd ed.). New York: McGraw-Hill.

Wolins, L. (1962). Responsibility for raw data. *American Psychologist, 17,* 657–658.

Woodman, R. W., & Sherwood, J. J. (1980). The role of team development in organizational effectiveness: A critical review. *Psychological Bulletin, 88,* 166–186.

Woodman, R. W., & Wayne, S. J. (1985). An investigation of positive-finding bias in evaluation of organization development interventions. *Academy of Management Journal, 28,* 889–913.

Yin, R. K. (1984). *Case study research: Design and methods.* Beverly Hills, CA: Sage.

Yule, G. V., & Kendall, M. G. (1957). *An introduction to the theory of statistics* (14th ed.). London: Griffin.

DEVELOPMENT AT THE TOP:
A REVIEW AND A PROSPECT

Robert E. Kaplan, Joan R. Kofodimos and
Wilfred H. Drath

ABSTRACT

An executive's strengths and weaknesses are relative to a particular job and particular circumstances yet a broad class of requirements can be identified as pertaining to executives in general, and developmental needs do arise in executives when these requirements are not met. In addition to knowledge of the business, economics, markets, and other technical abilities, these requirements consist of managerial skills and what might be called psychological preparedness. Because of their elevated position in the organization, executives face unique difficulties in addressing such deficiencies and doing anything about them, though unique opportunities for development also exist for executives. The chapter introduces a method, Biographical Action Research, for conducting intensive research into the managerial character, the organizational milieu, and the resulting developmental prospects of individual executives.

Research in Organizational Change and Development, Vol. 1, pages 229–273.
Copyright © 1987 by JAI Press Inc.
All rights of reproduction in any form reserved.
ISBN: 0-89232-479-9

INTRODUCTION

When considering organizational development, one must also consider managerial development, and perhaps especially, executive development. Organizations themselves cannot change or develop; the people who make up the organization must create and manifest change through their own behavior and attitudes. Considered in these terms, organizational development is predicated upon changes in organizational members, in addition to changes in structure, economics, technology, and so forth. Of these members, the executive ranks comprise a group of people whose behavior and attitude is crucial to the success or failure of organizational development. These are the people with the power to intitiate fundamental organizational change, the people who spend their time dealing with broad issues of policy or with operational problems that raise issues of policy. These are the managers with the power to authorize initiatives for change coming from below, the sponsors of change whose support for mid- and lower-level mavericks, change agents, and product champions is crucial (Kanter, 1982, 1983). The extensive literature on the relationship between behavior change in the CEO and the success of OD efforts shows clearly the central role of the very top executive (Mann, 1957; Jaques, 1952; Guest, 1962; Seashore & Bowers, 1963; Blake et al., 1964; Dalton, 1969; Kaufman, 1971; Golembiewski, 1972; Argyris, 1973; Boss & Boss, 1985). This relationship also works the other way—that is, OD can facilitate executive developments—as we will discuss in the conclusion to this chapter.

We cannot hope to write about research on executive development without dealing in some way with the problem of the terms "executive," "development," and "executive development." By executives we mean roughly the top one or two percent of an organization's population, the people with general management responsibility or those who head up major staff functions such as finance, strategic planning, and R&D.

By development we mean the actualization of some potential ability, the bringing out of latent strengths, usually for the purpose of correcting a weakness that is blocking effectiveness. Effectiveness we in turn define as the ability to have an effect consistent with goals. Thus, a manager who intends to open up communications with subordinates and in fact, does so, is in that instance, effective. In other words, effectiveness is related not to global qualities of some hypothetical, perfect manager, but rather to goals, intentions, and achievements. Development promotes effectiveness; it does not create paragons. Many types of learning, formal and informal, pedagogical and experiential, may lead to development.

The term executive development—already saddled with the uncertainties of its component terms—is ambiguous on its own merits as well. Sometimes it means the development managers undergo on their way to the top, at other times it means the development executives may undertake once they become executives.

In this chapter we will address executive development in the latter sense. In this sense executive development is important only to the extent that one makes the assumption, as we do, that highly capable and successful executives (and their organizations) can profit from continued learning and development, that they are not—and perhaps cannot be—fully prepared for executive work before reaching the top.

In this chapter, then, we will discuss the current state of our understanding of executive development, and we will look at a way of studying executive development that we think has the potential for bringing about a better understanding of this phenomenon. We will first discuss the developmental needs that are more or less particular to the executive job, then discuss the forces—within the executive's psyche and impinging upon it from without—that can affect his prospects for development by influencing whether or not he will pursue development or by influencing his agenda for it. To illustrate this, we will present examples from among the executives we studied using an intensive research-cum-development method that we call Biographical Action Research (BAR). To conclude, we will describe this method briefly, including a few warnings for those who would consider using it or any method related to it.

DEVELOPMENTAL NEEDS

Though most executives are extraordinarily capable people, they cannot escape the human condition: they are imperfect, with some highly developed skills and abilities, but also with weaknesses and limitations. Because developing complex skills to a high degree requires a great deal of time and energy, the weaknesses of many highly developed people tend to be mirror images of their strengths. To spend a life developing one's ability at logical analysis, for example, can well leave one with a limited capacity for—or at least little patience with—inspired guesswork. There is thus a clear limit to development in as much as there will always presumably be some pattern of mirror weaknesses for whatever set of skills we may develop. The issue is: what abilities and skills do we need to do what we aspire to do?

Where executives are concerned, strengths and weaknesses are always relative to a particular job, or type of job, or to a particular organization (Mintzberg, 1973). An executive's deficiency in one job might serve as a strength in another: an entrepreneurial, risk-taking executive might be a disruptive influence in a stable organization, yet he could perfectly fill the bill in an organization needing a turnaround. What we consider to be an executive's developmental needs are also relative to our values regarding effectiveness. In other words, in assessing need we always take into account what we see as being ideal, effective behavior. We may, for example, hold achievement in high esteem and thus assume that achievement is tantamount to effectiveness. We might then define needs in terms of behaviors or deficiencies deterring achievement. But as Levinson has pointed out, the drive to establish one's place in the world is stronger before mid-life than after it (Levinson, 1978). If we define effectiveness in terms of an executive's changing life goals, we may find, for example, in older executives, that their need for rising through the organization has cooled, that the desire for that kind of achievement is replaced by wishes to nurture and develop younger managers, and we should assess their developmental needs accordingly.

Related to this, and another factor in considering developmental needs, is the relativity of perception, the fact that a need is not a need until someone sees it as such. This in turn raises the question of the bias of the perceiver. An executive who wants to see himself in a favorable light—as we all do to some extent—may not be a good judge of his own developmental needs. An executive's boss, often the one responsible for assessing developmental needs, may be equally biased. People inevitably apply their own standards when measuring others (Kelly, 1955). As an example, one executive we know of was strongly influenced by his boss to try to become more attentive to detail through formal training. The development specialist in charge of the program later had second thoughts about the boss's diagnosis of the problem when he ran across a test result on the boss that placed the boss on the 95th percentile in attention to detail. Was the executive's need real, or merely a projection by his boss? In this way and others, developmental needs are often determined through a negotiated social process that can produce distortions.

The process of determining developmental needs is also complicated by the fact that success in some areas can overshadow weaknesses in other areas. Certain developmental needs may exist and yet not be taken seriously (even though they may cause problems in the organization) because the presence of certain strengths may lead people to underestimate the importance of the weaknesses: "He's hard on people, but he sure gets them to perform!"

We will look at developmental needs in two broad classes. First we will examine a set of skill deficiencies that research has shown to be detrimental to executive performance. Second we will look at certain attitudes and orientations that are dysfunctional in the executive role.

External Developmental Needs of Executives

Strategic Skills

One possible deficiency is the inability to provide a strategic perspective, a vision, for an organization. Kotter (1984) used the term "agenda" to refer to the plans and purposes, not necessarily formal or explicit, that a leader creates. Based on his research with Sears executives, Bentz (1985) placed importance on planful thinking, which equips the executive with a "loose but purposeful framework within which he makes decisions" (p. 11). Peters and Waterman (1982) stressed the few basic values with which top managers must inculcate their organizations. A deficiency in strategic skills can arise when, in earlier management jobs, an executive has made progress primarily by taking action, by trouble-shooting, by meeting problems with quick, tactical plans. In mastering a tactical art, such activist managers can fail to develop the ability to think and operate strategically (Bennis, 1985). This deficiency is relevant because providing strategic direction is one of the important functions of organizational leadership.

In their study of derailed executives—managers who had made it near the top but who failed to reach the top—McCall and Lombardo (1983) found that one of the telling weaknesses in these executives was the inability to think strategically. This is often manifested as a tendency to get bogged down in details, as a tendency to continue to manage by doing, or as a failure to learn how to manage through plans.

Kaplan and colleagues conducted an interview study of general managers in a large, diversified corporation. The sample consisted of 10 general managers and 15 other executives who worked closely with general managers. One of the questions asked for a short description of an effective and an ineffective general manager the resondent had actually known. Of the 21 general managers cited as being effective, several were credited with strategic ability; but of the 16 cited as being ineffective, none were credited with this ability, and several were described as being short-term or crisis-oriented (Kaplan, 1986).

Perhaps related to a short-term, detail orientation is the tendency some managers show to avoid risk whenever possible. This can spell trouble strategically for executives, who must often take calculated risks to move an organization forward in an uncertain environment. In this connection, Kaplan (1986) found that several general managers described as being effective were also characterized as being confident, decisive, or aggressive; while several of the GMs described as being ineffective were characterized as being insecure, unassertive, indecisive, or as having "no guts."

Managing a Large Organization

Another class of problems for executives are those connected with managing system and structure on a large scale (Kotter, 1982; Bentz, 1985). The need to direct, organize, coordinate, monitor and reward the efforts of many people engaged in a variety of interconnected functions demands a strong administrative ability. This ability is not universally present in high-level managers. In his research with Sears, for example, Bentz (1985) discovered a type of executive whom he called the "natural leader": a charismatic, action oriented manager who says all the right things but who fails to create the proper organizational structure for following through on plans.

Perhaps more common is a simple failure to delegate well (Bentz, 1985). McCall and Lombardo (1983) concluded that an inability to delegate was a major cause of executive failure. In our study of general managers, we found that of the 16 regarded as not effective, six did not delegate well or were too detail-oriented. Jenks (1984) has seen a tendency among founders of high-growth, high-tech firms to stay intimately involved in matters that they should turn over to subordinates. Effective executives do not keep their distance from everything happening in their organizations. Instead, as a complement to their general practice of "proficient superficiality" (Mintzberg, 1973), they pick a few strategically important projects to get heavily involved with (Mintzberg, 1973; Bentz, 1985).

Managing in large organizations calls for excellent ability in communicating and presenting. This is especially true for high-level executives who must be able to communicate strategy to people who had no hand in formulating it (Bennis & Nanus, 1985). Effective executives are able to get their strategic points across in memorable and compelling ways. In our study of GMs, several of the 21 effective GMs were described as being good communicators who could effectively sell their ideas; many of the ineffective GMs were seen as lacking this ability or as simply being noncommunicators or out of touch.

Another aspect of the executive's job that places a premium on communication skill is the need to have a spokesperson for the organization and a figurehead who can preside at official and ceremonial occasions. Some managers are uncomfortable or unhappy in this role—some because they have poor speaking ability, others because they shy away from public scrutiny. As one executive in our study complained: "The spotlight is always on you. . . . I'm uncomfortable being the center of attention. I escape to the men's room."

Handling Scope and Scale

Some managers fail to make the transition from manager of a smaller unit to leadership of a large organization because of the tremendous complexity that confronts them. The sheer breadth of the job may require more intelligence and analytical ability than a manager can call upon. In the world of the leader, any given problem (or opportunity) breaks down into parts that bear interesting, but often conflicting, relations to one another. Each problem is closely or distantly related to many other problems, and the inter-relations are either complementary (and therefore something to be exploited) or contradictory (and therefore something to be resolved). Sometimes the interrelation is between the concrete, day-to-day and the abstract, strategic. The required ability for multidimensional thinking, or handling cognitive complexity (Streufert, 1983; Isenberg, 1984; Bentz, 1985) may be something a manager is born with, but clearly not all managers possess this ability to the extent required by the executive job.

Another problem in making the transition to leadership is that of transcending the functional specialty in which a manager grew up in the business. As Cleveland (1980) put it: "Leaders are by function generalists, yet there is no such thing as a generalist ladder to leadership. . . . To graduate from specialist to leader is a wrenching, demanding, sometimes traumatic 'change of life.'" Failing to rise above a former specialty can result in strategic thinking that is distorted by a specialist point of view (Gabarro, 1985). Also, old rivalries and jealousies among specialties may linger, making it difficult for an executive to work effectively with experts in specialized areas.

Finally, managers can fail in this regard by not learning the business broadly enough, by not keeping up with the diverse aspects of production, marketing, personnel, and so forth.

In our study of general managers, those seen as effective included a few mentioned as knowing the business well or taking the broad view; this group also included five described as curious, open-minded, and open to change. On the other hand, some of those seen as ineffective were described as not having an adequate grasp of the business. Our study was conducted in an organization that made a strategic shift toward a greater emphasis on new product development, thereby putting a premium on technical knowledge in GMs and rendering those incumbent executives who lacked this knowledge inadequate in this respect (Kaplan, 1986).

Managing a Large Network

Effective executives build, nourish, and use a very large set of contacts inside and outside the organization. Kotter (1982) found that the 15 general managers he studied each boasted networks with hundreds of members. Similarly, the mayors that Kotter and Lawrence (1976) studied possessed large networks, although the size varied with how ambitious and proactive the mayor's agenda was. Networks provide the power, resources, and support needed to help get things done; as such, they are a vital ingredient in executive success.

There are numerous ways in which executives can mismanage their networks. Chief among these is insensitivity to people, which McCall and Lombardo (1983) found was the chief culprit in the demise of executive careers. In less successful Sears executives, Bentz (1985) found a common personality flaw: insensitivity to people, abrasiveness, or overaggressiveness. Another common flaw is a lack of integrity, defined variously as being untrustworthy, too political, or too concerned with the next career move (McCall & Lombardo, 1983). In our general managers study, several of those classed as ineffective fell into this category (Kaplan, 1986). These flaws damage networks by undermining the trust, reciprocity, and give-and-take that is the foundation of effective working relationships (Sayles, 1964; Kaplan, 1984).

Another kind of developmental need has to do with the degree to which executives develop and use different sectors of their networks. With limited time and considerable latitude, executives may specialize in one sector (e.g., relationships with superiors) and neglect another (e.g., subordinates or peers). Ineffective executives cut themselves off from important constituencies and, as that part of their network atrophies, so does the success of the business associated with that part. Just as executives may isolate themselves, they may also become insulated—cushioned against certain sets of people with their attendant problems and needs and therefore ill-prepared to deal with those constituencies.

Using Power with Finesse

With the formal role of the executive comes considerable power, and the way it is exercised may spell success or failure for a leader. A major difficulty for executives is balancing the need to assert their power with the need to modulate their use of power, knowing when to exercise their strengths and when to exercise restraint. In other words, an executive's power, though it needs to be fully available to them, needs to be "socialized," in McClelland's (1975) terms so that it is put primarily in the service of the organization and other people. To use power skillfully, to possess a wide repertoire of influence tactics and an ability to call upon these tactics appropriately (Kotter, 1982), is not an ability that all managers possess in equal proportions.

At one extreme are those managers who abuse power, who take advantage of their control over subordinates' careers, who push their own plans and aims at the expense of others, who fail to recognize the ease with which their power and position puts them in a talking rather than a listening mode (Kaplan, Drath, & Kofodimos, 1985). Bork (1984) has noted a tendency among wealthy heads of family businesses to assume that they are the only source of workable ideas. The hard-driving self-assurance that enabled these entrepreneurs to build their businesses often defeats them when they reach the point where they must rely heavily on other people.

Managing Oneself in the Role

An executive's effectiveness depends on his ability to call upon his internal resources—skills, knowledge, interests, drives—as well as to hold in check his limitations and dysfunctional qualities. To deploy himself best, the executive must manage his own mix of strengths and weaknesses, and to manage the mix he must be aware of what it is (Maccoby, 1981; Bennis & Nanus, 1985; Kaplan, Drath, & Kofodimos, 1985). But one of the occupational hazards of being in a high position is that the position itself can work against realistic appraisal of the individual's leadership practices, either by the individual or by others. In both a sociological and psychological sense, the executive can become elevated in his eyes and other people's eyes. Factors that contribute to this elevation include the prestige, power, and perquisities of the high position, the steep ascent pattern that led to this position, and the need for accomplishment and advancement that propelled the individual forward (Kaplan, Drath, & Kofodimos, 1985). If as a result of these factors the executive becomes overly impressed with his own importance, it will become difficult for him to acknowledge limitations or to admit mistakes.

Another way in which executives must manage themselves in a role is in the relation between their highly demanding jobs and their private lives. A near-total absorption in work creates an immediate "negative spillover" at home (Kanter, 1977a; Evans & Bartolome, 1981). It also plants the seeds for delayed reactions in one's spouse and children. Although it may take years, underinvestment at home may ultimately lead to divorce, personal health problems, or adjustment problems for children (Kofodimos, 1984). A Wall Street Journal survey of 476 wives of senior corporate executives told the story of commitment: "The most important test for many wives is how the husband's . . . investment in his career compares with his commitment to . . . his wife and children. The women who are most unhappy contend that . . . their husbands [are much more committed to their work]" (Allen, 1981). Despite the inordinate demands of most executive jobs, executives' marriages and families do not have to suffer. Effective executives find a way to invest in both work and home (Vaillant, 1977; Evans & Bartolome, 1980). A key to effectiveness at home is a capacity for emotional awareness and close, personal relationships outside of a context of achievement and advancement. This is what Bakan (1966) called a capacity for communion.

Inner Developmental Needs

From the foregoing account of potential problems, we get a picture of the executive's needs as deficiencies in skills or abilities. From this we can define developmental needs in terms of behaviors such as framing strategy, innovating, altering structure, exercising power, making decisions, getting cooperation, allocating resources, organizing time and so on. These are the external attributes with which many management researchers concern themselves (Campbell, Dunnette, Lawler, & Weick, 1970; Kotter, 1982; McCall & Kaplan, 1984; Mintzberg, 1973; Sayles, 1979).

But these behavioral abilities do not exhaust the possibilities of what an executive might need to improve her performance. Complementing the set of behaviors required of an effective executive is the person's emotional life, deep inner needs, and fundamental relation to herself and to others. The executive's inner life has a great deal to do with how she behaves as an executive. The literature on management deals only minimally with the inner life, the deep-seated patterns, of managers or executives.

This is not the place to expound at length on personality. It should be enough to point up some of the basic internal patterns that shape, or misshape, executive behavior. To make the point, we have adapted a relatively simple model of personality that Barber (1968) developed to describe U.S. presidents. As adapted, the model rests upon two dimensions: active-passive, which distinguishes between people who put a lot of energy and initiative into their work and those who are withdrawn and unassertive; and positive-negative, which distinguishes between people who feel fundamentally good (pleased, optimistic, fulfilled) about their situations and those who feel fundamentally bad (alienated, discouraged, unfulfilled). From these two axes of personal make-up comes a fourfold

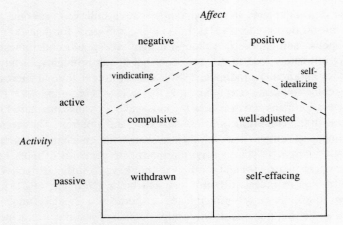

Figure 1.   Personal Styles of Executives

typology (see Figure 1). Each personal type is in effect a basic solution to the problem of how to make one's way in the world. In Barber's terms, each is a "bundle of strategies for adapting [and] for protecting and enhancing self-esteem" (1968, p. 52). Although one solution often predominates in an individual, others are always present to a lesser degree. Also, since these are dimensions and not dichotomies, an executive can be placed anywhere on each dimension. Finally, since our emphasis here is on developmental needs, we will focus on the liabilities of each of the four types and overlook the assets.

Active Negatives

The active-negative category is what Barber called the compulsive type, which he characterized as being oriented primarily toward personal ambition. Barber (1968) cited the example of Herbert Hoover, who as President worked extremely and compulsively hard yet was chronically discouraged. His barely suppressed aggressive feelings hindered his ability to form genuinely cooperative lateral relations with other leaders, and this failure undoubtedly fed his frustration. Former President Richard Nixon is another example of the active-negative type. So as not to stigmatize the active-negative type, we point out that charismatic leaders capable of making drastic changes in organizations—what Burns (1978) calls the transformational leader—also fall in this category. A mild example of the active-negative comes from the extensive observational research done by Hodgson, Levinson, and Zaleznik (1965) in a psychiatric hospital. The hospital's superintendent, an effective institutional leader overall whose attention was turned mostly to the outside world, adopted a "paternal-assertive" role. He was capable of being blunt to the point of occasionally being brutal. He cultivated a reputation in the hospital as being tough and aggressive yet, in reality, his behavior did not usually live up to this billing.

This type exhibits one of the three basic needs—moving against people— which Horney (1945) saw reflected in overdeveloped ambition and a craving for power and prestige. In a later book, Horney (1950) described the extreme case of the "aggressive vindictive" or "arrogant-vindictive" individual who defends himself against an underlying feeling of self-contempt by compulsively attempt- ing to prove his self-worth, to vindicate himself, hence the "vindicating style." In the process he treats others shabbily and then rationalizes this behavior by externalizing responsibility for it by cloaking himself in self-righteousness. In the extreme case the arrogant-vindictive person cannot tolerate anyone more powerful or more accomplished and responds rivalrously to anyone who is. In reaction to unresponsive or rejecting parents in childhood, the individual has undergone a hardening process that is designed to seal him off from further injury. As an adult he tries to live down the reputation foisted upon him as a child.

In their clinical research on executives, Kets de Vries and Miller (1985) found roughly the same extreme phenomenon which they called "reactive nar- cissism." "Reacting" against (or compensating for) being mistreated and other- wise diminished in childhood, the executive wages a campaign in adulthood to elevate himself at the expense of others. This blatant form of the active-negative includes grandiosity, domination, exploitation, and abuse. Levinson (1968) identified the equivalent of the active-negative executive in the angry, au- thoritarian individual who "spews anger, is unnecessarily critical, and argues too long and too much" (p. 278). Levinson noted that the anger is often caused by the environment as well as the executive's personality. Levinson (1968) also discussed "self-centered" executives, who were so concerned about maintaining or increasing their own status they will resort to attacking or exploiting others.

Of the many ways in which an active-negative executive can hurt his effective- ness, we will mention just a few. Active-negative executives are likely to err on the side of over-using or abusing power, by being demanding taskmasters, by encouraging conformity and yesmanship, or, in the extreme case, by running roughshod over people (Kets de Vries, & Miller, 1985). Their networks are likely to suffer because active-negatives tend to be mistrustful and therefore undermine the reciprocity needed to build strong relationships, their low need to please makes them less likeable, and their limited empathy keeps them from tuning into other people's needs (Horney, 1950). At their worst, active-negatives are the abrasive, intimidating individuals who damage their relationships and their careers. On the strategic front, active-negatives have a weakness for grand if not grandiose plans, formulated on the basis of too little investigation and too little input from others. Should the plan run into trouble during implementation, these executives have difficulty accepting disconfirming evidence (Kets de Vries

& Miller, 1985). Finally, the compulsive nature of active-negatives make them candidates for work addiction.

Passive-negatives

This is a withdrawn type oriented toward minimal performance of duty (Barber, 1968). Passivity and negativity feed each other. Expecting little, passive-negatives do not exert themselves, and attempting little, they get little in return. President Calvin Coolidge typified this style. He spent much time alone, looking out of his office window. He avoided problems; his motto was: "Let well enough alone." A delegator in the extreme, he unloaded much of his work on others. His relationships were cool and distant (Barber, 1968, p. 55). The passive-negative personality is also characteristic of some mayors whose limited aspirations and engagement are manifested in modest strategies for their terms of office and small networks (Kotter & Lawrence, 1976).

The passive-negative category amounts to what Horney (1950) called the resigned solution to inner conflicts. These individuals cope with inner conflicts by retreating from them. In the worst cases, they are characterized by the "absence of any serious striving for achievement and the aversion of effort" (p. 261). They may have aspirations, which are often fulfilled only in their imagination. They have a distaste for expectations, deadlines, and conflict of any kind. They are not given to goal-setting and planning. Their relationships, while perhaps smooth on the surface, are characterized by emotional distance.

The passive-negative type tends to originate from an overly confining and demanding family life during childhood. The child pulls back from a situation that threatens to overwhelm her by asking too much of her emotionally or in the way of achievement and by paying too little heed to what she needs as an individual (Horney, 1950).

Passive-negative executives are at best custodians of their organizations, who distinguish themselves by attempting little in the way of strategizing, of managing their large organizations, of making use of the power available, of delving into complex problems, or of building relationships.

Passive-positives

Executives of this variety are generally compliant people oriented toward being on harmonious terms with others (Barber, 1968). Horney discovered an equivalent category, which she called "moving toward" (1945) and later "self-effacing" (1950). These are people who surrender their own ambitions and claims to mastery in favor of drawing support from other (powerful) people. These self-minimizing individuals restrict themselves by placing a taboo on being expansive, superior, or aggressive. Having probably grown up in the shadow of a powerful and at least somewhat benign individual (e.g., older sibling or parent), the self-effacing person opted for winning the favor and affection of others. Rather than struggle for his place in the sun he chose to be compliant, ingratiating, lovable, and good. Self-effacing types are susceptible to active, conscious feelings of self-doubt and worry. By restricting their power, they purchase good relationships at the expense of good feelings about themselves (May, 1972).

As executives, they are liable to set their organization's sights too low (Horney, 1950). Bearish rather than bullish, they would be likely to underestimate, rather than overestimate, what their organizations can do. Best at responding to the strength of others, they would have trouble taking the initiative (Levinson, 1968). This type of individual makes a better number two executive than a chief executive. Prone to being self-critical, passive-positives would have trouble making hard choices and being decisive. Their self-doubt and self-minimizing tendencies also have a way of handicapping them and making them inefficient in the performance of their jobs. They fail to make full use of their resources because of the need to keep themselves down (Horney, 1950). In the worst case, a self-effacing executive can become utterly immobilized.

The passive-positive personality has its redeeming qualities, however. The clinical director of the psychiatric hospital mentioned earlier (Hodgson, Levinson, & Zaleznik, 1965) specialized in a democratic style of leadership that bordered on the passive. He was also known for his way of nurturing his subordinates, who included psychiatric residents, in a way that the authors described as being maternal.

Active-positives

These are executives whose primary motivation is to have productive and rewarding work and relationships (Barber, 1968). Active-positive executives, whom Barber labeled "adjusted," pour themselves into the strategic and administrative aspects of their work, set challenging but attainable goals, form strong, mutual relationships with the members of their networks, use power in such a way that work gets done and relationships are maintained or enhanced, and in general operate off a basic drive to be competent and to get the job done. The 15 general managers that Kotter (1982) studied intensively appear to be a collection of active-positives. Although they vary somewhat in effectiveness, they show an enviable ability to set appropriate short- and long-term strategy and to call upon a vast collection of contacts in their organizations and industries first to frame strategy, and then to act on it. As a group, their basic personalities demonstrated high activity in the form of ample needs for power and achievement and strong career ambition. Their personalities demonstrated a highly positive affect in the form of marked optimism, even in the face of adversity, and a large capacity to enter into successful, cooperative relationships. Almost all of the 15 general managers came from families in which they were close to one or both parents and from which they received a legacy of high expectations for themselves.

Although Barber (1968) did not consider it, there is a possibility that executives of this type will display counterproductive tendencies—by being excessively active and positive. This is a way of saying that some active-positive executives take that type's characteristic orientation towards being productive a step further and become almost totally absorbed with attaining mastery. In this respect, the extreme active-positives are similar to the extreme active-negatives (see the arrogant-vindictive and reactive-narcissistic types). Both fall prey to the "appeal to mastery" because both represent attempts to vanquish doubts about oneself by becoming masterful, powerful or successful in one way or another (Horney, 1950). Horney also called these patterns "expansive" solutions because they all lead the individual to try to become a big or superior presence. Horney (1950) described those people who choose an expansive solution as follows:

> The feeling of superiority that goes with this solution is not necessarily conscious but . . . largely determines behavior, strivings and attitudes toward life in general. The appeal of life lies in its mastery. It chiefly entails his determination, conscious or unconscious, to overcome every obstacle—in or outside himself. . . . He should be able to master the adversities of fate, the difficulties of a situation, the intricacies of intellectual problems, the resistances of other people, conflicts within himself. . . . When looking superficially at the expansive types we get a picture of people who . . . are bent on self-glorification, on ambitious pursuits, on vindictive triumph, with the mastery of life through intelligence and will power as the means to actualize their idealized self (pp. 191–2).

The two types of expansive solutions part company along the affective dimension. (Kohut's theory of personality would distinguish between the two by tracing the origin of the extreme active-negative type to the child's unmet grandiose-exhibitionistic needs which, when frustrated, kick up aggression and rivalry in later life; and the extreme active-positive type to the child's overidentification with an ideal other, which imbues the person with the positive motivation to climb to great heights [Kahn 1985]). Horney (1950) called the active-positive version of the expansive solution "narcissism," which applies to the person who seeks to become her idealized self, hence the "self-idealizing" style. The narcissistic person exudes self-confidence and shows little or no self-doubt. Her relationships, even including generosity towards others, tend to be governed by the need to stimulate devotion or admiration—that is, confirmation of the person's ideal self.

Kets de Vries and Miller (1985) refer to the same personality types as the "self-deceptive narcissist," an extreme case which originates with parents who treat the person in childhood as if she were perfect. She may be the favored or admired child (Horney, 1950), and the parents thus overburden the child with their high expectations.

In his therapy with successful people, Jung found something comparable to narcissism as defined by Horney and self-deceptive narcissism as defined by Kets de Vries and Miller (Hall & Nordby, 1973). By "persona," Jung meant the mask a person puts on to make a good impression on others. The narcissistic version of the persona is what Jung called "inflation," or an overblown sense of one's own reputation or importance.

Finally, Maccoby's (1976) research on corporate character unearthed a type that he named the "gamesman," which contains elements of Horney's category of narcissism. What stands out about the gamesman is his strong need for mastery put in the service of task accomplishment and career progression. The benefits of the gamesman's single-minded pursuit of mastery include a talent for understanding and acting on complex sociotechnical problems in a complex social system, coupled with a cool and confident manner and a knack for winning the cooperation of others. But, reminiscent of the narcissist in Horney's terms and the self-deceptive narcissist in Kets de Vries and Miller's terms, the gamesman builds shallow relationships and takes an overly analytical, unemotional approach to decision-making.

While the extreme active-positive can be extraordinarily successful and productive (because she is so positive about her prospects and so active in pursuing them), and although this type is highly valued by organizations as executive material, she is susceptible to characteristic difficulties. As with any extreme type, this person may not know how to work well (that is, how to manage oneself in the executive role). She may take on too much and spread herself too thin, or she may work erratically, making up for lost time by dispatching a backlog in one fell swoop. This pattern is self-perpetuating because it feeds the narcissist's appetite for the heroic gesture, for making a big splash. Because of their sense of themselves as special, these individuals may have trouble not only with making the consistent effort to turn out work but also with attending to detail, which they may feel is beneath them (Horney, 1950).

Different from the reactive narcissist, the executive with this kind of narcissism carefully scans the environment and solicits input from others in making decisions and setting strategy, so much so that she runs the risk of becoming paralyzed (Kets de Vries & Miller, 1985). This type is motivated not only by the need to be admired and loved but also by the fear of failure, which can slow down the decision-making process and also make for conservative strategy-making (Kets de Vries & Miller, 1985). At the same time, this benign narcissism is associated with a responsible use of power and a moderate openness to influence, not seen in the extreme active-negative.

It is not surprising that self-idealizing tendencies would be found in some executives and other highly successful people. The executive position is in fact a rare and elevated niche that accords the individual a special standing, and individuals who would want that position badly enough to work for many years to achieve it might be prone to a sense of self that accentuates the positive and strong in themselves and suppresses the negative and weak.

While recognizing the potential for self-idealization in executives, we do not want to overplay the point. Some research has found, for example, a small negative correlation between leadership and conceit and between leadership and eagerness for admiration (Bass, 1981). If high-level positions tends to attract people with self-idealizing tendencies and then to reinforce those tendencies, we do not yet know in what proportions.

FORCES AFFECTING EXECUTIVE DEVELOPMENT

Having discussed some of the possible developmental needs of executives, we turn to the question of how such needs can be met. Assuming that an executive has already reached a high organizational level, how does he go about continuing his development?

We will assume that for development to happen, four conditions must be met. First, an executive must receive information from those around him that helps him decide whether or not his behavior is effective. Second, an executive must be able to look inward, to find within himself the reasons and values that guide his behavior or that will motivate future behavior. Third, an executive must be able to accept criticism. That is, he must be able to admit weaknesses and see the value in working to correct them. Finally, for development to take place, an executive must change his behavior or attitudes or both. Change is the proof of development. (See Figure 2 for a schematic view of these forces and how they operate.)

Whether or not these conditions can be met depends largely upon the degree to which an individual executive and those around him are open to the possibility of development. An executive who is open to change is more likely to solicit feedback than an executive who is relatively resistant to change. Subordinates, peers, and superiors of the executive who are open to development are more likely to give feedback than others who are relatively closed to the idea of change and growth. The same goes for the other three conditions. In each case, the more open an executive is to the need for change, and the more open those around him are, the more likely that the conditions for change and development can be met.

Were this the extent of the problem, however, we would need merely to address the issue of openness versus resistance to change. Yet our research suggests strongly that more than this is involved. Our examination of forces affecting executive development is based on a study that consisted of a literature review and 40 interviews with executives and people who work closely with executives (Kaplan, Drath, & Kofodimos, 1985). There are certain forces inherent in the organization and in the nature of an executive's job and position that also affect the prospects for development. Although some of these forces can encourage growth and development, we will discuss here those forces that tend to inhibit development. We should remember however that these forces operate within the context of the executive's overall attitude toward development and change. Here is one way that the Biographical Action Research method we describe later shows its value. If we are to understand why a certain executive is

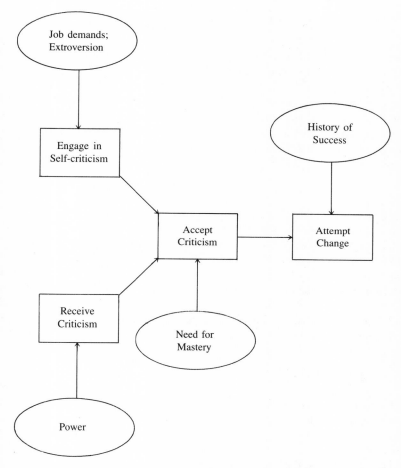

Figure 2. Factors Affecting Conditions for Executive Development*

Note:

*An arrow from a circle to a box indicates a causal relation. An arrow from a box to a box indicates a chronological relation.

relatively resistant to change and why another executive is more open to change, we must acquaint ourselves with the character of the person as well as with the nature of the organization in which the person operates.

We will look at the four conditions needed for development and see how certain organizational and personal forces may inhibit the formation of these conditions.

Condition One: An Open Flow of Information and Criticism

Where executives are concerned, getting behaviorally focused information and criticism is affected to some degree by the executive's way of exercising power. Our research suggested that there are four factors related to the exercise of power which tend to inhibit "feedback." These factors are highly interrelated, which means that in discussing them separately we will be slighting somewhat the effects created by the way these factors act in concert. Yet an analytical discussion will help us see the contribution each factor makes to the process by which power can inhibit criticism.

The Executive's Demeanor

Although a certain air of authority is probably necessary if executives are to carry out their jobs, we found that often an executive's bearing, his way of conducting himself with others, can inhibit feedback. Whether it is related to mental acuity, command of the issues, or a history of success; an exaggerated, dominating presence often chokes off criticism. The attitude underlying such a demeanor may be one of entitlement of sorts; that is, an executive may feel that her achievement entitles her to an exemption from criticism. As one executive development specialist we interviewed put it, the executive may be thinking, "I've made it to the top . . . and people don't swing my door open and tell me how to do my job."

The Executive's Impact

One theme we heard again and again in our interviews centered on the fact that many people seem to be especially sensitive to the statements made by powerful people. Comments can be interpreted as commands; inquiries become injunctions (Laing, 1967). This effect can become so pronounced that some executives feel they must guard the expression on their faces. "If I don't smile," one told us, "people think the business is going bad." This effect can make executives reluctant to say anything not thought out beforehand, and a lack of spontaneity can have the effect of adding distance to the relationship between an executive and those around him. In such cool relationships, people feel less free to offer criticism. The executive's exaggerated impact can thus restrict feedback.

Another effect of the executive's impact can be to create cheerleaders, subordinates and others who for reasons of self-interest tell the executive only what they imagine he wants to hear and omit what they do not want him to hear, including news of problems that might reflect badly on them (Read, 1962; Burns & Stalker, 1961). There is also the problem of a kind of unconscious cheerleading, when subordinates do not withhold information, but become blind to any faults in a highly-placed superior. This is a form of collusion in which subordinates, because of their dependency on the executive, support the image of himself he wishes others to see (Goffman, 1959). Thus, together, the subordinates and the executive create a "delusionary system" (Kets de Vries, 1979). This is not likely to be fertile ground on which an executive can learn and grow.

The Executive's Isolation

The structure of the organization tends to bring executives, as they move upward, into contact with fewer and fewer people inside the organization. From his research on top executives, Burns (1957, p. 60) found a "uniform segregation of three or four persons" at the top of organizations. A human resources director we interviewed told us, "Most executives have very few people they have contact with (inside the organization)—20 or 30 people in a 20,000 person organization—and those people tend to be high-level executives who also tend to be isolated." There is also the matter of insulating executives, protecting them from the little indignities and problems of everyday life. Sometimes such insulation can result in the executive losing touch with much of the organization below (Townsend, 1984, pp. 6–11). Although executives need a certain amount of isolation to make their jobs feasible, isolation takes a toll on communication and tends to inhibit criticism upward because the absence of contact guarantees the absence of communication, especially of sensitive information. Moreover, whatever communication does take place probably happens on the executive's turf, complete with the symbols of power and isolation (such as an office on the top floor) that can add to the discomfort of subordinates who would speak out (Steele, (1983).

The Executive's Autonomy

Executives must have a certain amount of autonomy to function effectively, but executives are granted autonomy along a wide spectrum, from the extreme of the chief executive who is only a functionary of the board or its chairman, to the top person who has no board or whose board "rubber stamps" her decisions. Executives with a great deal of autonomy can use that power to screen criticism, in effect if not by intent. Executives who have the autonomy to hire whomever they please can—and some do—use that power to hire people whose backgrounds, sex, and education promise to make them compatible and sympathetic. Executives who do this are likely to end up with the cheerleaders we have already discussed, subordinates who tell them only what they want to hear, (Zaleznik & Kets de Vries, 1975; Bennis, 1976; Kanter, 1977b).

Executives with much autonomy can also in effect or in fact put themselves outside of the performance appraisal system. As DeVries et al. (1981) found in their review of appraisal practices in organizations, appraisals tend to thin out at high levels. Executives can have the power to define what is appropriate to discuss in appraisals; they can also have the power to define appraisals so that they themselves are not even included.

The exercise of power can impede the open flow of information and criticism, yet power must be exercised if executives are to do their jobs. So the issue here is not how to reduce the power an executive needs, but rather how to manage the aspects of its exercise that impede criticism.

Condition Two: The Ability to Look Inward

Introspection is a necessary step in the process of development, whether we look inward to make sense of criticism and information from others, or whether we look inward to gain fresh insights about ourselves and our behavior. Yet the extent to which an executive is likely to look inward must be considered in light of the fact that the demands of his work usually preclude time for reflection and reflection is not immediately relevant to an executive's performance. Self-reflection is not correlated with the vitality of one's business.

The typical executive's day does not leave much time or energy for introspection. The former CEO of BankAmerica wrote that his job was virtually four full-time jobs in one: desk work, meetings with employees, meetings with customers, civic and other public functions—each could take 100 percent of his time (Lundborg, 1981; p. 6). Though high-level managers may see fewer people within their own organization, the number of people they see outside the organization increases dramatically (Dubin & Spray, 1964). A survey of brigadier generals found that they were "too busy to have time for any reflection; [instead they were] putting out brush fires and reacting rather than thinking or planning ahead" (USARI, 1978, p. 8).

But lacking time for introspection may not be the whole story. After all, the executive's day is less hectic than that of some lower-level managers, whose day is crammed with as many as 500 discrete episodes (McCall, Morrison, & Hannan, 1978). Despite the demands on their time, executives may have greater latitude than lower-level managers to decide how to spend that time.

As Jenks (1984) pointed out, lacking time may be partly a matter of the perception of time. Executives may not be able to find the time for introspection because looking inward is not immediately relevant to their work. Executives are concerned with tangible, external results—profits, productivity, market share. The role of introspection in achieving such results may be hard for an executive to see, if indeed looking inward plays a role at all.

Executives may even be suspicious of introspection. Jennings (1965) asserted that executives get satisfaction from doing rather than contemplating; "dreamers seldom make it to the top." One CEO we interviewed told us "I am not conscious of doing any kind of in-depth reflecting . . . there [are] always so many things to do." Many executives share this sense of being always immersed in action. They are men and women of action, not reflection, and certainly not self-reflection (Mintzberg, 1973; Sayles, 1979). In Jung's (1959) terms, they are extroverts, in the sense that they invest chiefly in the external world and care much less about their internal world of feelings and bodily states. For organizational and business purposes this is probably as it should be, yet the effect on development is problematic.

To be effective, executives must be oriented toward action, but this may lead many executives to discount the benefits of introspection. The issue is not how to turn executives into navel-gazers, but how to help them use introspection as a tool for processing information about their own performance so that they might become more effective.

Condition Three: The Ability to Accept Criticism

To grow and develop, we must do more than receive information and be able to reflect inwardly. We must also be able to accept the validity and importance of criticism, and we must be able to admit, if only to ourselves, that we can fail, that we have shortcomings and weaknesses that could stand redressing.

On this issue the executive has come in for much abuse. Many people seem to assume that an executive is not likely to admit weakness or accept criticism. The assumption seems to be that executives are simply the kind of people—powerful, egomaniacal—who will simply not admit failure out of stubborn pride. Our study suggests that the reason for an executive's reluctance to admit failure, where such reluctance exists, may be strongly related to the executive's powerful need to be competent and at the same time to appear to others as highly competent. In extreme cases this need for competence may be fueled by narcissistic tendencies.

Several factors contribute to this need. One factor is the set of expectations that come with the territory. An executive told us, "[The CEO] needs to be above everybody, never wrong . . . he has to act [as if he were] perfect." A consultant we interviewed explained it this way: "Executives in general are not supposed to have problems. They are supposed to be strong and competent and adequate to most situations." Another factor is that executives, as holders of high position, incur high risks. The potential damage an executive may do in terms of losing money or hurting people makes competent performance vitally important. In addition to the factors that make competence necessary is the fact that executives must also demonstrate their competence for all to see. The opinions an executive renders and the decisions he makes are often highly visible. Executives want to build a reputation as people who know what they are doing. If an executive makes a habit of publicly being seen to be wrong, he will erode people's confidence in his competence, which can make it difficult for him to do his job. The need to save face can therefore become powerful, and can also impede the executive's ability to accept criticism.

The executive who admits weakness and error may also erode his confidence in himself. In fact, the passive-positive or self-effacing personality type, which has, relatively speaking, no problem accepting criticism, is perhaps too ready to take criticism to heart and at the expense of self-confidence. In other types of people, the ambition to be competent and powerful may arise from a need to ward off underlying feelings of inadequacy (Zaleznik & Kets de Vries, 1975). To the extent that this is true, criticism may be rejected because it touches off unconscious feelings of inadequacy. According to Kets de Vries and Miller (1985), the reactive narcissist (that is, the extreme active-negative) tends to become enraged by criticism and the self-deceptive narcissist (the extreme active-positive), hurt by it. Discussing the expansive types, which includes both the extreme active-negatives and the extreme active-positives, Horney (1950) attributed their difficulty with criticism to their tendency to overrate their abilities and the quality of their work. "Any criticism, no matter how seriously or conscientiously given, is felt as a hostile attack. And, because of their necessity to choke off any doubts about themselves, they tend not to examine the validity of the criticism but to focus primarily on warding it off in this way or that" (p. 311). She argues that a narcissistic individual "uses all available means to denying his 'failures' to himself. . . . He must maintain in his mind a picture of himself of which he can be proud. He must . . . live with the pretense of being all knowing, all generous, all fair, etc. He must never . . . be aware that by comparison with his glorified self he has feet of clay" (pp. 192–3).

Thus, executives who combat self-doubt by adopting an expansive solution and seeking maximum mastery over their work and over themselves will characteristically resist criticism and therefore sacrifice the chance to become aware of disturbances in their work. As Bandura (1982) discovered in research on self-efficacy in people in general, a strong sense of self-efficacy helps in the performance of tasks the person already knows how to do, but hinders learning. (Bandura also found the converse to be true: self-doubt bestirs learning but hinders performance.) Although failure can be a great teacher, expansive types will have difficulty learning from the implied or explicit criticism that emanates from failure because they are not inclined to take responsibility for their piece of it. What we have here is a self-sealing mechanism that has a low capacity for self-correction (Argyris & Schon, 1974). Extreme active-negatives have a tendency to blame others for mistakes and failures. Extreme active-positives, because of their strong need to be right, are hypersensitive to being held responsible for problems (Kets de Vries & Miller, 1985).

Because of the internal and external pressures for executives to be masterful, they can begin to believe that they are nearly infalliable. As pointed out in a report by the Society for Personnel Administration (1965, p. 24), "At heart we are all egotists and we are—to ourselves—important individuals. As important individuals, we don't feel we have many faults." As people who are in fact important, executives are perhaps even more susceptible than most to this way of thinking. According to Kotter (1982), the highly successful track records of the general managers he studied lulled them into what he called an "I-can-do-anything" syndrome. Hague (1974, p. 93) has pointed out that "the executive may get conceited about his successes and blame his failure on external circumstances, but worst of all, he will cease to be self-critical and to learn from his experiences."

The single largest factor in this issue may be the link too often forged between making a mistake and being judged incompetent. If executives are to more willingly accept criticism, this link must be weakened, if not broken (Peters & Waterman, 1982). Too often a mistake, if large enough, brands a manager as being unequal to the task. Yet, McCall and Lombardo (1983) have shown that successful managers often make many serious mistakes, and that the lessons they learn from such mistakes may be critical to their success. Executives need to understand that admitting weakness or error can be the beginning of further development and increased effectiveness.

Condition Four: The Ability to Change

To become an executive in the first place means that one has succeeded. Managers who have succeeded in the past are expected to continue to succeed in the future, and are therefore usually given choice assignments which lead to further success. Frequently, such managers were always highly regarded, and therefore got off to a good start, being well situated in the "opportunity structure" (Kanter, 1977b). This string of success followed by opportunity, opportunity followed by success, stretching over a manager's career, is what Kotter (1982) called the "success syndrome." Such a career history may leave an executive with the idea (in some cases justified) that changing his way of managing, even a little, could hurt his chances for continued success. Thus it may be that success itself is a powerful impediment to the ability to change, which is the final condition that must be met if development is to take place.

In our interviews we found evidence that successful executives instinctively play hands off with their style of management. As one executive we interviewed said, "Fundamentally my management style is cast, and I'm not about to risk changing it and jeopardize the success I've achieved." This executive may have been worried, perhaps rightly so, about losing his effectiveness by changing. Such an anxiety might be coupled with a general fear of failure that researchers such as Jennings (1965) have noted in executives—an anxiety that they will not accomplish what they have set out to do. A consultant we interviewed described an executive as being, "cautious about changing, saying that he knows the organization talks about a more humanistic approach, a greater emphasis on human relationship skills, but 'If I lose some of my toughness, am I really going to be successful?' "

The significance of an executive's "winning formula" is better appreciated in the light of Barber's (1968) finding that U.S. Presidents first form the leadership style they later use in office early in their adult lives. A product of strong personal needs, resources available from their pasts, and present opportunities, leadership style is not easy to come by and is not readily relinquished.

It is not the executive alone who has this attitude; the people with a stake in the success of the executive may feel the same way. In our interviews we heard that trying to change an executive was "playing with dynamite." We were asked, "Is the potential improvement worth the risk of losing a reasonably effective executive?" One respondent commented, "I'm impressed with the danger of changing [executives]. I've seen executives try to change and get lost because they get away from their management style—the way they grew up and manage best." The executive's boss, who may be in the best position to precipitate work on the problem, may choose to overlook a serious behavioral problem because the executive is seen as too valuable to lose (Levinson, 1968).

In fact, rather than correcting weaknesses, many executives seem more interested in building on strengths. This can be a worthwhile pursuit of development, but it can also be a way of avoiding confronting painful deficiencies that could be corrected with perhaps equally worthwhile effect on overall performance.

Facilitators of Development

The forces that act to dampen executive development can also be manipulated to encourage it. These forces can be converted into facilitators by the executive himself, other people and the organization. Events, including setbacks and challenges, can also propel development.

The Individual

The executive is obviously a key factor because without his active cooperation, development is impossible. His values matter greatly. If, for example, the executive comes to value introspection, then he will have a reason to order his priorities so that he can find the time to introspect. His treatment of others is key. It is only if he recognizes, for example, the potentially restricting effect of power on the flow of sensitive information that he can work to cut back on those restrictions. People around him will not funnel him criticism, unless he actively encourages it. Similarly, the supply lines of constructive criticism are limited by the extent of the network he develops. The evidence is that effective general managers avoid the isolation which is the occupational hazard of executives by developing, maintaining, and using extensive networks (Kotter, 1982).

Probably the most fundamental aspect of the executive vis-á-vis his own development is his self-orientation and self-worth. If the executive takes himself too seriously, if his confidence depends on leading a mistake-free existence, then criticism and failure will be hard to take and hard to benefit from. A key, then, to a developmental attitude, is for the executive to detach himself from the need for perfection so that he sees the value of mistakes and failures as a vehicle for increasing mastery and not just as a threat to mastery. To achieve this attitude could itself require a major intervention. It is worth noting that Bandura (1982) has found through his research on self-efficacy that the ideal combination in a person is a strong sense of efficacy to help in withstanding failure and a measure of uncertainty about one's abilities to spur learning.

Other People

The condition of the executive's relationships also make a difference for his prospects for development. To have a confidante, a sounding board, encourages introspection by giving the executive a chance to talk out loud about private material. Similarly, if the executive has one or more friends or close associates at work or outside of work, then constructive criticism is more likely to flow from those sources. Note that this will happen only if the close association is defined as one in which honesty and openness are valued (Maccoby, 1976).

The executive's boss is in an excellent position to help if he can overcome his own reluctance to intervene. In the case of a hostile executive, for example, the superior may be intimidated by the subordinate's anger; the superior may himself get angry to the point where he holds back out of guilt over his own anger; or the superior may worry about his ability to keep his own feelings in check if he confronted the subordinate (Levinson, 1968, p. 281).

Criticism is also more likely to come the executive's way if he works with one or more individuals bold enough to confront him and if he is receptive enough to allow it to happen. The chances that the executive will accept the personal criticism go up when it comes from someone whose motives the executive trusts and whose perspective he respects. The executive's spouse can fulfill this role, but it is not uncommon for the executive to disregard the spouse's observations. All these conducive relationships assume that the executive can enter into certain relationships in which he can disclose and in which others can confront. An executive whose problem is that he alienates other people and cannot enter into close, open relationships will have this avenue closed off to him.

The Organization

Organizations also have a big impact on the course of executive development. How organizations treat the power variable, for example, has a direct relation to the likelihood that executives will receive criticism from below. If organizations segregate executives less and remove some of the trappings of power, then the executive becomes more accessible and personal criticism more likely. One factor is executive offices. Organizations can reduce the power differential by making executive offices less impressive and locating these offices in closer proximity to the rest of the organization (Steele, 1983). Intel, for example, deliberately diminishes the power difference between high-level managers and others by eliminating such executive perks as limousines, plush offices, and private dining rooms (Grove, 1983).

Another thing organizations can do is create mechanisms for feeding constructive criticism to executives. For starters, organizations can include executives in standard personnel practices like performance appraisal that apply to the rest of the organization. The key here is whether the CEO takes the system seriously and personally uses it. The same thing applies to training programs that include a self-diagnostic component. Organizations can go against the tendency to offer such programs to lower- and middle-level managers but exempt high-level managers (Digman, 1978). Basic to whether appraisal practices are applied to executives is the organizational culture, especially at the top, and whether its values and practices support the self-development of the executive.

Organizations can help executives accept criticism by moderating the use of status symbols that feed the executive's sense of his importance. Organizations can also help in this regard by encouraging norms that legitimize a certain amount of justifiable mistakes and failures (Peters & Waterman, 1982). Successful executives make mistakes and, as importantly, learn from their mistakes (McCall & Lombardo, 1983); organizations should convey the message to their executives that admitting ineffectiveness can be salutary and conducive to further development.

Challenges and Setbacks

Apart from self-conscious and deliberate attempts to develop, executives can and do grow in response to the regular challenges that their jobs deal them. The executive's job does not remain constant but changes according to what the organization's problems, opportunities, and crises require of him (Dubin & Spray, 1964). In addition, new jobs present new challenges, which bring out new response capacities in the executive. At the same time executives have a fair amount of latitude (Stewart, 1982) so that the advantage they take of new experiences varies considerably. A pivotal factor is whether the executive is inclined to do what Gardner (1963) calls self-testing or whether he stays safely within the set of things he can do comfortably.

Setbacks and crises in the executive's worklife or personal life can also precipitate development. There is nothing like a career setback, such as being demoted or fired, to prompt soul-searching and redirection. The same is true of personal crises such as divorce or a troubled child. The precipitating event need not necessarily occur in the executive's life but can happen to someone in the immediate vicinity and touch off the same reaction vicariously. Examples include having a close associate get fired or a close friend lose a loved one or develop a serious health problem. There is nothing, however, about naturally occurring stresses that guarantees learning about oneself. Executives regularly leave their jobs or their marriages without learning a thing. The determining factor is whether the executive is prepared to take the appropriate amount of responsibility for the setback. The expansive self-idealizing type of executive tends to take too little, and the self-effacing type, too much.

To overcome stiff resistance such as what the expansive or self-idealizing executive puts up, the only recourse may be a "manufactured crisis." When the executive denies the existence of a problem or shrugs off responsibility even when confronted, then other people may need to force the issue. This means applying only the minimum force needed to budge the immovable object. One form this can take is personal consultation, often mandated by a higher level executive, in which the executive is "overwhelmed by data" collected from him, his co-workers, and people in his private life (Kiel, 1986). In the case of an alcoholic or drug addict, the intervention may be a surprise confrontation. A corporate executive with an alcohol problem, found himself confronted by a number of his colleagues and the medical director who presented him with the choice of undertaking treatment or losing his job (Greenberger, 1983). Forcing the issue in this way is tricky at best but even more problematic when the target is powerful and a highly placed person. The founder and chief executive of what had been a large and fast-growing private company had a serious drug problem that seriously hurt his effectiveness and that his board (whose members he had selected and had under his control) chose to overlook (Behar, 1985). A manufactured crisis may seem like a drastic step to take but it is one of the few ways to strip away the layers of rationalization surrounding a troubled or troublesome and defensive executive. A caveat: only a highly skilled professional should attempt this kind of powerful intervention.

Executives with drug addictions (an increasingly widespread problem) are an especially interesting case of the challenges of confronting behavioral problems in executives (Flax, 1985). An executive might take a drug like cocaine in the first place because it enhances the feeling of mastery. The executive may not worry about becoming addicted because he is used to feeling masterful. Having become addicted, executives (and their families) are reluctant to own up to the problem because they feel they have so much to lose. Because of the executives' need to preserve an image of capability, they will be loath to go public in their organizations with the problem. Yet, the essential first step towards overcoming an addiction is to get the executive to admit that he has a serious problem and that he is powerless to solve it by himself. Once addicted executives undergo treatment, they have among the best prognoses of all addicts because they have so much going for them—jobs, families, money, supportive co-workers as well as their own personal characteristics and skills. Their skills can, however, work against treatment, if they are used to win over professional staff as a substitute for working on the problem; or if they take a detached, analytic approach to the problem instead of letting in the full emotional impact of the addiction (Flax, 1985).

The discussion of executives who abuse drugs or who have other pronounced behavioral problems raises the question of what about an executive is amenable to change and what is not. Is there any hope of reaching executives like the extreme active-negatives who are so well defended against and resistant to feedback? Kets de Vries and Miller (1985) suggested that it is very difficult to change this type of executive. Vaillant (1977) recognized the difficulty, rooted in their lack of motivation for treatment and their resistance to change. But he contended that these "defenses are not always the incurable bad habits that they appear on the surface" (p. 159). The defenses were developed in the first place as an adaptation to the person's circumstances and to the extent that circumstances change, the person can outgrow the adaptive mechanism: "immature mechanisms of defense can be dynamic modes of adaptation and not simply a rigid armor that deforms the personality" (p. 158). If we take a longitudinal perspective on an adult's development, we can see how executives can recover (as men in Vaillant's sample did over 30 years) from "seemingly intractable character disorders" in the same way that people move from adolescence to adulthood (Vaillant, 1977, p. 239). As a final note of hope for people with marked personality problems, Vaillant observed that the poor prognosis given for these types is a function of how poorly they are understood, which in turn stems from the fact that they are not liked.

BIOGRAPHICAL ACTION RESEARCH

In our attempts to understand executives and their development, we have evolved a research strategy we call Biographical Action Research (BAR). As its name implies, BAR is an intensive method that approaches biography in the scope and depth of information it allows us to gather. The method also combines inquiry with service to the person being studied. The service component helps us gain the extraordinary access to the person's life that we need by offering the executive something in return for his participation. In essence BAR involves collecting a large amount of information about an executive from the executive herself, from her colleagues at work—including subordinates, peers, and superiors past and present—and from her family. These various sources of data tell us about various aspects of the person being studied, as we will discuss in some detail in this section. The interviews are supplemented by direct observation. Our understanding and any insight we gain come from the information we collect and from the executive's reactions to being presented with what we have learned.

We have chosen to describe this particular method rather than focus on intensive clinical methods in general, because BAR has been tailored specifically to illuminate two interrelated issues: the personality of the executive and the conditions affecting self-insight and development. Thus, with BAR, we study individual executives in the context of their work environments. The method is idiographic; in using it we aim to understand individuals as a whole, to understand "individual traits or variables and their patterned relationship within the individual" (Runyan, 1984, p. 167).

These are the questions we are trying to answer with BAR:

1.   What is the executive's makeup? What are his characteristics as a leader and manager?

2. What are the executive's developmental needs? In what areas could she stand to develop, to become more effective in carrying out her role?
3. What forces influence the likelihood and course of such development? In what ways is development deterred by the nature of the executive's personality, role, relationships, and environment, and in what ways is it facilitated? What role do the executive's resistance or openness to change and the resistance or openness of those around him play in his development?

BAR also has a purpose beyond the research goal inherent in these questions, namely, individual change: to facilitate the self-awareness and growth of the executive we study by providing her with feedback about her managerial character and also by directly discussing possible avenues for change. Few of the studies investigating individual lives in depth also have development as a goal. In contrast, we see these goals as being complementary. As we work to address an executive's developmental needs, we also gain insight about the processes involved in development.

BAR involves a process of individual diagnosis and development which parallels the process of organizational diagnosis and development in several respects (Alderfer, 1980; Alderfer, Brown, Kaplan, & Smith, in preparation). As does organizational diagnosis, BAR consists of several stages: entry, data collection, data analysis, feedback, and action planning.

Entry

Our choice of research subjects is opportunistic. We generally make initial contact through our network of executives and training and development professionals who know of executives interested in pursuing their own development. Sometimes executives participating in training programs at the Center for Creative Leadership may seek further self-understanding and development, in which case they are referred to us. Someone from the executive's organization—usually someone from the training and development function—agrees to play a liaison role for the duration of the project.

After discussing the project with the executive and verifying his interest, the liaison arranges for an initial entry meeting. This meeting is attended by the executive, the liaison, and the research team. In this meeting we elicit the executive's wishes and needs for the study, and we explain the general sequence of activities. We emphasize the applied nature of the project: although we expect to obtain research data from the study, the executive's prime motivation to participate is that we offer him an opportunity to learn about himself and improve his capacities as an executive.

Two important issues must be discussed in the entry meeting: confidentiality and publication. It is necessary, for the validity and usefulness of the data and the security of the executive, that we work with the executive under conditions of privacy and confidentiality. We only share information with others in the organization—including our liaison—when the executive chooses to do so; the executive controls what information is shared, when, and with whom.

We expect to publish our findings, however so we must come to an agreement about our right to use the research data in our writing. Since this work essentially involves detailed case studies, we agree at entry that if and when we write about our work with this individual, we will negotiate a disguise with him that protects his privacy without doing violence to the essence of his character and development.

In addition to this initial entry meeting, we must go through an entry process with every individual whom we interview about the executive. Before the interviews, the executive meets with these respondents as a group or individually to describe the project and to explain that he, and we, are asking them to talk candidly with us about his character and his strengths, and weaknesses, and that their openness will contribute greatly to his learning. He also explains to them our stand on confidentiality. For these others our pledge of confidentiality is that all information will be fed back to the executive at a group level. For instance, we cluster together the perceptions of all subordinates, or all peers, or all members of a particular functional group, such as the marketing staff. No quotes or statements which identify individuals are used later in feedback.

In addition, at the beginning of each interview with these others, the interviewer repeats a brief description of the study, stating our policy regarding the interviewee's anonymity and confidentiality, and eliciting any concerns or questions the interviewee might have.

Because of the role of the executive's implicit agenda—and those of others involved—on the progress of the study, we need to remain especially careful about the study's image in the organization, so that it is not seen either as a plum for fast-trackers or as a remedial course for problem children, because this can undermine motivation to participate for the sake of self-learning. And, we need to emphasize the primacy of our relationship with the executive, not with the organization, and our adherence to the principles of confidentiality, so that there is no fear that our data will fall into the hands of other organizational members, such as decision makers on executive succession.

Data Collection

The intensive nature of our study puts us in the tradition of research such as White's (1966) and Vaillant's (1977) studies of lives, Levinson's (1978) work on adult development, the examination by Bray et al. (1974) of managerial life, and Maccoby's (1976) investigations of leaders. Our methodology calls for in-depth data collection on each executive we study. We spend a total of 70 to 80 hours actually collecting data on a particular executive. We hope that this will allow us to gain a rich understanding of each executive's life and work patterns.

We study the individual in all areas of her life. We interview the executive regarding her work life, and also her family and community life—in short, we want to know about her as a whole person. We make the assumption that the issues and problems that a person faces may vary in her roles as an executive, spouse, parent, or community leader. And, the person may behave differently in each of those roles, but the person herself does not change. In fact, looking at how a person's behavior varies or remains constant in such different situations can help us understand the underlying forces driving that behavior.

For example, we interviewed Frank Lindler (not his real name) about his work and his personal life, learned about his community involvement and leisure activities. We found that to understand his makeup as an executive, we had to understand him as a person. It turned out to be important to investigate his patterns of involvement in the community, because his compulsive, heavy involvement in community work paralleled his approach to his job. Similarly, it was important to investigate his family relationships, because the quality of his relationships with wife and children directly related to the role that work played in his life and how he approached it: his marital relationship was unsatisfying, and he used his work relationships to meet his needs for relatedness. However, one reason his marriage was not working was that it was very difficult for him to be vulnerable and close with others, including his wife. Thus, focusing on work relationships allowed him to associate (without becoming intimate) with people who respected him for his accomplishments and were unaware of his vulnerabilities.

The parallel we found between his interpersonal distance and invulnerable demeanor at work and those same qualities at home helped us see his general defense against intimacy, a defense that limited the depth of knowledge others acquired about him and thus limited the feedback they could give him.

Our understanding of how the individual behaves as an executive in the present can be illuminated by exploring his past. Thus, we ask the executive about family, childhood experiences, and relationships in youth and throughout his life. On our list of others to be interviewed we include people who knew the executive at different points in his past. This can include parents, siblings, childhood friends, college chums, and colleagues from early worklife. In the case of Frank Lindler, for example, we found that his relationship with his parents helped to explain much of his current behavior. His interpersonal distance at work derived in part from the nonintimate nature of his relationship with his parents. His high need for mastery, competence, and respect is rooted in their subtle pressures and expectations for achievement and excellence, and the lack of clear praise for meeting those expectations.

In this work, we need the executive to share himself with us—to talk candidly, and to allow us to interview others who will also talk candidly. To do this, we need to build a relationship of mutual trust. This takes time. We find that by the fifth or sixth interview the executive is disclosing information about himself that he would not, and did not, disclose to us in the first or second one. For example, for the first few months we knew Lindler, he described his parents as exceedingly respectful and supportive of him. Not until we had known Frank for several months did he acknowledge that he had felt unsupported by his parents in his youth and that this had affected his self-esteem, ambition, and feelings of competence. Another example is related to Frank's initial presentation of himself as having been an obedient and nonrebellious adolescent. It took a year for us to learn (from others) about his drinking and dating activities in high school. Further, in both of these examples, not only is it useful for us to learn the information that has been held back, but the very fact that Frank withheld these particular pieces of data provides us with clues regarding his character. For example, we gather that part of the image Frank hopes to portray is that of a wholesome and obedient "good son," while his rebellion remains cloaked and compartmentalized.

It is not realistic to hope for complete objectivity in our view of the executive. Rather, we can gain insight by understanding how the relationship we form with the executive influences our view of him. The intensive contact with the executive throughout the study inevitably leads us to identify with certain characteristics we find desirable. All of us identified with Lindler's intellectual bent and his high need for achievement. In fact, we frequently communicated with him by giving him copies of articles on management, ostensibly because this would be consistent with his mode of learning about the world, but also because this was a way we ourselves liked to learn.

The research team and the executive influence one another. We influence the executive by working with him, asking him to think about particular issues and events, and guiding his self-perceptions in certain directions, simply making him more reflective. He changes us by provoking us to think about ourselves in relation to him, about our reactions to his personality and his work. Sometimes there are unanticipated changes. Over the course of our work with Frank, he became more introspective, and made some major changes in his life—a divorce, a job change, an overseas move—as well as smaller changes in his managerial style. These changes can in part be attributed to the development work we did with him, but they are also the result of Frank's increasing self-awareness.

We changed, too. As we got to know Frank, our feelings about him changed from extremely positive, when we were impressed by the smoothly polished surface of his character, to quite critical, when we began to discover that the smooth surface covered flaws and we felt perhaps a bit betrayed. Eventually we came to a balanced view; we saw a human, although by many standards a very effective one, with virtues and failings like all other humans. This evolution has influenced our perspective on the other executives we are studying by making us more aware that our perception of character is influenced by the maturity of our relationship with the person.

As we have indicated, we also talk with the executive's colleagues, family members, and friends. We ask the executive to give us a list of such people who know him in different ways and can therefore give us a range of perspectives. In doing these interviews with others, we assume that people reveal different aspects of themselves to various others, and that each of those other people perceives the individual through the unique lenses of his or her own personality. Synthesizing these varying perceptions of others and comparing them with our own perceptions helps us get a rounded portrait of the executive in question. This rounded portrait is a departure from most of the intensive studies of lives that focus primarily on self-description (see, for example, Vaillant, 1977; White, 1966; Levinson, 1978). Our use of multiple perspectives is informed by the field of biography (Maurois, 1930; Edel, 1959). Biographers, of course, rely to a large extent on the reports of others regarding their subject. In part, this is because their subjects are no longer living, but also because of their belief that perceptions always vary across observers. We all present different aspects of ourselves to different people, thus these perceptions "are valuable only insofar as they are put face to face with each other and with the complete picture of the man's personality" (Maurois, 1930, p. 87).

In studying Frank Lindler, we talked with about a dozen co-workers, superiors, subordinates, and peers. We talked with several co-workers from Frank's previous job. We talked with his wife and personal friends. In getting these names from Frank, we asked him to consider people who would have a variety of opinions about him based on a variety of perspectives. This produced many interesting results. For example, in doing these interviews with others we found that Frank was consistently seen in a more favorable light by his superiors than by his subordinates. Because several superiors shared the same favorable perceptions and several subordinates shared a more critical one, we were led to conclude that the difference in perception was unlikely to be due primarily to idiosyncratic distortions of the perceivers. It was more likely, of course, that Frank actually behaved differently towards superiors than he did towards subordinates. In this case, using information we had from his own self-reports in combination with the interviews with others, we surmised that Frank's presentation of certain key favorable aspects of himself to superiors was telling us something about his ego ideal. This was the way he wanted to be seen and to see himself; this was indicative of how he felt about superiors and other authority figures. The picture of himself he was painting for his superiors represented not just the way he would like to be seen, but the way he would like to be: intelligent, obedient but iconoclastic, ambitious, and honorable.

The historical elements in our method and its multiple perspectives are mutually reinforcing. This is because our understanding of the executive's varying relationships with different groups can be enhanced by understanding his life history. All relationships contain an element of what Sullivan (1954) calls "parataxic distortion"—that is, one's response to people is influenced not only by who they are, but by what kinds of people they represent from one's past. Where Frank Lindler was concerned, his desire to please authority figures harkened back to his youth as an only child growing up in an environment of parents and grandparents and their friends. His perceptions of his superiors and his behavior toward them were influenced by their inevitable representation of earlier authority figures, such as Frank's father and grandfather.

Our use of multiple perspectives is one way of dealing with what Erikson (1968, 1969) refers to as "relativity." The perceptions of the researcher, subject, and other interviewees are all unique, influenced by their current circumstances and needs and by their histories as well. Thus, for example, when we interviewed a former co-worker regarding an event in Frank's past, we could count on the fact that the co-worker's recollection of the event was being influenced by circumstances in her life at the time of the event, by the way she felt about the event at the time, by her relationship with Frank then, by her relationship with him now, by conditions in the organization then and now, and on and on.

The executive being studied inevitably sees himself subjectively, relative to his own desires for himself, and these distortions can undermine the researcher's ability to paint a truthful portrait. Or they can, if properly taken into account, help the researcher understand the person even better. For example, subjective views sometimes intrude in the area of the person's motivation for taking part in the study, and this motive influences how he presents himself to us. He may have reached a dead end in his career, for example, and he may consciously or unconsciously use his participation in the study to try to convince us and others of his worthiness for promotion.

This is another reason why multiple perspectives are useful to our understanding of an executive. Like all of us, an executive has in mind a particular "persona" that he or she wants to present to the world (Jung, 1959). The researcher's job is to get behind this self-presentation, to recognize it as a picture of an ideal persona, and to find out something about the "real" self that lies behind the mask. For example, much of what Frank told us in early interviews, much of the so-called factual information we recorded in our notes was tempered by his desire to present to us the picture of an executive who was virtuous and honorable—the same qualities which he portrayed to superiors. This led him to suppress certain information that he felt might have damaged the persona while emphasizing other information that supported it. This distorted our emerging portrait, but when we recognized what Frank was doing (by contrasting other perceptions of Frank's behavior with his own) it helped us understand him all the better.

The very subjectivity of the information we get answers one of our research questions. The executive's attitude toward growth and change, and the attitudes of those around him, influence his response to our effort to understand him, and thus distort our data. Yet, this distortion is also data in itself: by understanding the executive's response to our investigation, we can gain insight about his orientation towards his own development. For example, by looking for patterns in what is withheld and disclosed, and under what circumstances, we can begin to understand the forces influencing openness and resistance to development. When Frank withheld information that was inconsistent with the characteristics of his desired persona, when he systematically failed to tell us about his youthful rebellions, or his self-doubts, or his mistakes, or his anger, we drew certain conclusions about why he was unwilling or unable to acknowledge these things about himself. In addition, these unacknowledged aspects, as long as they were denied, would remain outside the scope of developmental efforts.

We supplement the information gained through interviews with direct observation and with psychological testing. A team member spends a few days with the executive at work, observing and recording her behavior and interactions. We administer psychological tests such as the Meyers-Briggs, FIRO-B, and Career Anchors Inventory, and discuss the results with the executive. These test scores can be illuminating. For example, Frank's FIRO-B scores in the area of Control were 8 "Expressed" and 1 "Wanted," which supported our hypotheses regarding his need for control and his drive for mastery in spite of his apparently delegating style.

We take advantage of opportunities in obtaining data. For one executive who attended a workshop at the Center, we had the results of a battery of a dozen or so tests which were administered for purposes of the workshop, and which the executive made available to us. Another executive, who characteristically communicated by memo in his organization, had documented his worklife by saving every memo he wrote, as well as all written communication he received, all ordered chronologically and bound in notebooks. Sifting through these provided us with interesting glimmers into the texture of his life at work.

Data Analysis

We try to let our framework emerge from the unique psychological makeup of each of our subjects. Each of our studies, like a biography, "should take its form from its material" (Edel, 1959). We try to look at each individual's life on its own terms. Hence, we approach the data with our own theories and predispositions in the background. We try to let our categories of managerial characteristics and situational forces emerge from the data. In the case of Frank Lindler the categories that emerged from analysis included Attitudes Toward Work and Career, Types of Relationships, Use of Authority, Approach to Conflict, and Emotional Control, among others, not because we think these are the primary units for analyzing executives in general, but because these were the areas that stood out in the data on Frank Lindler.

Throughout data collection and analysis, team members constantly try to look into themselves in the service of understanding the executive and his development. We explicitly recognize our subjectivity and try to take it into account in every aspect of the study. We are mindful that our perspective on the research is influenced by our identity and our individual and group agendas for undertaking the study (Alderfer, 1985).

The fact that there are three of us on the research team provides a check on the subjectivity of our individual perceptions. Like the interviewers referred to in White's "Lives in Progress," we are "of somewhat different backgrounds and training [and] to a considerable extent . . . cancel each other's personal rigidities of judgment" (1966, p. 105). We also use the variation in our own perspectives to discuss the varying aspects of the executive's personality which our own individual identities evoke. For example, the woman on the team became aware of a certain ambivalence in herself regarding Frank Lindler. This took the form of an alternating inclination to protect him from the pain of discoveries about himself on the one hand, and to break down his defenses and expose his vulnerability on the other. This ambivalence came in part from her own personality and needs, but also paralleled the dynamic that occurred in Frank's relationship with other women.

Vaillant (1977) on the subject of researcher subjectivity praised the "mosaic interview, produced by several observers [as] more accurate than one could be alone" (p. 52). He gave an example of a member of the study who "was always seen as dynamic and charismatic by the female staff members and as a neurotic fool by the men" (p. 52).

As we try to make sense of the individual, we try to remain aware of the ways in which our values, as well as our personalities and inner conflicts, influence our interpretation of the data. Since we cannot remove the bias, we must continually seek to understand how it influences our work and our conclusions. Early in our work with executives, for example, we took what we now see as an overly critical stance. We have come to understand this as a product of a counter-dependent attitude towards these powerful figures, and we are now aware that we must continually guard our research findings from this bias.

In one sense or another, everyone uses work to "work on" personal issues, and the biographical researcher is no exception. Our choice of executives and development as our focus, the kinds of data we evoke from people, the findings and conclusions we choose to perceive, are all influenced by our identities and personal goals. On one hand, as researchers, we must analyze our own motivations so as not to "refashion the other person in [our] own image" (Edel, 1959). On the other hand, valuable insights can be gained when we discover something about the subject's personality by virtue of identifying with him.

Data analysis involves combing the interviews for salient quotations, copying these quotations onto cards along with ideas and hypotheses generated over time, then sorting the cards into conceptual or issue-oriented categories, slowly working toward the final set of categories. The data analysis process involves moving back and forth between hypotheses and data. The inarticulable quality of this process is described by the biographer Leon Edel: "[The biographer] is called upon to take the base metals that are his disparate facts and turn them into the gold of the human personality . . . [and] no chemical process has yet been discovered by which this change can be accomplished" (1959, pp. 8–9).

This alchemical process of data analysis and synthesis must be approached with a vigor that is appropriate to the nature of the work. "Relativism does not mean that one ignores evidence or throws out procedures of critical inquiry, but rather that empirical evidence and logical inference are employed within the context of a particular perspective" (Runyan, 1984, p. 38). For example, behavior is typically "overdetermined," having multiple causes and meanings. Thus psychological and cultural explanations are complementary, not competing. BAR is ideally equipped to provide multiple explanations through its attempt at comprehensive investigation of phenomena and circumstances. But this does not mean we can accept all possible interpretations. We need to evaluate alternative hypotheses on the basis of their logical soundness, the adequacy with which they account for the evidence, their consistency with the evidence and with other hypotheses, and so on. The explanations—multiple or not—that survive the tests of plausibility and consistency will survive.

Action

The "action" in Biographical Action Research as we have practiced it consists of activities involving insight-generation and planning. We present the findings of our research to the executive to help him absorb and interpret the data and to draw implications for change in his behavior.

As the first step in the action phase, we prepare a feedback report based on our data analysis. The report consists of our findings on the executive's make-up as a leader and, to a lesser extent, on the executive's openness to constructive criticism and continuing development. The feedback report to Frank Lindler contained several inductively derived categories for characterizing his leadership style, with each category and its subcategories illustrated by a number of quotations from Lindler and his coworkers. The major categories in the report were:

1. Image in the organization.
2. Task orientation.
3. Work relationships.
4. Style of delegation.
5. Decision making and problem solving style.
6. Manner of dealing with conflict.
7. Work ethic.

To take an example, within the "Decision Making Style" category there were a number of subcategories such as "Slow to Decide," "Thorough," "Logical Thinker," and "Promotes Consensus." For "Slow to Decide," supporting quotes included, "He sometimes waits too darn long before he makes a decision. It's frustrating," and "He likes to follow protocol, question, probe, make every decision perfect."

In addition to an analysis of interviews with people at work, the report includes the results from psychological tests. If we are able to interview as many as five members of the executive's family, the report also includes categorized quotations about the executive away from work and the relation of private life and work life.

As a second step in the sequence, we go over the report with the executive privately. The executive controls further distribution of the report. In some cases the agreement with the executive and the organization calls for sharing the developmental needs identified by the study with the executive's superior. Ownership of the data is a ticklish issue because the executive needs to be afforded privacy so that he can enter freely into the learning experience, but the upshot of the study may need to be made available to other individuals who are interested in furthering the executive's development. This tension arises whenever self-learning occurs in a hierarchical context (Meyer, Kay, & French, 1965; Kaplan, 1982).

Following the private feedback session, one option is a meeting or meetings with the executive's colleagues to clarify the findings, which, because they are presented in general terms and on an aggregated basis, may need to be grounded in concrete instances in particular relationships. In Lindler's case, he held feedback sessions with three groups of subordinates. In each session he summarized those findings he wanted to discuss with the particular group, left the room so that the group could address the issues freely, and then returned for a discussion of the issue. The group sessions reinforced some of the things that came out in the report, for example, the perceived need for him to get out of his office and interact informally with staff and his tendency to use an aggressive questioning approach when challenged. One group Lindler met with consisted of subordinates two levels down from him, with whom he had a poor relationship. The session cleared the air and resulted in a joint decision to take certain specific actions to improve the relationship.

How many group sessions we hold and with what groups varies with the executive. With one executive, we held one stormy group session that the subordinates viewed as productive but the executive did not. With another executive, we held no group session at all. In the latter case, the executive was near retirement and not receptive to open discussions of his leadership style. In the former case, the executive was fairly resistant to criticism and change, which made the group session difficult and which cut into his interest in exploring the issues further. He was also affected by a corporate culture that made owning up to weakness unlikely and risky.

The feedback sessions provide additional data on the executive for purposes of both action and research. Feedback meetings are especially useful in illuminating forces influencing development. For example, we can see evidence of the executive's defensiveness in her response to feedback in the meeting. We can also notice when subordinates withhold criticism, or when their criticism influences the executive counterproductively. With Frank Lindler, we saw in a feedback session our first direct evidence of how he uses a challenging, argumentative style to defend, by counter-attack, against criticism he receives.

Out of the feedback in its various forms usually come problems that the executive wishes to do something about. The change he makes may simply be to take a weakness into account, so that he might work around it. Or he may choose to make concrete behavioral changes designed to increase an underdeveloped capacity or to tone down a self-defeating behavior. Because of its emphasis on research, our work has tended to end with planning for change. We have generally left implementation to the executive and developmental professionals in or outside his organization.

Power of the Intervention

BAR is a potent intervention into an executive's work and life. The collecting of data alone can kick up a reaction by bringing previously unacknowledged feelings to the surface. A not too unlikely example occurred as a result of an interview with one of Frank Lindler's friends. Because of questions asked during our interview with her, she became aware of her feelings of anger and unhappiness with him. Later she expressed this to him in no uncertain terms. Though bearable, the incident caused Frank some considerable pain.

The feedback report is powerful, zeroing in as it does on the executive's character as a manager and person. Group feedback sessions are similarly potent, since they are settings in which coworkers and perhaps even family members openly discuss the executive's behavior and its effect on them.

In Harrison's (1968) terms, the action phase of BAR qualifies as a combination of level three and level five in his model of intervention depth, with five being the deepest. Level three interventions focus on work relationships. Level five focuses on the individual, including questions of identity, basic drives and inner conflicts, along with the deep feelings evoked by the exercise. With Harrison, we believe that to operate at level five requires considerable clinical expertise and sensitivity. In using BAR, one must dedicate oneself to the maxim: primum non nocere (first of all, do no harm). The power of the intervention must be harnessed for constructive ends.

On top of the effects of data collection and direct intervention, BAR creates another powerful impact if the study is to be published. Not only does BAR mean that the executive is confronted with a behavioral science analysis of herself, she must also deal with the possible ramifications of having the case study published. To protect the executive from possible harm on this count, we take a number of steps, including: (a) disguising the executive and her organization, (b) review by the executive to guard against distortions, and (c) review by others in the organization who advise us on the likely impact of publication. With Frank Lindler, who is the first executive we have written up, we found it helpful to give the pre-publication manuscript to one of his colleagues inside the organization who had Lindler's best interests at heart and who also had a stake in the success of the research. We have found that there is no ultimate authority on whether we have discharged our responsibility to the executive where publication is concerned. As in studying the individual in the first place, we inevitably operated in a web of perspectives from which we constructed our own view of this reality.

CONCLUSION

We developed the BAR method to study executives' developmental needs, internal and external, and the forces influencing their development. We believe that the BAR method is uniquely well-suited to uncovering information regarding these issues. Where external needs are concerned, the method's use of multiple perspectives overcomes the inevitable bias executives—and all of us—have regarding their own abilities and liabilities. Gathering information about personal life in addition to worklife allows us to see how leadership style and developmental needs play out in settings outside of work. Finally, observation lets us witness the impact of these needs on effectiveness. BAR's emphasis on understanding the whole person in all his complexity allows us to see an executive's character and behavior in configuration, as opposed to seeing them as separate elements. In the case of Frank Lindler, this led us to an understanding of his managerial style that tied together his consensual approach to decision making, his delegation of responsibility and authority, and his challenging style of questioning subordinates—all of which revolved around an aptitude for analytical thinking, a reluctance to exercise direct control, and a strong need to be right.

An intensive method is necessary if one hopes to learn about the executive's inner world. By investigating the executive's life history, we can learn about the building blocks of the past—family relations and significant childhood events—on which this external character is built. We can develop hypotheses about inner needs driving external behavior, and we can further elaborate and test these hypotheses as our relationship with the executive becomes closer over time and the information shared becomes more personal. For example, in our interviews we discovered that Frank Lindler's parents treated him as a special child, that they held especially high expectations for him, particularly in regard to moral standards and principled behavior; as a result, he became a high achiever in school, was active in many organizations and clubs, and eventually became that child who is esteemed more by parents and authority figures than by peers. The outcome of this in Frank's executive character is that he places great importance on being highly respected, especially by authority figures, and he values being competent, exceptional, masterful, and worthy of praise. These attributes he desires are most easily achieved by what we have described earlier as an active-positive approach, which Frank exhibits to a great degree—even to the degree that he can sometimes become susceptible to the extreme variation of the active-positive type, which leads him to self-idealization, to the magnification of his strengths in his own eyes and the suppression of his awareness of his weaknesses.

Earlier we discussed the forces affecting prospects for executive development: power, which tends to deter the giving of feedback; the nature of the executive job, which limits the executive's inclination and skill at introspection; the pressure for competence, which inhibits the executive's capacity to accept feedback; and success, which dampens the executive's motivation to change. In each case, aspects of the individual executive and his environment interact to produce an effect on his developmental prospects, sometimes to cloud those prospects, but sometimes to brighten them. Many of the same features of BAR that enabled us to understand external and internal needs also help us to learn about how the forces affecting feedback and change operate. In addition, the action phases of BAR (feedback and development planning) allows us to see these forces operate as we try to help the executive develop.

Frank Lindler's prospects for continuing development were affected by his makeup as an individual and by his circumstances. His personal style tended, for example, to discourage constructive criticism because other people saw him as being so secure that he had no need for help. On the other hand, his style enhanced self-learning because his controlled use of power made him approachable and open to feedback. His environment enabled his further development. For example, two superiors adopted him and counselled him. On the other hand, his environment constrained his development by reinforcing him strongly for what he had become.

In the introduction we said that one cannot develop an organization without developing its executives. Now we see that one cannot develop executives without developing the organization, since to get around the forces that inhibit development one must intervene into things such as structure, goals, and organizational values. Thus, organization development and executive development are inextricably interwined. In fact, if the goal of organization development is to improve organizations, then OD practitioners and researchers must acknowledge the role of organizational forces in limiting the development of executives, and must see that the limits on executive development can undermine the success of OD efforts. This means that a primary goal of organization development should be to help organizational members manage the forces that affect the development of executives.

ACKNOWLEDGMENTS

We would like to thank Clayton Alderfer, Morgan McCall, William Pasmore, Leonard Sayles, Jeffrey Sonnenfeld, and Richard Woodman for their helpful comments.

REFERENCES

Alderfer, C. P. (1980). The methodology of organizational diagnosis. *Professional Psychology, 11,* 459–468.

Alderfer, C. P. (1984). Taking our selves seriously as researchers. In D. Berg & K. Smith (Eds.), *The clinical demands of social research.* New York: Sage.

Alderfer, C. P., Brown, L. D., Kaplan, R. E., & Smith, K. K. (in preparation). *Group relations and organizational diagnosis.*

Allen, F. (1981, December 15–18). Executive's wives describe sources of their contentment, frustration. *Wall Street Journal.*

Argyris, C. (1973). The CEO's behavior: Key to organizational development. *Harvard Business Review, 51,* 55–64.

Argyris, C., & Schon, D. A. (1974). *Theory in practice: Increasing professional effectiveness.* San Francisco: Jossey-Bass.

Bakan, D. (1966). *The duality of human experience.* Chicago: Rand McNally.

Bandura, A. (1982). The psychology of chance encounters and life paths. *American Psychologist, 37,* 747–755.

Barber, J. D. (1968). Classifying and predicting presidential styles: Two "weak" presidents. *Journal of Social Issues, 24,* 51–80.

Bass, B. M. (1981). *Stogdill's handbook of leadership.* New York: The Free Press.

Behar, R. (1985, December 30). The open secret. *Forbes,* 31–33.

Bennis, W. (1976). *The unconscious conspiracy: Why leaders can't lead.* New York: AMACOM.

Bennis, W. (1982, May 31). Leadership transforms vision into action. *Industry Week,* 54–56.

Bennis. W., & Nanus, B. (1985). *Leaders: The strategies for taking charge.* New York: Harper & Row.

Bentz, J. (1985). *View of the top.* Unpublished manuscript.

Blake, R. R., Morton, J. S., Barnes, L. B., & Greiner, L. E. (1964). Breakthrough in organization development. *Harvard Business Review, 42,* 133–155.

Bork, D. (1984, August). Developmental dilemmas at top levels of family-controlled companies. In R. Kaplan (Chair), *What's different about developing executives (once they've already become executives)?* Symposium conducted at the 1984 Annual National Meeting, Academy of Management, Boston.

Boss, R. W., & Boss, L. S. (1985). The chief executive officer and successful OD efforts. *Group & Organization Studies, 10,* 365–382.

Bray, D. W., Campbell, R. J., & Grant, D. L. (1974). *Formative years in business: A long-term AT&T study of managerial lives.* New York: John Wiley and Sons.

Burns, J. M. (1978). *Leadership.* New York: Harper & Row.

Burns, T. (1957). Management in action. *Operational Research Quarterly, 8*(2), 45–60.

Burns, T., & Stalker, G. M. (1961). *The management of innovation.* London: Tavistock Publications.

Campbell, J. P., Dunnette, M. D., Lawler, E. E., & Weick, K. E. (1970). *Managerial behavior, performance, and effectiveness.* New York: McGraw-Hill.

Cleveland, H. (1980, August). Learning the art of leadership. *Twin Cities.*

DeVries, D. L., Morrison, A. M., Gerlach, M. L., & Shullman, S. L. (1981). *Performance appraisal on the line.* New York: John Wiley & Sons.

Dalton, G. W. (1969). Influence and organizational change. In A. R. Negandhi (Ed.), *Modern organizational theory.* Kent, OH: Kent State University and the Comparative Administration Research Institute.

Digman, L. A. (1978). How well-managed organizations develop their executives. *Organizational Dynamics,* Autumn, 63–80.

Dubin, R., & Spray, S. L. (1964). Executive Behavior and Interaction. *Industrial Relations, 3,* 99–108.

Edel, L. (1959). *Literary biography*. Bloomington, IN.: Indiana University Press.

Erikson, E. H. (1968). On the nature of psychohistorical evidence: In search of Gandhi. *Daedalus, 97*, 695–730.

Erikson, E. H. (1969). *Gandhi's truth*. New York: W. W. Norton.

Evans, P., & Bartolome, F. (1981). *Must success cost so much?* New York: Basic Books.

Flax, S. (1985). The executive addict. *Fortune, 111*(13), 24–31.

Gabarro, J. J. (in press). Taking charge: Stages in management succession. *Harvard Business Review*.

Gardner, J. W. (1963). *Self-renewal: The individual and the innovative society*. New York: W. W. Norton.

Goffman, E. (1959). *The presentation of self in everyday life*. Garden City, N.Y.: Doubleday.

Golembiewski, R. T. (1972). *Renewing organizations: The laboratory approach to planned change*. Itasca, IL: Peacock.

Greenberger, R. S. (1983, January 13). Sobering method: Firms are confronting alcoholic executives with threat of firing. *Wall Street Journal*, p. 1.

Grove, A. S. (1983, October 3). Breaking the chains of command (my turn). *Newsweek*.

Guest, R. H. (1962). *Organizational change: The effect of successful leadership*. Homewood, IL: Irwin & Dorsey.

Hague, H. (1974). *Executive self-development*. New York: Wiley & Sons.

Hall, C. S., & Nordby, V. J. (1973). *A primer of Jungian psychology*. New York: New American Library.

Harrison, R. (1968). *Some criteria for choosing the depth of organizational intervention strategy*. Paper delivered at the Fourth Annual International Congress of Group Psychotherapy, Vienna.

Hodgson, R. C., Levinson, D. J., & Zaleznik, A. (1965). *The executive role constellation: An analysis of personality and role relations in management*. Boston: Harvard University Graduate School of Business Administration.

Horney, K. (1945). *Our inner conflicts: A constructive theory of neurosis*. New York: W. W. Norton & Co.

Horney, K. (1950). *Neurosis and human growth*. New York: Norton.

Isenberg, D. J. (1984). How senior managers think. *Harvard Business Review*, November–December, 81–90.

Jaques, E. (1952). *The culture of a factory*. New York: Dayden.

Jenks, S. (1984, August). Solving the executive development dilemma: The case of high-tech entrepreneurs. In R. Kaplan (Chair), *What's different about developing executives (once they've already become executives)?* Symposium conducted at the 1984 Annual National Meeting, Academy of Management, Boston.

Jennings, E. E. (1965). *The executive in crisis*. New York: McGraw-Hill.

Jung, C. G. (1959). *The basic writings of C. G. Jung*. Edited by Violet Staub de Laszlo. New York: Random House.

Kahn, E. (1985). Heinz Kohut and Carl Rogers: A timely comparison. *American Psychologist, 40*, 893–904.

Kanter, R. M. (1977a). *Work and family in the United States: A critical review for research and policy*. New York: Russell Sage.

Kanter, R. M. (1977b). *Men and women of the corporation*. New York: Basic Books.

Kanter, R. M. (1982). The middle manager as innovator. *Harvard Business Review*, July–August, 95–105.

Kanter, R. M. (1983). *The change masters: Innovation for productivity in the American Corporation*. New York: Simon & Schuster.

Kaplan, R. E. (in press). *The warp and woof of the general manager's job*. (Technical Report #27). Greensboro, NC: Center for Creative Leadership.

Kaplan, R. E. (1982). Intervention in a loosely organized system: An encounter with non-being. *Journal of Applied Behavioral Science, 18*, 415–432.

Kaplan, R. E. (1984). Trade routes: The manager's network of relationships. *Organizational Dynamics,* Spring, 37–52.

Kaplan, R. E., Drath, W. H., & Kofodimos, J. R. (1985). *High hurdles: The challenge of executive self-development* (Technical Report #25). Center for Creative Leadership, Greensboro, NC.

Kaufman, H. (1971). *The limits of organizational change.* University, AL: University of Alabama Press.

Kelly, G. A. (1955). *A theory of personality: The psychology of personal constructs.* New York: Norton.

Kets de Vries, M. F. R. (1979). *Managers can drive their subordinates mad. Harvard Business Review,* 57(4), 125–134.

Kets de Vries, M. F. R. & Miller, D. (1985). Narcissism & leadership: An object relations perspective. *Human Relations 38,* 583–601.

Kiel, G. F. (1986, August). Executive counselling program. In R. E. Kaplan (Chair), *Zooming in on executive development: Intense, intensive methods for research and intervention.* Symposium to be presented at the 46th Annual National Meeting of the Academy of Management, Chicago.

Kofodimos, J. R. (1984). A question of balance. *Issues & Observations.* The Center for Creative Leadership, Greensboro, NC, 4(1), pp. 1–9.

Kofodimos, J. R., Kaplan, R. E., & Drath, W. H. (in preparation, 1986). *Anatomy of an executive: A close look at one executive's managerial character and development.* Greensboro, NC: Center for Creative Leadership. Technical Report.

Kotter, J. P. (1982). *The general managers.* New York: The Free Press.

Kotter, J. P., & Lawrence, P. R. (1976). *Mayors in Action: Five approaches to urban governance.* New York: Wiley.

Laing, R. D. (1967). *The politics of experience.* New York: Ballantine Books.

Levinson, D. J. (1978). *The seasons of a man's life.* New York: Ballantine Books.

Levinson, H. (1968). *The exceptional executive: A psychological conception.* New York: Mentor Books.

Lundborg, L. B. (1981). *The art of being an executive.* New York: The Free Press.

Maccoby, M. (1976). *The gamesman.* New York, NY: Simon & Schuster.

Maccoby, M. (1981). *The leader: A new face for American management.* New York: Simon & Schuster.

Mann, F. C. (1957). Studying and creating change: A means to understanding social organizations. In C. M. Arensburg (Ed.), *Research in industrial human relations.* New York: Harper.

Maurois, A. (1930). *Aspects of biography.* New York: Appleton.

May, R. (1972). *Power and innocence: A search for the sources of violence.* New York: Delta.

McCall, M. W., Jr., & Kaplan, R. E. (1984). *Whatever it takes: Decision-makers at work.* Englewood Cliffs, NJ: Prentice-Hall.

McCall, M. W., Jr., & Lombardo, M. W. (1983). What makes a top executive. *Psychology Today,* February, 26–31.

McCall, M. W., Jr., Morrison, A. M., & Hannan, R. L. (1978). *Studies of managerial work: Results and methods.* (Technical Report #9). Greensboro, NC: Center for Creative Leadership.

McClelland, D. C. (1975). *Power: The inner experience.* New York: Irvington Publishers.

Meyer, H. H., Kay, E., & French, J. R. P., Jr. (1965). Split roles in performance appraisal. *Harvard Business Review, 43,* 123–129.

Mintzberg, H. (1973). *The nature of managerial work.* New York: Harper & Row.

Peters, T. J., & Waterman, R. H., Jr. (1982). *In search of excellence.* New York: Harper & Row.

Porter, M. E. (1980). *Competitive strategy: Techniques for analyzing industries and competitors.* New York: The Free Press.

Read, W. H. (1962). Upward communication in industrial hierarchies. *Human Relations, 15,* 3–15.

Runyan, W. M. (1984). *Life histories.* New York: Oxford University Press.

Sayles, L. R. (1964). *Managerial behavior: Administration in complex organizations.* New York: McGraw-Hill.

Sayles, L. R. (1979). *Leadership: What effective managers really do . . . and how they do it.* New York: McGraw-Hill.

Seashore, S. E., & Bowers, D. G. (1963). *Changing the structure and functioning of an organization.* Ann Arbor, MI: University of Michigan Survey Research Center.

Society for Personnel Administration. (1965, June). *Executive development in action.* Pamphlet No. 9, 1–31.

Steele, F. (1983). The ecology of executive teams: A new view of the top. *Organizational Dynamics, 11,* 65–78.

Stewart, R. (1982). *Choices for the manager.* Englewood Cliffs, NJ: Prentice-Hall.

Streufert, S. (1983). The stress of excellence: Why our best decision-makers may face the greatest risk of heart attacks. *Across the Board,* October, 8–16.

Sullivan, H. S. (1954). *The psychiatric interview.* New York: Norton.

Townsend, R. (1984). Further up the organization. *New Management, 1,* 6–11.

U.S. Army Research Institute. (1978, April). General officer's views of continuing education/updating program for general officers. *Research Problem Review 78-3.*

Vaillant, G. E. (1977). *Adaptation to Life.* Boston: Little, Brown & Co.

White, R. W. (1966). *Lives in progress: A study of the natural growth of personality,* (2nd ed.) New York: Holt, Rinehart & Winston.

Zaleznik, A., & Kets de Vries, M. F. R. (1975). *Power and the corporate mind.* Boston: Houghton Mifflin.

SELF-DESIGNING ORGANIZATIONS:
TOWARDS IMPLEMENTING
QUALITY-OF-WORK-LIFE INNOVATIONS

Thomas G. Cummings and Susan A. Mohrman

ABSTRACT

This chapter develops a strategy for implementing innovations requiring fundamental organizational change. Referred to as self design, the strategy is particularly suited to quality-of-work-life (QWL) innovations that cannot be fully specified prior to implementation, and consequently a great deal of experimentation and learning are needed to implement them. As an introduction to self design, the chapter first describes the more widely-used innovation-adoption perspective on organizational innovation. Although organizations prefer to emulate this rational approach to innovation, its general applicability is limited to highly-certain innovations whose implementation can be preplanned and programmed. QWL innovations are highly uncertain, and thus require a radically different implementation strategy like self-design. The different phases of the self-design process are de-

Research in Organizational Change and Development, Vol. 1, pages 275–310.

scribed and operationalized, and the chapter concludes with future research areas
that need to be addressed to increase its success.

INTRODUCTION

The 1980s can be characterized as a time of widespread organizational innovation. Organizations are faced with unprecedented foreign competition, environmental change, societal pressure for more efficient operations, and employee
demands for more meaningful work lives; thus, better ways of designing and
managing organizations are needed. Change programs are focusing on creating
leaner, more efficient and adaptable organizations, better able to utilize human
resources.

These changes often involve quality-of-work-life (QWL) techniques aimed at
enhancing both organizational effectiveness and employee fulfillment, such as
quality circles, self-regulating work groups, gain sharing, and job enrichment.
Although the success of QWL methods is frequently extolled in the popular
media, organizations can experience problems applying the change programs if
they use an inappropriate implementation strategy. The techniques cannot simply
be adopted like other, more clearly-specified organizational innovations, such as
new accounting practices and manufacturing technology. Rather, existing research is relatively weak in offering specific prescriptions for designing QWL
innovations; it provides only general guidelines for organizational improvement.
Consequently, organizations need to engage in considerable experimentation and
learning in order to apply the techniques to their specific situations. They need to
learn how to translate the general practices into organizationally-relevant behaviors, structures, and processes.

This chapter presents a strategy for implementing QWL innovations. Called
"self design," this approach is particularly suited to QWL innovations which
tend to involve: organizational changes that can only be generally defined prior
to implementation; an implementation process that is relatively uncertain and
requires on-going adjustment and refinement of the innovation; and considerable
learning in order to enact the behaviors implied by the innovation. The self-
design strategy contrasts sharply with the more traditional innovation-adoption
approach to implementation which underlies much of the literature on organizational innovation. This strategy is best suited to innovations which involve clearly-defined designs and relatively straightforward implementation processes.

As an introduction to the self-design strategy, the first part of the chapter
examines the more widely-accepted innovation-adoption perspective and explains why that approach is ill-suited to implementing QWL innovations. Specific characteristics of innovations which impact the effectiveness of implementation strategies are identified; these can serve as contingencies in choosing an
appropriate strategy. The second part of the chapter presents the self-design

strategy and shows why it is more applicable to QWL programs than the innovation-adoption approach. Particular attention is directed at describing the process through which self design is carried out in organizations; so far, researchers have focused primarily on the conditions giving rise to self design while providing few actual descriptions of the process itself. This section explains what is already known about the self-design process. The last section addresses research issues that need to be addressed to increase its success, as well as the nature of action research in a self-design context. Particular attention is paid to the dynamics of the relationship between organizational members and action researchers.

INNOVATION-ADOPTION PERSPECTIVE

The extensive literature on organizational innovation has relied primarily on an innovation-adoption perspective to describe how organizations implement new ideas, practices, and technologies. This viewpoint tends to treat innovations as clearly-defined entities that simply can be adopted by organizations. The key issues in innovation adoption are to stimulate interest in change, to choose an appropriate innovation, and to replicate it within the adopting organization. According to this perspective, organizational improvements, such as new production machinery, improved accounting methods, and novel management practices, are essentially copied from early innovators or developers of the innovation (Rogers, 1983). A frequent criterion for adopting an innovation is whether other, high-status organizations are using it (Kimberly, 1981).

Much of the research on innovation adoption has focused on the diffusion of innovations, beginning with the initial conception of the innovation and extending through phases of adoption by others (e.g., Rogers & Shoemaker, 1971; Zaltman et al., 1973; Rogers, 1983). This research has assumed a decidedly "pro-innovation" bias (Rogers, 1983). It has treated an innovation as worthy of adoption and has not addressed either the possibility of a need to reject or radically alter it. Considerable research has been devoted to identifying factors which facilitate the adoption process, including characteristics of the innovations themselves and of the adopting organizations (e.g., Hage & Aiken, 1967; Corwin, 1972; Hage & Dewar, 1973; Moch & Morse, 1977; Kimberly, 1978; Kanter, 1983; Pinchot, 1984). Most of this research has been cross-sectional, and has tended to generalize poorly from one situation to another, however.

Assuming that innovations are definable entities that can be adopted by organizations, the task is to develop a strategy for introducing the innovation into the organization. A generalized innovation-adoption strategy is outlined in Figure 1, and includes four stages: (1) diagnosis and search, (2) adoption, (3) implementation, and (4) evaluation. This rational sequence conforms closely to the expectations and preferences of practitioners who are responsible for the introduction of change into organizations. The stages closely resemble the innovation-adoption

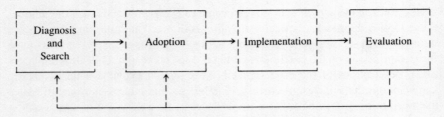

Figure 1.   Innovation-Adoption Perspective

procedures which are formally encouraged and reinforced in most organizations (Mohrman & Cummings, 1983).

Diagnosis and Search

In this initial step, organizations analyze their current situation to uncover sources of problems or opportunities for improvement. This sometimes involves a comparison between desired and actual levels of functioning to detect performance gaps. Such gaps either stimulate the search for innovative courses of action (March & Simon, 1958) or provide motivation to adopt an innovation (Rogers, 1983). The contextual understanding provided by the diagnosis lends impetus and direction for searching for and adopting innovations to solve problems and/or improve organizations.

Adoption

The image conveyed by the innovation adoption framework is that innovations are defined well enough so that organizations can adopt them. Based on an understanding of the situation, the organization has searched for and chosen an appropriate innovation. The design of the innovation is generally well-developed and maximally specified in advance of adoption. This includes identifying the various features of the innovation, and specifying how they should fit together to make the innovation operative. Ideally, the adoption process is guided by relatively complete knowledge of how the innovation is supposed to work when fully implemented. In this way, decision makers have a clear idea of what they are adopting, what is required to make it work, and how it will impact other aspects of the organization. They can make an "informed" adoption decision.

Implementation

Because the designs of innovations are fully specified, implementation generally involves constructing the innovation from detailed knowledge of its design features and how they should work together. This construction process typically involves specified steps for introducing the innovation into a particular situation which serve as instructions for constructing the innovation anew in the organization. They may include aspects as diverse as training for organizational members, installation of equipment, establishment of structures and special roles, and the development of communication techniques. All of these elements are frequently organized into an elaborate "road map" such as a PERT chart which specifies time tables, milestones, and responsibilities for "putting each of the pieces in place." This planning is often orchestrated by a staff group which then "rolls out the innovation" into the organization. Organizations typically attempt to remove ambiguity from the implementation process, and rely heavily on the authority structure of the organization to motivate and oversee implementation activities (Zaltman & Duncan, 1973).

Evaluation

Once innovations are implemented, organizations evaluate their overall effectiveness in order to find out if the innovation "worked." They assess the extent to which the innovation is performing as expected, and such understanding provides organizations with feedback about the accuracy of the initial diagnosis and/or the appropriateness of the innovation. If the innovation is ineffective, for example, organizations may undertake additional diagnosis and/or choose an alternative approach, as shown by the feedback loop in Figure 1. Alternatively, the innovation may simply be abandoned. If the innovation is judged effective, continued use and/or further dissemination are possible.

This relatively straightforward model of innovation adoption makes it appear deceptively simple for an organization to find a suitable innovation, implement it, and assess its effectiveness. It portrays the innovation process as more linear and rational than it is likely to be (Kimberly, 1981; Rogers, 1983). Rationales for innovation may only emerge retrospectively (Weick, 1979). Awareness of an innovation may stimulate discontent with current organizational performance, which may in turn lead to diagnostic activities to justify innovation adoption (Zaltman & Duncan, 1973). Organizational innovation may be characterized as a "garbage can" where an unordered assortment of organizational members, innovations, and problems interact in unpredictable ways. It may also be seen as a political process (e.g., Wilson, 1969; Pfeffer, 1981), and as an arena for idea champions or "change masters" (Kanter, 1983). In actuality, organizational innovation is probably a combination of rational problem solving, opportunism, and politics.

Despite these divergent viewpoints, organizations tend to prefer the rationality underlying the innovation-adoption process outlined in Figure 1. They seek the control and certainty inherent in innovation adoption, and encourage practices which emulate it (Mohrman & Cummings, 1983). Given this propensity to prefer an innovation-adoption process, it is important to understand where that approach can most effectively be applied and where it might encounter limitations.

INNOVATION UNCERTAINTY AND
IMPLEMENTATION-STRATEGY APPLICATION

The general applicability of the innovation-adoption perspective can be explored by considering the kinds of innovations organizations can adopt successfully using this approach. Borrowing from Galbraith's (1977) information-processing model of organizations, innovations can be characterized in terms of their degree of uncertainty. This refers to how much is known about the innovation prior to implementation. The greater the uncertainty of the innovation, the more organizations need to learn about the innovation *during* implementation. If the innovation is highly certain and organizations fully understand it, much of the implementation process can be preplanned and standardized. If the innovation is highly uncertain, however, organizations must engage in considerable problem solving and experimentation in order to learn how to implement it. Thus, the degree of innovation uncertainty affects the amount of problem solving and learning that must occur during implementation if the innovation is to be implemented successfully.

Because innovation uncertainty involves how much is known about the innovation prior to implementation, at least three key factors can contribute to such understanding: (1) the degree to which the innovation is clearly defined, (2) the degree to which there are specified steps for implementing the innovation, and (3) the degree to which the learning required to make the innovation operational is rudimentary. Innovations scoring high on these dimensions are highly certain. They are understood well enough that implementation can be preplanned and include relatively programmed steps to introduce the innovation into the organization. Innovations scoring low on these characteristics are highly uncertain, and require a great deal of trial-and-error learning during implementation. This involves considerable information processing and decision making as organizations learn how to enact the innovation, typically modifying it in light of information about how the implementation process is progressing.

The innovation-adoption perspective seems particularly suited to innovations falling toward the highly-certain end of the innovation-uncertainty continuum. In terms of the first factor impacting innovation uncertainty—the degree to which the innovation is clearly defined—organizations must clearly understand how an innovation is designed and supposed to work if they are to adopt it. This includes understanding the specific features of the innovation and knowing how they operate together to produce expected results. Moreover, if organizations are to choose an innovation applicable to their particular situation, they must clearly understand the conditions upon which expected results are contingent, and whether those conditions exist in their organization.

In regard to the second feature contributing to innovation uncertainty—the degree to which there are specified steps for implementing the innovation—organizations will have difficulty recreating the innovation in their own setting unless they know the precise steps for implementing it. Such knowledge enables organizations to plan and control the implementation process because it shows them how to enact the innovation and make it operational.

In terms of the third characteristic affecting innovation uncertainty—the degree to which the learning required to make the innovation operational is rudimentary—if organizations are to adopt an innovation, learning about how to operate it must be relatively straightforward. The behaviors needed to make the innovation work must be clearly understood and readily acquired, otherwise the organization will have difficulty making the innovation work in its own setting.

The three factors contributing to innovation uncertainty help to explain why organizations prefer and seek to utilize an innovation-adoption strategy. Organizations tend to perceive the myriad of technical and procedural improvements that they adopt continuously as scoring low on these dimensions almost as a matter of course. Such innovations are seen as highly certain, and are generally well-understood in terms of design features, operating mechanisms, and expected results. In many cases, the innovations derive from a solid body of scientific knowledge, and have been thoroughly tested before they are considered for adoption. Also, they often include detailed steps for implementation, clearly specified operating behaviors, and training programs for learning the behaviors. Organizations have become so accustomed to perceiving innovations as displaying these features that a major criterion for adopting innovations is the degree to which they appear well-developed and packaged for easy adoption, and are characterized by well-defined and limited costs (Cherns, 1979; Cole, 1982).

The innovation literature has also recognized that adoption occurs more readily to the extent that innovations are highly certain. Such innovations have been referred to as "routine" (as opposed to "radical") because they do not entail extensive alteration in the status quo (Normann, 1971). Similarly, they have been called "programmed" (as opposed to "nonprogrammed") because they can be accommodated by existing organizational routines and procedures (Knight, 1969). Such innovations have also been contrasted with those that are "discontinuous" involving the development of new behavior patterns, and "pervasive" requiring changes in many aspects of the social system (Lin & Zaltman, 1973).

Although the innovation-adoption perspective seems applicable to innovations that are highly certain, it can encounter severe limitations when applied to less certain organizational improvements. Indeed, research suggests that organizations can have problems trying to adopt even relatively routine innovations. Eichholtz and Rogers (1964), for example, found considerable resistance to the introduction of audio-visual equipment into classrooms. Even this relatively simple technical aid challenged prevailing teaching habits and practices. In her extensive studies of the introduction of computer systems into organizations, Mumford (1983a; 1983b) found that the successful introduction of even the most simple computer system is characterized by considerable on-site design by organizational members. Systems designed by external designers/inventors frequently clash with values, practices, and politics of the adopting unit. A review of research showing similar difficulties with trying to introduce various technologies into organizations led Rogers (1983) to conclude that even rather straightforward innovations undergo a great deal of "reinvention," being modified and adjusted to fit the situation.

Given these limitations of the innovation-adoption perspective, methods currently being used to improve productivity and employee well-being can be expected to pose severe problems for organizations using such as strategy. QWL innovations, such as quality circles, participative management, self-managing work teams, and job enrichment tend to be highly uncertain, falling at almost opposite ends of the continuum favoring innovation adoption. They generally lack the clarity and developed knowledge base to permit ready adoption from one situation to another.

In terms of the first factor favoring innovation adoption—clearly-defined innovation—reviews of the relevant literature suggest that QWL methods tend to be ill-defined and poorly understood (Cummings & Molloy, 1977). The key features of the innovations are often not clearly specified, and there is ambiguity about how the features should combine or interact to produce expected results. Common approaches are applied quite differently in different organizations. For example, despite the widespread application of and research about self-regulating work groups and quality circles, there is still considerable uncertainty about their necessary design features and about how they produce observed results (Cummings, 1978; Pasmore et al., 1982; Mohrman, 1983). In a comprehensive study of participative management practices in the United States, Cole (1982) found that adopting decisions regarding such techniques were characterized by lack of specification of goals and only partial understanding of the practices being considered. Moreover, because QWL innovations typically involve complex and multifaceted organizational changes, evaluative studies have had difficulty determining whether the innovations actually produced observed results, and if so, which features of the innovations were responsible for positive results (Cummings, Molloy, & Glen, 1977). In the absence of such empirical knowledge, the innovations tend to be relatively abstract and offer only general prescriptions for organizational improvement.

The second characteristic favoring innovation adoption—highly specified steps for implementation—is rarely applicable to QWL innovations. Because the innovations provide only general prescriptions for change, organizations must do considerable experimentation on site in order to implement them. They must discover how to translate the abstract concepts into specific organizational changes. This typically involves considerable monitoring and adjustment as organizations modify the change program in light of information about how it is progressing. The implementation process is relatively uncertain and often involves responding to unanticipated consequences in novel and complex ways.

For example, attempts to implement a relatively straightforward innovation, such as quality circles, may lead to modifications in wider aspects of the organization, such as reward systems, selection practices, and leadership styles, in order to make the context more supportive of the innovation (Lawler & Mohrman, 1985).

The kinds of innovations used to improve productivity and employee fulfillment also do not easily fit the third feature favoring innovation adoption— requirement for only rudimentary organizational learning. Organizations tend to underestimate the amount of learning required to implement and sustain QWL innovations (Mohrman & Cummings, 1983). Most of these innovations include, either implicitly or explicitly, an underlying philosophy promoting employee participation and egalitarian practices. In order to implement the innovations, organizational members must learn both the underlying philosophy and the behaviors implied by it. For example, quality circles may be effective only when employees have the necessary skills, knowledge, opportunities, and willingness to participate and when managers have the skills, knowledge, and willingness to respond. Because these values and behaviors are generally quite different from those commonly found in most organizations, such learning typically requires significant changes in people's world views and work behaviors (Argyris, 1970; Cole, 1982). There is currently little understanding about how to change the way people see or respond to their environment or attach value to certain outcomes (Smith, 1982). Similarly, research suggests that changing people's behaviors is an exceedingly time-consuming and complex process (Watzlawick et al., 1967, 1974; Argyris & Schon, 1974).

The features of the QWL innovations clearly do not fit an innovation-adoption perspective. They tend to be ill-defined and not well understood; they are relatively abstract and offer only general prescriptions for organizational improvement. The innovations do not include clearly specified implementation steps, but rather involve an uncertain implementation process requiring considerable experimentation and adoption on site. Finally, the innovations entail large amounts of organizational learning; people must often change their world views and work behaviors, a time-consuming and complex change process.

Given these characteristics, organizations must rely on a strategy different than innovation adoption for implementing QWL innovations. The strategy must take into account the relatively undeveloped knowledge base underlying these innovations. It must provide a method for translating general prescriptions for organizational improvement into situation-specific change programs. The strategy must account for an inherently uncertain implementation process. It must provide guides for monitoring and adjusting the change program in light of new information and unanticipated consequences. Finally, the strategy must recognize the need for considerable organizational learning. It must help organizational members gain the necessary skills and knowledge to change values and relevant work behaviors.

The following pages develop, in a preliminary manner, an implementation strategy meeting these requirements. Called *self-design*, the strategy is aimed at implementing the kinds of innovations currently being used to improve productivity and employee fulfillment.

SELF-DESIGN MODEL

The strategy needed to implement QWL innovations derives from field studies with organizations trying to improve effectiveness and employee quality of work life. The research sites included manufacturing plants of firms in the glassmaking, aerospace, pharmaceutical, munitions, communication, and pulp and paper industries. The authors served as action researchers, helping the organizations design and implement improvements while studying the change process itself (see Cummings et al. [1985] for a description of this action research process). The typical research project began when organizational members expressed an interest in implementing QWL innovations such as self-regulating work groups, quality circles, or gain-sharing. Each organization was able to take concepts and ideas from the experiences of other organizations. The process of implementing these concepts, however, was less an innovation-adoption strategy and more a process of the organization designing a new way of operating for itself. A major research interest for the authors was operationalizing what such a self-design strategy actually entails in an organizational setting. This contrasts with organizational theorists who have made strong conceptual arguments for self design, while leaving the operational details to more action-oriented researchers (Hedberg et al., 1976; Weick, 1977).

The self-design model is aimed at helping organizations translate general prescriptions for organizational improvement into situation-relevant change programs. Because this involves considerable experimentation and learning by organizational members, the self-design process, as the name implies, involves considerable participation by managers and employees. They essentially implement and manage the change program, typically with the help of professionals having relevant expertise. The role of OD practitioners/researchers in the self-design process is discussed in the next section of the paper. This section describes the five main phases of the self-design model as depicted in Figure 2: (1) value clarification, (2) diagnosis, (3) innovation generation, (4) implementation learning, and (5) feedback measurement.

Value Clarification

This preliminary phase of the self-design process is concerned with clarifying the values which will guide the choice of organizational innovations. Which (whose) values will guide the process is a key element of any innovation process, having ethical, political, and practical ramifications (Taylor & Vertinsky, 1981).

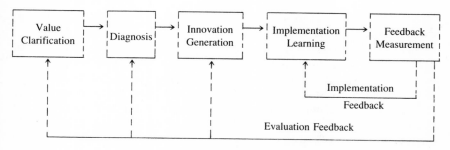

Figure 2. Self-Design Process

Multiple stakeholders, such as managers, employees and unions, are generally interested in the outcomes of QWL innovations, and consequently they introduce an expanded set of values into the design process.

Values determine which kinds of organizational outcomes are desirable or undesirable. Because they are used to judge, either explicitly or implicitly, the outcomes of organizational innovations, it is important to clarify as early in the design process as possible the values which the innovations are intended to promote or satisfy. For example, QWL innovations typically imply values of high-quality performance, innovation, and employee involvement, satisfaction and well-being.

Value clarification can make explicit the value premises underlying design choices and can help organizations make informed choices about the values they want to guide the design process. When values are implicit, organizations are unlikely to question them; they are likely to rely on whatever values have guided past choices about organizational improvements. This may limit the range of values that designers take into account, and constrain the kinds of innovations that are considered. For example, organizations have traditionally relied on technical or economic values to judge innovations (Gerwin, 1981). This can lead to a strong technological imperative in designing organizations, and a relative neglect of important social/psychological considerations.

Value clarification is a particularly important part of the design of QWL innovations. Their implementation generally requires changes in some of the assumptions and values that are embedded, often tacitly, in traditional hierarchical modes of organizing. Evaluative differences between "managers" and "workers," for example, can lead to a myriad of differences in how these two groups of employees are treated in organizations and in beliefs about their legitimate expectations from work. Successful implementation of various participative practices may require shifts in these underlying values, as well as changes in managerial practice. Clarifying values early in the design process can make these issues explicit, and enable organizational members to become more aware of value-constrained behaviors. Actual changes in values typically begin later in the design process, but sensitization to the issues and awareness of current values should frame the entire innovation process.

There are numerous values that organizations might take into account in designing QWL innovations. Value clarification can help organizations identify and explore a wider range of values than is typically considered, and is usually accomplished in two stages. First, potential stakeholders having vested interests in the outcome of the innovation are identified (see Mason and Mitroff [1981] for a full description of stakeholder analysis). They might include managers and employees, as well as key groups from the organization's task environment, such as labor unions, customers, regulators, and suppliers. A key point is to identify those stakeholders whose support and resources are necessary for implementing the innovation. The inclusion of multiple stakeholders with varying perspectives is likely to increase both the range of values that will be considered and the probability that the innovation will depart from the status quo (Zaltman et al., 1973).

Second, the values of these stakeholders are surfaced and potentially taken into account in the design of the innovation. Because values are deep-seated and often not discussed explicitly, it may be necessary to infer stakeholders' values from statements or observations of their behaviors and preferred modes of organizational functioning. Also, because stakeholders can have divergent values for judging the outcomes of organizational improvements, the process of arriving at an acceptable set of values can create conflict. Conflict resolution may require considerable process intervention aimed at helping the participants understand each other's values. It may also require bargaining solutions in those situations where agreement cannot be reached through informal interaction (Walton, 1969; Shepard, 1984).

A tangible outcome of value clarification is an explicit list of values that the QWL innovation is intended to satisfy. Some organizations have embodied the values in a statement of philosophy jointly created by the stakeholders; the statement communicates desirable organizational outcomes and/or a vision of the desired future state of the organization (e.g., Poza & Marcus, 1980). Because the values serve to guide the self-design process by providing standards against which to judge the current outcomes of the organization and the potential outcomes of alternative designs, all further design, implementation, and evaluation activities are referenced in terms of those values.

This initial value clarification phase does not typically resolve the value issue forever because organizational members are generally unaware of differences between the values they espouse and those that they actually use (Argyris & Schon, 1974). Consequently, they will frequently agree to a set of values which appear somewhat noncontroversial (like "motherhood and apple pie"), but will later disagree strongly with design features or operational consequences of those values. Value clarification is thus an ongoing part of any organizational innovation. Fortunately, experience appears to shape values just as values shape action choices (Cole, 1983). As the innovation process proceeds, the new experiences to which organizational members are exposed become the basis for the development of new attitudes and values (Kelman & Warwick, 1973). Indeed, participation in new structures that are created to perform the multi-stakeholder design process can be the source of some attitude and value shaping for members who have not participated in such a collaborative effort before.

Diagnosis

The next step in the self-design process is to assess the organization in order to understand its functioning. Diagnosis provides a foundation for the identification of performance gaps as well as for the design of a transition to innovative practices (Beckhard & Harris, 1977). Diagnostic data are the stimuli for organizational members to collectively interpret how the organization is operating. Participants must share their interpretations and arrive at a sufficiently agreed upon view of the organization to proceed in self design.

Because diagnosis generally proceeds from a conceptual model or theory of organizational functioning (Nadler, 1980), organizational members must gain a basic understanding of such diagnostic frameworks if they are to gain the capacity to self design. In QWL innovations, diagnosis tends to follow a socio-technical systems perspective (Trist et al., 1963; Cummings & Srivastva, 1977). This framework includes three key organizational dimensions that have been shown to affect the success of such innovations: (1) technology, (2) task environment, and (3) people.

Technology

This dimension includes the tools, techniques, and methods for transforming raw materials into finished products or services. Researchers have identified two key technological variables as affecting whether innovative work designs, such as job enrichment or self-regulating work groups, are appropriate to the organization: technical interdependence and technical uncertainty (Susman, 1976; Cummings, 1978; Slocum & Sims, 1980). Technical interdependence refers to the relationship among the different parts of a technological process. To the extent that technical interdependence is high and employees must work together to complete an overall task, work should be designed for groups rather than individualized jobs. Technical uncertainty refers to the amount of information processing and decision making that must occur during task execution. To the extent that technical uncertainty is high and employees must process information and make decisions during task performance, work should be designed for employee self-control rather than for external forms of control, such as hierarchy, standardization, and schedules.

Task Environment

This includes those external factors impacting the achievement of organizational goals, including the demands of customers, competitors, suppliers, and regulators (Dill, 1958). Researchers have described the environment along a static-dynamic dimension (Emery & Trist, 1965; Terreberry, 1968). They have shown that as the environment becomes more dynamic in terms of complexity and unpredictable change, organizations must become more organic or flexible if they are to adapt to such conditions (Burns & Stalker, 1961; Lawrence & Lorsch, 1967). Because many QWL innovations are intended to provide employees with the autonomy, information, and flexibility to respond to changing conditions, assessing the degree to which the task environment is dynamic is an important element in diagnosis.

People

This includes those individual differences affecting how people react to QWL innovations, such as participative structures, job enrichment, and self-regulating work groups. Researchers have identified at least two personal characteristics impacting reactions to these kinds of innovations: growth needs and social needs (Hackman & Oldham, 1980; Brousseau, 1983). Growth needs refers to the desire for personal accomplishment, learning, and development. In general, the more people have growth needs the more favorably they react to enriched work providing high levels of discretion, task variety, and feedback about results. Social needs involve the desire for significant social relationships. People having high social needs generally favor working in interactive groups, while those with low social needs tend to favor working on individualized jobs.

Diagnosing these kinds of variables provides knowledge for developing innovations appropriate to the situation. The contingencies specify the technological, environmental, and personal conditions that organizational designers must take into account in developing innovations to promote particular outcomes. In effect, the situational contingencies place limits on the kinds of innovations that will result in desired outcomes. For example, if organizational designers intend to promote outcomes of high performance and employee satisfaction in situations characterized by high levels of technical interdependence and uncertainty, of environmental change, and of employee growth needs and social needs; then participative group structures, such as self-regulating work groups, will best promote those values. More traditional designs, such as standardized jobs on an assembly line, would not enhance performance or employee satisfaction in these situations (Cummings, 1985). Table 1 summarizes how innovation features fit with different combinations of the diagnostic variables, with particular examples from work design.

Table 1. How Innovation Features Fit with Diagnostic Variables

| | DIAGNOSTIC VARIABLES | | | | |
| | Technology | | Environment | People | |
Innovative Features	Interdependence	Uncertainty	Dynamic	Growth Needs	Social Needs
• Individual Level • External Forms of Control • e.g., Traditional Jobs	Low	Low	Low	Low	Low
• Individual Level • Employee Self-Control • e.g., Enriched Jobs	Low	High	High	High	Low
• Group Level • External Control • e.g., Traditional Work Groups	High	Low	Low	Low	High
• Group Level • Employee Self-Control • e.g., Self-Regulating Work Groups	High	High	High	High	High

289

Innovation Generation

This step in the self-design process concerns generating alternative innovations to meet the situational contingencies and to achieve desired outcomes. Although this step involves considerable creativity, there is a growing body of organizational-design knowledge which can be used to guide this process (e.g., Cummings & Molloy, 1977; Hackman & Suttle, 1977; Nystrom & Starbuck, 1981). This design literature provides two kinds of information necessary to create effective QWL innovations: knowledge of organizational features that can be changed to achieve certain outcomes and knowledge of contingencies upon which positive results are dependent.

The first kind of knowledge involves various organizational components which can be designed to produce particular outcomes, such as productivity and employee satisfaction. Among these factors are: work design, organizational structure, reward systems, personnel practices, participative structures, selection, and training. Specific combinations of these components include such popular QWL innovations as quality circles, skill-based pay, job enrichment, self-regulating work groups, and gainsharing. Although it is beyond the scope of this chapter to review this extensive literature, two issues are particularly pertinent to generating innovations.

The first issue concerns the quality of research findings underlying the QWL innovations appearing in the literature. Ideally, existing research findings would provide specific prescriptions for organizational improvement; they would serve as a definitive blueprint for generating organizational innovations. Reviews of the relevant research suggest, however, that the findings cannot be used to maximally specify QWL improvements in advance of their implementation (Cummings & Molloy, 1977; Porras & Berg, 1978; Woodman & Sherwood, 1980; Nicholas, 1982). Plausible threats to the internal validity of the findings raise serious doubts about whether specific change programs actually produced the observed results. Moreover, most of the change programs involved multiple changes and it is difficult to disentangle either the effects of specific changes or interaction effects from the global, overall results of the change program.

Given these problems inherent in evaluating organizational improvements, existing research is relatively weak in offering specific prescriptions for designing QWL innovations. Rather, it can offer only general guidance for generating alternative innovations. The studies can provide rich case descriptions of change programs; they can help designers consider novel designs and frames of reference. The findings can provide warnings and checklists of issues to consider in designing and implementing organizational innovations. Organizational members typically want to know how innovative ideas and practices have worked in other organizations. Case studies, visitation to innovating companies, and attendance at practitioner conferences can all be useful exposure to new practices. At minimum, such exposure increases awareness that other organizations are successfully utilizing QWL approaches. Ideally, it can also help to generate minimally-specified designs to begin the innovation process. The designs can be further defined and elaborated during implementation as organizational members gain experience with the general prescriptions and learn how to enact them in their situation.

The second issue involving knowledge about organizational changes that can produce certain outcomes concerns the congruence or fit that must occur among the design components if positive results are to occur. As mentioned above, many QWL innovations include multiple changes. For example, a job enrichment program might include changes in technology, work flow, reward systems, training, and supervisory practices. A growing body of research suggests that these separate changes must be congruent with each other to achieve positive results (e.g., Nadler & Tushman, 1983; Mohrman & Lawler, 1984). This means that in generating alternative designs, the different features of the innovations must be mutually reinforcing. Designing a high-involvement plant, for example, would likely include several of the following compatible design features: a flat organization structure, enriched jobs, open job posting, realistic job previews, training in both technical and interpersonal skills, skill-based pay, and egalitarian personnel practices (Lawler, 1982; Walton, 1985). Full congruence in such an organization would ultimately entail altering most of the traditional personnel systems (Mohrman et al., 1986).

The second kind of knowledge that can guide generation of innovations involves contingencies upon which the success of innovations depends. As discussed earlier, researchers have identified a variety of situational variables impacting the general applicability of QWL innovations. These technological, environmental, and personal factors can be assessed during diagnosis, and the resulting information can guide the choice of alternative designs. Reviews of the relevant literature suggest, however, that organizational designers are likely to encounter a multitude of unanticipated contingencies during implementation (Srivastva et al., 1977; Cummings & Molloy, 1977; Zaltman et al., 1973). Consequently, designers must be prepared to adjust or modify innovations as unanticipated contingencies are encountered. Again, this argues for minimally-specified designs that are flexible enough to permit on-going adaptation to the situation. The general features of such innovations are specified before implementation, and the details of these features as well as of remaining dimensions are left free to vary with the circumstances.

While designing innovations to account for certain contingencies has been advocated widely in the literature, this may inadvertently constrain the generation of organizational innovations. When contingencies are treated as design imperatives, they become fixed constraints to which innovations must be fitted or adjusted. Such constraints may limit the kinds of innovations that are considered.

For example, many QWL innovations are aimed at enhancing employee participation, discretion, and flexibility. These designs would be inappropriate in situations where technology is highly certain, or where the environment is static, or where people have low growth needs. More traditional, routinized kinds of designs would better fit these situations. Rather than treat contingencies as design imperatives, organizational designers may want to consider them as design variables which can be altered if necessary. Indeed, socio-technical systems theorists have long advocated that both technology and people be treated as design variables (Trist et al., 1963; Cummings & Srivastva, 1977). This would open the design stage to a wider range of possible innovations. If existing contingencies are too constraining, they could be included as key elements of the change program. The contingencies, along with the other design features, would undergo change during implementation.

Implementation Learning

This stage of the self-design process concerns implementing organizational innovations. As discussed above, the deficiency of the existing knowledge base and the likelihood of encountering unanticipated consequences make it difficult to maximally specify designs in advance of their implementation. Rather, the general features of the innovation can be specified and implementation involves translating them into situation-relevant behaviors, structures, and processes. This translation process involves considerable experimentation and learning.

The iterative nature of the innovation process has been described in most literature on change and innovation. However, the introduction of one innovation as a solution to an existing organizational problem often creates new problems which become the impetus for another change, and so on (Zaltman et al., 1973). This cycle is especially prevalent when an organizational innovation stimulates learning, which in turn leads to further changes. There are at least five distinct areas in which such learning can stimulate innovation and change.

First, learning can lead to modification of the innovation itself. It is often impossible to understand fully what a change encompasses until it is experienced. For example, it is relatively easy to describe a computerized design system to an engineer, but only after trying it out will the engineer fully understand how it changes the nature of the engineering job, the information needed to perform it, and the altered interfaces with others in the organization. Managers adopting quality circles often do not realize until after the process has started that the innovation entails an alteration in the way they spend their time (Mohrman, 1982). Therefore, implementation of an innovation is often necessary for organizational members to learn what it actually entails.

Second, learning can lead to changes in the behaviors, values, and understandings required to enact the innovation. Organizational members must invariably develop new skills and behaviors in order to implement an innovation. In the example of a computerized design system, the engineer must learn how to use the new work station. In the case of quality circles, the participants must learn group process skills, and supervisors must learn to handle requests from groups. Learning these new behaviors is not a straightforward training process. Many of the requisite behaviors achieve significance only within the context of a new set of values and a new way of understanding the organization (Benne, 1985; Lewin & Grabee, 1945). Organizational members may have to engage individually in trial-and-error learning in which new behavior is tried out and the individual relies on feedback from others to determine if the behavior is congruent with the espoused values (Argyris & Schon, 1974).

Third, learning can result in discovering the situational contingencies impacting innovation success. Implementation can lead to failure. Self-regulating work groups, for example, may be ineffective when implemented without careful consideration of the contingencies determining their success. Research may not yet specify the important contingencies, and organizations may inadvertently design an innovation inappropriate for the situation. The organization may successfully implement the innovation, however, if it can first discover and then learn to alter the contextual conditions constraining the innovation's effectiveness.

Fourth, learning can lead to additional organizational changes needed to support the innovation. Work redesign, for example, may require supporting changes in personnel practices, leadership styles, and reward systems. Many QWL innovations require behavioral changes that are incongruent with most aspects of traditional organizations (Mohrman et al., 1986). Teamwork, cooperation, and risk-taking, for example, run counter to many of the control and incentive systems in large bureaucratic organizations. Traditional personnel practices, information systems, and job designs, to name a few, frequently result in individual suboptimization, competition, and low risk taking. Because the different features of an organization tend to reinforce a particular mode of operating, changing that way of functioning generally requires multiple interventions, and will eventually require alteration in most aspects of the organization (Nadler & Lawler, 1977). The transitional phase can be difficult because organizational members are likely to experience conflicting behavioral demands (Wilson, 1966).

Fifth, organizational members can learn about changes in the wider environment that require modification of the innovation. Because of the complexity of today's innovations and the rapid changes occurring in many organizations' environments, organizations may experience new pressures for adaptation before innovative practices are fully implemented. Organizational members can learn about these changes, and make necessary refinements and alterations in the innovation.

In summary, organizational learning can occur in all five areas. Thus, the implementation of an innovation is really an evolving process of learning how to enact the requisite changes through time. This means that members cannot simply adopt a well-developed innovation, but must learn how to develop it themselves in situ. Similar approaches to organizational learning have been proposed for governmental policies (Campbell, 1969; Lindblom, 1959), factory management (Box & Draper, 1969), and organizational reforms (Warner, 1981; Staw, 1978).

Implementation learning can be considered a feedback-adjustment cycle. Members start from general design prescriptions and try to enact the specific changes needed to implement the innovation. They subsequently learn how well those changes are progressing, and make necessary modifications in behaviors, structures, and processes. This feedback-adjustment cycle continues until the innovation and resultant changes are implemented sufficiently. The dynamic quality of the process is underscored by the fact that the environment itself can change, thus altering the adaptation needs of the organization. Consequently, implementation is an on-going learning process carried out by organizational members who continue to self design through time. To be capable of self design, members must be proficient at three kinds of learning.

Single-Loop Learning

The first type is called "single-loop learning" and involves detecting and correcting errors between the innovation's current and desired states (Argyris & Schon, 1978). Such learning takes place within an existing frame of reference— a set of values, cognitions, programs, and interpretive schemes (Bateson, 1972; Cyert & March, 1963; Morgan & Ramirez, 1983). When deviations from the desired state are discovered, designers must engage in inquiry to find the causes of the error and to devise appropriate actions to correct it. The outcomes of single-loop learning are behavioral (Fiol & Lyles, 1985). Such inquiry can involve a complex learning cycle, especially when applied to implementing QWL innovations. Because knowledge of such innovations provides only general prescriptions for change, designers may have relatively vague understanding of what the desired or developed state of the innovation should resemble.

In such a highly uncertain change process, single-loop learning is of limited benefit. For example, detection of errors may only be possible within a new frame of values, which generally has not been fully learned and is only partially adhered to during the early stages of change. Consequently, organizational members may have difficulty detecting errors; there may be ambiguity about whether particular innovation features are actually being implemented correctly. Moreover, because multiple stakeholders, such as employees, managers, and staff specialists, tend to participate in the self-design process, there may be conflicting opinions about the presence of error, the causes, and the appropriate remedies. Resolution of these ambiguities and conflicts requires norms promoting open exchange of information and active listening. Many of the process interventions prevalent in organization development, such as team building, process consultation, and conflict resolution, can facilitate the development of requisite learning norms (e.g., Huse & Cummings, 1985). Similarly, interventions aimed at group problem solving can help participants gain the skills and knowledge needed to detect and correct complex implementation errors (e.g., MacCrimmon & Taylor, 1976). Ultimately, however, the participants must progress to a new level of learning.

Double-Loop Learning

The second type of implementation learning is referred to as "double-loop learning" and is concerned with changing existing organizational values or norms (Argyris & Schon, 1978) and the development of new frames of reference (Shrivastava & Mitroff, 1982), or interpretive schemes (Bartunek, 1984). Typically, it arises when designers encounter value conflicts during implementation—for example, in trying to implement participative management, which promotes values of employee discretion and involvement, designers may discover that providing employees with more task discretion runs counter to prevailing organizational values promoting managerial control. In order to resolve this conflict, designers must first recognize that it cannot be corrected within the framework of existing organizational norms. Rather, they must undertake inquiry that results in changing the values, either by setting new priorities and weighting of values or by modifying the values themselves. The difficulty of this inquiry has been dealt with in great detail by Argyris and others (Argyris, 1982; Argyris & Schon, 1978), who proposed that a time-consuming process of individual change must precede organization-level change. Others, such as Lewin and Grabbe (1945) and Benne (1985) suggested that change in values and cognitions is essentially a social process in which the group is the fundamental source of support.

The need to confront and resolve value conflicts seems particularly salient when implementing QWL innovations. There is evidence to suggest that some innovations may not be robust enough to promote both economic and social/psychological values (Cummings, 1981; 1985); designers may need to make trade-offs between these two kinds of values. Further, many of the innovations, such as job enrichment, participative management, and self-regulating work groups are likely to require significant changes in traditional organizational values if they are to be implemented (Mohrman & Cummings, 1983; Cole, 1982). Although designers may set new values during the value-clarification stage of self design, underlying conflicts between those values and existing organizational norms may not emerge and need to be resolved until designers attempt to implement innovations promoting the new values. Then, existing values may block implementation of innovations; they may offer strong resistance to making necessary changes in behaviors, structures, and processes. Unless designers undertake double-loop learning and confront and resolve such value conflicts, the likelihood of successful implementation seems low.

Deutero-Learning

The third type of implementation learning is called "deutero-learning" and involves inquiring into previous attempts at organizational learning so that the learning process itself can be improved (Bateson, 1972). In essence, it is concerned with learning how to learn. Deutero-learning includes discovering factors facilitating and inhibiting single- and double-loop learning and creating new strategies for more effective learning (Argyris & Schon, 1978). Because implementation learning is likely to involve many reiterations of the feedback-adjustment cycle, designers should have ample opportunities to examine their on-going learning process so they can improve it. An important norm supporting organizational learning is the surfacing of valid data which provides feedback to the organization about how well it is accomplishing its goals and enacting its values. The final aspect of the self-design process deals with that feedback process.

Feedback Measurement

The last stage of the self-design process involves providing relevant measures of innovation features and outcomes to guide the learning process. This surfacing and interpretation of data is actually an integral part of implementation learning. Organizational members must have on-going knowledge about how the implementation process is progressing if they are to learn how to enact the innovation correctly. Referred to as "implementation feedback" or "process evaluation" (Stufflebeam, 1967), such information allows designers to make necessary adjustments in behaviors, structures, and processes in light of information about whether the innovation is being implemented correctly. Designers must also have knowledge about whether the innovation is having intended effects and whether it is promoting desired outcomes. Referred to as "evaluation feedback," such information helps designers decide whether to continue to invest resources in the innovation or whether to rethink the self-design process, perhaps changing values, rediagnosing the situation, or choosing an alternative innovation. The two kinds of feedback are shown in Figure 2. They are frequently collected through a systematic, action-research program, often with assistance from external action researchers.

Implementation Feedback

This information is used to guide implementation learning and consists of two kinds of data: measures about whether the different features of the innovation are being implemented properly, and information about their immediate effects. Traditionally, QWL innovators have focused on outcome measures, while neglecting to assess whether the innovations were implemented as intended, whether organizational members have mastered the new skills and behaviors, and whether there are unanticipated consequences that require additional design elements and/or implementation steps (Cummings & Molloy, 1977). This makes it difficult to determine if outcomes result from the intended innovations. Moreover, it provides little guidance for making the kinds of behavioral and organizational changes needed to implement the innovation or for adjusting the features of the innovation to situational contingencies. Consequently, effective self design relies on measures of innovation features, contextual dimensions, and outcomes. The first can be used to assess the different elements of the innovation so designers can learn whether they are being implemented as intended; the second to identify anticipated and unanticipated contextual consequences; the third to evaluate whether the features that are actually being implemented are having expected results.

Because implementation feedback is used to guide the self-design process, it must be obtained repeatedly and with little delay. Repeated and timely assessments of innovation features and outcomes help organizational members learn how to enact the innovation and make necessary on-going adjustments. This need for an almost continuous cycle of implementation feedback places heavy demands on the measurement process. Organizational designers need valid and reliable measures of innovation features and outcomes; however, all measurement techniques contain inherent biases. Therefore, several independent methods should be used to obtain valid measures, such as questionnaires, in-depth interviews, structured observations, and archival data. Less formal methods such as multi-stakeholder discussion groups can also be useful in gathering and interpreting information. The different methods can be used to triangulate on variables—if the different measures converge, the variables are likely to have been measured validly. Organizational members can design and validate their own measures, or they can rely on a growing number of standardized methods for measuring the features and outcomes of QWL innovations (e.g., Hackman & Oldham, 1980; Lawler et al., 1980; Seashore et al., 1983). These methods can be used in total, or they can be adapted to specific organizational circumstances with some on-site validation testing.

In order to obtain reliable measures of innovation features and outcomes, it is necessary to account for random measurement errors that are likely to occur when data are collected repeatedly at short intervals. Because these measurement errors might be mistaken for actual changes, designers can aggregate different measures of the same variable, thus averaging out much of the random error (Waters et al., 1978). For example, productivity outcomes could be observed with an index combining such elements as product quality, machine utilization, and production costs. Similarly, a job-satisfaction index might combine such components as absenteeism and questionnaire and interview responses. When using repeated, self-report measures, however, it is also necessary to distinguish between alpha, beta, and gamma changes (Golembiewski & Munzenrider,

1976). Because QWL innovations are likely to produce all three kinds of perceptual change, analytical methods for distinguishing among them should be used (see, for example, Bedeian et al., 1980; and Terborg et al., 1982).

Evaluation Feedback

This information is used to assess whether the innovation is having intended effects. It generally occurs after designers have some confidence that the innovation is being implemented correctly, and consists of longer-term evaluation of outcome measures. Such assessment helps designers determine whether the innovation is promoting desired outcomes, and thus whether it should continue to be supported. When evaluation feedback shows innovation success, designers may expend effort institutionalizing the innovation by making it a permanent part of normal organization functioning (e.g., Goodman & Dean, 1982). They may also decide to diffuse the innovation to wider segments of the organization (e.g., Walton, 1975). On the other hand, when evaluation feedback suggests that the innovation is not having expected results, designers may decide to drastically alter it or to choose an alternative innovation. They may also decide to modify the values or outcomes that the innovation is supposed to promote, either by changing their priority or weighting, or by replacing or discarding them altogether.

By the time the innovation is sufficiently implemented to enable evaluation feedback, it is likely change has occurred in multiple aspects of the organization. Thus, a decision to discontinue an innovation does not leave the organization as it was prior to the self-design process. In fact, abandoning the innovation implies new design efforts. It is also possible that an innovation that contributed to improved organizational effectiveness may eventually outlive its usefulness as organizational and environmental conditions change. This may call for a whole new design process, an iterative process that Schein (1970) has called an "adaptive-coping cycle."

The effective use of evaluation feedback rests on at least two requirements. The first is the need to design evaluation feedback so that it permits relatively strong causal inferences about innovation results. Otherwise, designers can draw erroneous conclusions from the information. Although randomized evaluation designs allow the strongest causal inference, they are difficult to apply in organizational settings because work units generally have a choice about implementing innovations. Furthermore, random selection of innovating units can decrease the probability that there will be sufficient levels of commitment to enact a self-design strategy. Organization designers often rely instead on quasi-experimental evaluation designs which, although not as strong as randomized designs, offer some control over threats to causal inference (e.g., Campbell & Stanley, 1966; Cook & Campbell, 1966). A nonequivalent control-group design using time-series data is probably the strongest quasi-experimental design organizations can expect to apply to evaluation feedback (Cummings et al., 1985). Even with a well-designed, quasi-experiment, however, organizational members may have problems interpreting results because the innovation has been through a series of iterative changes, and has consisted of evolving practices and supporting changes. Thus, the most that can be concluded is that the organization has been more or less effective in achieving valued outcomes through a series of changes that it has been able to implement (Hedberg et al., 1976).

The second requirement for the effective use of evaluative feedback is the need for a strong commitment to learning how to improve organizations rather than to defending specific innovations. There is a tendency for organizational innovators to become "trapped administrators" (Campbell, 1969), and to defend their innovations regardless of the actual outcomes. They tend to eschew valid, long-term evaluation of their innovations and to defend them rigidly. Such unswerving defense of innovations arises primarily because top managers often judge designers based on the outcomes of their innovations (Cummings & Molloy, 1977), and because designers tend to commit increasing resources to failed courses of action, especially when they have publicly committed to such actions (Staw, 1976; 1981). When designers become trapped administrators, they are too concerned with appearing successful to risk the failures inherent in learning. They also become committed to the structures and mechanisms that are associated with a particular innovation, and are insensitive to the processes which enable successful performance through time. Although there is no ready solution to this problem, organizations can promote learning from evaluation feedback by explicitly separating the evaluation of innovations from the assessment of innovators. They can also promote a learning culture that views short-term innovation failures as contributions to long-term learning (Waters et al., 1978).

Summary

In summary, the self-design process differs substantially from the innovation-adoption perspective. In innovation adoption, the innovation is viewed as a well-defined entity which can be adopted by an organization that has determined that it fits a need. The major challenge is developing a willingness to try out something new. The self-design strategy approaches innovation as a *process* rather than as a discrete event. Innovative practices in other organizations or in the literature help the organization generate its own designs. The question is not whether to adopt an innovation, but whether the organization can use existing concepts and practices to design a situationally-relevant innovation. The innovation-adoption perspective seeks highly certain and thus easily copied innovations. The self-design process is aimed at highly uncertain innovations which provide only general prescriptions for change needing further development and refinement during implementation. The goal of innovation adoption is successful

Table 2. Contrasts Between Innovation Adoption
and Self-Design

	Innovation Adoption	*Self-Design*
Stages	Diagnosis and Search	Value Clarification
	Adoption	Diagnosis
	Implementation	Innovation Generation
	Evaluation	Implementation Learning
		Feedback Measurement
General Applicability	Clearly-Defined Innovation Knowledge	Poorly-Defined Innovation Knowledge
	Highly-Specified Implementation Steps	Highly-Uncertain Implementation Steps
	Rudimentary Learning	Complex Learning

implementation of the innovation. The self-design model looks at innovative practices as design elements to enable an organization to better attain its goals. Table 2 summarizes these contrasts between the two innovation perspectives.

FURTHER RESEARCH NEEDS

The self-design process is an attempt to manage the fundamental problems of organizational change that organizations can experience trying to implement QWL innovations. The strategy is still in a development stage, and considerably more research and conceptualization are needed to increase its success. Specifically, further research is needed in at least three major areas: (1) the dynamics of self design, (2) measurement of innovation features and outcomes, and (3) the nature of action research in a self-design context.

Dynamics of Self Design

The first area for further research concerns the need to study the implementation process itself rather than simply innovation outcomes. Traditionally, most research in the QWL field focuses on evaluating the outcomes of innovations while paying relatively little attention to the processes through which they are actually implemented (Cummings & Molloy, 1977; Nicholas, 1982). Many evaluative studies measure only outcomes and assume that the innovation has been implemented as intended. This assumption is not only open to empirical question, but grossly underestimates the complexity and uncertainty inherent in implementing QWL innovations.

Research should be concerned with the underlying dynamics of designing and implementing organizational innovations as well as with the effects of those change programs. It would study innovation as a developmental/learning process involving on-going inquiry and reflection. This contrasts sharply with much of the traditional innovation research which tends to treat innovations as discrete events occurring at a single point in time. Further, such research would require abandonment of the traditional variance approach to doing research and require the further development and application of a process approach (Rogers, 1983; Mohr, 1982; Ledford, 1984). Although some conceptualization and research has proceeded in this direction (e.g., Kolodny & Stjernberg, in press; Argyris et al., 1985; Warner, 1984; Cummings, 1981; Herbst, 1966), there is considerable need for systematic theory and research on the following kinds of issues: How do organizational stakeholders come to value certain types of innovations and outcomes rather than others? What diagnostic models are most relevant for different organizational settings? How do organizational members translate diagnostic information into alternative design choices? What dimensions constitute minimal-specification designs for the different kinds of innovations considered here? How do organizational members learn how to enact the innovations? What is the role of implementation feedback in the learning process? How can innovations be realistically and honestly evaluated? This list could easily be expanded; the main point is to direct attention to the self-design process itself, in addition to outcomes.

Measurement

A second area for further research is the development of valid and reliable measures to guide the self-design process. The strategy places heavy demands on data gathering. Measures of both innovation features and outcomes must be collected repeatedly and at short intervals. As discussed earlier, these data requirements call for multiple measures in order to triangulate on specific variables, as well as indices comprised of different measures to account for the random error inherent in short-interval data.

So far, measurement has tended to focus on innovation outcomes. Although there are increasing attempts to expand the focus to the design features comprising various kinds of QWL innovations (e.g., Hackman & Oldham, 1980; Seashore et al., 1983), there is considerable need for further measurement development in this area. Similarly, most research has relied primarily on single measures of innovation and outcome variables derived mainly from questionnaire and archival data. There is a need for multiple measures of variables, and for the development of unobtrusive measures of people's reactions to QWL innovations. Unobtrusive measures are nonreactive and could supplement questionnaire data which are so prevalent in this field (Webb et al., 1966). They could help to provide more valid measures of innovative features and outcomes, as well as to construct indices of relevant variables (e.g., Seashore et al., 1983).

Action Research and Self Design

The final and perhaps most important area for future research concerns the nature and conduct of research in QWL innovation. Research about designing and implementing QWL innovations has typically followed an action research perspective (Lewin, 1946). It has been concerned both with generating new knowledge and with helping organizational members solve important practical problems. As such, it requires that researchers bridge the epistemological and world-view gaps that traditionally separate them from practitioners (Bennis, 1983) and action from science (Sarason, 1978). Generating knowledge that is useful and applying "scientific" knowledge to action both demand that action researchers transcend the bounds of academic disciplines and comprehend practical issues from the position of practitioners. In short, the action researcher exists in two worlds.

Ideally, practitioners will also develop the ability to function both in the role of doer and observer. The self-design process demands the establishment of a learning community capable of taking action and learning from it. This learning community must be able to assess its own functioning, and to move between roles of implementor and assessor. The action researcher is generally called upon to help create as well as to be a part of that learning community.

Action research includes both a "content" and "relationship" component (Cummings et al., 1985). The content aspect is concerned with generating research questions, designing relevant methods, and collecting and analyzing data. The content of research about the self-design process deals only partly with the particular design choices, systems, and techniques that are applied as design components in self-designing organizations. Equally important are the process questions: How does an organization self-design? What processes are required to enact the iterative cycles of design, implementation, and redesign in a multistakeholder setting? Knowledge of both the process and substance of design is the goal of the action researcher and the source of his/her legitimacy as a member of the learning community. Research content is the substantive link between the action researcher and the organization.

The relationship component involves the nature of interactions between researchers and organizational members, including the role of researchers in the change process and their position vis-à-vis other stakeholders. Because the relationship aspect of action research is relatively tacit and serves as a context for the research content, it can easily be neglected in favor of the more tangible content component. There is considerable evidence, however, that the relationship between researchers and organizational members can have a powerful impact on the research findings as well as on the usefulness of the research for organizational members (Argyris, 1980; Kilmann et al., 1983; Lawler et al., 1985). The relationship provides a frame for interpretation of all communication between parties. For example, information provided by the researcher about design options or trends in the feedback data are likely to be interpreted differently by organization members depending on whether there is a relationship of trust or skepticism between them. The observation of a meeting will be experienced differently if the researcher is viewed as neutral or partial, as a co-learner or as an authority. The relationship issue is paramount, as it impacts the quality of information that is willingly shared, and consequently may limit the ability of the researcher to collect meaningful data. Consequently, researchers must explicitly address and manage the relationship component of action research.

When action research is applied to self-design situations, there are at least three key features of the research relationship that need to be taken into account (Mohrman et al., 1983). First, the relationship requires relatively long-time commitments from researchers and organizational members. They are jointly engaged in clarifying values, diagnosing the situation, generating alternative innovations, learning new behaviors, and evaluating results. These activities generally take considerable time, and researchers must be prepared to develop long-term relationships with organizational participants. Second, the research relationship involves high levels of psychological intensity. This is inherent in any professional relationship where one party is helping the other to change. Psychological intensity is especially prevalent in the self-design process, where researchers and members are often exploring new ground both scientifically and practically. The stakes are high for both parties, and researchers should be prepared to manage the psychodynamics underlying the research process. Third, because action research is aimed at the joint goals of producing knowledge useful to organizational members and relevant to the scientific community, multiple stakeholders are interested in the research process. Researchers must establish relationships with the interested parties; they must actively involve them in designing and executing the research. The self-design process must provide data useful to organizational members engaged in self design and useful to organization development practitioners and researchers in learning to help organizations self design. Collaboration in the research increases the likelihood that relevant stakeholders will support the research and see it as relevant to their values and objectives (Elden & Taylor, 1983).

As might be expected, the role demands facing action researchers in self-design situations are complex and difficult (Cummings et al., 1985). Researchers must establish a legitimate and relatively active role in the self-design process. They must earn the right to engage with organizational members in joint learning, usually by establishing a "professional relationship" where privileged access to the organization is attained by providing useful services (Emery & Trist, 1973). These services might include, for example, collecting and feeding back data to members, providing expert design information, and actively intervening in the design process. A professional relationship requires an active role in the design process. Such participation not only provides legitimacy and access to the organization, but increases the likelihood that researchers will gain the depth of information necessary to understand the dynamics of the design process.

Researchers whose role is as narrowly prescribed as collecting data fit the "scientific" expectations of impartiality and noninvolvement. They are likely, however, to have difficulty maintaining effective linkages with stakeholders. Data collection generally requires an on-going commitment of time and energy from organizational members, who are unlikely to continue to cooperate if they see no useful outcome and feel no ownership over the learnings. Indeed, such a hands-off research role violates the very premise of the self-design model that on-going data collection provides guidance in the iterative design process. The academically-based action researcher is thus caught between the standards of two worlds. In order to fulfill this role effectively, researchers need methodological skills appropriate to the research content as well as social/political skills relevant to establishing and maintaining the research relationship. Among the multiple skills and knowledge bases required of the action researcher are the following:

1. Exposure to a wide variety of situations and theoretical frameworks that offer a rich way of understanding organizations and viewing possible alternatives;
2. Communication skills for presenting this understanding to others in such a way that they can assimilate it into their own world views;
3. Process skills to help multiple stakeholders share their preferences, concerns, and understandings and arrive at agreement about action; and
4. Methodologies to observe and record the process systematically, and to share learnings with the professional academic community.

Because application of the full range of skills may exceed the capacity of a single researcher, a multi-disciplinary team of researchers may be needed to carry out action research in self-design situations. This requires yet another skill on the part of action researchers: the ability to create and maintain effective research teams of people who are able to challenge, yet complement, one another's viewpoints.

CONCLUSION

Organizations are increasingly undertaking change programs aimed at improving productivity and employee well-being. Despite widespread reports of success, many organizations are discovering that QWL innovations cannot simply be adopted like other types of organizational improvements, such as new machinery and accounting practices. The innovations have a number of features unsuited to an innovation-adoption perspective. They tend to be ill-defined and not well understood; they offer only general prescriptions for organizational change; and they involve an implementation process requiring considerable experimentation and learning.

This chapter presented an implementation strategy that is more responsive to those conditions than the traditional innovation adoption model. Referred to as *self-design*, the strategy is aimed at helping organizations translate general prescriptions for organizational improvement into situation-relevant change programs. It involves considerable participation by managers and employees in an on-going process or organizational change and learning. The self-design process includes five key phases: (1) value clarification, (2) diagnosis, (3) innovation generation, (4) implementation learning, and (5) feedback measurement. Although the phases are discussed sequentially, they may overlap and interact in application.

The self-design strategy is still in a developmental stage, and more experience and research are needed to clarify its features and application. Further understanding is needed with regard to the underlying dynamics of designing and implementing QWL innovations. Because implementation and evaluation are guided by data feedback, there is also a pressing need to develop valid and reliable measures of innovation characteristics and outcomes. Equally important, the self-design process points to the need for researchers to attend to both the content and relationship aspects of action research. They must actively engage with organizational members in a learning process characterized by long time commitments, psychological intensity, and multiple stakeholders. Researchers need to be responsive to these conditions. They need to form relationships with organizational members which allow for mutual trust, cooperation, and joint learning.

In many respects, the self-design strategy presented in this chapter is not new. Academics and practitioners have long called for similar approaches to designing and implementing organizational changes. Many organizations have undoubtedly discovered similar strategies through wise practice and probably some luck. What has been missing, however, are explicit descriptions of a self-design strategy and how it works. The relative absence of such concrete understanding leaves self-design more a metaphor than a specific change strategy. Hopefully, this chapter is a step towards translating that metaphor into a scientifically-sound approach for implementing and evaluating organizational innovations.

REFERENCES

Argyris, C. (1982). How learning and reasoning processes affect organizational change. In P. Goodman (Ed.), *Change in organizations*. San Francisco: Jossey-Bass.

Argyris, C. (1980). *Inner contradictions of rigorous research*. New York: Academic Press.

Argyris, C. (1970). *Intervention theory and method*. Reading, MA: Addison-Wesley.

Argyris, C., Putnam, R., & Smith, D. (1985). *Action science*. San Francisco: Jossey-Bass.

Argyris, C., & Schon, D. (1978). *Organizational learning.* Reading, MA: Addison-Wesley.

Argyris, C., & Schon, D. (1974). *Theory in practice: Increasing professional effectiveness.* San Francisco: Jossey-Bass.

Bartunek, J. M. (1984). Changing interpretive schemes and organizational restructuring: The example of a religious order. *Administrative Science Quarterly, 29,* 355–372.

Bateson, G. (1972). *Steps to an ecology of mind.* New York: Ballantine.

Beckhard, R., & Harris, R. T. (1977). *Organizational transitions: Managing complex change.* Reading, MA: Addison-Wesley.

Bedeian, A., Armenakin, A., & Gilson, R. (1980). On the measurement and control of beta changes. *Academy of Management Review, 5,* 561–566.

Benne, K. (1985). The process of re-education: An assessment of Kurt Lewin's views. In W. Bennis, K. Benne, & R. Chin (Eds.), *The planning of change* (4th Edition). New York: Holt, Rinehart and Winston.

Box, G., & Draper, N. (1969). *Evolutionary operation.* New York: John Wiley and Sons.

Brousseau, K. (1983). Toward a dynamic model of job-person relationships: Findings, research questions, and implications for work system design. *Academy of Management Review, 8,* 33–45.

Burns, T., & Stalker, G. (1961). *The management of innovation.* London: Tavistock.

Campbell, D. (1969). Reforms as experiments. *American Psychologist, 24,* 409–429.

Campbell, D., & Stanley, J. (1966). *Experimental and quasi-experimental design for research.* Chicago: Rand McNally.

Cherns, A. (1979). *Using the social sciences.* London: Routledge and Kegan Paul.

Cole, R. E. (1982). Diffusion of participatory work structures in Japan, Sweden, and The United States. In P. S. Goodman (Ed.), *Change in organizations.* San Francisco: Jossey-Bass.

Cook, T., & Campbell, D. (1976). The design and conduct of quasi-experiments and true experiments in field settings. In M. Dunnette (Ed.), *Handbook of industrial and organizational psychology.* Chicago: Rand McNally.

Corwin, R. (1966). Patterns of organizational conflict. *Administrative Science Quarterly, 14,* 507–522.

Cummings, T. (1985). Designing work for productivity and quality of work life. In D. Warrick (Ed.), *Contemporary organization development.* Glenview, IL: Scott, Foresman and Company.

Cummings, T. (1981). Designing effective work groups. In P. Nystrom and W. Starbuck (Eds.), *Handbook of organizational design,* Vol. 2. London: Oxford University Press.

Cummings, T. (1978). Self-regulating work groups: A socio-technical synthesis. *Academy of Management Review, 3,* 625–634.

Cummings, T., Mohrman, S., Mohrman, A., & Ledford, G., Jr. (1985). Organization design for the future: A collaborative research approach. In E. Lawler, III, A. Mohrman, S. Mohrman, G. Ledford, Jr., and T. Cummings (Eds.), *Doing research that is useful for theory and practice.* San Francisco: Jossey-Bass.

Cummings, T., & Molloy, E. (1977). *Improving productivity and the quality of work life.* New York: Praeger.

Cummings, T., Molloy, E., & Glen, R. (1977). A methodological critique of fifty-eight selected work experiments. *Human Relations, 30,* 675–708.

Cummings, T., & Srivastva, S. (1977). *Management of work: A socio-technical systems approach.* San Diego, CA: University Associates.

Cyert, R., & March, J. (1963). *A behavioral theory of the firm.* Englewood Cliffs, NJ: Prentice-Hall.

Dill, W. (1958). Environment as an influence on managerial autonomy. *Administrative Science Quarterly, 2,* 409–443.

Duncan, R. (1974). Modifications in decision structure in adapting to the environment: Some implications for organizational learning. *Decision Sciences, 5,* 705–725.

Eichholtz, G., & Rogers, E. M. (1964). Resistance to adoption of audio-visual aids by elementary school teachers: Contrasts and similarities to agricultural innovation. In M. Miles (Ed.), *Innovation in education*. New York: Teachers College Press, Columbia University.

Elden, M., & Taylor, J. (1983). Participatory research at work: An introduction. *Journal of Occupational Behavior, 4,* 1–8.

Emery, F., & Trist, E. (1973). *Towards a social ecology*. New York: Plenum.

Emery, F., & Trist, E. (1965). The causal texture of organizational environments. *Human Relations, 18,* 21–32.

Fiol, C., & Lyles, M. (1985). Organizational learning. *Academy of Management Review, 10,* 803–813.

Gerwin, D. (1981). Relationships between structure and technology. In P. Nystrom and W. Starbuck (Eds.), *Handbook of organizational design*, Vol. 2. Oxford: Oxford University Press.

Golembiewski, R., & Munzenrider, R. (1976). Measuring change by OD designs. *Journal of Applied Behavioral Science, 12,* 133–157.

Goodman, P., & Dean, J. W., Jr. (1982). Creating long-term organizational change. In P. Goodman (Ed.), *Change in organizations*. San Francisco: Jossey-Bass.

Hackman, J. R., & Oldham, G. (1980). *Work redesign*. Reading, MA: Addison-Wesley.

Hackman, J. R., & Suttle, J. L. (1977). *Improving life at work*. Santa Monica, CA: Goodyear.

Hage, J., & Aiken, M. (1970). *Social change in complex organizations*. New York: Random House.

Hage, J., & Aiken, M. (1967). Program change and organizational properties: A comparative analysis. *American Journal of Sociology, 72,* 503–519.

Hage, J., & Dewar, R. (1973). Elite values versus organizational structure in predicting innovation. *Administrative Science Quarterly, 18,* 279–290.

Harvey, E., & Mills, R. (1970). Patterns of organizational adaptation: A political perspective. In M. N. Zald (Ed.), *Power in organizations*. Nashville, TN: Vanderbilt University Press.

Hedberg, B. L. T., Nystrom, P. C., & Starbuck, W. H. (1976). Camping on seesaws: Prescriptions for a self-designing organization. *Administrative Science Quarterly, 21,* 41–65.

Herbst, P. (1966). *Socio-technical unit design*. Tavistock Institute of Human Relations, Doc. No. T899.

Huse, E., & Cummings, T. (1985). *Organization development and change*. St. Paul, MN: West Publishing Co.

Kanter, R. M. (1983). *The change masters: Innovation for productivity in the American corporation*. New York: Simon and Schuster.

Kelman, H. C., & Warwick, D. P. (1973). Bridging micro and macro approaches to social change: A social-psychological perspective. In G. Zaltman (Ed.), *Processes and phenomena of social change*. New York: Wiley-Interscience.

Kilmann, R., Thomas, K., Slevin, D., Nath, R., & Jerrell, S. (Eds.) (1983). *Producing useful knowledge in organizations*. New York: Praeger.

Kimberly, J. R. (1978). Hospital adoption of innovation: The role of interpretation into external informational environments. *Journal of Health and Social Behavior, 19,* 361–373.

Kimberly, J. R. (1981). Managerial innovation. In P. Nystrom & W. Starbuck (Eds.), *The handbook of organization design*, Vol. II. London: Oxford University Press.

Knight, K. (1967). A descriptive model of the intra-firm innovation process. *Journal of Business, 40,* 478–496.

Kolodny, H., & Stjernberg, T. (in press). The change process in innovative work designs: New design and redesign in Sweden, Canada, and the U.S.A. *Journal of Applied Behavioral Science*.

Lawler, III, E. (1982). Increasing worker involvement to enhance organizational effectiveness. In P. Goodman (Ed.), *Change in organizations*. San Francisco: Jossey-Bass.

Lawler, E., III, Nadler, D., & Camman, C. (1980). *Organizational assessment*. New York: John Wiley and Sons.

Lawler, E., & Mohrman, S. (1985). Quality circles after the fad. *Harvard Business Review, 63*(1), 64–71.

Lawrence, P., & Lorsch, J. (1967). *Organization and environment*. Boston: Harvard Business School.

Ledford, G. E., Jr. (1984). The persistence of planned organization change: A process theory perspective. Unpublished doctoral dissertation, University of Michigan.

Lewin, K., & Grabbe, P. (1945). Conduct, knowledge and acceptance of new values. *The Journal of Social Issues, 1*(3).

Lin, N., & Zaltman, G. (1973). Dimensions of innovations. In G. Zaltman (Ed.), *Processes and phenomena of social change*. New York: Wiley.

Lindbloom, C. (1959). The science of 'muddling through.' *Public Administration Review, 19*, 79–88.

MacCrimman, K., & Taylor, R. (1976). Decision making and problem solving. In M. Dunnette (Ed.), *Handbook of industrial and organizational psychology*. Chicago: Rand McNally.

March, J. G., & Olsen, J. P. (1976). *Ambiguity and choice in organizations*. Bergen, Norway: Universitetsforlaget.

March, J., & Simon, H. (1958). *Organizations*. New York: Wiley.

Moch, M. R., & Morse, E. V. (1977). Size, centralization and organizational adoption of innovations. *American Sociological Review, 42*, 716–725.

Mohr, L. B. (1982). *Explaining organizational behavior: The limits and possibilities of theory and research*. San Francisco: Jossey-Bass.

Mohrman, S. (1983). The impact of quality circles: A conceptual view. Working Paper G83-5. Center for Effective Organizations, University of Southern California, Los Angeles, CA.

Mohrman, S. (1982, August). Employee participation programs: Implications for productivity improvement. Paper presented at the American Psychological Association Annual Meeting, Washington, DC.

Mohrman, S., & Cummings, T. (1983). Implementing quality-of-work-life programs by managers. In R. Ritvo & A. Sargent (Eds.), *The NTL managers' handbook*, Arlington, VA: NTL Institute.

Mohrman, S., Cummings, T., & Lawler, E., III (1983). Creating useful knowledge with organizations. In R. Kilman, K. Thomas, D. Slevin, R. Nath, & S. Jerrell (Eds.), *Producing useful knowledge for organizations*. New York: Praeger.

Mohrman, S., & Lawler, E., III (1984). Quality of work life. In K. Rowland & G. Ferris (Eds.), *Personnel and Human Resources Management*, Vol. 2. Greenwich, CT: JAI Press.

Mohrman, S., Ledford, G., Lawler, E., & Mohrman, A. (1986). Quality of worklife: Implications for industrial psychology. In C. Cooper (Ed.), *Review of industrial/organizational psychology*. London: John Wiley & Sons.

Morgan, G., & Ramirez, R. (1983). Action learning: A holographic metaphor for guiding social change. *Human Relations, 37*, 1–28.

Mumford, E. (1983a). Participative systems design: Practice and theory. *Journal of Occupational Behavior, 4*, 47–57.

Mumford, E. (1983b). *Designing human systems*. Manchester Business School Press.

Nadler, D. (1980). Role of models in organizational assessment. In E. Lawler, III, D. Nadler, & C. Camman (Eds.), *Organizational assessment*. New York: John Wiley and Sons.

Nadler, D., & Lawler, E. (1982). Quality of work life programs, coordination and productivity. *Journal of Contemporary Business, 11*, 93–106.

Nadler, D., & Tushman, M. (1983). A general diagnostic model for organizational behavior: Applying a congruence perspective. In J. R. Hackman, E. Lawler, III, & L. Porter (Eds.), *Perspective on behavior in organizations*. New York: McGraw-Hill.

Nicholas, J. (1982). The comparative impact of organization development interventions on hard criteria measures. *Academy of Management Review, 7*, 531–542.

Normann, R. (1971). Organizational innovativeness: Product variation and reorientation. *Administrative Science Quarterly, 16*, 203–215.

Nystrom, P., & Starbuck, W. (Eds.) (1981). *Handbook of organizational design*, Vols. 1 and 2. Oxford, England: Oxford University Press.

Pasmore, W., Francis, C., Halderman, J., & Shani, A. (1982). Socio-technical systems: A North American reflection on empirical studies of the seventies. *Human Relations, 35,* 1179–1204.

Pinchot, G., III (1985). *Intrapreneuring.* New York: Harper and Row.

Porras, J., & Berg, P. O. (1978). The impact of organization development. *Academy of Management Review, 3,* 249–266.

Rogers, E. M. (1983). *The diffusion of innovations,* 3rd Edition. New York: The Free Press.

Rogers, E. M., & Shoemaker, F. F. (1971). *Communication of innovation: A cross-cultural approach.* New York: The Free Press.

Sarason, S. B. (1978). The nature of problem solving in social action. *American Psychologist, 33,* 370–380.

Schein, E. (1970). *Organizational psychology,* Second Edition. Englewood Cliffs, NJ: Prentice-Hall.

Seashore, S., Lawler, E., III, Mirvis, P., & Camman, C. (1983). *Assessing organizational change.* New York: John Wiley and Sons.

Slocum, J., & Simms, H. (1980). A typology of technology and job redesign. *Human Relations, 33,* 193–212.

Smith, K. K. (1982). Philosophical problems in thinking about organizational change. In P. Goodman (Ed.), *Change in organizations.* San Francisco: Jossey-Bass.

Srivastva, S., Salipante, P., Cummings, T., Notz, W., Bigelow, J., & Waters, J. (1977). *Job satisfaction and productivity.* Kent, OH: Kent State University Press.

Shrivastava, P., & Mitroff, I. (1982). Frames of reference managers use: A study in applied sociology of knowledge. In R. Lamb (Ed.), *Advances in strategic management.* Greenwich, CT: JAI Press.

Staw, B. (1981). The escalation of commitment to a course of action. *Academy of Management Review, 6,* 577–587.

Staw, B. (1978). The experimenting organization: Problems and prospects. In B. Staw (Ed.), *Psychological foundations of organizational behavior.* Santa Monica, CA: Goodyear.

Staw, B. (1976). Knee-deep in the big muddy: A study of escalating commitment to a chosen course of action. *Organizational Behavior and Human Performance, 16,* 27–44.

Stufflebeam, D. (1967). The use and abuse of evaluation in Title III. *Theory Into Practice, 6,* 126–133.

Susman, G. (1976). *Autonomy at work.* New York: Praeger.

Taylor, R. N., & Vertinsky, I. (1981). Experimenting with organizational behavior. In P. Nystrom & W. Starbuck (Eds.), *The handbook of organizational design,* Vol. II. London: Oxford University Press.

Terborg, J., Howard, G., & Maxwell, S. (1982). Evaluating planned organizational change: A method for assessing alpha, beta, and gamma change. *Academy of Management Review, 7,* 292–295.

Terreberry, S. (1968). The evolution of organizational environments. *Administrative Science Quarterly, 12,* 590–613.

Trist, E., Higgen, G., Murray, H., & Pollack, A. (1963). *Organizational choice.* London: Tavistock Publications.

Walton, R. (1985). From control to commitment in the workplace. *Harvard Business Review, 63,* 76–84.

Walton, R. (1975). The diffusion of new work structures: Explaining why success didn't take, *Organizational Dynamics, 3,* 3–21.

Warner, M. (1984). *Organizations and experiments: Designing new ways of managing work.* New York: John Wiley and Sons.

Warner, M. (1981). Organizational experiments and social innovations. In P. Nystrom & W. Starbuck (Eds.), *Handbook of organizational design,* Vol. 1. London: Oxford University Press.

Waters, J., Salipante, P., & Notz, W. (1978). The experimenting organization: Using the results of behavioral science research. *Academy of Management Review, 3,* 483–492.

Watson, G. (1973). Resistance to change. In G. Zaltman (Ed.), *Processes and phenomena of social change*. New York: Wiley-Interscience.

Watson, G. (1971). Resistance to change. *American Behavioral Scientist, 14,* 745–766.

Watzlawick, P., Beavin, J., & Jackson, D. (1967). *Pragmatics of human communication*. New York: W. W. Norton.

Watzlawick, P., Weakland, J., & Fisch, R. (1974). *Change*. New York: W. W. Norton.

Webb, E., Campbell, D., Schwartz, R., & Sechrest, L. (1966). *Unobtrusive measures: Nonreactive research in the social sciences*. Chicago: Rand McNally.

Weick, K. E. (1979). *The social psychology of organizing*. Reading, MA: Addison-Wesley.

Weick, K. E. (1977). Organization design: Organizations as self-designing systems. *Organizational Dynamics, 6*(2), 30–46.

Wilson, J. Q. (1966). Innovation in organization: Notes toward a theory. In J. D. Thompson (Ed.), *Approaches to organizational design*. Pittsburgh: University of Pittsburgh Press.

Woodman, R., & Sherwood, J. (1980). The role of team development in organizational effectiveness: A critical review. *Psychological Bulletin, 88,* 166–186.

Zaltman, G., & Duncan, R. (1977). *Strategies for planned change*. New York: Wiley-Interscience.

Zaltman, G., Duncan, R., & Holbeck, J. (1973). *Innovations and organizations*. New York: John Wiley and Sons.

BIOGRAPHICAL SKETCHES OF
THE CONTRIBUTORS

Chris Argyris is James Bryant Conant Professor of Education and Organizational Behavior at Harvard University. He was awarded the A.B. degree in psychology from Clark University (1947); the M.A. degree in economics and psychology from Kansas University (1949); and the Ph.D. degree in organizational behavior from Cornell University (1951). From 1951 to 1971, he was a faculty member at Yale University, serving as Beach Professor of Administrative Sciences and as chairperson of the Administrative Sciences department during the latter part of this period.

Dr. Argyris has written a number of well-known books including *Personality and Organization, Intervention Theory and Method,* and *Theory in Practice.*

Argyris is currently working on a project that will relate his perspective to the ideas of other researchers and practitioners. Argyris has earned honorary doctorates from the Stockholm School of Economics (1979), the University of Leuven, Belgium (1978), and McGill University (1977).

L. David Brown is Professor and Chairman of the Organizational Behavior Department at the Boston University School of Management, and President of the Institute for Development Research. He received a B.A. in Social Relations from Harvard College and an LL.B and a Ph.D in Organizational Behavior from Yale University. He has served on the faculties of the Harvard Institute for International Development, the Public Enterprises Centre for Continuing Education (New Delhi), and Case Western Reserve University. His research and consulting activities focus on problems of institutional development and social change, especially in Third World settings. He is an author or coauthor of several books and monographs (e.g., *Strengthening Ministries of Health for Primary*

Health Care, Managing Conflict at Organizational Interfaces, Learning from Changing) and many professional articles and chapters on planned change, conflict management, and action research.

R. J. Bullock is an Assistant Professor of Psychology at the University of Houston. He received his Ph.D. at the University of Michigan in Organizational Psychology and a Masters Degree from Michigan State University in Industrial Organizational Psychology. He teaches and researches organization development with a focus on research methods in OD, gainsharing, employee suggestions, and productivity measurement.

David L. Cooperrider is assistant professor of organizational behavior in the Weatherhead School of Management, Case Western Reserve University. He received his B.A. degree (1976) from Augustana College in psychology; his M.S. degree (1982) from George Williams College in organizational behavior; and his Ph.D. degree (1985) from Case Western Reserve University in organizational behavior. Recently he has been engaged in research on the relationship between organizational ideology, executive power, and the management of change. Cooperrider is the author of a number of articles on alienation and authenticity in organizations and is coauthor of an experiential book and training manual, *Developing Organizations for High Performance* (1985). He is also very active as a management educator and consultant.

Jane Gibson Covey is Executive Director of the Institute for Development Research. She has a B.S.N. from Georgetown University, an M.S.N in Psychiatric Nursing from Yale University, and an M.B.A. from Case Western Reserve University. She has served on the staffs of the Connecticut Mental Health Center, the Cleveland Public Health Department, and St. Johns College, and been an organizational consultant for the Public Enterprises Centre for Continuing Education in New Delhi and for Goodmeasure, Inc. She has consulted to private, public, and nonprofit organizations. She presently works with private voluntary organizations involved in development and social change in the Third World and in the United States, especially on problems of managing change and cultural differences. She has written papers on difference management, empowerment, and strategic planning as well as change processes in social change and development organizations.

Thomas G. Cummings is Professor of Management and Organization at the Graduate School of Business Administration, University of Southern California. He received a Ph.D. in socio-technical systems from the University of California at Los Angeles. Dr. Cummings was previously on the faculty at Case Western Reserve University. He has co-authored or edited seven books: (1) *Job Satisfaction and Productivity;* (2) *Management of Work;* (3) *Improving Productivity and* *the Quality of Work Life;* (4) *Systems Theory for Organization Development;* (5) *Labor Relations: A Multi-Dimensional Perspective;* (6) *Organization Development and Change;* and (7) *Research for Theory and Practice.* Dr. Cummings has also written over 30 scholarly articles. He is Associate Editor of the *Journal of Occupational Behavior,* Past-President of the Western Academy of Management, and Past-Chairman of the Organization Development Division of the Academy of Management. Dr. Cummings' major research and consulting interests include designing high-performing organizations, planned organization change, transorganizational systems, and occupational stress.

Wilfred H. Drath is a Research Project Leader and is the Publication Editor at the Center for Creative Leadership. He is also the editor of the Center's quarterly publication, *Issues & Observations.* He has fourteen years experience as a writer and editor, including six years as a freelance writer. With Robert Kaplan and Joan Kofodimos, he is currently a principal member of the research team conducting an intensive study of executive character and development. Bill holds an A.B. in English from the University of Georgia and has completed graduate work in English Literature at the University of North Carolina at Chapel Hill, where he was an instructor in English composition in the Adult Education curriculum. He is co-author of *High Hurdles: The Challenge of Executive Self-Development* and also *The Looking Glass Experience.*

Robert E. Kaplan is Behavioral Scientist and Director of New Program Development at the Center for Creative Leadership in Greensboro, North Carolina. He has a Ph.D. in Organizational Behavior from Yale University.

Kaplan has a longstanding research interest in the uses of openness for maintaining relationships, building teams, equipping people with interpersonal and managerial skills, and diagnosing and changing organizations. Kaplan has also investigated managerial work at middle and upper levels. With Wilfred Drath and Joan Kofodimos, he is now involved in a long-term project to study executive character and development.

Kaplan is also active as a group facilitator, management trainer, and organizational development consultant. He is a member of NTL and Certified Consultants, Inc.

Joan R. Kofodimos is a Program and Research Associate at the Center for Creative Leadership. In addition to her work using biographical methods to understand executive character she conducts research and workshops in the areas of balancing work and personal life, stress and wellness and peak performance. She has taught organizational psychology at Yale University and served as a counselor and administrator in community mental health agencies. She was a founding partner of Nexus, a consulting group specializing in the implementation of automated office systems. She received a BA in Psychology and an MA in

Sociology from Stanford University, and a Ph.D. in Organizational Behavior from Yale University.

Susan A. Mohrman is a Senior Research Scientist at the Center for Effective Organizations at the Graduate School of Business Administration, University of Southern California. She received a Ph.D. in Organizational Behavior from Northwestern University. She has been a Visiting Lecturer at the Ohio State University, and has taught on the Faculty of Organizational Behavior at USC. Dr. Mohrman's research and publications are in the areas of innovative management practices, change and organization development, participative design, and innovative research methodologies. She is an editor of *Research for Theory and Practice*.

Jerry I. Porras is an Associate Professor of Organizational Behavior in the Graduate School of Business, Stanford University. He received a BS in electrical engineering from the Texas Western College of the University of Texas in 1960, an MBA from Cornell University in 1968, and a Ph.D. from U.C.L.A. in 1974. His research focuses on planned organization change, specifically the assessment of organizational change processes and the development of theoretical models describing the dynamics of planned change. He has been or is currently on the editorial board of the *Journal of Applied Behavioral Science, Academy of Management Journal, Academy of Management Review*, and *The Business Review*. Presently he is working on two books—one for the Addison-Wesley series on OD and the second a text book on Organization Development.

Peter Robertson is a Ph.D. candidate in Organizational Behavior at the Graduate School of Business, Stanford University. His research interests include the underlying dynamics of effective planned organizational change, and the relationship between the values and behavior of organizational members and their impact on organizational performance. In addition to the present chapter, he has co-authored the chapter on Organizational Development for the Handbook of Industrial and Organizational Psychology, 2nd edition, and an article (currently submitted for publication) exploring conceptually the relationship between technology change and individual behavior change. He has worked since 1984 as a consultant with Lockheed Missiles and Space Company in their internal Organizational Effectiveness group.

Suresh Srivastva is professor of organizational behavior in the Department of Organizational Behavior of the Weatherhead School of Management, Case Western Reserve University, serving as chairman of the department from 1970 to 1984. He received his Ph.D. degree (1960) from the University of Michigan in social psychology. In addition to his work as a consultant for industrial enterprises and health care systems in the field of organization development, he is the author of numerous articles in the area of psychology and management problems. His major books include *Behavioral Sciences in Management* (1967), *Human Factors in Industry* (1970), *Anatomy of a Strike* (1972, with I. Dayal and T. Alfred), *Job Satisfaction and Productivity* (1975, with others), *Management of Work* (1981, with T. Cummings), and *The Executive Mind* (1983, with others).

Mark E. Tubbs is an Assistant Professor of Psychology and Management at the University of Missouri-St. Louis. He received his PhD in I/O Psychology at the University of Houston in 1985. His doctoral dissertation, a meta-analysis of the goal setting literature, appeared in the *Journal of Applied Psychology* in 1986. His major interests are in the areas of employee motivation and research methodology. Mark has also worked with a number of business and governmental organizations on research and change projects over the past several years.